Developments in British Politics 5

Edited by

Patrick Dunleavy
Andrew Gamble
Ian Holliday
Gillian Peele

First published 1997 by
MACMILLAN PRESS LTD
Houndmills, Basingstoke, Hampshire RG21 6XS
and London
Companies and representatives
throughout the world

ISBN 0–333–67775–7 hardcover
ISBN 0–333–67776–5 paperback

A catalogue record for this book is available
from the British Library.

This book is printed on paper suitable for recycling and
made from fully managed and sustained forest sources.

10	9	8	7	6	5	4	3	2	1
06	05	04	03	02	01	00	99	98	97

Copy-edited and typeset by Povey–Edmondson
Tavistock and Rochdale, England

Printed and bound in Great Britain by
Creative Print and Design (Wales), Ebbw Vale

Published in the United States of America 1997 by
ST. MARTIN'S PRESS, INC.,
Scholarly and Reference Division
175 Fifth Avenue, New York, N.Y. 10010

ISBN 0–312–21010–8

046503
28.1.98

Developments in British Politics 5

Contents

List of Contributors   ix

Preface   xii

1 Introduction: 'New Times' in British Politics
   Patrick Dunleavy   **1**
   Electoral Change and Stability   2
   The Conservatives' Crisis   5
   Labour Ascendant and the Centre Ground   11
   New Directions in British Governance   16
   Conclusion   18

2 Britain, Europe and the World   *John Peterson*   **20**
   The Theoretical and International Context   21
   Britain in the European Union   24
   The Special Relationship   32
   The Legacy of Empire   35
   Britain as an International Actor   38
   Conclusions   40

Part I: Political Behaviour

3 Voting and the Electorate   *David Sanders*   **45**
   The Survey Data Perspective   46
   The Aggregate Model Approach   62
   Conclusions   71

4 Political Communications   *Pippa Norris*   **75**
   The Decline of the Pre-Modern Campaign   76
   The Evolution of the Modern Campaign   80
   The Development of the Post-Modern Campaign?   87
   Conclusions   88

5 **Political Parties**   *Gillian Peele*   **89**
   'New Labour'   91
   The Conservative Party   98
   The Liberal Democrats   108
   Conclusion   109

6 **Political Participation**   *Mark Evans*   **110**
   Political Participation in the UK: A Snapshot   110
   Unconventional Political Participation in the UK   114
   New Forms of Political Opportunity Structure   118
   Explaining Changes in Political Participation   121
   New Labour, New Politics?   123

Part II: Political Institutions

7 **The Constitution**   *Patrick Dunleavy*   **129**
   The Centralization of Power   133
   The Devolution of Power   136
   The Declining Legitimacy of Government   140
   Rebuilding Faith in Government   144
   The Unresponsive Voting System   147
   The Future of Electoral Reform   150
   Conclusions   154

8 **Parliamentary Oversight**   *Philip Norton*   **155**
   The Role of Parliament   155
   Marginalization?   158
   Assertiveness?   160
   Scrutiny by the European Parliament   172
   Conclusion   176

9 **The Central Executive**   *Christopher Hood and*
      Oliver James   **177**
   Recent Changes   177
   Four Fundamental Control Mechanisms in Central
   Governance   185
   Assessing Public Service Change   192
   Conclusion   202

10 The Regulatory State *Martin Loughlin and Colin Scott* **205**
Privatization and Regulation 208
Deregulation and Self-Regulation 210
Euro-Regulation 211
Regulating the Public Sector 212
Conclusion 218

11 Territorial Politics *Ian Holliday* **220**
Territorial Politics in the UK 221
Territorial Politics and the 1997 General Election 223
Territorial Politics in the Conservative Years 225
Implementing Labour's Programme 229
Territorial Politics and the British Party System 230
Managing Territorial Political Change 236
The Future 238

12 Northern Ireland *Arthur Aughey* **241**
The Downing Street Declaration 241
Reaction to the Ceasefires 242
The Framework Document and Decommissioning 244
Elections and Talks 246
The Talks 248
Conclusion 252

13 Local Governance *Peter John* **253**
The Restructuring of Local Politics 253
Central–Local Relations in the 1990s 257
Towards Community Governance? 266
Centralized Local Administration and Local Government Decline? 270
The Future 274

Part III: Public Policy

14 Economic Policy *Gavin Kelly* **279**
After the ERM: Rebuilding the Institutions of Macroeconomic Policy 281
Evidence: Macroeconomic Policy and Trends 284

Policy Debates   286
Conclusion: New Debates   301

15 Social Policy   *Catherine Jones Finer*   **304**
The Stakeholder Idea   305
'Stakeholder' Social Policies   308
Conclusion   324

16 Crime and Public Order   *John Benyon and*
   Adam Edwards   **326**
The Politicization of Crime and Public Order   327
Law and Order Under the Conservatives   328
Labour's Law-and-Order Strategy   335
Problems and Prospects   338

17 BSE and the Politics of Food   *Wyn Grant*   **342**
BSE: The Disease and a Chronology   343
The Politics of Expertise   348
BSE and Devolution   350
Britain's Relations with the European Union   351
Conclusions   353

18 Conclusion: Politics 2000   *Andrew Gamble*   **355**
The End of the Nation-State   359
The End of Ideology   361
The End of Tradition   364
The End of the Public Realm   366
The End of Government   368
The End of Security   371
New Beginnings   373

Further Reading   377

Bibliography   384

Index   408

List of Contributors

Arthur Aughey is Senior Lecturer in Politics at the University of Ulster at Jordanstown. Recent publications include *Northern Ireland Politics* (co-edited) and three chapters in Philip Norton (ed.), *The Conservative Party*.

John Benyon is Professor of Political Studies and Director of the Scarman Centre for the Study of Public Order, University of Leicester. Research interests include collective violence, social protest and political stability; the politics of law and order; and crime and policing in the European union. Books include *The Roots of Urban Unrest* and *Police Co-operation in Europe*.

Patrick Dunleavy is Professor of Government at the London School of Economics and Political Science. Recent works include *Prime Minister, Cabinet and Core Executive* (co-edited), *Democracy, Bureaucracy and Public Choice* and numerous journal articles on public choice, urban politics and electoral systems.

Adam Edwards is a Research Officer at the Scarman Centre for the Study of Public Order, University of Leicester. Research interests include public policy change, learning and transfer; local governance; crime prevention; and the politics of law and order.

Mark Evans is Lecturer in Politics at the University of York. Recent publications include *Charter 88: A Successful Challenge to the British Political Tradition?* and journal articles on British public policy and state theory.

Andrew Gamble is Professor of Politics at the University of Sheffield. He is the author of *Hayek: The Iron Cage of Liberty* and co-editor of *Regionalism and World Order* and *Stakeholder Capitalism*.

Wyn Grant is Professor of Politics at the University of Warwick. His most recent books are *The Common Agricultural Policy* and *Autos, Smog and Pollution Control*.

Christopher Hood is Professor of Public Administration and Public Policy in the Department of Government, London School of Economics and Political Science. Recent articles related to the UK central executive include 'Deprivileging the UK Civil Service in the 1980s: Dream or Reality?' (in Jon Pierre (ed.) *Bureaucracy in the Modern State*) and 'Bureaucratic Regulation and New Public

Management in the UK: Mirror-Image Developments?' (co-authored) (*Journal of Law and Society*, 1996).

Ian Holliday is Senior Lecturer in Government at the University of Manchester. Recent publications include *The British Cabinet System* (co-authored) and journal articles on British politics and policy. He co-edits the journal *Party Politics*.

Oliver James is Research Officer in the Department of Government, London School of Economics, and Research Associate of the Institute for Public Policy Research. Recent publications related to the UK central executive include 'Explaining the Next Steps Reform in the Department of Social Security' (*Political Studies*, 1995) and 'Reinventing the Treasury' (co-authored) (*Public Administration*, 1997).

Peter John is Lecturer in Politics at the University of Southampton. Recent publications include *Analysing Public Policy* and articles on public administration in the EU.

Catherine Jones Finer is Reader in Comparative Social Policy at the University of Birmingham. Recent publications include *Promoting Prosperity: The Hong Kong Way of Social Policy* (edited) and *New Perspectives on the Welfare State in Europe*. She edits the journal of *Social Policy and Administration*.

Gavin Kelly is Research Officer on the Corporate Governance Project at the Political Economy Research Centre, University of Sheffield. Recent publications include *Stakeholder Capitalism* (co-edited) and articles on British economic policy.

Martin Loughlin is Professor of Law at the University of Manchester. Recent publications include *Public Law and Political Theory* and *Legality and Locality: The Role of Law in Central–Local Government Relations*.

Pippa Norris is Associate Director (Research) of the Joan Shorenstein Center on the Press, Politics and Public Policy at the Kennedy School of Government, Harvard University. Recent publications include *Electoral Change since 1945* and *Passages to Power: Legislative Recruitment in Advanced Democracies*.

Philip Norton is Professor of Government and Director of the Centre for Legislative Studies, University of Hull. Recent publications include *Does Parliament Matter?* and *The Conservative Party* (edited).

Gillian Peele is Fellow and Tutor in Politics at Lady Margaret Hall, Oxford. Recent publications include *Governing the UK* and

Developments in American Politics (co-edited). She is currently working on a study of John Major and the contemporary Conservative Party.

John Peterson is Jean Monnet Senior Lecturer at the Department of Politics, University of Glasgow. Recent publications include *Europe and America: The Prospects for Partnership* and *Decision-Making in the European Union* (co-authored).

David Sanders is Professor of Government at the University of Essex. Recent articles include 'Economic Performance, Management Competence and the Outcome of the Next General Election' (*Political Studies*, 1996) and 'New Labour, New Machiavelli: A Cynic's Guide to Economic Policy' (*Political Quarterly*, 1996).

Colin Scott is Lecturer in Law at the London School of Economics and Political Science. Recent publications include *International Regulatory Competition and Coordination* (co-edited) and articles on British public administration.

Preface

For this fifth *Developments in British Politics* volume the editorial teams remains unchanged from *Developments 4*, but as ever our list of authors is entirely new.

The task we set contributors this time was to analyse the challenges facing Britain's first Labour government for nearly two decades in the context both of the Conservative legacy and of the main theories and models developed by political scientists to explain British politics. All chapters are thus focused squarely on the late 1990s, and on the emerging political agenda of the twenty-first century.

Our Introduction (Chapter 1) examines the key contemporary approaches to understanding British politics, and our Chapter 2 explains Britain's place both in Europe and in the wider global order. The book then divides into three main parts. Part I analyzes constituent elements of British political behaviour. Part II investigates the key institutions of the British state. Part III examines central aspects of British public policy. Our final chapter (Chapter 18) considers the political agenda Britain will face in the twenty-first century. This structure is somewhat different from that employed in previous editions, chiefly because it integrates shorter issues chapters into the main parts of the book. New topics covered in this edition include political participation, crime and public order, and a special case study of BSE and the politics of food.

The timing of the 1997 general election made what is in any event a tight publishing schedule almost unmanageable. We are grateful to our contributors for meeting our very demanding deadlines. We are also grateful to David Butler and Nigel Allington for advice at a late stage in the process. Our greatest thanks go, however, to our publisher Steven Kennedy, who on top of his customary efficiency and enthusiasm was critical in keeping the book on schedule when it seemed all too likely to fall behind.

It is no exaggeration to say that this book would not have been published on time without the hard work put in by Steven and his team at Macmillan. We are more than usually grateful to him. Comments, suggestions and criticism are always helpful and would be greatly welcomed by us. We are currently planning a *Developments in British Politics* web site for 1998. When ready, this will be accessible through the Macmillan web site: http://www.macmillan-press.co.uk.

Patrick Dunleavy
Andrew Gamble
Ian Holliday
Gillian Peele

1

Introduction: 'New Times' in British Politics

PATRICK DUNLEAVY

Elections are the key means by which citizens in a liberal democracy can signal their preferences and intentions to political elites. But like the oracles by which ancient Greek gods divulged glimpses of the future to mortals, election results can sometimes be famously ambiguous – their meaning requiring to be picked over and reassessed for an extended period. This warning seemed thoroughly otiose in the first flush of Labour's landslide victory in the May 1997 general election. The emphatic character of the outcome, with its dramatically reconstructed and feminized House of Commons, was apparently confirmed in significance as a radical change by the distinctive character of the new ministers' initial policy announcements.

But impressive as the new government's mandate undoubtedly was, the underlying pattern of political alignments also retained more continuities with the past than simple constituency outcomes suggest. And interpretation of the electors' subtle intentions remained tricky. Labour won the election, many commentators remarked, because it was not the Tories, but it was at the same time very like the Tories. The new government was most like its predecessor in its programme of mild (not to say disconcertingly timid) changes in substantive policies – such as education, health, welfare and public spending. Yet Labour also came to power with a potentially radical programme of constitutional reform, the implementation of which was in some respects facilitated by its huge majority, as with devolution, and in some respects undermined by it, as with electoral reform (Chapter 7).

1

For the system of British democracy as a whole, the electorate's decision to will a 'leadership succession' after an unprecedented 18 years of one-party predominance also contained mixed messages. On the one hand, the alternation of parties in government seemingly restored the effective competition between political elites for mass endorsement which Schumpeter defined as the essence of liberal democracy. In the process the switch of ministers may further refurbish the centrist Conservative–Labour consensus destroyed in the Thatcher years, and rebuilt to some degree under Major. On the other hand, the new viability of the Liberal Democrats, the pre- and post-election divisions in the Tory party and the first signs of an emerging 'hegemonic project' for Labour may all signal a possibility for more fundamental realignment in British politics away from Conservative predominance. This chapter briefly considers the implications of the new political era for electoral trends, for the main political parties and for the overall character of British government.

Electoral Change and Stability

The 1997 election was a historic result which broke records in several different respects. It brought about only the third ever Labour government with a clear legislative majority in British history, and gave Labour its highest share of Commons seats. Compared with the party's previous landslides in 1945 and 1966, Labour's share of votes in Britain was lower (44 per cent instead of 49 per cent). But of course the earlier results occurred before the growth of third-party support in the early 1970s, which has remained fairly stable ever since. In the current British three-party system, Labour achieved a larger lead over the Conservatives in both seats and votes than ever before (Table 1.1).

TABLE 1.1   Labour lead over the Conservatives

	% of GB votes	*Commons seats*
1997	12.9	254
1945	9.5	183
1966	7.4	109

In the post-war period Labour had never increased its support by more than 4 per cent, but in 1997 its share of the vote grew by nearly 11 per cent. Since the party's electoral nadir in 1983 (when it got just 28 per cent of the vote under Michael Foot's leadership), Labour has now regrown 16 percentage points over three general elections, with its greatest increases coming in London and south-east England, the regions where it lagged so badly throughout the 1980s. The answer to analysts who had asked if the 1992 election was *Labour's Last Chance?* (Heath *et al.*, 1994) could not have been more emphatic.

However, there is also a strong sense in which Labour's apparent strength was just the mirror image of exceptional Conservative weakness. Labour's sweeping landslide was achieved on half a million votes less that the total which brought John Major only a narrow victory in 1992. Table 1.2 shows that the Tories lost a massive 4.5 million votes in just five years, the biggest

TABLE 1.2   The results of the 1997 general election in Great Britain

	MPs elected	Votes	Share of GB vote (%)
Labour	419	13 541 400	44.4
change from 1992	*+ 148*	*+ 1.98m*	*+ 10.8*
Conservative	165	9 591 100	31.4
change from 1992	*−171*	*−4.50m*	*−11.3*
Liberal Democrats	46	5 243 500	17.2
change from 1992	*+ 26*	*−0.76m*	*−1.1*
Scottish/Welsh Nationalists	10	783 300	2.5
change from 1992	*+ 3*	*+ 0.00m*	*+ 0.1*
Referendum Party	0	811 800	2.7
change from 1992	*0*	*+ 0.81m*	*+ 2.7*
Others	1	525 900	1.7
change from 1992	*+ 1*	*+ 0.20m*	*+ 0.3*

Note: Vote totals figures are rounded to the nearest hundred votes. The Referendum Party contested seats for the first time in the 1997 election. SNP won 6 seats and Plaid Cymru 4 seats. The total number of seats increased by 7 in the 1997 Commons. In Northern Ireland there were an additional 1.7 million votes (2.5 per cent of the UK total), and 18 seats won by distinctive Northern Ireland parties.

recorded change this century (dwarfing the 3 million lost by Labour in 1983 and the 2.6 million lost by the Tories across the two general elections of 1974). In the period 1900–92 the Tories averaged 44 per cent of the vote, and only when times were very poor did they slip as low as 38 per cent of the poll – a level they reached in February 1974 and three times in the 1920s. Conservative support previously slipped lower than this base score only once in the twentieth century, in October 1974 when an incumbent Labour government called a second election at a time least suited to the Conservatives (who were in crisis after losing power six months earlier). So most political scientists before the election felt that the Tories would again gain at least 36 per cent of the vote – whereas in fact their vote was 4.5 per cent lower.

Explaining the Conservatives' astonishing loss of support is no easy task. After all, the economy in 1997 was booming (as Tory election slogans constantly reminded voters), unemployment was falling fast, inflation was low, and economic growth was high. These conditions all provided a strong contrast to the gloomy economic circumstances of the 1992 election, when John Major survived with a 'normal' Tory party vote of 42 per cent. The conventional wisdom in political science has long been that economic performance determines government re-election chances. But this process simply failed to operate from 1993 through to the general election, generating predictions of a Tory vote 6 per cent higher than the party actually achieved (Chapter 3). Two important electoral factors may help to explain some of the Conservatives' collapse in support. First, as Table 1.2 shows, 0.8 million people voted for the Referendum Party, and just under half of them were previously Conservative supporters. Together with a similar share of the 0.1 million votes cast for the UK Independence Party, this growth of right-wing fringe parties may have cost the Conservatives nearly half a million votes. Second, turnout fell by 6 per cent in 1997, from nearly 78 to under 72 per cent. Conservative supporters were almost certainly more numerous among the stay-home electors than supporters of other parties, but the net Tory loss due to differential turnout is hard to calculate (since people who admit to being non-voters are also under-represented in election surveys). It almost certainly was far less than might be thought from the raw turnout change alone, perhaps accounting for another half million votes. Thus we might be able to explain away 1 million out of the Conservatives' 4.5 million 'lost' votes as due to special factors, the intervention of right-wing fringe parties and temporary disillusionment due to a floundering government having been in power for too long. But explaining the remainder of the party's dramatic unpopularity remains a problem.

As in previous elections only just over 1 in 20 UK voters switched directly from one major party to another, but the flow of the vote was all one way. One in every 7 1992 Conservatives backed Labour 5 years later, and a further one in 10 switched to the Liberal Democrats. The proportion of Conservatives backing the same party fell from the normal major party level of 80–90 per cent to just 71 per cent in the NOP exit poll conducted for the BBC, comparable with the Liberal Democrats' re-voting level of 65 per cent. The same survey showed that the Tories did disastrously amongst new voters (picking up less than a quarter of their support) and amongst people who were previously non-voters. Labour attracted most support amongst all non-pensioner age groups, while people aged over 65 were the only age group still to give the Tories a lead. In occupational class terms Labour attracted most support amongst routine non-manual people, and skilled and unskilled manual workers. Only the 'upper' middle-class AB group (comprising just over a quarter of the population) still gave the Conservatives a strong lead over Labour. Amongst non-manual people as a whole, Labour and the Conservatives were level-pegging, while Tory support among manual workers fell below a quarter compared to Labour's convincing majority support in this group. Conservative voters split between non-manual and manual people in a 7:3 ratio, while Labour drew support in equal numbers from both social groups, lending credence to Tony Blair's claim that it was now the 'one-nation' party. The Liberal Democrats drew support fairly evenly across age groups, but in class terms their support base was also two-thirds non-manual.

The Conservatives' Crisis

The problems facing the Tories were not just attributable to their sharply declining support, however. In Britain's peculiarly unfair and unpredictable voting system (called 'plurality rule' voting) there is only an erratic link between parties' vote shares and seat shares across successive elections (Chapter 3). Table 1.2 shows that Labour gained nearly two-thirds of the seats nationally, but on the basis of less than 45 per cent of the votes. So there was a massive 'leader's bias' in Labour's favour, partly achieved by the Conservatives being under-represented in the Commons – for only the second time in the post-war period. Instead of both the major parties being over-represented at the Liberal Democrats' expense, the Tories got nearly 6 per cent fewer seats than their share of the vote would warrant. And the Liberal Democrats secured an extra 26 seats at the Conservatives' expense, creating a solid area of third-party MPs in the south-west and pushing up into urban areas of south-east England and some London seats. The Liberal Democrats' normal under-representation in terms of seats dramatically reduced. Their share of seats was 15 per cent less than their share of votes in 1992, yet by 1997 it was only 10 per cent less, and the party was treated proportionately by the electoral system in its key south-west heartland.

The nightmare threat for the Conservatives in these changes is that by letting their support drop so low they may have placed themselves at a critical disadvantage. Under plurality rule with multi-party competition a party which sinks below about 33 per cent of the vote will very rarely be treated proportionately. Instead it may be severely under-represented. At the least Tony Blair's government can look forward to its opposition being fragmented between the Tories and the Liberal Democrats, just as Margaret Thatcher stayed in power in the 1980s partly because of the divisions in the non-Tory vote between Labour and the Liberal Democrats. At the worst for the Tories, there is a real danger that the Liberal Democrats might be able to displace the Conservatives as the main alternative to Labour in substantial areas of the country, just as they have done in much of local government. With 46 MPs and coherent representation in south-west England and other areas to add to their traditional 'peripheral' seats in Scotland and Wales the Liberal Democrats may be able for the first time to consolidate their parliamentary representation, building local support bases and 'digging in' at the Westminster level in a way that Labour previously could not do in southern England.

For the first time, too, the Conservatives ceased to be a credible national party in 1997. They elected no MPs in Scotland or Wales. And across 160 seats in the great metropolitan areas of England (covering Liverpool, Manchester, Newcastle and its surrounds, the West Midlands conurbation, south and west Yorkshire, and inner London) the party could only muster 8 MPs. Even in a traditional heartland area, the outer London suburbs, the party hung on to less than a quarter of all seats. A majority of the 165 Tory MPs elected represented only the most countrified areas of south-east England and East Anglia. This poor performance in terms of seats owed a great deal to Labour's clear leads in the opinion polls, which solved the 'tactical voting' problem for people who wanted to get John Major's government out. In 1992 across the whole of south-east England outside London the Conservatives won 97 per cent of the seats on the basis of just 55 per cent of the votes, and the two opposition parties won hardly any seats. But in 1997 the Conservatives on 40 per cent of the vote won less than two-thirds of the region's 117 seats, and Labour and the Liberal Democrats elected 42 MPs between them. The south-west went from being a Conservative heartland area with a solid Tory advantage in terms of seats to being the region of the country where all parties' votes were mostly fairly translated into seats. These twin trends spell problems for the Conservatives, with the electoral system becoming more deeply disproportional in Labour's heartland areas, while the system for translating votes into MPs becomes fairer in the areas where the Conservatives are still dominant, eroding their historic advantages.

To overcome Labour's large majority and win back power in 2001–2 the Conservatives need to surmount a series of daunting hurdles. With an 8 per cent swing from Labour to the Tories a hung Parliament would result, but only with a 9.5 per cent swing would the Conservatives become the largest party. To gain a Tory overall majority of 1 would require an 11.6 per cent swing, far more even than Labour's 10.5 per cent swing in 1997. There have been sharp pro-Conservative swings before, notably after Labour's previous landslide victory in 1966. In the 1968 local elections the Conservatives scored historic gains and went on win the 1970 general election, but both changes reflected the Labour government's crisis devaluation of sterling in 1967 and were achieved on much smaller swings. Many analysts have thus already concluded that the Conservatives cannot realistically hope to return to government at the next election, and that Labour can probably look forward to two terms of office – unless a catastrophe equivalent to the 1967 devaluation should sour Blair's leadership.

These gloomy prognostications formed an important part of the backdrop to John Major's immediate announcement that he was standing down and the launch of a Tory leadership race between five candidates, one on the Europhile left, Kenneth Clarke; one on the centre or centre-right, William Hague; and three on the Eurosceptic right, Michael Howard, Peter Lilley and John Redwood. Hague's eventual victory in this election did not prevent many Conservatives from criticizing the decision to carry on electing the party leader using a method which gave votes to only the 164 remaining Tory MPs, since so many Conservative constituency parties had no MP left to lobby. The many calls for the Conservatives to adopt an electoral college system which would give constituency activists as well as MPs a share in choosing the leader is a significant example of belated Tory convergence on the practices of the other two main parties. A re-run of the Tory leadership election on a new system would almost certainly have the same effect as Labour's electoral college system, entrenching the winning leader much more securely than a system based solely on the parliamentary party's votes.

In substantive policy areas also the party will have to reconsider many of the positions which were maintained under John Major, but which it was clear from many sources were unpopular with voters. The party's opposition to Scottish and Welsh devolution, which seemed sustainable after Conservative MPs survived there in 1992, ended in disaster five years later – despite Major's bizarre conviction that it was a vote-winner (Chapter 11). With its large majority Labour can now legislate for devolution largely unhindered, forcing the Tories onto the back foot. Will the Conservatives accept defeat and change their policy, and could they anyway seriously promise to abolish the devolved assemblies or restrict their powers if they returned to government? These issues caused serious rifts in Conservative ranks within weeks of the election outcome, and the same cleavage between 'compromisers' and 'irreconcilables' already looks certain to appear over elections for a London mayor and strategic authority. On a whole range of other issues, the Labour government can push through changes which are hard to reverse, setting a new agenda for which the Conservatives are woefully unprepared. Gordon Brown's immediate decision to vest control of interest rates in the Bank of England is one major example where Conservative frontbenchers were left floundering and divided about what their stance should be. Some of these issues highlight the substantial problems which the Conservatives got into by the mid-1990s in setting policy. Tory ministers became used to 'bouncing' the electorate into accepting things which were unpopular, notably with successive privatizations, each of which was opposed by public opinion before it happened but then accepted reluctantly after the fact. But the London governance problem was always a telling counter-example to this misplaced confidence that public opinion could be defied. The abolition of the GLC in 1986 was staunchly opposed by a majority of Londoners, and the series of ineffective and ad hoc arrangements put in place by Tory ministers to replace the GLC always attracted public opposition. In the 1997 election the *London Evening Standard* called for a Labour vote to sort the mess out, and although specifically London dissatisfactions probably played only a small role in the Tories' large losses in the capital, the issue was undoubtedly a negative factor. It is hard to think of any sensible reason why Conservative ministers came to this pass, or why they should have ignored overwhelming evidence that their policies were inadequate. Why not concede the return of a streamlined strategic authority? What great Conservative principle hung on defying public opinion in this matter?

The same problem of understanding why the Conservatives became locked into unpopular positions, and repeatedly failed under Major to make low-cost and perfectly acceptable policy adjustments to respond to public opinion, hangs over the whole of the party's European stance. Egged on by chauvinist national newspapers, and perhaps misled by the anti-Europeanism of Tory activists whose average age was 61, Conservative ministers and backbenchers alike became convinced that public Euro-scepticism was much more developed and salient in influencing voters' choices than turned out to be the case. British public opinion has a normal 'resting state' which is to be Euro-critical, to grumble about 'Brussels bureaucrats' and swap outlandish stories about their often mythical regulation proposals. But on the only three occasions where the major parties have offered British voters the chance to opt out of Europe, the outcome has always swung heavily in favour of retaining British involvement. Thus in the 1975 referendum on UK membership of the then EEC, public opinion swung briefly towards Euro-enthusiasm, delivering a healthy 'Yes' majority, before returning to its normal Euro-scepticism within a few weeks. In 1983 Labour offered an immediate exit from the EEC, and went down to its worst defeat since 1931. Again voters adjusted their views on Europe during the election period to fit with the majority decision to vote Tory or Liberal Democrat. Finally in 1997, the Referendum Party and UK Independence Party failed to attract more than 1 in 20 votes for leaving the EU. And the Conservatives' obvious Euro-scepticism (buttressed by two of the oddest party election broadcasts in British history focusing on European themes) seemed to have no effect in insulating them from disaster. The lesson drawn by many Europhile Conservatives has been that most British voters may talk or think idly in a Eurosceptic vein when the issue of withdrawal is remote, but they soon change their minds (or can have their minds changed by elite groups) once the question becomes a serious practical one.

The main significance of the contest to replace Major as Conservative leader lies in the signal it gives about the party's future policy, especially if Blair's government should decide to commit the UK to joining the EMU – either in a first wave in 1999 (which seems highly improbable), or in a second wave in 2002 or thereabouts if the Euro should have become successfully established by then. The Conservative divisions run deep on this issue, just as they did over free trade and protectionism in the disastrous 1906 defeat by the Liberals, or the split over the corn laws' repeal in the 1840s. On both these previous occasions there was a real threat to the Tory coalition's character as the most successful integrated party of the right in the western world – the party's ability to link together urban–industrial and agricultural interests, small and large business, domestic and international capital, and big business and the middle classes. The party's previous official policy on European Monetary Union, John Major's 'wait and see' position, failed to contain those Conservative voices who wanted to rule out British membership on principle. If EMU is now delayed or fails to materialize, the Conservatives' division on Europe will be manageable, especially since the party is in opposition. But if EMU progresses, and becomes more popular with British voters so that British entry after a referendum begins to look more feasible, the incompatible Tory positions could once again create the prospect of a party visibly divided by factional warfare. In this respect as in many others, the Conservatives in opposition may find that in losing control of government they have also lost control of the political agenda, making them heavily reliant on Labour mistakes or external misfortunes to spark a Tory revival, rather than controlling much of their own future.

Labour Ascendant and the Centre Ground

In every previous Labour government the battle between left and right groupings inside the party has been one principal determinant of the government's character with the left almost permanently suspicious of leadership sell-outs and deradicalization, and often able to command significant numbers in the Parliamentary Labour Party (PLP) and support in the trade unions (Seyd, 1987). Tony Blair is the first Labour premier not to have serious worries about trouble on the left, partly because his majority is so large and the scale of the left presence in the PLP is relatively small, and partly because there is not much of a coherent left agenda around today. Since the fall of Communist regimes in eastern Europe in 1989 and the triumph of capitalism as the world's only modern mode of production, the left's traditional ideological prescriptions (for nationalization of industries and extensions of the welfare state financed by taxation) have looked increasingly threadbare. The longer a Labour government endures the more a set of organizing issues and an alternative left agenda may develop which can unite different left strands in the party. But on present form a left revival is likely to be too little, too late to bother the Prime Minister much – unless his centrist policies trigger some unforeseen misfortune.

In managing the Labour Party Tony Blair also has unique advantages as leader which have never been available to his predecessors. He is the first Labour PM to be elected by the whole party via an electoral college, making him virtually immune to any damaging speculation about the PLP displacing him in a leadership contest (a problem which persistently clouded Harold Wilson's government after the 1967 devaluation). Only if he badly fails to get Labour re-elected as the government will Blair's leadership be in serious question. The trade unions' previously dominant voting influence at the party conferences and in elections for the National Executive Committee has been greatly reduced in favour of the constituency membership, which in turn has been greatly increased and become somewhat more representative of voters generally. Party management issues have been toiled over by Blair, and before him by John Smith and Neil Kinnock, creating a much simpler internal party structure, with clearer influence by the party leader and PLP leadership over party policy than ever before. At the 1997 conference final arrangements for how the NEC operates under a Labour government will be agreed that should remove a constant source of tension plaguing the Wilson and Callaghan governments of the 1970s. Entryism by Trotskyist and other sectarian left groupings has been strictly controlled. And by changing the Labour party's famous 1918 constitution Clause IV (which committed Labour to public ownership) Blair removed a potent left organizing call from debate. Submitting the party's 1997 election programme to a vote of the party membership a whole 6 months before the election means that Blair need not even be closely bound by the party conference when coming up for re-election in 2001 or 2002. He can repeat the same exercise, and probably secure similar levels of mass membership support against any dissenting activists or MPs. Blair also ran a very personalized and personally-directed New Labour election campaign, so that he can rely on solid support from the raft of new MPs brought to Westminster on his coat-tails, often in unexpected seats. And protected both by his relative youth and by the electoral college endorsement, he has no serious challengers for the Labour leadership to worry about over the next five years at least.

Instead of focusing on traditional left/right factionalism and party management issues, the main area of future interest in Labour's internal politics is likely to lie on the party's position in relation to the Liberal Democrats and to the centre ground in

British politics. The most potent meanings associated with the famously ambiguous marketing concept 'New Labour' lie in Tony Blair's repeated proclamations that his party is a party of the centre and (after a pause) centre-left, and in the slogan of 'one nation' politics which blatantly seeks to capture a Disraelian theme back from the Conservatives. These apparently symbolic new acquisitions in the Labour armoury were backed up by an extensive party leadership effort to woo business people, industrialists and City interests. Prominent business figures were persuaded to star in party election broadcasts and subsequently to get involved in the Labour government's work, a few in ministerial or permanent advisory positions and others in task forces working on long-term issues. Once in power Labour ministers have pledged to seek consensus and to revive the centre ground as the keystone of policy making in many different spheres of government action.

But above all the theme of modernizing centrism has an ideological momentum behind it which the old right rarely commanded in previous Labour administrations. New Labour's centrism now reflects an outward-looking response to globalization, to the reduced powers and competencies of the nation state in the modern age. It re-focuses on the 'core competencies' of national governments in the 'post-modern' period, conceived as facilitating the UK's economic competitiveness via re-skilling and education, encouraging long-term investment, creating flexible and adaptive labour markets and industrial structures, and retuning the welfare state to reduce dependency and encourage self-reliance. These are glittering modern concepts, to which the welfare left and the union left have no comparably fluent or convincing alternatives, especially since only part of the centrist agenda is realizable at the UK nation state level. Many of these ideas require considerable concertation amongst the European or G8 (advanced industrial) countries if they are going to have a chance of success. New Labour centrism has a clear target, the 'casino capitalism' of the Thatcher era, and a well-worked out creed (expressed for instance in books like Will Hutton's *The State We're In*, published in 1995). Economic conditions for implementing an alternative strategy are quite benign, especially with the 'death of inflation' in most advanced industrial countries, which wrong-foots the influential monetarist and new right ideas of the last 20 years. And the political conditions of New Labour's majority and the Tories' disarray could hardly be bettered. Advocates of Labour's move towards the centre ground have two alternative hegemonic projects in view. The dominant view in the Labour leadership, strongly espoused by Peter Mandelson and apparently endorsed in its essentials by Blair and Chancellor Gordon Brown, accords a fairly minor role to constitutional reform in appeasing the Liberal Democrats and the 'chattering classes'. In particular, encouraging devolution of welfare state and regional development issues will allow the central government to focus intensively on 'competition state' policies designed to increase the UK's effectiveness in global markets. Many of the 'social market' ideas first (weakly) expressed by the breakaway Social Democratic Party in the 1980s return under the guise of developing a 'stakeholder' society (Chapter 15). Labour would ostentatiously trespass on the Liberal Democrats' centre terrain, putting them under pressure to converge on government policies and perhaps effectively merge with Labour in the future to form a new centrist bloc. Implicit in this long-term project is the departure of Labour's left wing into a political wilderness at some stage, hence the need to maintain the current House of Commons voting system to ensure that any left grouping which separated from Labour had zero political future as a fourth party. This approach relies on Labour in power demonstrating superior leadership, management and ideological skills to maintain its popularity, and on continuing Tory divisions and ideological fetishes to stop the Conservatives' support from bouncing back. It essentially envisages that Tony Blair's three-year trajectory in opposition can be maintained and developed using Labour's position in government.

The second hegemonic project is a minority centre-left view, held most notably by Robin Cook. It accords a much more fundamental role to constitutional changes in achieving a once-for-all reduction in the Conservative dominance of twentieth-century politics, in particular by changing the voting system for Commons elections to some form of proportional representation. Given the rancorous Conservative divisions over Europe, it would be feasible to expect that PR would trigger a reconfiguration of politics – the departure of the Tory Europhiles to form a new grouping or perhaps join the Liberal Democrats, and the effective 'entrenchment' of a centre-left majority in British politics. The lessons this grouping draws from the 1997 general election is not that PR means Labour can never form a majority government again (always having to rely on Liberal Democrat support), but that if Tory fragmentation could be engineered New Labour could itself become a dominant bloc in a much more fragmented politics – for instance, as the Swedish Social Democrats have been for most of the post-war period with around 40–45 per cent support. This position gains some support from the clear movement by the Liberal Democrats and the nationalist parties in Scotland and Wales to offer 1997 policy programmes in many ways more left-wing than New Labour's manifesto – such as pledging tax rises to finance public service improvements. For the centre-left these moves both make these parties more attractive coalition partners and prove that a New Labour hegemonic project which does not involve electoral reform cannot work. It will leave the party vulnerable to being outflanked on the left, as well as threatened by the kind of strong Conservative revivals which occurred within a couple of years of both the 1945 and 1966 Labour landslides.

At the leadership level, however, it is still European policy which has most potential to cause trouble for the Labour government, despite ministers' apparently united proclamations of a 'fresh start' in Europe and an end to British isolationism. When Labour was in opposition Gordon Brown was widely believed to be keen on Britain signing up for EMU in the first wave, and reluctant to concede the need for an explicit pledge to hold a referendum on EMU entry. Brown's early actions as Chancellor, in particular transferring day-to-day control of interest rates from the Treasury to the Bank of England and increasing the Bank's independence, could reflect a continuing concern to facilitate EMU entry since an independent central bank is a Maastricht criterion. However, Foreign Secretary Robin Cook has been keener on efforts to reorientate European integration around progress on jobs and boosting growth, and takes a sceptical line about first-wave EMU entry, while conceding that delaying entry beyond a few years would also be dangerous. Blair has so far followed an intermediate course between these opposing poles on European issues. But the Labour government will have to be either incredibly skilful or very lucky in the way that the European agenda develops to avoid the acute variable-geometry tensions between PM, Foreign Secretary and Chancellor which continually divided successive sets of Conservative ministers from the mid-1980s up to the 1997 election.

The divergent Labour voices still leave the Liberal Democrats rather on the sidelines of British politics. Like Labour's centre-left, they place a great deal of reliance on the voting systems referendum, and to a lesser degree on devolution, to move their agenda on and help them extend their new representation of 46 MPs in the Commons at the next election. But the Liberal Democrats also have a leadership problem, Paddy Ashdown having fought two general election campaigns already, an electoral support problem, with their support amongst manual workers dwindling back to 1979 levels, and above all an ideology problem. Much as Liberal Democrat spokespersons proclaim that their party is a radical one, their ideas are principally now distinct in retaining some of the 'tax and spend' and welfare statist style of 'old' Labour, and sharing none of the shiny modernism of Blair's 'New Labour'. Only on Europe have the Liberal Democrats remained distinctive, with their MPs almost uniformly prepared to advocate moves towards EMU and further policy integration across member states.

New Directions in British Governance

It already seems clear that New Labour in government will accomplish some significant and permanent changes in the structure of governance. Devolution to Scotland and Wales, and new institutional structures in the English regions and London should extensively disperse power which was over-centralized in Whitehall under the Conservatives (Chapters 7 and 11). On a benign scenario for Labour this movement of powers will allow the central government to focus more specifically on its 'competition state' agenda, without being constantly distracted by managing the numerous smaller issues which Whitehall had scooped up under the Tories. At the same time pushing powers away from the centre could help defuse some of the over-optimistic expectations of change built up in the run-up to Labour's election victory, and reduce spending pressures on central budgets (rather than regional or local government finances). Within Whitehall, too, the new government has sought clearer lines of accountability. Blair's style is quite different from Major's loosely coordinated government, with Number 10 being more activist in concerting policy and setting priorities, especially for the legislative programme. Departmental reorganizations have brought Transport and Environment back together, as they were originally in the 1970s, and there is a clear push behind long-term welfare state reform, notably in Frank Field's appointment at the Department of Social Security. Cook at the Foreign Office issued a long-term 'mission statement', stressing relations with Europe and apparently downplaying relations with the USA. Brown at the Treasury vested interest rates policy with the Bank of England, but then enraged the Bank's Governor two weeks later by stripping it of regulatory control of the banking sector, creating a new super-regulator in the reconstituted Securities and Investments Board. The Major government's refusal to admit that a crisis in consumer confidence over food required reforms to remove the issue from the Ministry of Agriculture (Chapter 17) was replaced by a clear commitment to an independent Food Standards Agency. All these initial steps suggest a willingness to move ahead decisively on institutional issues which the previous government had evaded or left unresolved. With five full years in which to work, and a possible second term as well, the Blair government may yet make a major impact on institutional patterns at the centre.

In other ways the new government's policies remain undefined, however. Under the Tory governments there were strong 'new public management' (NPM) trends in the civil service and quasi-governmental agencies (Chapter 9). These radical changes were opposed by many trade unions and criticized in the past by Labour spokespersons, but it is not clear how much policies will alter under Labour ministers. In one prominent case a minister has revoked a responsibility previously delegated from a Whitehall department to a 'Next Steps' agency, when Jack Straw resumed direct control of the Prisons Agency. But the agency system looks likely to remain more or less intact. Nor has the government ruled out continuing privatization of functions or contracting out, an issue that briefly disrupted the even tenor of

Labour's electoral campaign when a speech by Tony Blair seemed to promise continuing activity on this front. Pressures for greater savings inside the public services have been maintained by sticking with potentially unrealistic Conservative-set spending targets until 1999. The most likely outcome under Labour seems to be the emergence of a 'humanized NPM' approach, similar to that in Australia under Labour governments in the 1980s and in the US federal government under President Clinton's National Performance Review. Humanized NPM does not require the strong anti-public sector prejudice characteristic of the Thatcher years, nor a dogmatic belief in privatization as a solution. More attention is paid to preserving government's ability to carry out key tasks, incorporating employees into cooperative processes of change and providing high-quality services for public service consumers. But the financial regime in humanized NPM remains tight, competition for blocs of work occurs regularly, public employees are not guaranteed 'cushy' conditions, and annual 'efficiency savings' are still expected. Some policy areas will show greater change in this direction, and others less. Ministers have acted faster in regulatory areas, announcing clamp-downs on privatized rail and water utilities and the national lottery operators. But Labour's criticisms of the NHS 'internal market' in opposition have produced rather slow-moving proposals for simplification and cost-savings in office. The 'regulatory state' may thus be easier or cheaper to reorientate than large-scale public services (Chapter 10).

Conclusion

The currently feasible scenarios for British politics at the turn of the century depend on:

- how the Labour government fares in office
- whether either of the Labour 'hegemonic projects' is taken seriously by the leadership and makes progress
- if the Conservative opposition succeeds in re-grouping, around its new leader, William Hague
- and how far European integration and the European single currency develop

What is already clear is that Labour's election draws a clear line under a period of unprecedented Conservative predominance. It reaffirms two-party alternation in government, promises major constitutional change, and responds to a new set of low inflation economic conditions. These changes are already sufficient to judge Blair's victory as the end of an era, and the start of a new one.

2
Britain, Europe and the World

JOHN PETERSON

In the late 1990s, British foreign policy became caught up in a new and different kind of domestic political debate. Party political competition turned far less on economic ideology and far more on constitutional issues, particularly regional devolution and European integration. The 'politics of national identity' moved to the forefront of debates about Britain's future, with considerable knock-on effects for foreign policy.

As a backdrop, the wider world was a fundamentally different place from the one in which three basic principles of postwar British foreign policy had been developed. First, the Soviet threat had to be contained, if not curtailed. Second, the North Atlantic Treaty Organisation (NATO) needed to be preserved as the principal western collective security organization. Third, a 'special relationship' with the United States required constant nurturing, while moves to make the European Union more than a loose and ostensibly economic organization usually were shunned.

By the mid-1990s, the Soviet threat was gone. NATO had not lost its relevance, but the lack of a clear and present military threat to the west reduced its salience. Meanwhile, the EU became a more weighty and highly political organization which developed ambitions (even pretensions) to a Common Foreign and Security Policy. The US under President Bill Clinton liked to argue that it was 'more supportive of European integration than any administration since Kennedy's' (Peterson, 1996, p. 98).

This chapter offers a broad, interpretive look at Britain's role in the world. Its central argument is that the United Kingdom continues to punch above its weight as an international actor. However, its political class has been slow in responding to sweeping changes in both international politics and Britain's essential foreign policy interests. Given the climate of debate over 'Europe', the new Labour government's sudden and enthusiastic turn towards 'constructive engagement' with the EU after the 1997 election was almost as striking as the scale of its landslide victory. It also highlighted the difficulty – even futility – of maintaining Britain's international standing without fundamental changes in its foreign policy.

The Theoretical and International Context

The transformation of the international system after 1989 recast debates between advocates of competing theories of international relations. Against the odds, neo-realism remains the dominant approach to international politics. Its proponents assume that the international system is 'anarchic' in nature, marked by relentless competition between self-interested states, and characterized by relatively weak international organizations. Neo-realists are stubbornly pessimistic about the durability of Cold War alliances in a post-Cold War world. In particular, conservative American commentators forecast the 'collapse of the West' and insist that 'the days of allies are over' (Harries, 1993; Steele, 1995).

'Neo-liberalism' denotes a broad, alternative theoretical church. It includes 'institutionalists' who insist that international organizations such as the EU and United Nations have become important actors in their own right (Keohane *et al.*, 1993), as well as liberals such as Fukuyama (1992) whose forecast of the 'end of history' after 1989 is now notorious. The essential neo-liberal argument is that the interests of states are fundamentally altered by economic interdependence, which emerges from open markets for global commerce. By nature, open markets require co-operation between relatively liberal states, which are unlikely to compete with each other militarily. Military force, over which states usually exert monopoly control, becomes a less important source of power. Economic power, knowledge and the ability to process information, which are shared between states and firms, are more important tools of influence.

Many neo-realists concede that economic competition between states has become a more important dimension of international politics. Still, most argue that the decline of military strength as a central medium of international politics has been exaggerated. Economic sanctions, for example, could not get Iraq out of Kuwait. Neo-liberals respond that a neo-realist model of state-centred competition ignores the structural shift in power from governments to markets in the 1990s. Deregulation, privatization and declining subsidies became the hallmarks of domestic economic policies in Britain and elsewhere, while external policies focused on expanding trade and attracting foreign direct investment. Most states appeared to lose both the will and capacity to steer their domestic economies as the falling costs of transport, communications and technology transfer yielded an increasingly seamless, 'globalized' economy.

Perhaps paradoxically, globalization appears to weaken governments, while making their policies – on investment, education and infrastructure – more crucial determinants of the competitiveness of their national firms. With investment flowing more freely across borders, and non-western states developing modern infrastructures and workforces, the same production techniques become available to businesspeople in Bombay, Bangkok or Basingstoke. Governments that make bad decisions are punished quickly and ruthlessly by globalized markets which channel investments elsewhere (Bryan and Farrell, 1996).

In this context, Britain's economy has become highly integrated with the global economy. Compared to most states, it has both more to gain and more to lose from its relative international economic position. On one hand, the UK is better-placed than many of its rivals. Its labour market is the most flexible in Europe. Britain attracts about 40 per cent of all investment in the EU by foreign companies, which account for about 15 per cent of all British jobs and tend to offer good salaries and working conditions. After a painful shake-out in the 1980s, British industry is now more specialized, internationalized and competitive. The UK leads Europe in computer ownership per capita and is strong in telecommunications, the world's fastest growing industry. By many economic measures, it is no longer losing ground to other industrialized countries.

On the other hand, Britain's competitive edge reflects the

deterioration of other advanced economies, particularly in Europe, more than its own improvement. It was the only industrialized nation that was spending less of its national wealth on research in the mid-1990s than it did in 1981. Investment in manufacturing remained sluggish. Britain still ranked near the bottom (just ahead of Greece) of advanced states in terms of the percentage of 18-year-olds in full-time education and training. Increased labour market flexibility did little to break down class barriers which made Britain a less socially mobile society than Australia or the US. Britain's 'persistent and large rise in earning inequality' in the 1990s was unequalled by any other industrialized country (OECD, 1996). The poverty rate continued to rise, after very sharp increases in the 1980s. Yet, at the 1995 Copenhagen international summit on social development, the former Social Security Secretary, Peter Lilley, insisted that Britain did not need new anti-poverty measures.

Of course, it is impossible to assess Britain's role in the world on the basis of economic criteria alone. Even if one accepts the argument that 'as the economy weakens, the country's international prestige is waning' (Hutton, 1995, p. 1), the thesis is too simple. The UK remains an important military power and a core member of leading international organizations. 'New' security issues such as crime, terrorism and ethnic conflict have risen on the international agenda, and the UK offers special expertise on all of them. For example, following the terrorist bombing at the 1996 Olympic Games in Atlanta, Britain responded to American overtures with proposals to build on its experience in Northern Ireland in organizing new international anti-terrorist measures.

For Britain, more than most other states, the post-Cold War world implies new dilemmas. According to its Foreign Secretary, Robin Cook, the new Labour government was determined to confront them above all by ending the 'sterile, negative and fruitless conflict' between the UK and its EU partners (quoted in *Financial Times*, 9 May 1997). More than previous Conservative governments, Labour appeared ready to acknowledge the irreversibility of Britain's interdependence with Europe, the increased primacy of economic over traditional security issues, and the long-standing paradox of Britain's stubbornly nationalized policy and increasingly globalized economy.

Britain in the European Union

On 'Black Wednesday' in September 1992, enormous turbulence in currency markets forced the pound sterling out of the European exchange rate mechanism (ERM). The government of John Major had staked its entire economic strategy on maintaining sterling's value within the ERM, which was intended to keep currency rates stable and facilitate trade in the EU's internal market. The ERM also provided a platform for full Economic and Monetary Union (EMU) and a single currency, one of the most audacious and dramatic steps mooted in the postwar history of European integration. Black Wednesday marked a watershed: from this point forward, 'Europe' dominated domestic political debate in Britain (Chapter 14).

Over the next four years, Major and members of his cabinet often seemed forced to scorn the EU just to occupy a middle ground within the Conservative party. British negotiating positions on a range of key issues were perceived in Brussels and Strasbourg as extreme and miles from the European consensus. In London, British withdrawal from the Union was favoured by a hard-core of around a dozen Conservative MPs. They held considerable sway over a government which enjoyed a much smaller majority than its predecessors (Wallace, 1995).

The debate over 'Europe' heated up as a general election approached and the Union imposed a ban on exports of British beef. The beef ban was intended to reassure frightened consumers across Europe after the Major government acknowledged new evidence which suggested that BSE, or 'mad cow disease', could be passed to humans. The cause of the epidemic appeared to be the uniquely British practice of feeding cheap, contaminated offal to cattle in the late 1980s. Previous Conservative governments had played down the problem and demurred from adopting a comprehensive eradication policy. Reported rates of BSE elsewhere in Europe were suspiciously low, but the disease appeared essentially to be a British problem which had been exported to the continent (Chapter 17).

Beef markets collapsed across Europe. EU cash for BSE eradication, plus a ban on British exports, similar to those imposed by the US and even Hong Kong, seemed logical policy responses. Yet the Major government astonished its partners by announcing a 'non-co-operation policy'. The UK vetoed all proposed EU measures which required a unanimous vote, whether related to beef or not, while demanding that a timetable be agreed for lifting the ban. London further infuriated its partners by refusing to accept a large-scale culling of British herds and doing little to justify its policy in other European capitals. By the time of Major's announcement of 'non-co-operation', the Netherlands – which had only a fraction of the BSE cases reported in Britain – had slaughtered more cattle than the UK. Eventually, Britain agreed to a much larger cull than it initially argued was politically feasible.

A vague and non-committal declaration to seek an end to the ban was agreed at the Florence European summit in June 1996. Major thus declared victory and suspended 'non-co-operation'. By this point, the Foreign Office had received urgent expressions of concern from countries such as Mexico and Slovenia whose EU trade or aid agreements had been delayed by British vetoes. Britain had blocked a total of about 100 different measures, including several for which previously it had lobbied heavily on deregulation, police co-operation and fraud prevention.

Thinking Beyond Beef

From the Major government's point of view, the British non-co-operation policy was an extraordinary strategic blunder. It was adopted as the Union's decision-making rules were being scrutinized in an intergovernmental conference (IGC) with a view to reforming them. British non-co-operation highlighted the ability of one member state to blackmail all others and block decisions taken unanimously. It redoubled the determination of a majority of member states who favoured expanded majority voting. Requiring unanimous agreement on all but constitutional issues seemed impractical in a future, enlarged EU which included some or all of the 10 Eastern and Central European states plus Cyprus which had applied for Union membership by the time of the IGC.

Major (1996) would give no quarter on expanded majority voting. He insisted that the British veto meant 'we cannot be forced where we do not want to go'. Pro-European Conservatives, such as Kenneth Clarke and Michael Heseltine, were in retreat as the general election campaign began in earnest. Evidence that only one-quarter of all Tory candidates fighting the 1997 election agreed with the government's policy to 'wait and see' before deciding whether the UK would join a single currency suggested that EMU 'posed probably the greatest threat since the split over the corn laws in the 1840s' (*Daily Telegraph*, 16 December 1996). Labour Eurosceptics were not as influential as their Tory counterparts, but placed political limits on the Blair government's policy of 'constructive engagement' in the EU. Labour, like the Conservatives, took the politically safe route of trying to avoid the EMU issue by promising a referendum on whether Britain would join a single currency when and if it was created. Even the Blair government was probably going to need cross-party support to secure parliamentary ratification for joining EMU. One of the most important anomalies of British politics was that a large pro-EU majority persisted in the House of Commons.

This cross-party consensus had emerged as the EU had evolved into a far more 'comfortable' international organization for the UK after 1985. With a British Commissioner in the lead (Cockfield, 1994), the EU launched the single market programme. The Common Agricultural Policy (CAP) underwent significant reform during a successful world trade round. Germany, which usually shared British economic interests, became a more significant player. France gradually abandoned its Gaullist ambitions to make the EU into a defence organization. The EU took in Austria, Finland and Sweden in 1995, all of which broadly shared Britain's agenda on budgetary and enlargement questions.

The European Commission and Court of Justice (ECJ) were both active in enforcing EU rules which most member states observed less diligently than Britain. In 1994, the Commission made 89 referrals to the ECJ for violations of internal market rules, with only one case involving the UK. Regardless, Conservative Eurosceptics were outraged when the Court held against Britain in several high-profile cases in 1996, especially one concerning an EU directive which mandated a maximum 48-hour work week.

Under British pressure, the directive had been watered down to the point where it was essentially voluntary and subject to a seven-year delay before implementation in the UK. Britain still abstained in a vote on the directive. Then, the Major government sought (unsuccessfully) to overturn it in the ECJ on the grounds that legislation on working conditions should not be subject to majority voting rules reserved for health and safety matters. Britain gave ammunition to its critics by voting in favour of mandatory rest stops for transported animals but going to great lengths to oppose mandatory rest breaks for workers. More generally, Britain began to isolate itself in debates about the EU's future. Major's vision of the EU of the future stressed the need for 'flexibility' in a loose partnership of nations. Eventually, the French, Germans and others began to extol the virtues of flexibility, but in the sense of establishing an avant garde of countries which could move ahead faster than others in integrating specific policies, particularly in an enlarged Union. It was hard to think of policy areas (besides agriculture) where the UK stood to benefit from being on the periphery of a Franco-German led 'hard core'. Such thinking inspired Cook's plea, within a week of the 1997 election, for the emergence of 'three main players in Europe, not two' (quoted in *Financial Times*, 8 May 1997).

The 1996–7 IGC was the Union's third in just over 10 years. Its outcome was a very modest set of reforms which fell far short of any leap forward in European integration. However, after British 'non-co-operation', the Blair government, and its Minister for Europe, Doug Henderson, seemed determined to make a fresh start and to stamp Britain's influence indelibly on debates about the EU's future.

How Isolated is Britain?

It is probably too easy to view Britain as uniquely isolated or opposed to European integration. One poll in late 1994 found more German than British citizens opposing 'closer political links between EU members' (MORI poll in *Financial Times*, 5 December 1994). Several polls in late 1996 suggested that clear majorities of Germans opposed a single currency, while popular support for EMU was falling in France.

Moreover, the 1995 enlargement of the Union clearly made the UK less of an outlier in terms of public opinion. According to the EU's own polls, British citizens remained markedly more 'Eurosceptic' than, say, Dutch or Italian citizens (see Table 2.1). However, public opinion in both Austria and Sweden had turned sharply against the EU only a short time after they joined the

TABLE 2.1   Support for EU membership in selected member states, 1995
(%)

Member state	Is your country's EU membership a		
	'good thing'	*or*	*'bad thing'*
Netherlands	80		5
Italy	69		6
EU 15 average	53		15
United Kingdom	42		24
Sweden	31		40
Austria	29		29

Source: European Commission (1996).

Union, even though accession in each country had been ratified by popular referendum.

Even the UK's natural northern allies became progressively less tolerant of the Major government's foot-dragging on the environment, social policy and immigration in 1995–6. On these and other issues, the 'swing vote' often belonged to France. The election of Jacques Chirac as French President in 1995 led to a *frisson* within the British Conservative party about the prospects for an Anglo-French *entente cordiale*. France and Britain, so the logic went, were old nation-states with imperial traditions. Both instinctually guarded their national sovereignty. Both were medium-sized nuclear powers with permanent seats on the UN Security Council (along with the US, Russia and China). Together France and Britain could neutralize German-led, federalist impulses in EU debates. On defence questions, the Clinton administration's support for plans to loan US military assets to exclusively European forces in future coaxed the French closer to NATO. In announcing swingeing cuts in France's defence budget in 1996, Chirac even expressed hope for a volunteer French army that was as good as Britain's.

Concerns in Bonn about the severity of French military cuts was soothed by a stepping up of bilateral Franco-German exchanges on military issues. More generally, the French and Germans continued to see eye-to-eye on far more numerous and fundamental issues, particularly EMU, than did the UK and France. In sharp contrast to Britain, France and Germany continued to look to the state generally, and the EU specifically, to provide public goods ranging from protection for farmers, research subsidies and support for home-grown European films and television programmes. The UK remained a major player in EU politics. It often allied with France, which by itself was an increasingly ineffective counterweight to Germany. But the Blair government clearly had much to do before the Franco–German alliance was to be supplanted, let alone subsumed, by some new 'triangle'.

'Europe' as a Domestic Political Issue

By 1996 it was hard to argue that the domestic debate about Britain's place in Europe had not deteriorated to a level of ill-informed dogma. A virulently anti-European press – much of it under non-British ownership – found EU-bashing to be a comfortable and even popular theme. The rhetoric of Conservatives, such as the party chairman, Brian Mawhinney, was sharp: 'if you want to reduce Britain to the level of a poodle, trotting at the heels of others, letting them set Europe's agenda, then you can vote Labour' (*Financial Times*, 15 May 1996).

The Labour Party approached EU matters with great caution as the general election approached. Blair looked hesitant and uncertain as he refused to condemn the Major government's non-co-operation policy during the beef crisis. Labour seemed firmly united on few EU matters besides the need for the UK to annul its 'opt-out' of the Social Chapter, a framework for agreeing EU social and employment legislation. One of Labour's first announcements in office was that Britain would sign the Social Chapter. On a range of other policies, particularly a single currency, Labour was however deeply split (Baker *et al.*, 1996). Regardless of Blair's landslide and subsequent 'turn towards Europe', the British electorate was uniquely ill-prepared to pass judgement on EMU, which constituted one of the most dramatic and historic political choices facing the UK since the War.

Nonetheless, Labour began to resemble a European Social Democratic party. Under Blair, it tried to attract the political loyalties of younger voters, many of whom appeared to support both a more European-style polity in Britain and European integration in principle, if not always in practice. Despite his moderately Eurosceptic position on EMU, Cook launched a

'Business Agenda for Europe' in the teeth of the beef crisis. It promised Labour government activism on extending the single market, strengthening EU competition law and launching new competitiveness and employment measures. Blair himself gave a strongly pro-European speech which extolled the traditional Tory virtues of free trade, deregulation and open markets to a somewhat shocked German employers' federation.

Many of Britain's EU partners were so bitterly disappointed with the Major government that they simply stopped negotiating on many vital issues within the IGC until Labour was in power. Major's problem was partly one of expectations raised in 1990–1 when he replaced Thatcher and pledged to put Britain 'at the heart of Europe'. By 1996, European leaders no longer treated Major as someone with whom they could do business. Most viewed his non-co-operation policy as a wheeze to unite the Tories and embarrass Labour. The beef crisis probably opened up as wide a gulf between Britain and the rest of the EU as had ever existed during the Thatcher years. Labour's election was warmly welcomed in national capitals across the EU, but it remained an open question whether Blair and Cook could reverse the domestic tide of Euroscepticism and truly put Britain 'at the heart of Europe'.

Theory and Practice in EU Politics

A neo-realist perspective gives succour to Tory scepticism about European integration. The EU could be viewed as a Cold War institution which lost much of its relevance after 1989. While the economic effects of Britain's EU membership are difficult to quantify, they probably are not large. On the other hand, considerable evidence can be marshalled to suggest that EMU and continental labour market policies would do considerable damage to the British economy.

In contrast, neo-liberals would point to 'the dramatic reorientation of Britain's trade towards Europe in the postwar period' (Chisholm, 1995, p. 167). From a base of about 10 per cent in 1950, about half of British exports went to other EU member states by the mid-1990s. The EU clearly had what economists call 'trade creation effects', thus mutually enriching both Britain and her EU partners. With economics becoming a more important dimension of international power, neo-liberals argued that the real litmus test for Britain as a political force in Europe was EMU.

A single European currency by 1999 was far from certain, but no other actual or mooted EU policy in history threatened to sap so much of Britain's capacity to control its economic destiny. The assumption that the UK could survive outside an EMU without any great costs was challenged with considerable force when European banking officials voted in 1996 in favour of discriminating against countries outside a payments system which would facilitate trade in Euros, the foreseen new currency. It was hard to imagine that London's position as a financial capital would not be damaged if the UK opted out.

EMU offered a clear illustration of the paradox which European integration poses for Britain and its EU partners. The EU empowers them by making them part of a rich and influential collective, while also limiting severely their margin for independent action. Global trade negotiations also highlight the paradox. As an EU member state, often in alliance with Germany, the UK can push the world's largest trade bloc to adopt more liberal positions than usually are preferred by southern member states (especially France), even if EU positions are rarely identical to British preferences. Outside the EU, Britain's voice on trade issues would be a weaker and lonely one.

EU membership also raises problems of political legitimacy and transparency. Instead of weakening national executives, the Union often strengthens them by allowing them to 'hide' from domestic interests and adopt policies which would be impossible on a purely national level. The EU is a remote and technocratic political system, as illustrated by the byzantine discussion on British beef. It was conducted mostly within a committee of veterinary experts who also acted as the political agents of their member states.

By the mid-1990s, the EU clearly needed to enlarge, reform and democratize itself. In debates on these issues, officials from other member states often spoke of the need for more British-style common sense and pragmatism in EU negotiations. However, the UK's unique sense of national identity made it harder for her than for other member states to come to terms with questions which EU membership inevitably posed about national independence and political legitimacy. Under the second Major government, the British response to these questions often comprised defensive, muscle-bound arguments about the sanctity and superiority of its domestic institutions. The problem is by no means a new one. In the view of one long-time British ambassador, the decision of the UK not to join new European institutions in the early post-war period was its biggest strategic mistake of the late twentieth century. The EU thus developed a set of institutions untouched by British influence and dominated by French practice, law and leadership (Renwick, 1996). A former European Commission envoy to Washington concurred that London 'could have had the leadership of Europe for a song' in the 1950s. Instead, according to his view, 'on the world stage, Britain will end the century little more important than Switzerland. It will have been the biggest secular decline in power and influence since seventeenth-century Spain' (Denman, 1996, pp. 1–2).

The Special Relationship

Britain's troubled relations with Europe have always been, in part, a consequence of the assumption that relations between the US and Britain exist on a different, 'higher' plane than relations between any other two industrialized countries. No other allies share so much in terms of history, language and culture. In political, military and intelligence terms, the closeness of the 'special relationship' is sometimes illustrated in dramatic fashion. Henry Kissinger claimed that he often kept London better informed on global developments than the State Department when he served as US National Security Adviser in the 1970s.

The special relationship has helped Britain maintain its position of global influence despite its economic decline. Without American intelligence, for example, the Falklands War could not have been won so quickly and decisively. The personal and ideological affinity between Ronald Reagan and Margaret Thatcher could hardly have been closer. Even after both were out of power, the Bush administration found the UK to be its most reliable ally during the Gulf War. Despite the Major government's overt support for Bush in the 1992 US election, as well as powerful tensions over Bosnia, the Clinton administration showed itself to be protective of the so-called 'special relationship'. Clinton often just skirted ruptures with London as he involved himself in the Northern Ireland peace process, particularly when he allowed Sinn Fein's Gerry Adams to visit America. Still, Clinton stated repeatedly that the UK was a valued American ally, and has formed an important bond with Tony Blair.

However, the extent to which any ally had 'special' influence in America became subject to new doubts. Crushing domestic problems were reflected in US rates of poverty, homelessness, infant mortality, violent crime and imprisonment, all of which were the highest of any industrialized country in the world. The logical result was a general turn inwards, away from foreign policy and the wider world, particularly after Clinton was elected in 1992. Meanwhile, his administration's focus on the North American Free Trade Area (NAFTA) and the Asia Pacific Economic Cooperation (APEC) forum suggested that it saw America's economic future lying in Asia and the Americas. Europe, including Britain, appeared to offer only stagnant markets and political squabbles over EMU and trade with Eastern Europe. Clinton's first Secretary of State, Warren Christopher, declared that 'Western Europe is no longer the dominant area of the world' (Peterson, 1996, p. 137). The stunning seizure of Congress by the US Republicans in the 1994 mid-term election threatened to shift US foreign policy towards 'aggressive unilateralism', particularly on trade and Bosnia.

An earlier series of European initiatives to stop the civil war in ex-Yugoslavia had failed miserably. During its 1992 Presidency of the EU, Britain took the lead in seeking a peace settlement in Bosnia, where the worst inter-ethnic fighting and atrocities took place, but without success. American proposals to 'lift and strike' – lift an arms embargo on Bosnian Muslims and strike Bosnian Serbs with air power – were summarily rejected by European states. The UK and others had large contingents of troops in Bosnia delivering humanitarian aid who were an easy target for Serb reprisals. At this point, the special relationship seemed a joke: Clinton even told an interviewer that Major had rejected 'lift and strike' because his government would have collapsed if its internal divisions about keeping British troops in Bosnia had been exacerbated. More generally, the durability of both NATO and America's strategic commitment to European security became subject to new and serious doubts.

Eventually, a collective western decision was taken to bomb the Bosnian Serbs to the negotiating table in August 1995. NATO was used both to organize the bombing campaign and then to enforce a cease-fire. However, the Dayton Peace Accord was brokered almost exclusively by the Americans, with British and other European diplomats literally locked out of rooms in which the warring Bosnian factions negotiated at a US air force base in Ohio. While a blow to British pride, the Dayton peace deal showed that America clearly remained a European power, at least for the time being, while NATO remained a central pillar of US foreign policy. Both results were viewed as positive reinforcements to British policy and the 'special relationship'. Meanwhile, NATO's success under US leadership in Bosnia inspired continued British scepticism about alternative European security arrangements, including the West European Union (WEU), which obliged its members to accept a robust mutual security guarantee (that is, stronger than NATO's), excluded the Americans and was closely linked to the EU.

Despite intensive transatlantic military co-operation in Bosnia, trade became a serious source of transatlantic tension in 1996. American trade policy became increasingly unilateral and aggressive. In particular, the so-called Helms–Burton Act tried to punish non-American firms for doing business in Cuba. With initial encouragement from London, the European Commission designed countermeasures modelled on existing British legislation. Then, citing concerns about the Commission's legal competence on the matter, the UK threatened to veto the proposals. The Major government was accused by an outraged Commission of bowing to Tory Eurosceptics, who loathed anything which pitted the UK with the rest of Europe against America.

Certainly, European integration posed new challenges to old assumptions about the 'special relationship'. In this context, Major's Foreign Secretary, Malcolm Rifkind, was one of the first of many leaders on both sides of the Atlantic to call for a political relaunch of transatlantic relations after 1994. Rifkind himself had slithered away from his past Euroenthusiasm even before he replaced Douglas Hurd in the Foreign Office. Yet he clearly viewed closer US–EU ties as desirable both in strategic terms and as a political gesture to make Britain's EU membership more palatable to right-wingers in his party.

Rifkind could rightly claim a measure of credit for the new 'Transatlantic Agenda' and Action Plan agreed between the Clinton administration and EU in late 1995. By this time, total US non-military spending on international affairs was only half its 1984 total. Pooling American resources with those of the EU, particularly on new security issues such as terrorism, environmental protection and development aid, made sense from the point of view of America, which increasingly became a 'superpower on the cheap'.

Despite its frequent and often maddening disunity, the EU became viewed in Washington as a more reliable and resourceful partner than any other on offer. Gradually, if very slowly, American policy became more EU and German-centred and less NATO and Britain-oriented. In this context, one American opinion leader described the UK's non-co-operation policy during the beef crisis as a 'hissing fit' (Hoaglund, 1996). Raymond Seitz, the respected former US ambassador to Britain, warned that British influence in Washington would in future depend as never before on British influence in Europe. He was joined by Sharp (1996, p. 1) in pleading with the British political class to realize that 'the only way Britain is going to influence world events in the future is as a major European power working closely with France and Germany, and dealing with the US as a power committed to Europe'.

Looking ahead, it may prove significant that Clinton and Blair are both relatively young leaders and former Oxford men who share similar ideologies. However, the importance of shared affinities between American and British leaders probably has been exaggerated since the Reagan/Thatcher years. Ultimately, until Britain learns to maximize its influence in the EU, the central problem of the 'special relationship' – the glaring asymmetry in power between the US and UK – will persist.

The Legacy of Empire

Regardless of one's view of the extent of the UK's 'decline', Britain's global role and assets are clearly vestiges of its imperial past more than monuments to its recent economic success. Britain remains a highly influential member of the United Nations in large part because about one-quarter of all of its members are former British colonies or territories. The importance of the Commonwealth is a subject of debate, with detractors pointing to its inability to cope in the 1980s with apartheid in South Africa. Still, it includes 53 states or territories which account for about one-fifth of the world's population. Britain retains putative leadership of the Commonwealth, even if the reorientation of British trade towards Europe has reflected a rapid decline in the economic importance of its former colonies.

One of the most enduring legacies of the empire has been the 'lost generation' of modernization by British industry in the early post-war period. Imperial and then commonwealth preferences gave British industry privileged access to relatively undynamic and undemanding markets in the 1950s and 1960s. After Britain's entry into the Common Market in 1973, many of its industries were overwhelmed by continental competition which had been sharpened by 15 years of tariff-free trade between the Community's original members. In some respects, British industry never recovered, with the costs becoming clearer as the UK began to trade more with other industrialized countries. Ironically, by most measures, Britain now has weaker trade links to the developing world than do most of its EU partners (Clarke, 1992, p. 46).

Other remnants of the empire have helped to balance the ledger. First, English is spoken in at least a basic way by something like 20 per cent of the world's people. Second, the BBC World Service has a global audience of nearly three times the population of the UK itself. Britain's foreign aid budget is not generous, but it is the sixth largest in the world and is more focused than those of other major powers on the very poorest countries. Clare Short, Secretary of State for International Development, has pledged to increase Britain's aid budget.

Yet the UK's claim to be the enlightened voice of the west on North–South issues is considerably undermined by an entrenched 'liberal militarism' in its domestic industrial policy (Reynolds and Coates, 1996). Its effect is to make a large section of British industry dependent on arms sales to the less-developed world. By 1993, the defence sector still accounted for nearly 10 per cent of the total value of British manufacturing and employed about 400 000 people. Britain ranked second only to the US as an arms exporter and controlled about one-fifth of the total global market (Lee, 1996, p. 59).

Britain's international reputation was tarnished by the revelation of scandals connected with the arms trade in the mid-1990s. The Scott inquiry into the so-called Matrix Churchill affair saw private businessmen scapegoated for selling arms to Iraq despite the government's blessing of exports. The UK gave soft loans to an unsavoury Malaysian regime so that it could hire a British firm to build the Pergau Dam, with the entire deal underpinned by an agreement to buy British arms.

More generally, Britain's relations with South East Asia, where much of its empire once lay, were complex and often contradictory. The 'return' of Hong Kong to China in 1997 was always going to be fraught with tensions and charges of a British sell-out of the island's citizens. Yet it is difficult to imagine that any other major western state would have handled the negotiations with more skill, at least until Chris Patten, the final British Governor of Hong Kong, sought to renegotiate much that already had been agreed with the Chinese (Cradock, 1994).

The UK remained a magnet for inward investment from Japan and other states in the region, whose economic growth rates far surpassed those of Europe. The National Audit Office calculated that each pound spent on promoting trade with South East Asia generated 80 pounds in British exports. Yet Michael Heseltine's dire warnings in autumn 1995 about the threat to British prosperity posed by the Far Eastern Tiger economies seemed a blatant attempt to unite the Tories against a common enemy.

In short, the UK's imperial history continued to inform policy choices in ways which were usually subtle but sometimes not. The decision in the 1980s to send the British navy halfway around the world to defend a small and geopolitically meaningless group of islands in the South Atlantic clearly could not have been taken without recourse to familiar arguments about the need to defend Britain's foreign assets. The Major government's somewhat desperate defence of the pound against the overwhelming will of currency markets in 1992 recalled Britain's habitual post-war defence of an overvalued currency for the sake of broader foreign policy prerogatives. The successful export of the Westminster model of government to states across the world during the transition from empire to commonwealth will continue to colour

debates about Labour's plans to reform the British state. The legacy of empire remains palpable, particularly for critics of post-war British foreign policy, who often claim that 'the pursuit of an independent and major world role for the British state proved immensely costly and self-destructive over time: in high defence spending, the maintenance of a strong currency, and the failure to modernize the British state machine' (Reynolds and Coates, 1996, p. 257).

Britain as an International Actor

By some measures, such as ranking as an exporter, Britain's global position has stabilized. It continues to exercise considerable influence in many of the more than 120 international organizations of which Britain is a member. Its seat on the Security Council gives Britain veto power on virtually all important UN matters. As a financial capital with historical roots to much of the less-developed world, Britain is an influential member of both the World Bank and International Monetary Fund (IMF). The British vice-president of the European Commission, Sir Leon Brittan, was an important architect of the World Trade Organisation (WTO) created after the Uruguay Round of global trade talks. The UK remains a mainstay of NATO, playing a strong understudy to the US and often neutralizing French eccentricities.

The price paid for Britain's international role has been steep. Late entry into the EU, after its expensive (and wasteful) Common Agricultural Policy was in place, meant that the UK would always be a net contributor to the EU's central budget. The Major government volunteered the second largest contingent to allied forces in both the Gulf War and Bosnia. British taxpayers footed an annual £90 million bill for Britain's national subscriptions to international organizations.

Above all, Britain remained a nuclear power despite its limited means. Even before the Cold War ended, the UK faced a difficult choice between buying American nuclear systems or developing them co-operatively with European partners. Both options inevitably made Britain dependent on others for its own security. For example, furious diplomacy was unleashed on the Germans when the latter sought to reduce their contribution to the collaborative European Fighter Aircraft, after unification put enormous strains on German public spending. 'Buying American' was sometimes equally problematic. The Thatcher government's decision to buy the Trident submarine system in 1980 at first seemed to highlight the advantages of the special relationship, as the Americans clearly would not have sold the system to anyone else. However, the subsequent US decision to upgrade Trident to suit its own needs had the effect of landing the UK with a more expensive and sophisticated system than it needed.

Nuclear weapons continue to be a source of considerable status and power in international politics. Neo-realists are quick to point out that dismantling Britain's capability would invite questions about why it deserved special status in the UN. They scorn the neo-liberal argument that the UK could rely on the US or an integrated European nuclear capability to defend itself, and insist that permanent alliances do not and could not ever exist in international relations.

Cuts in British defence spending have mirrored those under-taken in most western states since the end of the Cold War. Arguably, however, they have had special implications for Britain. An independent UK military operation on the scale of the Falklands war was already technically impossible by the early 1990s (Clarke, 1992, p. 53). Whether or not neo-realists are right to be cynical about the durability of alliances, neo-liberals are on strong ground in arguing that Britain's formal military sovereignty brings her very little military independence.

Still, there is no question that Britain retains important, if somewhat intangible, levers to influence international politics. One is certainly the competent, professional and highly-respected cadre of British officials serving both in the foreign service as well as in myriad international organizations. British civil servants with international responsibilities usually deserve their reputation for tolerance, pragmatism and incorruptibility. However, it is hard not to conclude that they have been undermined repeatedly by their political superiors, as when British officials were forced to 'non-co-operate' during the beef crisis. The mentality reflected in a 1977 Central Policy Review Staff report, which criticized British officials abroad for doing their jobs 'to an unjustifiably high standard', was indicative of a general lack of clear purpose which hampers British diplomacy (Clarke, 1992, pp. 70–71). In this context, no wholesale review of Britain's foreign policy was undertaken in the afterglow of the Cold War. A defence review published in 1990 assessed military needs and priorities narrowly, but took little account of wider questions of economic, political and security strategy (Sanders, 1993, p. 288). Thatcher's foreign policy ethos underwent no systematic revision under the Major governments.

For its part, the Blair government pledged to upgrade Britain's international profile by adopting Clinton-style export promotion, putting more into the Commonwealth, and, above all, ending the UK's isolation in Europe. Labour probably won very few votes on the basis of its new thinking on foreign policy. Its focus during the election was overwhelmingly on domestic policy. But concern for Britain's global role is cross-party, instinctual and a crucial part of its national identity.

Conclusions

Any nation-state's identity and global role are derived in large part from history and geography. It clearly matters that Britain has not been invaded since the eleventh century and is an archipelago of north-western Europe. However, these factors are not determinant. Arguably, Britain's failure to produce a political class able to lead in a way that is appropriate to an increasingly interdependent world explains more about British foreign policy than any other factor.

Any state which aspires to international influence disproportionate to its economic power must be supported by an outward-looking, internationally-minded citizen-public. In 1996, Labour party strategists insisted that the electorate (and newspaper editors) were so ill-educated in the complexities of multilateral diplomacy that Labour had no choice but to support Major's non-co-operation policy. Far more British citizens either wanted to pull out of the EU or renegotiate the UK's membership than supported closer British ties to the Union (NOP poll in *Sunday Times*, 17 March 1996). The *British Social Attitudes Survey* (1996) found that around 60 per cent of Britons favoured limits on imports to protect the British economy. One-third thought foreigners should not be allowed to buy land in the UK.

The popular British press nourished a national identity based on equal parts of insecurity and pride. Its proclivity for blaming foreigners (especially 'Europeans') for problems with domestic roots recalled Pat Buchanan's American nativism. Tabloid caricatures of a jackbooted German Chancellor, Helmut Kohl, and openly racist headlines as Britain prepared to meet Germany in the 1996 European football championships led the President of the Confederation of British Industry, Sir Brian Nicholson, to lament 'this pungent atmosphere of romantic nationalism and churlish xenophobia' (*Financial Times*, 25/26 May 1996).

Conservative Eurosceptics claimed that they were 'internationalists' at heart. Yet, the writings of John Redwood, twice a Eurosceptic challenger for the party's leadership in 1995–7, were perhaps illustrative of his and his followers' attention to the world beyond British shores. Redwood (1994) predicted that North Vietnam would collapse in the 1990s, leading to Vietnamese unification, evidently not realizing that it already had occurred 20 years previous. His insistence that European integration would lead to a 'country called Europe' to which 'we would all have to swear allegiance', while the former British army 'went into battle under the European flag, marching to the European anthem' became almost a mainstream view in the British press (Redwood, 1996).

Ironically, it was difficult to see the logic of fighting an election on a fiercely Eurosceptic platform. The EU was ranked as one of the top five most important issues by few voters. Polls suggested that voters blamed the Major government, as opposed to the EU, for the beef crisis by a margin of three to one. The effect of the crisis on voting preferences actually appeared negative for the Conservatives (ICM poll in *The Observer*, 26 May 1996). Yet a minority wing of the Conservative Party became almost obsessively anti-European. The Blair government's 'constructive engagement' with the EU was certain to find no shortage of critics among the opposition.

Meanwhile, even when the Major government was insisting that it had reversed Britain's decline, a series of leaked government briefing papers predicted that the UK's status as one of the world's seven biggest economies would be lost within 20 years.

India, Brazil and Indonesia were set to pass Britain, with China emerging as the world's largest single economy. These states were certain to demand greater political representation in major international organizations. Pointedly, as Ireland took over the EU's rotating presidency in 1996, its government made much of evidence which suggested that Ireland's per capita income would overtake that of the UK in less than 15 years.

A neo-realist's assessment of British power would highlight the fact that the UK is the leading trading partner of no European country besides Ireland. British goods account for less than 10 per cent of the imports of the other member states of the Union. As such, the Eurosceptic billionaire James Goldsmith's urgings that the UK should act to 'convert or split Europe' grossly exaggerates British power to determine the EU's future.

From a neo-liberal perspective, Britain's role in the world is a valued asset. It can be preserved if British diplomatic excellence is backed by political leadership which nurtures popular interna-tionalism and alliance building in multilateral diplomacy, parti-cularly within the EU. From this point of view, the debate about whether Britain should remain a member of the Union appears pointless, especially to those outside the British Isles.

The claim that Britain's international decline has continued unchecked is not beyond dispute. The UK's future decline is not inevitable. But in recent times the only clear purpose of British governments in international affairs often has seemed to be insisting that Britain matters more than it really does.

Part I

3
Voting and the Electorate

DAVID SANDERS

Has the 1997 election, with its stunning Labour victory, long foretold in record Labour opinion poll leads, produced a genuine realignment of British electoral politics? Does it foreshadow a decisive alteration in the Conservative hegemony in British politics over the last two decades, and stretching back in a weaker way before that to the 1950s? Or is the third outright Labour majority government to be seen as no more than the periodic swing of a weighted pendulum always predisposed to swing back to Conservative predominance for another long period if the Labour government runs into difficulties? Is New Labour a qualitatively different electoral force from old Labour, or just an amorphous coalition temporarily assembled by the combination of Tony Blair's novel leadership qualities and the Conservatives' exhaustion and disarray in government? And do the ironies of John Major's electoral fortunes – re-elected in the teeth of economic recession in 1992, but ignominiously turfed out of Downing Street during the economic boom times in 1997 – signal a change in the conventional wisdom that 'It's the economy, stupid!' which decides UK general elections?

These central questions continue to be debated as New Labour grapples with government, and attempts to put through constitutional changes which may influence future electoral outcomes, and the Conservatives come to terms with leadership change and internal policy divisions over Europe. No definitive answer can yet be given, but electoral analysis does provide the basis for exploring possible answers in two ways – first looking in detail at survey data to see how voters' different social backgrounds, values and preferences influence their alignment; and second constructing aggregate models of how groups of voters behave, especially tracing how the views of the electorate as a whole evolve and change over time in response to political events and economic performance.

The Survey Data Perspective

Theories about voting preferences focus primarily on what goes on inside the individual voter's head; on the various factors, both conscious and unconscious, both explicit and implicit, that enter into the voter's decision to vote in a particular way. Survey data provide the key evidence for these individual-level analyses which, as their name implies, seek to assemble data which measure the voting behaviour, attitudes and perceptions, and dominant socio-demographic attributes (age, gender, class, education and so on) of a representative sample of individuals. Individual-level analysis consists in relating these individuals' voting preferences to their attitudes, perceptions and attributes. This analysis is effected either through a series of simple cross tabulations of the sort presented here or through more complex multivariate techniques (such as logistic regression) which attempt to determine whether or not the possession of a particular characteristic affects the probability that a given respondent will vote for a particular party. The crucial feature of survey-based individual-level data is that they allow for the direct testing of theoretical propositions about the relative importance of different attitudinal and perceptual variables on the probability that observable individual voters will support party A rather than party B.

We apply this approach to three key questions. What changed in the parties' fortunes in the 1997 general election? How does the apparently greater cross-class appeal of New Labour in 1997 shed light on the academic debate about the alleged (but contested) decline of social class as the dominant influence on British voters' long-term political alignments? And does the 1997 result put at rest the fears about the inaccuracies of political opinion polls which sprang up in 1992, when the polls inaccurately seemed to predict a hung Parliament or Labour victory?

Analysing the 1997 result

The 1997 general election was clearly an electoral triumph for New Labour. The party was returned with 419 MPs – 102 of them women – and a majority of 179, the largest since 1931. The Conservatives were reduced to a rural English rump of 165 MPs, securing no seats whatever in either Scotland or Wales and only a handful in urban England. The Liberal Democrats, whilst receiving a slightly smaller share of the national vote, more than doubled their Commons representation. Their 46 seats reflected the success of a targeting strategy that concentrated their campaigning efforts on 'winnable' seats in the south-west, Scotland, Wales and pockets of southern England.

The Conservatives' share of the national vote fell from 43 per cent in 1992 to 31 per cent. Labour's rose from 35 per cent to 44 per cent, a swing of 10.5 per cent. This was the largest swing to Labour since Attlee's victory in 1945 (a 12 per cent swing) and almost twice the size obtained by Margaret Thatcher (5.3 per cent) in 1979. Although turnout fell to below 72 per cent (from 78 per cent in 1992), there is no reason to suppose that this decline implied either a gain or a loss for any one party.

The Conservatives do appear to have been damaged, however, by tactical voting. A clear verdict on the full extent and implications of tactical voting is impossible without access to high quality individual–level data on voters behaviour, which is not yet available. That said, the raw constituency results suggest that both Labour and Liberal Democrat supporters did indeed vote tactically for the other party in seats where, on the basis of the 1992 results, one of them was in a strong position to challenge the incumbent Conservative. A measure of the costs in seats to the Conservatives of tactical voting can be gleaned from the fact that a uniform swing of 10.5 per cent to Labour should have left the Conservatives with around 195 seats in the House of Commons. The fact that 30 additional seats were lost suggests either a powerful tactical voting effect, or a misallocation of Tory campaign resources which caused them to lose more seats than they need have done.

Such a stunning victory for Labour – and such an improved showing for the Liberal Democrats in terms of Parliamentary seats – was a clear indication that the Conservatives' electoral hegemony of the period since 1979 had finally, and decisively, been broken. In a sense, however, the general election result merely delivered the *coup de grace* to a party which had experienced little electoral success of any kind – and which had been far behind in the opinion polls – for almost five years. Throughout the 1992 Parliament, the Conservative party lost every by-election contest that it fought. It performed badly both in local elections and in the 1994 election for the European Parliament. In local council by-elections (which were held every month and were regarded by some observers as a good indicator of the real electoral strength of the major parties), the Conservatives rarely secured more than the equivalent of 30 per cent of the national vote. So the Tories' vote in 1992 was not an isolated feature, but part of a longer-run decline. After Labour's disastrous showing in the 1983 general election, when its support fell to 28 per cent, the party took 14 years to recover. What worried Conservative strategists as they picked over the bones of their defeat in May 1997 was that it might take them equally long to recover the electoral ground that they had just lost.

Table 3.1 shows how the 1997 vote was distributed by class, tenure, gender and age compared with 1992, and Table 11.2 (on page 223 below) shows the regional distribution of the vote. The tables clearly show that the whole country, across all groups and regions, swung decisively to Labour. Not surprisingly, the swings were smallest for those groups (men and DEs) and regions (Wales and Scotland) where Labour already had strong support in 1992. The largest swings, however, were amongst the kind of people whom Labour especially wanted to attract. The under 25s, whose entire political education had taken place under Conservative rule, swung clearly to Labour (15 per cent), auguring well for Labour's future prospects if it proved able to retain the allegiances thus expressed. Middle-class voters – the ABs and CIs that Blair's team had been so desperate to reassure throughout the long campaign – similarly shifted their loyalties towards New Labour, again with a 15 per cent swing. In 1997, the Conservatives' only redoubts (and they were by no means decisive ones) were in the South East (outside London), the South West, East Anglia (where Labour almost equalled them) and among the ABs. Labour led the Conservatives by a clear margin in every other socio-demographic category – even among owner-occupiers, traditionally

TABLE 3.1   Voting patterns by social background characteristics in the
1992 and 1997 general elections (%)

	1992			1997			1992–7
	Con	Lab	Lib	Con	Lab	Lib	Swing to Lab
Occupational class							
AB	56	20	21	37	31	24	15
C1	49	28	20	32	41	22	15
C2	39	40	18	29	52	12	11
DE	30	51	14	25	52	15	3
Tenure							
Owner-Occupier	49	23	19	35	41	17	16
Council Tenant	23	58	14	13	65	15	8.5
Gender							
Women	45	35	18	32	44	17	11.0
Men	40	38	17	31	44	17	7.5
Age group							
Under 25	38	35	22	24	52	17	15.5
25–34	37	41	18	27	46	19	7.5
35–44	38	38	21	28	49	16	10.5
45–64	44	35	19	31	40	20	9
Over 65	49	33	14	38	40	15	9

Source: For 1992: gender, class and age, Gallup Post-Election Survey. For
1997: BBC Election Results file; class, gender and age, Gallup Post-Election
Survey, figures adjusted to take account of the survey's over-estimate of the
total percentage of Labour votes; tenure, BBC/NOP Exit Poll.

a group upon whose support the Conservatives could rely.
Collectively, this was a rejection for the Conservatives on an
enormous scale.

But why had such a dramatic political reversal taken place
between 1992 and 1997? A definitive answer will have to await
the publication of the results of the 1997 British Election Study.
However, the picture that emerges from the survey evidence
available in the immediate aftermath of the election is one of
the Conservatives' inability to convince voters of their competence
to govern and of Labour's contrasting ability to reassure voters
that its new moderation meant that the government and economy
of the country would be safe in its hands. The Conservatives

sought to fight the campaign on what they believed were potentially their four strongest issues: taxation, which was widely
thought to have been the Conservatives' trump card in 1992;
the performance of the economy, which had experienced three
successive years of steady growth, low inflation, low interest rates
and falling unemployment; the integrity of the UK Union, which
the Conservatives claimed was threatened by Labour's plans for
devolution and constitutional reform; and the party's generally
sceptical stance on Europe, which the Tory leadership considered,
despite deep intra-party divisions, to be far more in line with
voters' views than the pro-Social Chapter position taken by
Labour. Labour, for its part – as in 1992 – focused on the issues
of education and the NHS (where it stressed the need to restore
good public service provision) and on unemployment (where it
promised an earmarked windfall tax on the privatised utilities to
pay for schemes aimed at permanently reducing youth unemployment by 250 000).

TABLE 3.2   Evaluations of the party best able to handle the issues

Question: 'I am going to read a list of problems facing the country. Could you
please tell me, for each one of them, which party you personally think would
handle the problem best?'

	1992			*1997*		
	Con	Lab	Lab lead	Con	Lab	Lab lead
Unemployment	30	46	+ 19	24	62	+ 38
NHS	32	49	+ 17	16	65	+ 49
Education	33	39	+ 6	17	56	+ 39
Pensions	35	44	+ 9	21	58	+ 37
Inflation	54	25	−29	42	40	− 2
Defence	59	18	−41	41	34	− 8
Strikes	54	27	−27	40	43	+ 3
Law and Order	47	25	−22	28	50	+ 22
Britain's relations with Europe	55	21	−34	32	44	+ 12
Taxation	49	20	−20	36	42	+ 6

Source: Gallup Post-Election Surveys, April 1992 and May 1997. Data for
1997 are adjusted to take account of the fact that the survey overestimated
Labour support.

Labour knew, however, that it had to do something more than just win over voters to its policies on education, health and unemployment. In 1992, these had been identified by voters as the three most important issues facing the country – and Labour had enjoyed a clear lead over the Conservatives on each of them. Yet Labour had proved incapable of converting such 'issue support' into concrete votes (Sanders, 1992). In the spring of 1997, the same three issues (along with Europe) remained at the top of voters' stated issue priorities (Gallup Political Index, March 1997). Labour's lead on each of them, moreover, had increased considerably. More importantly – as Table 3.2 shows – voters' perceptions of Labour across the entire range of key issues had been comprehensively transformed. The Conservatives still enjoyed small leads on inflation and defence. But in every other issue-area Labour was clearly ahead. This suggested a funda-mental shift in Labour's overall image as a potential party of government, a shift which had begun with John Smith's election as leader in the wake of the 1992 defeat and which had strength-ened and deepened under Tony Blair's leadership after July 1994. By the time of the 1997 election, New Labour's continued presentation of itself as the party of moderation and fiscal rectitutude had neutralized voters' concerns about its likely policies on inflation and strikes. On taxation, law and order, and Europe, it had even succeeded in turning what, in 1992, had been credibility deficits into distinct policy advantages. And, of course, by 1997 Labour also enjoyed an even greater lead on health, education, unemployment and pensions than it had (though to little effect) in 1992.

Three factors underpinned this extraordinary transformation of the Labour and Conservative images. The first of these was the Conservatives' loss of their previous reputation for *economic manage-ment competence*. This Conservative weakness on economic compe-tence was reinforced by Shadow Chancellor Gordon Brown's determination to present Labour's tax and spending plans as being no more threatening to 'middle Britain' than those of the Conservatives. In 1992, the Conservatives were seen by 52 per cent of voters as the best party if Britain got into 'economic difficulties', compared with Labour on 31. By March 1997, for reasons that are discussed later in this chapter, the position had been almost reversed, with Labour seen as the best party by 49 per cent and the Tories by 35.

The second factor underpinning Labour's transformation was undoubtedly Tony Blair's ability to present himself as a *competent political manager* who would preside over a moderate, centrist government. In contrast to John Major's utter failure to quieten the seething discontent over Europe that continually festered within Tory ranks, Blair was able to present himself as a leader who had not only removed the embarrassment of Clause IV from Labour's constitution but who had also modernized British social democracy to the point where it now firmly embraced monetary orthodoxy and fiscal conservatism. Anyone who could lead a united Labour Party so decisively to the centre-ground of British politics, it was claimed, was also qualified to lead the country into the twenty-first century. Enough voters accepted these claims for Labour to achieve victory. Fully 93 per cent of Labour voters considered Blair's leadership strength to have been either very or fairly important in their decision to vote Labour – complementing the 67 per cent who thought that Major's weakness was important (Gallup post-election survey). The sense that Labour had become 'more moderate and responsible' under Blair was seen as very important by two-thirds of Labour voters – and by 74 per cent of those who converted directly from Conservative to Labour between 1992 and 1997. Whether or not Labour's rather cautious reform plans genuinely merited it, the overwhelmingly majority of Labour voters (97 per cent) also cited the party's promises to improve the NHS and education as important reasons for voting Labour. This was a clear, and damning, indictment of the Conservatives' record on health and education over the previous 18 years.

A third factor which undoubtedly contributed to the changing images of the parties was *sleaze*. Throughout the 1992 Parliament, the Conservatives were hit by a series of sexual and financial scandals. Notwithstanding Major's decision to set up the Nolan Committee on Standards in Public Life in 1994, Tory ministers were consistently unable to quell the public disquiet that the various allegations of corruption engendered. The dispute over the propriety of the behaviour of Neil Hamilton, Conservative MP for Tatton, continued to act as a focus for the 'sleaze' issue up to the very end of the campaign. The sense that the various acts of individual corruption were the consequence of the arrogance of 18 years of power was widespread among electors. Four-fifths of Labour voters identified the Conservatives' sleaze and corruption as being an important factor in their voting decisions (Gallup post-election survey). Sleaze, moreover, symbolized the tiredness and ineptness of John Major's government. Small wonder that 89 per cent of Labour voters considered that their support was predicated in part on the idea that it was 'time for a change'.

But if the changed images of the main parties were at the root of the Conservatives' failure and Labour's success in 1997, what light, if any, did the result shed on one of the major academic disputes that had dominated discussion of previous general elections, the role of social class?

The Decline (or not) of Class Voting

Until the late 1960s, it was almost universally acknowledged that social class was a major determinant, if not the major determinant, of vote choice in Britain. The interests of middle-class voters were most obviously represented by a Conservative Party that sought to promote private enterprise and to keep taxation low – and they duly showed a greater than average tendency to vote Tory. The interests of working-class voters, on the other hand, were most obviously served by the Labour Party's emphasis on redistributive policies and by its connections with the trade unions – and their political loyalties were accordingly tied primarily to Labour. In the 1964 and 1966 elections, roughly two-thirds of electors voted for their 'natural' class party, so that the class influence was by no means universally decisive, but its influence was none the less impressive. During the 1970s, however, the position appeared to undergo quite radical change. The most obvious development was that the Liberal Party dramatically increased its share of the popular vote, from under 10 per cent in 1966 and 1970, to almost 20 per cent in the two general elections of 1974, and to well over 20 per cent in 1983 and 1987. Its growth, however, did not necessarily imply a reduction in class voting. After all, the Liberals could have drawn their increased support either from defecting working-class Conservatives or from

TABLE 3.3　Occupational class and vote, 1964–97 (%)

	1964		1966		1970		1974f		1974o	
	Non-manual	Manual	Non-manual	Manual	Non-manual	Manual	Non-manual	Manual	Non-manual	Manual
Conservative	62	28	60	25	64	33	53	24	51	24
Labour	22	64	26	69	25	58	22	57	25	57
Liberal (Democrat)	18	8	14	6	11	9	25	19	24	20
Absolute class voting index		76		78		64		64		59
Relative class voting index		6.4		6.4		4.5		5.7		4.8

Note: The relative class voting index is an odds ratio measure recommended by Heath *et al.*, (1985); *a* = the percentage of non-manual workers who vote Conservative; *b* = the percentage of non-manual workers who vote Labour; *c* = the percentage of manual workers who vote Conservative; *d* = the percentage of manual workers who vote Labour. The relative class voting index = $(a/b)/(c/d)$.

Source: Source for raw percentage data, 1964–92: Denver (1994, p. 61); for 1997 data: Gallup Post-Election Survey. Absolute class voting index defined in the text.

defecting middle-class Labour voters – or both – thus leaving Labour and the Conservatives with their respective working- and middle-class 'heartlands' intact.

In fact, successive surveys conducted by the main academic survey, the British Election Study (BES), showed that there was a progressive, if uneven, reduction in the extent of 'absolute' class-based voting between 1964 and the late 1980s. Using a simple manual (working class) versus non-manual (middle class) dichotomy, Table 3.3 shows how the proportion of each class group voting for its 'natural' class party did indeed decline during the 1970s and 1980s. For example, in 1964, 64 per cent of manual workers voted Labour. By 1979, this figure had fallen to 50 per cent and by 1987 to 45 per cent. The table also shows several indices which have been developed to describe the changing overall strength of the class–party relationship. The simplest is the index of absolute class voting, which is calculated by subtracting (1) the percentage of working-class voters who support the Conservatives plus the percentage of middle-class voters who

1979		1983		1987		1992		1997	
Non-manual	*Manual*	*Non-manual*	*Manual*	*Non-manual*	*Manual*	*Non-manual*	*Manual*	*Non-manual*	*Manual*
60	35	55	35	54	35	56	36	38	29
23	50	17	42	20	45	24	51	40	58
17	15	28	22	27	21	21	14	18	12
52		45		44		47		27	
3.7		3.9		3.5		3.3		1.9	

support Labour from (2) the percentage of voters who support their 'natural' class party. This index shows clear declines in 1970, (February) 1974 and 1983, a slight recovery in 1992 and a further decline in 1997.

This tendency for 'class dealignment' had potentially important implications for UK electoral politics (Sarlvik and Crewe, 1983). If class location was becoming less important as a determinant of political preferences, presumably other things were becoming more important. Freed from the bonds of their class-voting constraints, voters were becoming much more like consumers who could make an informed choice between (or among) the alternative political products on offer, paying more attention to parties' key policy positions, the leadership qualities of the party leaders, and the rival front bench teams' economic management capabilities and performance potential. The decline of class-based voting also implied an electoral danger for the Labour Party in particular, both from the decline of its levels of support among working-class people (Crewe, 1989) and shrinking of the traditional manual working class, as the UK moved towards a post-industrial economy and service sector jobs replaced employment in industrial manufacturing. In the absence of a suitable response from Labour itself, these two tendencies taken together implied a continuing haemorrhaging of Labour support – a development that appeared to be supported by Labour's woeful performance in the 1983 and 1987 general elections.

In the mid-1980s, Anthony Heath and his colleagues sought to alter the terms of the debate about class dealignment (Heath *et al.*, 1985 and 1991), arguing that the simple manual/non-manual class division was misleading; that measures of absolute class voting ignored the increasing role played in UK electoral politics by the Liberals; and that absolute measures also underplayed the significance of variations in the overall popularity of the major parties. When proper account was taken of all of these factors, the relationship between class and vote had remained broadly constant throughout the period since 1964 – and in their view the 'social psychology' of class voting had not changed at all. Heath and his associates argued that, when appropriate statistical controls were made for the changing sizes of the social classes and for the changing overall support for each party in each election, the magnitude of the effect of social class on vote preference did not change substantially (and certainly did not decline systematically) between 1964 and 1992 (Heath *et al.*, 1995).

While the accuracy of Heath's statistical conclusion is incontrovertible, some scepticism has been expressed about its theoretical relevance (Crewe, 1986, 1992). Crewe argues that Heath's analysis confuses cause and effect. The emergence of the Liberals during the 1970s and 1980s, together with Labour's disastrous performances in 1983 and 1987, are assumed by Heath to constitute autonomous changes in the political scene that need to be taken into account when a suitable measure of class voting is being devised. Crewe contends, however, that these developments were precisely the result of class dealignment – of voters becoming less committed to voting for their 'natural' class party. In Crewe's view, to argue that increasing Liberal success and/or periodic Labour failure need to be 'controlled for' prior to the measurement of the class–party relationship is absurd. What is of theoretical interest is not the relationship over time between class and party relative to the sizes of the classes and the overall vote shares of the parties, but the changes over time in the absolute class–party relationship. It is precisely because this relationship has weakened that the electorate has become more 'volatile' and that the fortunes of the Labour, Liberal (Democrat) and nationalist parties have fluctuated so markedly since the early 1970s.

What do the results of the 1997 election imply for the debate about class dealignment? The results shown in Table 3.3, reveal that class-based voting was markedly less important in 1997 than in any general election since 1964. Both the 'absolute' and 'relative' class voting indices show clear downwards shifts in 1997 in comparison with 1992. The 'absolute' index fell 20 points from the mid-40s – where it had been since 1983 – to 27. The 'relative' index – which averaged around 3.5 in the period from 1979 – fell dramatically to 1.9. These index changes reflect the unprecedented desertion of middle class voters (ABs and C1s) from the Conservatives to Labour. In 1992, 56 per cent of non-manual workers voted Conservative. In 1997, with the Liberal Democrats obtaining more or less the same level of middle-class support as in 1992, the Conservatives could muster the support of only 38 per cent of non-manual workers. Over the same period, Labour increased its share of the non-manual vote from 24 per cent to 40 per cent. This extraordinary increase in what had traditionally been regarded as fertile electoral territory for the Conservatives represented an important breakthrough for Labour. Tony Blair's centrist policy stances during the three years of his leadership had led some critics (as well as some admirers) to observe that it was now New Labour, rather than the Conservative Party, that represented the one–nation conservatism of the old Tory left. New Labour's success in gathering cross-class votes in 1997 suggested that large sections of the electorate – and in particular the middle class – took a similar view. Labour in the 1980s had good cause to worry about its long-term electoral prospects because of the declining size and commitment of the working class. But if the party could sustain and build upon its ability to appeal to middle class voters in 1997, then Labour leaders might be encouraged in thoughts of a new cross-class (and perhaps non–class) electoral coalition that would help to keep the Conservatives out of office for a decade or more. It remains to be seen, of course, whether these fond hopes can be translated into more permanent political support for New Labour.

Opinion Polls

The general election of April 1992 was notorious for the failure of the commercial opinion polls accurately to predict the result. Having promised a neck-and-neck contest right up to the end of the campaign, the pollsters found when the votes came in that they had seriously underestimated the Conservatives' share of the vote and concomitantly overestimated that likely to accrue to Labour. The implications of the failure, however, went well beyond a few red faces at Gallup, ICM, MORI and NOP. Academic analysts of course also depend on the survey method for the data needed to evaluate both competing theoretical models of voting behaviour and alternative explanations for the actual election outcome. If the pollsters could get the parties' likely vote shares so badly wrong, what were the prospects for the future? Were all surveys now flawed for accurately measuring other voter characteristics and for accurately determining the impact of those other characteristics on voting preferences?

A wide range of explanations for the polls' poor performance in 1992 have been advanced (Broughton, 1995). Three factors were given most credence by the Market Research Society's own special enquiry (MRS, 1993):

(1) Commercial pollsters employed quota samples, where their interviewers sought responses from pre-set categories of the population: for example, so many people from different social classes, tenure groups, in and out of work, and so on. The categories employed by the pollsters were based on out of date view of the social structure and the wrong category sizes. In particular, there was (1) wide variation in the proportion of council house tenants sampled across different polls (ranging from 17.5 per cent to 26 per cent); and (2) oversampling of manual workers and undersampling of professionals and managers as a result of using the National Readership Survey (rather than the then unavailable 1991 Census) as the basis for determining quota sizes.

(2) There was a significant swing in opinion in the last two days of the campaign (towards the Conservatives and away from Labour) which occurred too late to be factored into the pollsters' estimates of the state of electoral opinion.

(3) There was some evidence of the operation of a 'spiral of silence', in which respondents who held what they perceived to be unpopular views (notably supporting the Conservatives) were both less prepared to be interviewed in the first place and more likely to refuse to state their voting intention. The omission of these 'interview-refusers' and 'item-refusers' in calculating voting intentions led to a consistent underestimate of the Conservative vote share.

In the period after the 1992 general election, the polling organizations strove to correct those failings that were capable of being addressed. They could obviously do nothing about 'late swing', other than to plan to continue polling until the very last minute in 1997. Nonetheless, they made strenuous efforts, first, to ensure the accuracy of their quota sampling techniques – though they were always aware that, by 1997, even the 1991 Census statistics would be six years out of date. On the question of the spiral of silence, the pollsters could do something about the voting intention item-refusers. Rather than excluding them from the percentage base in calculating vote intention percentages, from mid-1994 the major polling companies began to report 'adjusted' party support figures. The adjustment involved counting support-item-refusers who admitted to voting Conservative in 1992 as current Conservative supporters. However, the great unknown in the 1992 fiasco was always the preference pattern of the interview-refusers. Throughout the 1992–7 period, the pollsters were unable to make any adjustment whatsoever for the potentially disruptive effect that these refusers might exert on their vote share estimates. It was always an empirical question as to whether their differential voting pattern in the actual election would be sufficient to result in another 'failure of the opinion polls' in 1997.

When the opinion polls' huge Labour leads in 1997 translated into an equivalent in terms of actual votes, the sense of relief among pollsters and academic psephologists alike was palpable. As Table 3.4 shows, the final 'poll of polls' estimate of the likely vote shares of the major parties was broadly in line with the level of accuracy generally attained in the period since 1970 – the previous occasion on which the polls had seriously underestimated the Conservatives' vote share. It is extremely difficult to know what this greater degree of accuracy in 1997 implies about the

TABLE 3.4   The accuracy of commercial opinion polls (the 'poll of polls')
and BES surveys in predicting Great Britain percentage vote
of the parties, 1970–97

	Result	*Poll of polls*	*BES post-election survey*
1970			
Conservative	46	44	46
Labour	44	48	44
Liberal	8	7	7
1974f			
Conservative	39	39	37
Labour	38	36	41
Liberal	20	22	19
1974o			
Conservative	37	35	36
Labour	40	43	43
Liberal	19	20	18
1979			
Conservative	45	43	47
Labour	38	39	38
Liberal	14	14	14
1983			
Conservative	44	46	45
Labour	28	26	29
Liberal	26	26	25
1987			
Conservative	43	42	44
Labour	32	34	31
Liberal	23	22	24
1992			
Conservative	43	38	43
Labour	35	39	37
Liberal	18	19	18
1997			
Conservative	31	31	
Labour	44	47	
Liberal	17	16	

David Sanders 61

Note to Table 3.4: It should be noted that BES surveys are in a relatively privileged position in comparison with the pre-election polls conducted by the commercial agencies. This is because the main BES survey (to which the data here refer) is always conducted *after* the election has been held. The 'spiral of silence' effect is accordingly likely to be absent from the BES data because the result legitimizes the preferences of those who were reluctant to admit voting for an apparently unpopular government or party.
Source: For 1970–87 BES data, Crewe *et al.*, (1991, p. 3); for polls data, Broughton (1995, pp. 86–8); for 1992 BES data, Heath *et al.*, (1994, pp. 2, 10). Poll of polls for 1997 is the average of the final polls produced by ICM, Harris, Gallup, NOP and MORI.

failures experienced in 1992. The factors that generated the failure in 1992 were clearly not present to the same degree in 1997. It is probably safe to assume that the pollsters' quota allocations were more appropriate in 1997 than they had been five years earlier. However, it is impossible to determine how far it was 'late swing' rather than the 'spiral of silence' that produced the underestimate of the Conservative vote in 1992. The spiral may have continued to produce a small underestimate in 1997 – but certainly not sufficient to discredit the polling exercise as a whole. Opinion survey evidence, of course, always needs to be treated with caution. And the pollsters will undoubtedly have to prove themselves yet again in 2001 or 2002.

The snapshot character of polls, the fact that they display only a cross-section of voters' views on one particular day, and give no definite predictions for the future, remains the major limitation of all survey-based, individual-level data. While polls usually occur monthly, high-quality, comprehensive surveys of the sort conducted by the British Election Study are carried out relatively infrequently. Typically, there is a gap of several years between surveys, though in the 1992–7 period two additional survey waves, six months apart, were conducted in the year preceding the election. The normal spacing of academic surveys means that individual-level analyses based on BES data can say little either about the gradual changes in opinion and perception that occur in the periods between elections or about the effects on opinion of 'unusual political events' (which almost by definition occur at unpredictable times). The key problem here is that many of the things that potentially affect the electorate's political perceptions (for example, the condition of the domestic economy; economic confidence; public perceptions of party unity, management competence and leadership potential) do change gradually. Their gradual effects on public opinion – and especially on voters' political preferences – can only be properly assessed by reference to models which seek to explain shifts in regular poll data throughout the inter-election period.

The Aggregate Model Approach

The accuracy of opinion polls is important because they provide the data foundations for a second stream of academic models, the aggregate model approach. While individual-level approaches base their explanations of vote preference on the characteristics of different voters (or groups of voters), aggregate-level analyses, on the other hand, try to explain how the views of the electorate behave dynamically, how the overall balance of party support changes over time. These models have tended to focus on the condition of the objective economy; on changes in economic perceptions (the 'subjective economy'); on the impact of 'significant political events' such as Britain's exit from the ERM in September 1992; and more recently, on leadership perceptions and party identification (Sanders, 1996; Clarke *et al.*, 1996). We review the general features of this approach, and then look back at the light these models shed both on how the Conservatives came to lose so badly in 1997, and how Labour improved its performance.

Strengths and Weaknesses of Aggregate-Level Models

Aggregate models in electoral analysis relate the political preferences of a group of voters to (1) other attitudinal characteristics of the group and/or (2) the objective circumstances of the group. The 'grouping' of voters considered is sometimes defined by geographical location (for example, why there are variations in the allegiances of electorates in different constituencies). But we concentrate here on analyses of all voters, whose preferences, attitudinal characteristics and objective circumstances are measured at a series of different time points. The starting point for

FIGURE 3.1 Graphical representation of two aggregate time-series variables, Conservative popularity and aggregate personal economic expectations

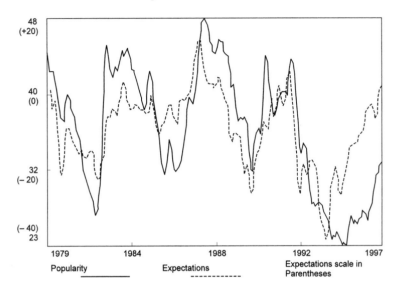

aggregate time-series analysis is the sort of relationship described in Figure 3.1. The graph shows fluctuations in the overall support between 1979 and 1992 for the Conservatives (as measured by the percentage of voters who tell a regular poll that they intend to vote Conservative 'if there were a general election tomorrow'). The graph also shows how, with notable exceptions, the level of 'personal economic expectations' (the difference between the percentage of voters who were optimistic about their personal financial prospects and the percentage who were pessimistic) tended to fluctuate broadly in line with Conservative support.

The first major strength of aggregate time-series analysis is that it allows the analyst to track the movements in any pair of variables very carefully in order to establish the character of the connection between them. If the theoretical proposition under investigation hypothesizes that the independent variable, X, exerts a causal effect on the dependent variable, Y, then we would certainly not expect to find that changes in Y precede changes in X. Equally, if changes in X consistently precede changes in Y, our confidence in the plausibility of the proposition that 'X affects Y' would clearly be reinforced. Aggregate time-series data, in short, allow for the analysis of the short-term dynamics of opinion change in a way that is simply not possible with individual-level BES data. A second, and related, advantage of aggregate time-series data is that they enable the analyst to examine the effects that 'political events' exert on public opinion in a very precise way. For example, with time-series data, it is a relatively simple task to look at the rise or fall in party popularity that occurs at the precise time of a particular event and then to observe (and indeed to model) how that effect either decays or endures over time.

A third strength of aggregate models relates to the question of 'measurement error' and its implications for the correlations between variables. Survey-based data such as opinion polls are in principle subject to measurement errors of two main sorts. First, a particular concept may not be properly measured for all respondents. For example, an operational measure of 'party identification' (which is based on a specific set of survey questions about respondents' feelings of 'closeness' to a particular party) may fail to correspond to the theoretical category (a 'stable and enduring affective attachment' to the party) which it is supposed to represent. Second, any given concept may be poorly measured among certain respondents in the sense that either the survey question(s) posed or the responses (or both) may mean different things to different groups of respondents. All survey data are likely to be contaminated, to varying degrees, by both these sorts of measurement error. However, with aggregate models, errors of the second type are less likely to present estimation problems because 'eccentric' or extreme responses are likely to cancel each other out. In these circumstances, it is possible that aggregate-level correlations, because the measures on which they are based are less prone to measurement error, represent better estimates of the average relationship between variables than correlations conducted at the individual level.

The major limitation of the aggregate approach to electoral politics stems from the gap between the theories that it develops (which, as noted above, are concerned with what goes on inside the heads of individual voters) and the data that are deployed to evaluate those theories (which refer to the characteristics of the electorate as a group). Aggregate analysis seeks to close this gap by assumption. It assumes (1) that the probability that any given voter supports party A at time *t* can be measured by the observed aggregate level of support for party A at time *t*; and (2) that the typical voter's subjective perceptions can be (variously) measured by the aggregate levels of a range of subjective perceptions variables at time *t*. Given these assumptions, the aggregate analyst can argue that an observed correlation between government popularity and aggregate personal economic expectations, of the sort described in Figure 3.1, provides empirical support for the claim that the average voter is more inclined to support the incumbent party when s/he is more optimistic about her/his personal financial prospects. The theoretical underpinning of this claim is that an economically optimistic voter is more likely in these circumstances to want to preserve the political status quo that produced her/his initial optimism. Critics of the approach argue that the assumptions made in this context are contentious. What an aggregate correlation between optimism and govern-ment support cannot show is whether the optimistic individuals are also the ones who support the government (while the pessi-mists back opposition). Only checks with individual-level analyses (of the sort discussed earlier in the chapter) can reveal this sort of information. So it is important to check out the findings of aggregate analyses against the more fine-grained data employed in individual-level surveys.

Other criticisms are directed to the stability of the relationships between variables in aggregate models. For example, looking back at Figure 3.1 it is clear that the Conservatives' popularity in government was closely linked to personal economic expecta-tions most of the time, but that in two periods, 1985–6 and from late 1992 onwards, Tory support was much lower than we would have expected, given people's views of the economy. These periods are not hard to explain in political terms: the first corresponded to the period around the Westland crisis in Mar-garet Thatcher's second term, while the second was inaugurated by Britain's forced exit from the European Exchange Rate Mechanism in autumn 1992, an event whose electoral implica-tions are analysed below. But, critics argue, if such political 'shocks' can make these big (and in 1992–7 long-lasting) changes in the relationships between such previously connected variables as perceptions of economic trends and government popularity, what is the point of elaborate models? If the model assumptions rely on constant relationships, they are useful but empirically wrong; whereas if the model assumptions can simply be revised to cope with whatever happens, then they are ad hoc and can explain anything. Defenders of aggregate models in turn rebut this position by arguing that they can use their models to pin down precisely when and why relationships between variables change, in a way that individual-level data cannot do.

What is sometimes perplexing to analysts of electoral politics is that both sorts of model appear to receive empirical support for their theoretical claims – even though the findings that are reported, using the different data types, are not always either complementary or compatible. How people see the economy as faring (subjective economic perceptions) have been seen as pivotal in explaining government support in several aggregate analyses (Sanders, 1991, 1995; Niemi *et al.*, 1996). However, although such perceptions have been found to be fairly important in individual-level models, they have not proved crucial as determinants of voting choice (Paulson, 1994). So is it possible to assess which approach is capable of telling the more plausible story about the character and origins of electoral change in Britain? The simple (perhaps unsatisfying) answer is that both approaches have advantages and disadvantages; that the decision about which should be used depends upon the nature of the problem that is being analysed; and that a comprehensive understanding of the dynamics of UK electoral change probably requires a familiarity with the assumptions and findings of both approaches.

Explaining the Conservatives' Downfall

To begin applying the aggregate approach, Figure 3.2 shows how support for the three major parties varied during the 1992 Parliament. The figures represent the monthly 'poll of polls' – the average percentage intending to vote for the party in question as reported by the major polling agencies (Gallup, MORI, ICM, NOP). While stated 'voting intention' is not necessarily the same thing as vote, support measures such as these undoubtedly represent the best available barometer of opinion among the electorate. Notwithstanding the 'failure of the opinion polls' in

FIGURE 3.2   Variations in support for the major political parties, 1992–7
(data are poll of polls averages of major commercial; polls)

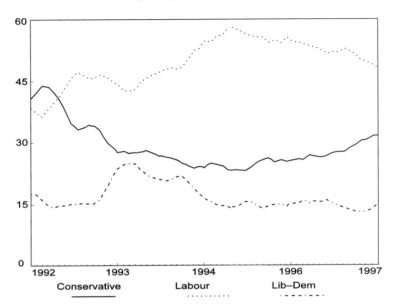

1992, it would be a brave politician indeed who dismissed the trend patterns in opinion poll findings as irrelevant or illusory. For instance, John Major took the Conservatives' consistently poor poll performance during 1995 and 1996 sufficiently seriously to delay holding the general election until the last possible minute.

After a brief initial 'honeymoon' after the April 1992 general election, Conservative support went into a long-term decline from which it only began to recover discernibly in late 1996 – a recovery which was not sufficient to produce yet another Conservative election victory. There can be little doubt that the sterling crisis of September 1992 had a decisive impact on the Conservatives' subsequent electoral fortunes. In the face of speculative pressure on the foreign exchange markets, the UK government was obliged to withdraw sterling from the EU's Exchange Rate Mechanism. The crisis itself seriously damaged the credibility of the government's macroeconomic strategy (Chapter 14). Between October 1990, when the UK entered the ERM, and 16 September 1992, the government had argued that low inflation, low interest rates and falling unemployment were only possible with Britain inside the ERM. After September 1992 the claim was reversed: these goals could only be achieved with Britain outside the ERM. Such a comprehensive volte face – without a plausible explanation to accompany it – was bound to reduce the government's credibility.

Yet the ERM crisis also probably acted as a 'crystallizing' moment for three other factors that were troubling British voters. First, the Conservatives had been re-elected in 1992, in part, on the promise that taxes would not go up. On the contrary, they had successfully portrayed Labour during the 1992 campaign as 'the party of high taxation'. By the late summer of 1992, it was already clear that public borrowing had grown so enormously over the two previous years that significant tax increases would be necessary in the autumn budget – increases that were indeed duly introduced. Second, the Conservatives had striven to give the impression during the 1992 election campaign that the recession, which Britain had experienced continuously since 1990, would be at an end: only a vote for Labour would prolong it. Again, by September 1992, voters were all too aware that the recession had not ended, and many of them saw no real signs of it coming to an end. Finally, in the early to mid-1990s there was a marked sense of economic insecurity among British voters. A poll conducted in December 1994 found that over 60 per cent of the electorate felt insecure about their own 'jobs, earning and homes'. Fully 93 per cent thought that 'at the moment . . . a lot of people are feeling economically insecure' (Gallup, 1994).

It is highly likely that these three factors together had already led voters to question the ability of the Major government to manage the economy effectively. The crisis itself mobilized their doubts. In the immediate aftermath of the crisis, the electorate's confidence in the Conservatives' economic management capabilities plummeted. Figure 3.3 shows how voters' assessments of the relative economic management skills of the Conservatives and Labour changed between 1991 and 1997. What is most apparent about this 'competence' time series is the marked downward shift that occurred in the wake of the ERM crisis. The survey question upon which the graph in Figure 3.3 is based comes from Gallup and has been asked continuously since January 1991: 'With Britain in economic difficulties, which party do you think could handle the problem best: the Conservatives under [leader] or

FIGURE 3.3   Variations in Conservative versus Labour economic
management competence, 1991–7

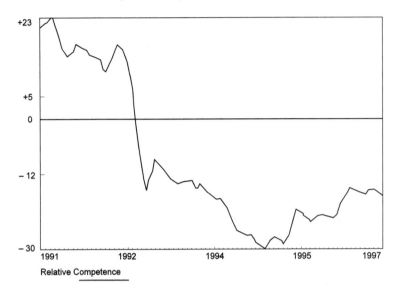

Relative Competence

Labour under [leader]?' But it had also been asked sporadically
before then and shown a Conservative lead over Labour (except
for March 1990, the month when Margaret Thatcher introduced
the poll tax). After the 1992 ERM crisis, in losing their reputation
for competent economic management, the Conservatives lost an
enormously important support cushion. Even when economic
'good news' came along, with falling interest rates during 1993–
4 and low inflation and falling unemployment from 1994 onwards, the Tories could derive little electoral benefit from it
(Sanders, 1996).

This failure to capitalize on improving macroeconomic conditions was underpinned by the government's continued failure to
manage its own political affairs more generally. Its poor reputation for economic management was extended to the political
sphere in 1994 by a steady stream of 'sleaze' stories about the
sexual peccadillos of certain Conservative MPs (this, from the
party which claimed to stand for 'family values') and the
questionable financial practices of others (Dunleavy *et al.*, 1995).
The government's overall management reputation was further

impaired by the widespread sense among voters that the Conservatives were increasingly a party torn by division and internal strife. In May 1992, two-thirds of the electorate considered the Conservatives to be a united party. By June 1993, this figure had fallen to under a fifth, a position from which the party failed consistently to recover. The continuing failure of the Conservatives to regain opinion poll support also caused periodic internal dissension about John Major's leadership, making matters worse. It was only when the election campaign actually began that Conservative MPs' traditional sense of loyalty and commitment to party discipline reasserted themselves – but by then it was too late.

The main ingredient in the very modest recovery in the Conservatives' electoral fortunes that took place in late 1996 and 1997 was the economic management skills of the then Chancellor, Kenneth Clarke, who assumed office in February 1993. His three predecessors, Geoffrey Howe, Nigel Lawson and Norman Lamont, had all greatly assisted the Conservatives' victories of 1983, 1987 and 1992 by reducing both interest rates and taxation levels during the run-up to each election, thus helping to create a sense of economic optimism among voters which appeared to increase levels of support for the incumbent party (Sanders, 1991, 1996). So Clarke wanted to follow a macroeconomic strategy that would give him sufficient flexibility to make similar reductions in the run-up to 1996–7. On the other hand, he also needed to restore the Conservatives' reputation for competent economic management, by pursuing a macroeconomic strategy aimed at boosting jobs and controlling inflation, and eschewing policies obviously geared only to the government's re-election. His solution was to try and engineer a surreptitious pre-election boom while at the same time presenting an image of responsibility. The trick worked to a very limited degree in that the Conservatives' economic management reputation was certainly rising in the last 12 months before the election. And voters' economic expectations had been rising almost continuously for over a year. The problem was that the hill to be climbed was too long and too steep. The Conservatives had dug themselves into such a deep hole of unpopularity during 1993–5 that even an expectations boom in 1996–7 was not sufficient to quell reservations about the Tories' management competence still felt by large numbers of voters.

Labour's revival

In political folklore governments lose elections rather than oppositions winning them. But the alternative team still have to make themselves potentially electable in order to be able to take advantage of a faltering government. Labour's success in 1997 owed at least as much to its own efforts to transform itself as it did to the errors made by the Conservatives. Like John Smith and Neil Kinnock before him, but in a much more sustained and successful fashion, Tony Blair demonstrated his leadership abilities to voters by pushing through internal modernization of Labour's policy positions and complex internal constitution. His strategy resolutely followed the prescriptions of Anthony Downs' famous book, *An Economic Theory of Democracy* (1957), which argued that the optimal position for any party to adopt in a two-horse race was as close as possible to the median voter – the person exactly in the middle of the electorate in left–right terms. Labour's repeated centrist moves successfully persuaded many voters that it was New Labour, removed from its previous left-wing policies. Partly as a result of these changes, and partly because of the Conservatives' failings, Blair's period of leadership witnessed a sustained and amazingly stable plateau of Labour popularity much greater than that experienced before, even under John Smith, creating an almost permanent lead over the Conservatives of around 20 points or more. The Conservatives might have expected to benefit slowly from three years of continuous economic growth, from their pre-election macroeconomic expansion and from the gradual restoration of their reputation for economic management. But their hoped-for comeback was slow, in fact almost invisible in terms of voting intentions, and set back by the loss of a safe Tory seat to Labour in the Wirral South by-election in February 1997, just over two months from the general election. Blair's ascendency was thus maintained through to the closing week of the campaign, with an almost static pattern of public opinion.

Conclusions

The size of the electoral humiliation suffered by the Conservatives in 1997 points in some respects to the fragility of their victory in

1992. In 1992, voters drawn from all socio-demographic groups remained suspicious that Labour had not truly divested itself of the unpopular radicalism that it had embraced in the early 1980s. Even though they were irritated with the Conservatives for having inflicted an unnecessarily long recession on the UK economy, voters in 1992 were still prepared to give the Conservatives the benefit of the doubt – to opt for security and vote for the devil they knew. In an important sense, the Conservatives lost the 1997 election in September 1992, when the cornerstone of their economic strategy dissolved in the face of international speculation against sterling and (as we now know) John Major seriously considered resigning as Prime Minister. Their continuing divisions over Europe prevented the Tory government from re-establishing its reputation for competent political and economic management, regardless of the heroic efforts of Chancellor Clarke. By the same token, Labour effectively won the 1997 general election in 1994 and 1995, when Tony Blair completed the party's modernization that had begun under Neil Kinnock and John Smith.

Blair's political triumph was to convince 'middle Britain' that New Labour carried very little of the baggage of old Labour's 'tax and spend' socialist past. The fiscal and monetary discipline advocated (if not practised) by the Conservatives since 1979 was imported directly into New Labour's programme. Labour now welcomed, and indeed sought to encourage, private-sector enterprise. Labour's policies on crime, defence and the trade-unions were, with minor exceptions, virtually indistinguishable from the Conservatives'. Labour was now a financially prudent, mainstream European social democratic party that posed no threat to middle- and upper-income voters. All of this was not lost on the electorate. They recognized a disunited and incompetent government when they saw one. They also recognized the attractions of an Opposition that was moderate, united, disciplined and clearly led – and which they believed would be likely to repair some of the damage that 18 years of Conservative rule had inflicted on the NHS and public education. New Labour's lack of policy difference from the Conservatives was a positive asset for middle Britain. Its promise to provide more competent government was attractive to voters across the board.

The most intriguing question for the next Parliament, of course, is whether New Labour can convert the votes that it obtained in 1997 into a new and permanent electoral coalition. As noted above, Labour obtained its biggest swings among women, home-owners, the middle class and voters in southern England. Will these groups stay loyal to Labour, or are they likely to defect if the Blair administration runs into the sort of problems – especially economic problems – that have been encountered by so many previous governments?

The danger for new Labour is encapsulated in the phrase 'easy come, easy go'. Over the last 30 years British voters have become much more volatile in their political preferences. Levels of partisan identification – thinking of oneself as consistently supporting one party rather than the others – have declined significantly. On one estimate (Brynin and Sanders, 1997), less than two-fifths of voters now 'identify' with either Labour or the Conservatives (and in roughly equal proportions). The conditions that have generated this decline, moreover, seem set to continue. Changing patterns of employment and their attendance consequences for changing class identities appear to have been at the root of declining partisanship – and these are processes which are likely to be reinforced by globalization and future technological change. The collapse of state socialism in eastern Europe and the end of the Cold War, in 1989, have weakened the ideological underpinnings of party politics throughout the western world, including the UK. Without a clear left–right cleavage to differentiate them, it is perhaps not surprising that the major parties should find that their reservoirs of loyal partisans are being increasingly eroded.

The corollary to this decline in identification is that voters have become much more consumer-like in their voting decisions. They compare the policy and leadership packages that are on offer from the various parties and cast their votes according to which appears (realistically) to promise the better deal. This tendency puts a premium on parties' rival claims to appear competent to manage the country's affairs. New Labour's ability to perform effectively in office will be far more important in determining its success in 2001 or 2002 than the fact that it made a successful electoral appeal to middle-class homeowners in southern England in 1997. Equally, the Conservatives' prospects will depend on the extent to which they are able to prevent themselves from being labelled as an insular, Europhobic fringe party, incapable either of managing the economy effectively or of adjusting to external (European) realities in order to maximize UK interests. The Liberal Democrats, as they did with some success in 1997, will undoubtedly seek to maintain their regional strengths and to position themselves as the pro-public services alternative to New Labour. In any event, it seems likely that 'the vision thing' will be less important in determining electoral preferences over the course of the coming Parliament than voters' perceptions of the managerial capabilities of the rival front-bench teams.

Acknowledgement

I am grateful to Patrick Dunleavy for very helpful editorial advice on this chapter.

4

Political Communications

PIPPA NORRIS

Since 1945 political communications has undergone a process of modernization which has transformed the relationship between parties, citizens and the media in democratic societies. The key changes have been:

- from ad hoc campaigns by local party organizations to planned co-ordination of the election by the party leadership
- from amateur party volunteers contributing time and shoe leather to paid, professional specialists skilled in marketing and polling
- from the month-long official contest towards the 'continuous campaign'
- from cleavage-based and issue-based conflict towards the character-based 'personalization' of politics
- from a campaign revolving around party platforms towards a poll-driven focus on the 'horse-race' strategy
- from a mass media subordinate to government towards a more autonomous, critical and powerful press driven by its own 'media logic'.

The evolutionary shift from a pre-modern to modern campaign has occurred in a wide range of countries, though the impact and pace of these developments have been speeded or hindered by the distinctive political culture, institutional structures and media systems of each one (Swanson and Mancini, 1996; Bowler and Farrell, 1992; Butler and Ranney, 1992). This process has often been termed an '*Americanization*' of campaigns, since many of these developments first became evident in the United States, but given the international exchange of campaign techniques and personnel

75

the term 'modernization' seems more appropriate (Negrine, 1996a, 1996b).

Some commentators believe that this development has had profound consequences for the British political system, disconnecting leaders and citizens, over-simplifying and trivializing political discourse, and ultimately producing a more cynical and disengaged public (Franklin, 1994). Others remain more sanguine, suggesting that changes in political communications have had little impact on the central institutions of the state, and that structural features of the British political system resist a wholesale 'Americanization' of election campaigns (Kavanagh, 1995). The central aim of this chapter is to consider how far political communications in Britain have been transformed by the process of modernization, and to evaluate the consequences for parties, the electorate and British democracy.

The Decline of the Pre-Modern Campaign

As illustrated in Table 4.1, three primary channels link parties and the public. In the post-war era, direct communications between citizens and their representatives – which we might term 'retail politics' – have been eroded by the decline of traditional mass membership party organizations. At the same time mediated communications have substantially increased in the modern campaign, due to the continued influence of the partisan press, the growth of radio in the 1920s, the rise of television in the 1950s and the evolution of new channels of electronic communication like the internet in the 1990s. As a result many believe that national elections in most industrialized societies have become contests revolving around leadership-centred media-campaigns.

Yet retail politics has not vanished in Britain, far from it. Elements of the traditional constituency campaign persist at the grass roots, with local party volunteers continuing to canvass and leaflet voters, in a pattern established with the evolution of party organizations following the extension of the franchise in mid-Victorian days. Local campaigning remains widespread: in the British Election Study almost half the electorate (47 per cent) report being canvassed in recent elections, while 82 per cent claimed to have read a party leaflet. Studies suggest local activism

TABLE 4.1   Changes in campaigning

	Pre-modern	*Modern*	*Post-modern*
Campaign organization	Local and decentralized	Nationally co-ordinated	Nationally co-ordinated but decentralized operations
Preparations	Short-term and ad hoc campaign	Long campaign	Permanent campaign
Central co-ordination	Party leaders	Central headquarters, more specialist consultants and party officials	More outside consultants, pollsters and specialist campaign departments
Feedback	Local canvassing	Opinion polls	Opinion polls, focus groups, internet web sites
Media	National and local press Local handbills, posters and pamphlets Radio leadership speeches	Television broadcasting through major territorial channels	Television narrow casting through fragmented channels, selective mailshots, selective advertisements
Campaign events	Local public meetings Limited whistle-stop leadership tours	Media management Daily press conferences Themed photo opportunities TV party political broadcasts Billboard wars	Extension of media management to 'routine' politics, leadership speeches, policy launches etc
Costs	Low budget and local costs	Higher costs for producing television party political broadcasts	Higher costs for consultants, research and television advertisements

continues to provide a vital boost in local support, promoting turnout and party votes in marginal seats and by-elections, although the exact size of the electoral bonus remains a matter of dispute (Denver and Hands, 1992; Seyd and Whiteley, 1992; Whiteley *et al.*, 1994).

Nevertheless, in the postwar era there has been a substantial erosion in the overall pool of volunteers: since the early 1950s Conservative party membership plunged from 2.8 million to 780 000 in 1992, while individual membership of the Labour Party declined from just over a million to its nadir in the 1980s, before recovering to 400 000 in 1997 (Norris, 1996). The core of active party workers is far smaller: studies have analysed who is frequently involved in election canvassing and have found this activity engaged about a third of Labour members, but only a tenth of Conservative members (Seyd and Whiteley, 1992; Whiteley *et al.*, 1994). Many European countries have experienced a modest shrinkage in party membership, although the fall has been more substantial in Britain than elsewhere. By the end of the 1980s, only 3.3 per cent of the British electorate belonged to a party, compared with about a fifth of the electorate in Austria and Sweden (Katz and Mair, 1994).

Does this decline matter? In mass-branch party organizations, grassroots members provide the volunteer life-blood for recruitment, fund raising and campaigning. In Britain the grip of constituency parties over selection for elected office continues undiminished: the key hurdle to a parliamentary career remains decisions at local level (Norris and Lovenduski, 1995). Moreover, local parties continue to provide an important although modest source of revenue. Estimates by McConnell (1994) suggest that through subscriptions, fund-raising events and donations, constituency associations channelled more than £1 million a year to Conservative Central Office, while Labour Party constituency affiliation fees provide about £600 000 a year to Walworth Road (although this represents, in both cases, only about 5 per cent of central party income).

In Britain constituency parties retain these important functions. Yet, although grassroots activists maintain traditional electioneering, the heart of the modern campaign has been transferred to television newsrooms and discussion programmes, where the core actors are a small team of party leaders, aided by backroom campaign managers at central party headquarters and flanked by an outer circle of paid professional consultants in marketing and opinion polling.

The transformation of campaigning can be shown by comparing recent elections with the pre-modern campaign in the post-war decade. In the 1945 general election, the campaign organization for all parties was highly decentralized, ad hoc and unco-ordinated. Rather than a single campaign, there were 640 separate contests. Voluntary helpers within each constituency remained the bedrock of the contest. Each constituency party functioned as an independent unit, with its own helpers, publicity, local agent, and candidate. Politics was soap-box retail: face-to-face canvassing on doorsteps, posters in household windows, leafleting at factory gates (Mitchell, 1995; McCullum and Readman, 1947).

Party headquarters played a marginal, and largely amateur, role in co-ordinating activity. They produced some slogans and coloured posters, but few other facilities for candidates. The first few opinion polls reporting voting intentions were produced by the British Institute of Public Opinion (Gallup) during the months leading up to the 1945 election, but these were widely ignored, even by the *News Chronicle* which published them. The Market Research Society was first organized in 1947, but it was not until the early 1960s that these techniques were seriously considered by the major British political parties. Policies were decided by party leaders without private polls, still less the paraphernalia of focus groups and market research to guide the presentation of campaign themes. The only feedback to influence party platforms came from conference debates, parliamentary post bags and informal soundings from constituency activists.

During the campaign party leaders toured the country, addressing public meetings in whistle-stop city tours. These speeches, often extemporary, were duly reported in the printed press, thereby reaching a national readership. Moreover, the introduction of radio broadcasting in 1924 had a major impact on the way elections were fought. The post-war audience could tune in to BBC radio on the Home Service or the Light Service, and just under 10 000 licences were distributed. Leadership broadcasts were heard after the main BBC news every weekday evening, allocated by agreement according to the party's share of the vote in the previous election, and the opening broadcasts set the tone for the subsequent campaign. BBC audience research reported that just under half the adult population heard each broadcast over the wireless. But television played no role during, or after, the campaign. Television services started by the BBC in 1936 and ran until 1939, but were suspended during the war and only resumed again in 1946. The first television party political broadcasts appeared in 1951, but television news did not cover the general election campaign until 1959.

Newspapers were the primary channel of mass political communications. The press had longstanding links with parties, especially in their editorial policies, although newspapers became independent of direct party control in the early nineteenth century, largely as a consequence of the growth of advertising (Curran and Seaton, 1993). Among national papers readers had the choice at the news agents of the Labour-leaning *Daily Mirror* and *Daily Herald*, with a total circulation of 4.5 million, the Conservative-leaning *Daily Sketch*, *Daily Express*, *Daily Mail* and *Daily Telegraph*, with a combined circulation of 6.8 million copies, and the Liberal-leaning *News Chronicle* and *Manchester Guardian* with a total circulation of 1.6 million. Independents even had *The Times*, traditionally Conservative although anti-Churchill in the 1945 election. Thus a range of tabloid and broadsheet national newspapers provided rough balance between parties.

The Evolution of the Modern Campaign

Changes in Newspapers

As the most partisan mass media, newspapers continue to be an important channel for party messages. Moreover about two-thirds of voters claim to follow the campaign in the print press (Norris, 1996). Coverage of the campaign in newspapers displays continuity with the past but it has been transformed over the years by three main developments: a modest fall in readership, accompanied by cut-throat economic competition among the tabloids, has led to down-market pressures towards populist sensationalism; shifts in the partisan balance of the tabloid press made it more difficult for Labour to get its message across in the Thatcher years, particularly to its working-class base; and some suggest a more autonomous journalism has developed, driven more by the economic market and 'media logic' than by the needs of parties, politicians and governments.

Newspaper readership remains fairly high since almost two-thirds of the British public (62 per cent) usually read a national newspaper every day. Total circulation figures remain fairly stable over the last two decades – about 13 million newspapers are sold every day – although circulation figures as a proportion of the population have steadily declined. In 1950, about a third of the British population bought a daily newspaper compared with just over a fifth today. Readership of tabloids, in particular, has declined over the last decade leading to fierce competition in this sector of the market. This has increased the pressures towards more sensational coverage focusing on personal scandals, sexual imbroglios or the monarchy (preferably all three). Tabloidization is less about the size of newspapers than an oversimplification of issues into black-and-white terms, a lack of proportion or qualification in news stories, and a focus on 'human interest'.

TABLE 4.2 Characteristics of newspaper readers

Who reads the tabloid press most?	*% who read*	*And who reads the tabloids least?*	*% who read*
Non-manual people	66	Graduates	31
People aged 21–24	66	Liberal Democrat voters	44
Labour voters	64	People aged 35–44	48
People aged 65 or more	63	Manual workers	49
Non-graduates	63	Conservative voters	55

Who reads the quality press most?	*% who read*	*And who reads the qualities least?*	*% who read*
Graduates	45	Manual people	6
Non-manual people	27	People aged 21–24	10
Conservative voters	26	Women	11
Liberal Democrat voters	24	People aged 65 of more	12
Men	20	Labour voters	13

Note: The question asked was 'Which daily or evening newspaper do you personally read regularly – at least two copies a week?'
Source: ITC, *Television: The Public's View*, 1995.

Secondly, the partisan balance in the press tipped significantly towards the Conservatives. In 1945, there were about 6.7 million readers of pro-Conservative papers compared with 4.4 million readers of pro-Labour papers. By 1992, total circulation of the Conservative-leaning press had risen to 8.7 million, while the circulation of Labour-leaning papers had dropped to 3.3 million. An important shift in the 1970s occurred with the transformation of the *Daily Herald* into *The Sun*, and with the more right-wing tone of *The Times* under Murdoch.

In the 1997 election, however, in a sharp reversal of fortunes Labour won the endorsement of 11 out of 19 papers. The *Daily Express*, the *Daily Telegraph* and the *Daily Mail* continued to back the Conservatives, with a combined circulation of 4.5 million. But the rest, with a tabloid circulation of 8 million readers, came out against the Tories. The defection of *The Sun* at the start of the campaign was a bitter blow for John Major. Even the *Daily Telegraph* and the *Daily Mail* mixed positive comments about the Conservatives with large helpings of criticism.

Lastly, it has been argued that the coverage of election campaigns by the American press has been affected by broader trends, in particular that economic pressures and 'media logic' mean that journalists are now focusing far greater attention on personalities than on party policies, party strategies and the 'horse-race' coverage of who is ahead and who is behind in the polls, rather than a serious and detailed debate about the issues (Patterson, 1993). It is difficult to establish whether this trend is also apparent in Britain without systematic content analysis of coverage over time. Nevertheless comparative studies suggest that this tendency has gone much further in the United States than in Britain, although the more commercially driven ITN news has moved somewhat towards the American model (Semetko, 1996).

The growth of the 'poll-saturated' campaign has been well documented (Crewe, 1983, 1992). Excluding election day surveys, private polls and regional or local surveys, there were 20 national polls published during the 1959 campaign. The number crept up to an average of 26 in the 1970s, doubling to 46 in 1983, and rising to 57 in 1992, before falling back to 42 polls in the 1997 campaign. There has also been a parallel proliferation in the number of agencies conducting polls, and different newspaper and television programmes commissioning this work. Not surprisingly this has had a major impact on the contents of news. The campaign coverage of the 'horse-race' (party strategy and opinion polls) in newspaper lead stories has steadily risen during the 1980s, from about a fifth to a third of all lead stories (Butler and Kavanagh, 1992). Given this front-page treatment, the fact that the polls spectacularly failed to predict the results in 1992 led to a major inquest into both survey methods and news coverage (Chapter 3).

Moreover, it is commonly suggested that campaign reporting has become more focused on the core party leadership, with the party managers placing more attention on the way that their leaders are packaged and presented (see, for example, Jones 1995). This has been termed the 'personalization' of campaign politics (Swanson and Mancini 1996), or the 'presidentialization' of British elections (Foley, 1993). Since the Labour Party moved towards the centre ground in the late 1980s, producing fewer differences between the major parties on the core issues of management of the economy, many journalists have suggested that differences between the leadership character and personalities of John Major and Tony Blair may have become more important for the outcome. Systematic evidence for the impact of the leaders on voting choice remains a matter of controversy (see Crewe and King 1994; Nadeau *et al.*, 1996). Nevertheless, evidence suggests that party leaders are receiving more coverage in recent campaigns, at least on television news. As shown in Figure 4.1, the main evening news programmes tripled their coverage of sound-bites from party leaders from 1979 to 1992. We can conclude that coverage of the campaign in newspapers has evolved slowly over the years, with moves towards more populist sensationalism in the tabloid and broadsheet sectors, less partisan balance across the print media, and more 'horse-race' and 'personality' driven campaign coverage in the press. Nevertheless, the changes in newspapers have had less impact on the conduct of the campaign than the growing influence of the electronic media, notably television.

The Rise of the Electronic Campaign

Although receiving little scholarly attention, radio has continued to play a significant role in political communications. BBC radio news, features, documentaries and current affairs have expanded

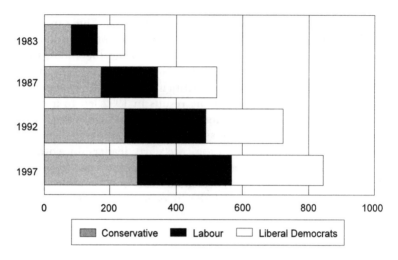

FIGURE 4.1   Campaign coverage of main party leaders

Source: Butler and Kavanagh (1992).

in recent decades, accounting for over a quarter of all output today. Prestigious news programmes like Radio 4's *Today* and *The World At One*, can continue to set the agenda for other media, and to influence the political elite. Early morning radio reaches a peak audience of just under a third of the population. Moreover, the growth of commercial radio has widened the availability of more diverse stations, including talk radio and local radio, and dramatically expanded the audience. During the last 40 years the amount of time people spent listening to radio, at least as background, has more than doubled, from seven to over 16 hours a week, with the strongest surge of interest in the 1990s.

Yet the most significant impact on political communications has come from the rise of television, since the first campaign coverage during the Rochdale by-election in 1958. The Independent Television Commission (ITC) has carried out an annual survey since the early 1970s asking the public about their sources of news. In a fairly stable pattern, people report a clear pecking order: television is regarded as the most important source for world, UK, and regional news, followed by newspapers, then radio. The only category where newspapers trump television is as a local news source, and even here newspapers have lost their edge during the last decade. Of course given the multiplicity and overlapping nature of news outlets, most of us are probably unaware of the exact source for specific stories, but this provides an indication of the public's perceptions. Moreover the ITC survey reveals that by a large margin television is widely regarded as the most comprehensive, fair and accurate source of national news (for details, see Gunter *et al.*, 1994). Television is believed to be influential in part because it is an all-pervasive medium which reaches all households. In the 1992 campaign the election dominated television news, absorbing two-thirds of the main bulletins. About half the population (27 million viewers) watched the BBC1 and ITV evening bulletins every evening during the campaign (Harrison, 1993, p. 158). In the 1992 British Election Study about eight out of 10 people said they followed the campaign on television, while about two-thirds of the electorate reported paying 'some' or 'a great deal' of attention to political news on television. Exposure to television news is fairly uniform throughout society, with few differences by gender, class and education, although younger groups are significantly less likely to tune in. Most importantly, there is also a significant partisan difference, with Conservatives voters slightly more likely than Labour to be regular viewers.

Yet people may watch the news for many different reasons, perhaps from an interest in sport or crime, or because this is a regular part of their evening routine at home. Viewers may pay little attention to coverage of party politics. If we analyse the audience who express an interest in the range of political pro-grammes, current affairs and news, a different pattern emerges. The attentive public focused on these programmes is sharply demarcated by gender, class, education, age and vote (see Table 4.3). Like other forms of political participation, the attentive public for television tends to be clustered among the older, affluent, well-educated and male population, and among Con-servative more than Labour voters. Differences in exposure and attention, combined with the Conservative edge in the print press, may have important consequences for party fortunes as it makes it even harder for Labour to gets its message across. Compared with the partisan press, television is a more neutral medium, which by law has to provide 'balanced' party coverage during elections. Yet the effects of who actually pays attention to political coverage on

TABLE 4.3   Interest in television programmes

	Politics	*% of category interested in* *Current affairs*	*News*
Who is most interested in television coverage of politics?			
Graduates	42	78	90
People aged 65 or more	33	63	93
Non-manual people	30	66	87
Conservative voters	29	65	93
People aged 45–54	29	58	88
Who is least interested in television coverage of politics?			
People aged 16–20	8	23	60
People aged 21–24	10	31	71
Manual people	15	42	82
People aged 25–34	17	46	82
Women	18	48	82

Note: The question asked was 'I am going to read out a number of different programme types and for each one I would like you to tell me how interested you personally are to watch that type of programme on TV'.
Source: ITC, *Television The Public's View*, 1995.

television mean that Labour voters are more insulated from its messages. In this media environment, the Labour Party has to work far harder than the Conservatives to communicate its meaning.

We can conclude that the heart of the modern British campaign, and the factor which dominates all other considerations by party strategists, is the battle to dominate the television agenda (see, for example, Butler and Kavanagh, 1992; Crewe and Gosschalk, 1995; Scammell, 1995; Kavanagh, 1995). As a result of these developments the potential influence of the media during the modern campaign has greatly increased, as has their function as an intermediary institution between citizens and the state. The actual impact of television on political information, agenda setting, framing responsibility for issues and, ultimately, voting choice, remains a matter of continuing dispute (see Norris, 1996; Miller, 1991).

The Development of the Post-Modern Campaign?

Political communications may be moving towards a post-modern phase. The *pre-modern* campaign was characterized by retail politics, local campaigns, and volunteer management. The *modern* campaign was characterized by a high degree of centralization, co-ordination and professionalization. In contrast, the *post-modern* campaign may be characterized by more specialized narrow casting leading to a greater fragmentation of media outlets, messages and audiences. The post-modern campaign contains new opportunities, but also new uncertainties and dangers, for party strategists, journalists and citizens. While it seems premature to claim that the British campaign has yet shifted into the post-modern phase, there are persuasive grounds to believe that this may be the direction in which it is moving.

In the late 1990s, the role of the British mass media has been affected by a series of technological, political and economic developments: the deregulation and erosion of public service broadcasting in many European countries, the rise of satellite and cable broadcasting systems which reached a growing proportion of UK households, changes in the franchising of ITV companies and increased economic pressures at ITN, the reorganization of the BBC news and current affairs division, (including the World Service) under the Birtian managerial ethos, the creation of Channel 5 and the development of new interactive media like the internet. The limited diversification of media outlets which have become available during the last decade in Britain seems likely to explode, as in the United States, if digital technology fulfils its promise. The global merger of international high-tech companies, – producing industries capable of integrating telephone, computer and television services – holds the potential for dramatically changing the familiar pattern of communications in Britain (for a discussion, see Negrine, 1994). The regulatory context may slow the process of technological change in Britain, but as in most advanced industrialized societies the future seems likely to produce a greater proliferation of media outlets. How far these developments influence the contents of political communication in the media, and thus the audience, rather than just its means of transmission, remains to be seen.

Conclusions

We can conclude that political communications in the modern
state can be understood as a process of dynamic interaction
between parties, citizens and the media. Parties aim to attract,
mobilize and reinforce public support by shaping the information
received by the public, defining the policy agenda, framing who
gets praised or blamed for policy problems, and ultimately
influencing people's voting choices. In turn, citizens sift, filter
and discount information, and weigh choices. Through the
process of opinion polling and focus groups the attitudes, opinions
and concerns of the public feed back into the policy making and
electoral process. Lastly the media provide an essential linkage
mediating between parties and voters. Journalists let citizens and
leaders talk to, and learn about, each other, albeit through the
filter of the news media. As direct channels of communication
have eroded, although not disappeared, the media has increased
its role as a primary linkage mechanism, like parties and pressure
groups, connecting citizens and the state. Amateur, ad hoc and
localized linkages between representatives and voters have been
increasingly mediated, professionalized and centralized. Whether
this has improved the flow of interactive communication, or
produced a barrier to mutual understanding, remains a matter
of continuing controversy.

5
Political Parties

GILLIAN PEELE

The 1997 general election result made clear that the erosion of the Conservative party's strength involved far more than a simple haemorrhage of electoral support. The Conservatives' crushing parliamentary defeat could be traced to a series of interlocking developments which together created a new opportunity for a resurgent Labour Party and presented the Conservative leadership with a fresh agenda for the post-election period.

The most important cause of Conservative decline was the increased salience of the European issue in British politics. Europe was the obvious cause of the Conservatives' acute ideological and policy differences throughout the 1990s and the dominant issue in their efforts to clarify the party's identity after the election. Secondly, there was a change in the relative organizational strengths of the two major parties. Traditionally the Conservatives have enjoyed an organizational and campaigning advantage over other parties. In the 1990s these advantages were eroded and in many spheres – especially membership recruitment and communications – Labour's performance was markedly better. Thirdly, Conservative morale was lowered by disunity, poor electoral performances and a series of embarrassing financial and sexual scandals.

Some of the problems which so plagued the Conservatives in the run-up to the 1997 election could perhaps be viewed as short term and likely to ease once the burden of government had been removed. Others, such as the erosion of the party's voluntary membership and its organizational difficulties, constituted a longer-term problem, particularly given the broader sociological trends which suggest that joining parties is an increasingly atypical activity for the average British citizen. Certainly the scale of their defeat seemed likely to concentrate the minds of Conservative leaders both in Parliament and the country, raising questions not merely about the direction of policy but also about the role of the voluntary party in relation to the parliamentary sector.

Labour, despite the euphoric mood created by its return to government, had internal conflicts of its own. Its long process of ideological revision and organizational reform generated internal disputes and resentments which were suppressed in order to win the election. How far that unity would be maintained in government remained, however, an open question. The multi-faceted issue of Europe which had so divided the Conservatives now threatened Labour, while the leadership's policy caution in key areas seemed bound to generate disillusion among its supporters.

The 1997 election confirmed the UK's multi-party character as the Liberal Democrats fought successfully to improve their parliamentary position in a campaign in which New Labour pre-empted much of the Liberal Democrat appeal. Scottish Nationalists, Plaid Cymru and Northern Ireland's parties brought a distinctive character to contests outside England (Chapter 11). Beyond the regular cast of smaller parties, an increasing number of tiny fringe parties, causes and candidates added colour, humour and confusion in 1997 as in 1992. In 1997 two of these smaller parties gained particular prominence. The anti-abortion movement fielded enough candidates to secure an election broadcast. James Goldsmith's Referendum Party fielded candidates with one aim only: to secure a wide-ranging referendum on Britain's relationship with the EU. In a period when finance was a problem for all parties, the Referendum Party was well-resourced. The *Guardian* calculated that it had £20 million at its disposal in 1996. The Referendum Party also attracted many disillusioned Conservatives, including a former Treasurer, Lord McAlpine, and Margaret Thatcher's personal economic adviser Sir Alan Walters, to its ranks. Initially some senior Conservatives feared that the Referendum Party could seriously damage the Conservative interest in highly marginal seats, and there were frantic efforts to secure a pre-election deal with Goldsmith. In fact the Referendum Party's impact was debatable. It secured an average of about 2000 votes per constituency and some 3 per cent of the total vote. Whether it made the difference in many seats captured from the Conservatives was however unclear. Certainly the Referendum Party added to Conservative nervousness in the run-up to the election, achieved further publicity for the European issue and underlined its capacity to disrupt normal party politics. Although theoretically neutral as between federalist and those who urged withdrawal from the European Union, in practice the Conservative party was overwhelmingly hostile to Europe (Young, 1996).

'New Labour'

Labour's 1997 election victory was built on a thorough-going reform of the party's ideology, structure and policies (Hughes and Wintour, 1990; Jones, 1996). Observers of the process which finally made Labour electable inevitably asked two inter-related questions. How far had Labour genuinely remade itself? And would the reforms make it easier for Labour to govern after the election? Advocates of change and supporters of Tony Blair's leadership naturally argued that Labour would succeed in government on the basis of its new agenda (Mandelson and Liddle, 1996). Others, from a variety of viewpoints, argued that the leadership would encounter difficulties in government. Press speculation about division inside Labour ranks intensified in 1997 after an anonymous *Tribune* article by a backbench Labour MP writing under the pseudonym Cassandra argued that Blair's authority was shaky and that he might be overthrown early in the new Parliament.

Under Blair's leadership, Labour has revised its fundamental doctrines and policies. Clause IV of the party's constitution has been consigned to history and replaced by a statement of values. Although the process of removing this clause from Labour's constitution still required courage and determination because of its symbolic significance, the reorientation of Labour policies which it signalled had already occurred well in advance of the special conference of April 1995. Long before then Labour had moved away from its commitment to public ownership and socialism, and had come to terms with market-based reforms of the Thatcher–Major years. To that extent, as a number of observers have noted, the revisionist project pursued by Hugh Gaitskell, Neil Kinnock and John Smith has succeeded under Blair. However, although Labour was by 1997 a free-market party, albeit one that believed market power and public purpose should be used together, its ideology was not altogether clear. It refused to reverse the Conservative privatisations and offered no more nationalizations. It backed away from a radical redistribution of wealth either through the taxation system or through higher public spending. Its foreign and defence policies remained solidly in line with NATO and (at least in opposition) it had become an enthusiastic supporter of European integration. Only in the field of constitutional reform did Labour display any real radicalism, although even at the time of the election the degree of the party's commitment to devolution and other constitutional reforms remained in doubt.

It was thus much easier to say what New Labour was not than what it was. Blair himself attempted to emphasize the ethical element in socialism and was apparently influenced by the writings of John MacMurray, a Scottish moral philosopher (Rentoul, 1995). Some of his parliamentary colleagues, such as Chris Smith, linked the reassertion of moral values with an explicitly Christian vision, although there were obvious dangers in stressing religious commitment in the context of a highly secular society such as Britain. Many in the Labour Party displayed an interest in the resurgence of communitarian ideas that occurred on both sides of the Atlantic in the 1990s as an alternative to unfettered market liberalism and individualism (Etzioni, 1995; Gray, 1996). Thus by the time of the 1997 election New Labour seemed to have adopted a political philosophy which was liberal rather than socialist in its orientation, pragmatic rather than dogmatic in its style, and a compromise between communitarian and market values.

Labour's 1997 manifesto confirmed this new policy orientation. It was an unusual document because a draft version was published earlier under the title *The Road to the Manifesto*. However, critics noted three stumbling blocks as Labour attempted to put its policies into operation. First, there was the question of how far its own parliamentary supporters could be kept in line behind the constitutional agenda. On the commitment to a Scottish parliament, which was thought to be the firmest of Labour's constitutional reform proposals, Blair's unilateral decision before the election to hold a dual referendum generated internal unhappiness and the resignation of John McAllion, initially an opposition spokesman but subsequently a critic of Blair and his agenda for reforming the party. Just a few weeks prior to the general election the Labour Party in Scotland was in disarray as supporters of 'the Network', a Blairite faction, attempted unsuccessfully to remove key left-wingers from the Scottish executive (Arlidge, 1997). Labour in Scotland remains much more deeply divided between 'new' and 'old' Labour forces than the party in England. Blair's supporters in Scotland have not been able to oust the left, and a parliament in Edinburgh might offer greater opportunity for old-style Labour politics to become dominant again. Thus with Labour in government there is a fear of further rumblings both in Scotland and from those English MPs concerned about the consequences of constitutional change for the rest of Britain.

Secondly, many observers wonder how far Labour's cautious approach to spending and taxing will alienate its activists. The threat of higher direct taxation has long been seen as a vote loser by the leadership and Chancellor Gordon Brown argues that additional income for Labour's spending plans will have to be met either from cuts in other spending programmes or additional revenue from such devices as a windfall tax on utilities' profits. Although Labour developed the rudiments of a distinctive approach to the economy using the notion of 'stakeholding' (subsequently not mentioned at all in the 1997 manifesto), it is not clear what the implications of this general approach are for concrete decisions about such tangible pressures as the rising costs of welfare or public-sector pay. The policy implications of these choices are likely to produce conflict in Labour circles because in its efforts to provide voters with assurance of its new financial responsibility, the party leadership has severely limited its own room for policy manoeuvre.

Thirdly, critics ask how long it will take before divisions over Europe open up on the Labour front benches. The urge to present a united front kept a lid on Labour divisions in the early and mid-1990s, but there was no doubt that divisions remained. Even Labour's late decision to commit itself to a referendum before taking Britain into a single European currency, while wrong-footing the Conservatives and reopening their internal debate, was criticized by Labour Europhiles as a needless hostage to fortune. A referendum, they argued, could seriously undermine the prestige and agenda of a Labour government in mid-Parliament. However, the referendum option seemed increasingly irrelevant in the run-up to the election as both Blair and Brown expressed scepticism about Britain joining the single currency in the first round.

Labour's Internal Divisions

Labour's preferred image in the 1992–7 Parliament was that of a well disciplined and united party preparing for government. Yet that image was in many ways deceptive, for during this time Labour's parliamentary party managers operated a regime in which many votes were one-line whips or free votes (Cowley and Norton, 1996). Such a practice would be impossible in government. Indeed towards the end of 1996 Labour adopted new disciplinary rules anticipating their coming to power which allowed the parliamentary party to withdraw the whip from any MP bringing the party into disrepute. The new code attempted to balance this restrictive approach to internal party debate with a commitment that Labour's backbench parliamentary committees would be given the right to be consulted by cabinet ministers before key policy decisions were taken.

Even with the luxury of opposition (and a strategy of allowing a good deal of free expression in the parliamentary party) some quite marked divisions appeared within Labour ranks, in addition to the more personal animosities which are to be expected in any political party. A total of 184 Labour MPs (70 per cent of the parliamentary party) voted against the leadership in the period 1992–6 on a range of issues such as economic policy, foreign policy, law and order, and welfare (Cowley and Norton, 1996). None of these problem areas was likely to disappear, and the question of European integration (on which Labour displayed divergent views) remained a constant difficulty. Nor had dissent in Labour's ranks come merely from the Campaign Group representing the hard left of the party. It had also come from backbench MPs who were not organized into any factional grouping. The Labour MPs who rebelled during the period 1992–6 were in every way a microcosm of the party as a whole except that they were slightly older than the average Labour MP (Cowley and Norton, 1996).

Blair's hope after the 1997 election was that the new intake of Labour MPs would share his vision of how to run a modernized

Labour Party and would be restrained in their opposition to the leadership. Analysis prior to the election suggested that the parliamentary face of New Labour would indeed be very different from that of old Labour and of the Conservatives (Criddle, 1996). Labour's use of all-women shortlists produced a massive expansion of women candidates in winnable seats. In addition the changed procedures for candidate selection, especially the introduction of one member one vote (OMOV) and the reduction in trade union influence in candidate selection, produced a new Labour intake with a strong background in local politics. Although the potential for left-wing factional activity has not been increased by these new entrants, they are also unlikely to be happy with the limited opportunities open to quiet backbenchers. Some persistent critics of Blair's leadership (such as Peter Shore) left the House of Commons in 1997, but most familiar rebels such as Dennis Skinner, Jeremy Corbyn and Ken Livingstone were re-elected. The Labour intake of 1997 will probably demand a positive policy role and be willing to demonstrate its independence in the voting lobbies. Party management will be more difficult because of the size of the Labour majority (179 seats), and because it will take time for the whips to get to know their new colleagues. Moreover, because the Labour landslide swept into Parliament candidates who had little hope of winning when originally selected, the character of the parliamentary party may turn out to be rather different from that anticipated by the leadership.

Labour has also displayed some marked personal conflicts, for example between Gordon Brown and Robin Cook. In some cases the divisions have both a policy and a personal dimension. Cook is a Eurosceptic, whereas Brown is not. However, many other Labour MPs are hostile to Brown's determination to impose financial constraints on Labour ministers. In many cases, though, the animosities are also the products of power struggles and stylistic differences.

Party Organization

A number of important structural changes initiated by Blair and his immediate predecessors affected Labour's 1997 election performance. The party's central bureaucracy is now managerially more efficient, building on initatives taken by Kinnock and Smith. The power of the trade unions within the Labour Party has been reduced, by cutting their vote at party conference to 50 per cent. From 1993 members of trade union delegations were in theory free to vote as individuals rather than as a block. Union sponsorship of individual MPs has declined in significance, although the unions still make significant contributions both to Labour's election funding and to constituency parties. Blair has thus continued the process of transforming Labour into a mass membership party operating a system of direct democracy based on the individual member rather than a federal and delegated democracy based on block votes. Suggestions that Blair was contemplating further constitutional distancing between the party and the unions fuelled a row at the TUC conference in 1996. Although the issue was said to be overblown, many trade unionists believed that Blair did indeed have an agenda which involved the severance of Labour's historic link with the unions. It remains to be seen how long a Labour government can avoid confrontation with trade union demands for pay rises in the public sector and whether Blair will consider further legislation in this field as he had suggested.

The composition of the Labour Party was visibly transformed by its election of 101 women to Parliament. The method used to achieve this proved controversial, but it also strengthened Labour's claim to represent women's interests and wrong-footed the Conservatives whose female parliamentary representation was dramatically reduced in the 1997 election.

One feature of the new Labour Party which was very evident – and controversial – was the enhanced power of the leadership. Ever since the leadership of Neil Kinnock there has been a contest between those who want to retain the traditional pattern of intra-party power and those who see a dynamic leadership as the key to modernization and electoral success. For those on the losing side of this battle, the leadership appeared to be extending its power and authority in a manner inconsistent with Labour's traditions (Heffernan and Marqusee, 1992). Under Blair there were accusations that power in the party had been personalized and that too many constitutional procedures had been circumvented in a drive to channel all policy-making and decision-making authority through the leader's office. Blair's reliance on spin-doctors (especially Peter Mandelson and Alistair Campbell) caused criticism, although their successes also provoked envy in the Conservative party.

There were a number of episodes in opposition which underlined the tension between Labour's strengthened leadership and the practices of a party with a vigorous tradition of internal debate. Blair unsuccessfully attempted to postpone the 1996 shadow cabinet elections in an effort to handpick the team that he would take into the election. There was also a clash over party funding. Labour made strenuous efforts under Blair to improve its its fund-raising capacity and to reduce its reliance on the trade unions. In March 1996 the party appointed Henry Drucker to mastermind the drive which was designed to raise £10 million prior to the 1997 election. However, he resigned in April 1996 after a disagreement about the continuation of a separate fund set up to finance the leader's office. Inevitably the row was about more than conflicts of fund-raising objectives. It reflected internal unhappiness about the leadership's determination to maintain an independent operating base which could be used to promote an agenda distinct from that of the party as a whole.

The potential for conflict between the party and the leadership was addressed head on with the publication in January 1997 of *Labour in Power*, which contained proposals for party reform. The document, drawn up Labour's general secretary Tom Sawyer and passed by its National Executive Committee with only Dennis Skinner voting against, had to be discussed by the 1997 party conference. But it was a pointer to leadership thinking about the future of party organization, aiming to reduce the possibility of embarrassing clashes between the party conference and NEC on the one hand, and a Labour government on the other. The reforms envisaged a reduced role for the NEC which would be obliged to support a Labour government's policies. The balance of strength within the NEC would be tilted towards ordinary members rather than the trade unions. Although the reliance on individual membership was a key to reforms of the party structure, some constituency parties remained strongly opposed to Blair's agenda. For instance Labour in Leeds remained very faction-ridden, despite the suspension of one of the constituency parties there.

Modernization has thus been achieved in the Labour Party and
further changes seem in the offing. Yet these changes have not
been cost-free. Certainly by the time of the general election
Labour was operating more effectively at the top and allowing
more individual participation at the grass roots. However, the
effort to change the party's traditional style and culture had
alienated some loyalists and it remained unclear whether New
Labour's formula for operating a heterogeneous political party
would work.

The Conservative Party

Few periods of internal division compare with that experienced by
the Conservative party in the 1990s. Not since the debate about
protection engulfed Balfour's leadership has the Conservative
party been engaged in so serious an internecine fight. At the root
of Tory turmoil was the issue of the UK's relationship with the
EU. Although it was the Conservative party which took Britain
into the European Community in the 1970s and into the Single
Market in the 1980s, the quickening pace of integration and the
prospect of monetary union exposed fundamental differences of
opinion within Tory ranks and bared the party's vein of neo-
nationalism. What was significant about the Conservative redis-
covery of nationalism was that it affected all generations of the
party. As well as appealing to the party's populist element, it had
intellectual support. In the unusual leadership contest of 1995
Europe was the defining issue between the prime minister and his
challenger, John Redwood (Sowemimo, 1996). After the 1997
election, Europe became central to the struggle to control the
future of the Conservative party and define its character and
ideology.

On one wing of the debate is a Eurosceptic group adamantly
opposed to further European integration and yearning for a
restoration of full British sovereignty in policy areas already
transferred to Brussels. Under Major's premiership, Eurosceptics
such as William Cash, Anthony Marlow, Sir George Gardiner
and Teresa Gorman were regular backbench critics of their own
government and part of a group of eight who had the whip
withdrawn, an act of collective punishment unprecedented in

twentieth-century Tory history (Norton, 1994). The wisdom of removing the whip was much disputed: as a strategy it had little impact on the dissident group's voting behaviour, reduced the government's already wafer-thin majority and was later abandoned without further sanctions or conditions.

The Eurosceptic tendency was not confined to the backbenches however. It was also represented inside Major's two governments of 1990–2 and 1992–7. In the cabinet John Redwood (until 1995), Peter Lilley, Michael Howard, Michael Forsyth and Michael Portillo were known sympathizers of a robustly anti-European approach and a recurrent threat to the unity of the government itself. The position below cabinet level was even worse. In the 1997 election campaign it became apparent that several junior ministers as well as some 150 backbenchers had signalled their opposition to a single currency in their electoral addresses to constituents; and, although ministers were reined back to conform to the government's official 'wait and see' line, Major as prime minister could do nothing to constrain his backbenchers.

There was also a strong element of Euroscepticism amongst Tory peers, where former ministers such as Lord Tebbit were able to mount savage attacks on any minister who seemed too subservient to Brussels. The former premier, Lady Thatcher, was also a frequent critic of any further moves towards a federal Europe. Her interventions were, of course, liable to be inflammatory because, whether intentionally or not, any contribution which she made to the debate was liable to highlight not merely her views on Europe but the deeper fault lines within the party and the difference between her style of leadership and Major's.

On the other wing of the party there were assertive supporters of European integration in the election run-up. On the backbenches figures such as Sir Edward Heath, Hugh Dykes, Edwina Currie, Ray Whitney and Peter Temple-Morris were enthusiastic and knowledgeable participants in the European debate, while most ministers in the cabinet (with a few notable exceptions) were generally more sympathetic to the European cause. Among senior members of the government Kenneth Clarke became the most high-profile advocate of the European cause and for that reason was seen by many Eurosceptics as an impediment to party unity. Opinion on European matters became increasingly polarized as the 1992–7 Parliament progressed. At its start the majority of

Conservative MPs adhered to neither extreme on the European issue (Baker, Gamble and Ludlam, 1993). However, by the time of the general election of 1997, Europe became had become a much more significant issue in Tory thinking and Euroscepticism had been absorbed into the wider culture of the party.

Why did outright antipathy to European integration become so much more evident over this period? Certainly the change of pace in the EU's own agenda, especially the radical proposals for monetary union, had the effect of moving the centre of Conservative opinion in a more Eurosceptic direction. The mass of Tory MPs was increasingly aware that there were two conceptions of the European 'project' and that the British interpretation of what was involved in membership was at odds with that of many other member states (Beloff, 1996).

On a more concrete level, there was also a growing realization about how far-reaching some earlier initiatives such as the Single European Act and the Maastricht Treaty had been for the EU. In addition Conservative MPs became more aware of the increased role of the European Court of Justice which, whatever its merits, operated in a manner unfamiliar to British constitutional practice. The prolonged conflict over British beef and fishing quotas highlighted the UK's isolation *vis-à-vis* its European partners but also created a new mood of public opposition to European decision making. Even if the mass of Tory MPs were not committed Europhobes or Europhiles, the handling of European issues frequently gave cause for concern. Thus in November 1996, many Tory MPs were highly critical of Major's initial refusal to allow a full parliamentary debate on monetary union prior to the European summit in Dublin and forced a debate to be held. Finally, Labour's conversion to the need for a referendum prior to taking Britain into a single currency increased the pressure on Major to put 'clear blue water' between the parties on the issue by giving an unequivocal rejection of British entry in the first phase.

Taken together these developments made the European issue intractable and unsettling for the Conservatives. Nor was this surprising. Tory governments frequently argued a line which was different from that of their European partners – for example on the social chapter and working hours. In some cases the government's line reflected backbench sentiment. More often it was a reflection of the distinct interest of the UK in the European policy process. In any debate on European issues, the UK's 'awkward' position put Europhiles at a disadvantage. Opposition to the EU's regulations had populist appeal: Brussels was an easy target to bash in the tabloid press. The ownership and outlook of the 'quality' press meant that *The Times* and the *Daily Telegraph* had become increasingly Europhobic.

In addition the European issue was a difficult one for Major's government to handle because it was dynamic rather than static so that formulas designed to bring about intra-party agreement were frequently shattered by events. And Europe subsumed an increasingly large number of other issues – prosperity, beef, fish, the role of judges, the power of bureaucrats, fraud, and sovereignty.

Other Ideological Divisions

Since Europe dominated the internal debates of the Conservative party in the late 1990s, other issues (such as the handling of the economy, the balance between tax cuts and public spending and intervention in industrial policy) lost much of their fervour. It was generally recognized that in the debate between 'wets' and 'dries' on economic issues, the 'dries' had won. Technical issues replaced doctrinal ones, and although in the 1990s there were still party divisions about economic policy, they tended to reflect the broad cleavage between those who wanted to advance the Thatcherite revolution and those who preferred consolidation. Thus some Conservatives prioritized tax cuts above all else. For them the reduction in the responsibilities of the state and the size of the public sector were key policies. But most Conservatives still wanted to achieve an electorally appealing, but difficult, mix of low taxation, low inflation and good public services.

Spending on welfare services generated particular ideological conflict although both Tory and Labour leaderships recognized the need to rethink the organization and funding of social policy (Chapter 15). For the right of the Conservative Party down-sizing and privatization were alternatives to public provision in such areas as pensions; and they wanted reform to be as radical as possible. For other Tories, the welfare state remained not merely a popular but a necessary protection against deprivation. Although Peter Lilley was keen to stimulate intellectual debate about the future of welfare, Conservatives generally did not rush to dismantle policies inherited from the years of post-war consensus. What did change, however, was the tone of debate. Major's government was keen to eliminate fraud from the social security system. There was some interest also in applying some of the ideas which had surfaced in American discussion of social policy, including linking unemployment benefit to a genuine commitment to seek work and using the welfare system to bolster traditional family structures. A job-seeker's allowance was introduced; and in the 1996 budget the government abolished the allowance for single-parent families.

The issue of single parents highlighted another potentially divisive theme in the Conservative party: moral attitudes. It was not that the 1990s saw a full-blown debate on this topic. Certainly some groups and individuals concerned with traditional family values became increasingly strident. Indeed Emma Nicholson saw the 1995 Tory conference debate on single mothers as a factor in her decision to leave the party and join the Liberal Democrats (Nicholson, 1996). Yet few Tories wanted either to defend libertarianism or to promote policies which were out of keeping with demographic reality. Most took a common sense view that families as institutions should be protected but recognized the dangers of a moral campaign backfiring on the party. There was general embarrassment when MP David Evans in the 1997 campaign described the children of his Labour opponent as 'bastards' and displayed a generally insensitive attitude to women. Evans lost his seat, as did Adrian Rogers, Tory candidate in Exeter who ran an explicitly anti-homosexual campaign against his Labour opponent.

Conservative Factions

Any schema of factions and tendencies in the current Conservative party runs into the problem that much of what divides the party concerns style and approach rather than explicit policy or ideology. Nevertheless, four basic tendencies in the Conservative party can be distinguished, constituting important sub-groups in Parliament and increasingly generating internal conflict and a muddied electoral image:

- 'Populists' are a relatively new and self-conscious attempt to appeal to anti-elitist sentiment in the electorate. The group is naturally iconoclastic, hostile to bureaucracy and disdains expertise especially in fields (such as education and social work) where it believes the values of professionals to be out of tune with common sense. On European policy and international matters it is supportive of a 'Little England' approach.
- The intellectual right has been heavily influenced by the free-market ideas associated with Thatcherism. Like the 'populists' the group is iconoclastic, but its iconoclasm tends to be rooted in intellectual argument rather than gut sentiment. Some members who fall into this group (for example David Willetts, John Redwood and Peter Lilley) were given office under Major. Others such as Iain Duncan Smith were not.
- The self-conscious progressive strand of the party was once prominent but is now on the defensive, although some new organizational efforts such as the formation of 'Conservative Mainstream' have occurred, and the 1997 intake brought in able new recruits such as Damian Green and Shaun Woodward. Some members of this group have moved towards an explicitly Christian Democratic vision of Tory philosophy. Others remain in the 'One Nation' tradition without any religious overtones.
- 'Pragmatists' self-consciously distance themselves from an ideological approach to politics and dislike populist appeals. Holding office tends to shift individuals into this category and the declining group of party 'grandees' (such as Douglas Hurd) also tends to be found there.

These groupings overlap and some MPs, not surprisingly, do not fit neatly into any one category. The Tory leadership must try to appeal to as many of these groups as possible, or at least to minimize the alienation of any of them. Edward Heath's support in the 1970s was firmly located in the progressive and pragmatic groups and he had very limited appeal beyond them. In the 1980s Thatcher based her support on the intellectual right and populist groups but was able to add to command some support from the pragmatists. Major attempted to gain support from all four groups but from 1992 onwards found that the European issue made him increasingly reliant on pragmatists and progressives.

In the early and middle 1990s, Conservative MPs mobilized around a range of groups such as the 'No Turning Back Group', the '92 Group' led in 1996 by John Townend and the Macleod Group as well as around dining clubs. These groups indulged in a range of activities from informal policy discussions to organized conferences and the publication of pamphlets. In some cases the groups constructed a slate of sympathetic candidates on key backbench committees (including the 1922 Committee) and tried to secure their election. Many of the groups also realized that the battle to control the future of the party would be determined by the character of the candidates selected in 1997. Thus the 92 Group urged prospective candidates to make their opposition to the single currency clear in their personal manifestos.

On European issues, the Euro-rebels in the 1992–7 Parliament organized through the 'Fresh Start' group which then contained about 50 members (Sowemimo, 1996). The sceptics also established an extra-parliamentary body – the European Foundation – with its own organ (*The European Journal*). The European Foundation was able to link sympathetic groups inside the Conservative party with non-party groups of similar persuasion. The pro-integrationists inside Parliament formed a Positive Europeans group and an extra-parliamentary Action Centre for Europe sponsored by Lords Howe and Kingsdown (Sowemimo, 1996). Factional groups operated independently of the formal party backbench subject committees which had a relatively low profile between 1992 and 1997 as a result.

Many MPs saw a marked change of atmosphere in the parliamentary party as increasing factional hostility made socialization more difficult. Retirements from the House in 1997 were in part driven by the decline of collegiality in Conservative ranks and one departing MP, Robert Hicks, underlined the damaging effects on the party of an increased number of aggressive new Thatcherite MPs. Major's decision to submit himself for re-election as party leader in 1995 followed a hostile reception at a 92 Group committee meeting. Emma Nicholson, one of three Tory MPs in the 1992–7 Parliament to cross the floor of the House, reported that she had been punched by a fellow Conservative after a vote on the Nolan Report. Julian Critchley highlighted the extent to which the 1992 intake of MPs had strengthened nationalism on the Tory benches: 'Thatcher's children are all Little Englanders

... what is so remarkable about the Conservative Party is the extent to which we hate each other' (quoted in *The Times*, 16 November 1996).

Parliamentary Dissent

Charting the scale of legislative dissent in the Conservative party is easier than precisely delineating its factions or tendencies. For all the drama of a declining governmental majority, conflicts over Europe and the breakdown in pairing arrangements in 1996, there was rather less Tory dissent under Major than in some other Parliaments. The incidence of Conservative dissent in whipped divisions was slightly lower than during Thatcher's second term in 1983–7 and much lower than under Heath's government of 1970–4 (Chapter 8). Nevertheless, Parliament was unusually difficult to manage for a variety of reasons. The government's declining majority made the handling of business – especially in committee – uncertain. The dominance of European issues created an image of Conservative disunity. And the weapons at the Conservative whips' disposal were seen to be blunt. The removal of the whip in the mid-term of a parliament exacerbated organizational difficulties and bad feeling inside the party. Although there were some efforts within Conservative local associations to deselect dissident MPs, only Sir George Gardiner at Reigate was in fact deselected for Eurosceptic criticisms and some pro-Europeans such as Hugh Dykes experienced constituency problems. (Gardiner stood as a Referendum Party candidate and was defeated; Dykes lost his seat.) Anticipated defeat helped to produce some compromise in Tory ranks; but it also created a nervous mood on the backbenches and a soured relationship between Major's government and his backbenchers. Backbenchers expected their criticism could be influential and were willing to press their ideological, policy and constituency causes on the crumbling government.

Leadership

Given the divisions the task of any Tory leader would have been difficult. But John Major's ability to contain the factionalism of his party was constrained by several factors. His own leadership style stood in marked contrast to his predecessor's. His decision making mode was that of a good manager: he was a skilled chairman, a good listener and had a rigorous regard for detail. Policy making for him progressed from the ground up and he was uncomfortable with sweeping visions or rhetorical flamboyance. Yet the organization he led was culturally schizophrenic. The Tory party had become more participatory and less deferential; but it remained wedded to the notion of strong leadership. The issues which divided the Conservatives in the 1990s, especially Europe, made clear and dogmatic statements impossible for a governing party; and they made attempts at heroic and forceful leadership unwise.

Major's difficulties were compounded by a weakening of the instruments of party management. The whips' office did not work particularly well during the 1992–7 Parliament. And one of the tools of leadership – patronage – was blunted by the prime minister's unwillingness to reshuffle his governments in a radical manner. Major was unwilling to sack weak ministers and his promotions displeased both loyalists and rebels who each felt the other side had been overly favoured.

The election result triggered Major's announcement that he would resign the leadership. The process of choosing a replacement involved further internal strife. Five candidates stood in the first ballot – Kenneth Clarke, Michael Howard, Peter Lilley, William Hague and John Redwood. Clarke offered a leadership from the Tory centre-left while John Redwood, Michael Howard and Peter Lilley promised leadership from the right and a strengthening of Euroscepticism. The youngest contender, William Hague, was on the centre-right of the party. The leadership contest turned into a surprisingly bitter affair. On the third ballot Hague beat Clarke by 92 votes to 70, despite an unexpected Clarke-Redwood pact after the indecisive second ballot. Clarke was the only leadership contender to refuse to serve under Hague, and returned to the backbenches, as did another major figure, Michael Heseltine.

Party Organization

Traditionally the Conservative party has been seen as better organized than the other parties. But during the 1990s this advantage declined partly for financial reasons. The Conservatives left the 1992 election with a deficit of some £19 million and although they were able to raise large sums of money as the 1997 election approached they were handicapped by the decline in constituency strength and by the reluctance of some firms to continue giving to the party. In addition a new climate was created in the wake of the Nolan Report which made it more difficult than before for the Tories to accept gifts from overseas and which also made large donations from individuals suspect. The advent of a Labour government made it likely that new rules governing party funding would be introduced and that the Conservative party would have to adapt to greater financial openness.

Central Office itself did not work well for much of the 1990s. Major's choice of Brian Mawhinney as his chairman for the run-up to the 1997 election showed his determination to get a grip on the party machine and resulted in some imaginative appointments, especially that of Danny Finkelstein as Director of the Research Department. But Mawhinney's abrasiveness itself created problems inside Central Office and in the cabinet. The well publicised resignation of Hugh Colver as Head of Communications was one result of Mawhinney's intervention in the management of publicity. Yet despite Mawhinney's efforts to get a grip on the organization, problems at Central Office persisted, especially in relation to communications and publicity where the Conservatives never seemed able to set the agenda. As a result after the 1997 election it was clear that the party's central organization needed attention and would claim time in opposition.

The party at the grass roots has withered in the 1990s. The Tories' traditional claim to be a mass party has been shaken by surveys which reveal a declining absolute membership and paint a portrait of party that is older and less educated than that of the revitalized Labour Party (Seyd *et al.*, 1992, 1994, 1996). The need to reverse this decline is evident. Although it might be argued that parties are becoming redundant in modern societies, the Conservative party needs its middle-level elites to raise money, choose parliamentary candidates, fight local elections and provide an attractive image to the electorate at large. The 1990s have seen a series of electoral defeats and a crumbling of party morale. One of the most urgent tasks in opposition is to rebuild the voluntary party. In the aftermath of defeat there has been much discussion of the need to learn from Labour's example and rebuild a democratic party based on strong individual membership. New leader William Hague has promised a greater role for the voluntary party, including a say in the selection of the leader.

The Liberal Democrats

In 1994 the Liberal Democrats abandoned policy 'equidistance' from the two major parties and made clear their preference for New Labour. For a radical party the logic of this move was clear enough, although it did not command universal assent within Liberal Democrat ranks. An accommodation with Labour reflected both a genuine intellectual and political sympathy with Tony Blair's aims and a desire to exert influence in government. In the run-up to the 1997 general election the Liberal Democrats engaged in a number of joint activities and initiatives with Labour, and close contacts developed between frontbench spokesmen such as Robin Cook and Jack Straw for Labour and Menzies Campbell and Alex Carlisle for the Liberal Democrats. Some of these initiatives covered specific policy problems, such as the banning of knives and the response to the Scott Report. More important, however, was the sustained discussion which occurred between the two parties in their Joint Constitutional Committee, which produced a measure of agreement on constitutional reform, including a possible referendum on the electoral system (Chapter 7).

However, convergence of opinion and agreements made at the top of the party organizations do not necessarily translate well to the parties' grass roots. Although tactical voting was clearly in the interests of both parties in 1997, it was not expressly endorsed as a strategy. Nor was there any agreement about whether Paddy Ashdown or any other senior Liberal Democrat should be invited to serve in a Labour government or indeed whether, if invited, they would accept the offer. In fact as the 1997 election results revealed, the Liberal Democrats' strategy of concentrating on a set of target seats paid impressive dividends and encouraged tactical voting for them in other areas. But whether it was a sufficiently strong performance to give the party real leverage over Blair's government remains unclear, as does the question of how long Liberal Democrat strength can be maintained if there is a

Conservative revival. For the immediate period after 1997 election the Liberal Democrats can celebrate their achievement of vastly enhanced parliamentary representation which complements their strong local government base.

Conclusion

The Labour Party's dramatic election victory signals a major change of personnel but its impact on broad policy remains an open question. Three new issues related to the British party system have risen to prominence at the end of the 1990s. First, will the Conservative party in opposition break with consensus and be transformed into an anti-European party, or will it be able to reunite around mainstream policies under a new leader? Second, how secure is Labour's transformation? Can it settle into being the natural party of government or is its own electoral success built on fragile foundations which could be smashed by internal dissatisfaction with the lack of substantive social reforms? Third, how far will the explosive issue of Europe and Labour's constitutional agenda change the context in which British party politics operates, dissolving old loyalties and behaviour patterns and creating new alignments? The answers to these questions remain obscure, though they will need to be answered in one way or another by the end of the century.

6

Political Participation

MARK EVANS

The late 1990s are witnessing a dramatic upsurge in single-issue protest activity and unconventional forms of political participation. At the same time, conventional forms of political activity are also changing. Europeanization of British politics and new styles of public administration have altered political opportunity structures and are reshaping the scope of citizen activity and the nature of contemporary protest and protest potential. In the late 1980s the bulk of survey data pointed to the 'steady state' of political participation in the UK (Jowell *et al.*, 1987; Topf, 1989; Parry *et al.*, 1992). In the late 1990s this is no longer the case.

Political Participation in the UK: A Snapshot

The British participation study undertaken by Parry *et al.* (1992) argued that participation is a 'multidimensional' phenomenon. However, it found that people were not involved in activities across the board but tended to focus on one type of action such as contacting a councillor or going on a protest march. Moreover, certain local communities were more attracted to certain types of activities than others. In short, participation in Britain is characterized by uneven practices across regions. Recent data support these findings. In 1993 a MORI poll showed that 33 per cent of those interviewed had helped to raise funds for a political purpose, 19 per cent had urged someone outside their family to vote, 19 per cent had urged someone to contact a local councillor or MP, and 4 per cent had taken an active part in a political campaign.

Even voting is not an activity in which all participate. Of those eligible to do so, 29 per cent did not vote in the 1997 general election. However, that election did mark an important stage in the evolution of British political participation, with 120 women elected to the House of Commons, at 18 per cent the highest intake ever. In 1992, 60 women (9 per cent) were elected to the Commons. Britain still lags behind Sweden (40 per cent) and Finland (38 per cent) in female representation in the lower house, but is now well ahead of France (6 per cent), Greece (6 per cent) and Italy (8 per cent). The number of non-white MPs also reached a new high at the 1997 general election, with 10 elected (9 Labour, 1 Conservative), but remains at a low level when placed in the context of an electorate which is 4.5 per cent non-white.

Recent studies suggest that one distinguishing feature of Britain is that it is more protest prone than any other state (Wallace and Jenkins, 1995). Putting protest participation (actual engagement in protest action) and protest potential (willingness to engage in protest action) together, the UK registers figures of 56 per cent for signing a petition, 35 per cent for attending a lawful demonstration, 25 per cent for joining a boycott, 15 per cent for joining a wildcat strike, 13 per cent for refusing to pay rent or taxes, 9 per cent for blocking traffic and 8 per cent for occupying a building or a factory. Use of personal violence (2 per cent) and damaging things (1 per cent) register very low scores. Within these overall measures differences of class, gender, age and race affect participation.

Class differences are often measured by trade union activity, which in Britain has declined markedly in the past 20 years. The peak union membership level of 53 per cent of the civilian workforce in employment was registered in 1978. It has since fallen to 30 per cent. Whereas men and women are almost equally likely to be trade union members, full-time employees are almost twice as likely to be union members as part-time employees. Strike activity has also declined since the late 1970s. In 1995 the number of working days lost to labour disputes was at its lowest level since records began at around 27 000 (*Social Trends*, 1996, p. 81). Nevertheless, in a comparative study Wallace and Jenkins (1995, pp. 96–137) found that union membership remained significant in Britain and Holland, where high levels of class voting, union organization and left party influence are exhibited. They also found that Britain is the leader in political strikes, with more than double the number of the runner-up, Italy. Hence, it would be wrong to disregard completely the importance of traditional forms of class politics in Britain. Indeed, a Gallup poll in August 1996 reported that 76 per cent of people asked believe that there is a class struggle in Britain. When Gallup asked the same question in 1964, during a period of partisan alignment and class voting, a figure of only 48 per cent was recorded. The Wallace and Jenkins (1995, pp. 120–35) study argues that the new class (of predominantly middle-class activists) is a significant source of protest in Britain as well as in the USA, Italy, Holland and Switzerland. In the UK it is viewed as a promoter of civil disobedience strategies in campaigns for animal rights and environmental protection. Education correlates positively with activism.

Gender studies show that men are more likely to engage in protest politics than women (Wallace and Jenkins, 1995, pp. 96–137). However, the gender gap in participation is narrowing, notably in the realms of political discussion and campaign work (Christy, 1994). This kind of change is reinforced by institutional change such as women-only shortlists in the Labour Party. One reason why women nevertheless still participate less than men is that they continue to be less formally educated and to earn less money than men, with the result that class differences begin to play a role. A 1995 OECD survey of 18 countries showed British women near the bottom in terms of average earnings relative to men. The gender gap in protest participation is partly a result of women's traditional commitments and is only slightly narrowed by new 'women on top' (Rowbotham, 1996, p. 12). While more sophisticated measures of female independence might tend to diminish further, or even reverse, the gender gap in protest activism, it seems likely that any further expansion in women's participation will only be achieved through improvements in economic conditions.

Age differences in participation are complex. The young are less likely to vote than the old (Heath *et al.*, 1991, p. 212), and are more likely to be alienated from conventional forms of participation (British Youth Council, 1995). However, they are more likely to engage in unconventional forms of participation, such as protest politics. In short, it is not that young people do not participate in politics, rather that they participate differently. Under-35s are particularly interested in help for the homeless (73 per cent), disabled rights (71 per cent), animal rights (66 per cent) and increased funding for the NHS (64 per cent) (Wallace and Jenkins, 1995, pp. 96–137). Young people have been prominent in championing environmental causes and civil rights (in, for example, campaigns against the Criminal Justice Bill in 1994). *Race* differences in participation are understudied, scarcely featuring in the British participation study which tried but failed to pick up the race issue (Parry *et al.* 1992, p. 358) and not featuring at all in a recent study of social movements in Western Europe (Jenkins and Klandermans, 1995). The limited salience of this issue in Britain results partly from the fact that the non-white population is small at 2.5 million and weak in terms of political resources at 4.5 per cent of the electorate. Attitudinal data also suggest that the interests of non-white voters coalesce with those of white voters on all issues except immigration, unemployment, housing, and law and order (Studlar, 1986). However, race is an important issue in urban Britain and local political arenas, where participation rates increase as non-whites have the chance to exercise some influence. The number of non-white elected local representatives has increased considerably since the mid-1980s (Saggar, 1992). Research also suggests that non-white groups can exercise significant influence on local policy development in housing and urban regeneration issues when non-whites are present within policy elites (Messina, 1989; Ball and Solomos, 1990). Participation rates for non-white Britons thus appear to be linked to perceptions of political efficacy. This may in part account for the most notorious, and exceptional, aspect of non-white participation, the politics of the street. Riots in 1981, 1985 and 1992 demonstrated that direct action remains the most effective mechanism of protest for minority groups lacking conventional organizational resources.

Among the most conventional forms of political participation is membership of *political parties* and *groups*. At the start of the 1990s political party membership in the UK was put at 2.3 million, or 7 per cent of the electorate (Parry *et al.* 1992, p. 112). This figure has certainly declined since then, chiefly because, while Labour Party membership has increased in the mid- and late 1990s, Conservative membership lists have declined. Moreover, the number of active party members is lower still. In 1993 the Labour Party was reported to have an active membership of 140 000 in a total membership of 280 000, and the Conservatives to have an active membership of 165 000 in a total membership of just over 750 000. The average age of Conservative party members is significantly higher (early 60s) than that registered for Labour (late 40s). Whiteley *et al.* (1994), who undertook the studies from which these figures are taken, argue that political parties have themselves contributed to their loss of membership by failing to provide either collective (policy) or selective (process/outcome) incentives to members. They focus particularly on the disintegration of local government as an explanatory factor (see Chapter 13). However, Britain continues to have a thriving associative culture: 'if there is a single key to political participation in Britain, it must be group memberships' (Parry *et al.* 1992, p. 422).

Unconventional Political Participation in the UK

As participation rates in conventional organizations (such as political parties) decline and as certain sections of the population (such as the young) become increasingly alienated from mainstream political processes, so forms of unconventional participation increase. There are many reasons for this, generating a wide variety of participatory forms.

Britain's membership of the EU, plus the broader globalizing processes which are now taking place, create new opportunity structures for, and barriers of entry to, political participation. Within the EU interest groups must operate within a multi-layered system. As the process of European integration has advanced – through, for example, the Single European Act 1987 and the Treaty on European Union 1993 – so interest representation at the EU level has increased. Now up to 10 000 Euro-lobbyists are thought to be operating. They are widely held to have a considerable impact on EU policies (Kohler-Koch, 1994, p. 166). Not surprisingly, the development of such activity has reflected the growth of EU competence. In some areas the European Commission is obliged to consult. Articles 193 to 198 of the Treaty of Rome provide for mandatory consultations with interest groups (McLaughlin, 1993, p. 27).

It is important to note, however, that 'sectional' or 'economic' rather than 'cause' or 'promotional' groups have historically been better represented at the European level. This is because sectional groups tend to be better equipped with personnel and financial resources, are more vigilant in defence of their interests and thus more adept at penetrating policy networks (Peterson, 1994).

Commission officials welcome good information and those groups with the resources to overcome structural impediments to transnational integration (such as divergent national experiences and language barriers) have a good chance of lobbying success. Organized sectional groups tend to focus their lobbying activities on what Peterson (1994, p. 154) has termed policy networks at the meso-level of policy development. The relatively new political arenas which are thereby created are dominated by the interaction of private and public elites, and are by implication elitist and exclusionary rather than participatory in nature.

Nonetheless, as Kohler-Koch (1994, p. 171) argues, 'Lowi's dictum that "policy determines politics" is as valid on the European as on any other level of policy-making. The more particular interests are affected by EC-policies, the more it is likely that they will strive to enter the arena.' As the process of political integration matures it is likely that patterns of interest intermediation will become broader. All types of interest groups will have to increase the range of their activities and adapt their organizational structures and lobbying strategies in order to survive. There is already some evidence that single-issue groups are attempting to organize issue-specific coalitions on an EU basis (Sandholtz and Zysman, 1992). Moreover, with the strengthening of qualified majority voting in the Council of Ministers the forging of coalition agreements between interests is likely to proliferate within European policy networks.

Domestically, new forms of youth participation are emerging. The British electoral system, which polarizes political competition and inhibits the development of new parties, is tending to alienate young people from traditional forms of politics. 'Rock the Vote', a campaign which aims to get young citizens to participate in the political process, is the latest example of the cross-over of popular music and politics which has taken place in recent years (Cloonan, 1996). It was inspired by a similar movement in the USA, and launched at the Ministry of Sound nightclub in London in February 1996. It had the simple objective of raising the proportion of the electorate under 25 who would vote at the 1997 general election by encouraging registration and turnout. In the event, that proportion stood at 71 per cent in 1997, precisely the national average across all age groups, though whether this campaign was in any way responsible for this change is hard to judge.

The nature of this movement reinforces the view that extensive use of popular media represents a new era in political communication, one engendered by profound changes in the character of electoral politics and political participation (see Chapters 3 and 4). Indeed, as the media in general plays an ever greater role in politics, this form of political activity is likely to increase. A more circumspect approach would, however, view Rock the Vote as a commercial activity, a cynical manipulation of young people more akin to establishing brand loyalty than mobilizing opinion.

The case of the Muslim parliament, created in 1992 with a majority of members from the Indian sub-continent, represents a further development of political participation. Chiefly, it is an expression of Muslim dissatisfaction with democratic arrangements in Britain. It is also a prudential response to the west's hostility towards Muslim peoples in the aftermath of the Gulf War. Beyond this, it is a strategic device for preventing the absorption of Muslim identity into western culture. Finally, in the aftermath of the 'Rushdie affair', it is a movement which takes issue with western secular liberalism and its emphasis on absolute freedom of speech at the expense of minority religious freedoms.

One major growth area in political participation during the 1990s has been environmental protest. The two salient characteristics of what might loosely be termed 'the environmental movement' are its commitment to postmaterial issues and its diverse range of political activities. In a typology of environmental protest, Grant (1995, pp. 24–5) distinguishes five types of groups: the animal protection movement (such as the Royal Society for the Protection of Birds (RSPB) and Chickens Lib); the amenity movement (Council for the Protection of Rural England); groups concerned with recreation and access (Ramblers' Association); organizations concerned with particular forms of pollution; and organizations focusing on transport issues. New social movements are said to be coalescing around postmaterial issues such as environmental protection. They adopt principled positions on single, but broad, issues such as care for the environment, peace and women's rights (Jenkins and Klandermans, 1995, p. 425). Many of these groups have grown considerably in recent years. In 1993 the RSPB had 850 000 members (up from 390 000 in 1985), Greenpeace had 411 000 members (50 000 in 1985), Friends of the Earth had 230 000 members (27 700 in 1985) and the World Wide Fund for Nature had 208 000 members (91 000 in 1985) (Rawcliffe, 1995).

Since the early 1990s a particular focus for the British environmental movement has been transport issues, in particular roads policy. These campaigns have brought together a very wide range of environmental groups, including Greenpeace, the World Wide Fund for Nature and the RSPB, none of which has a track record in this sphere (Rawcliffe, 1995, p. 32). By 1991 250 anti-roads groups had emerged in Britain under the umbrella organization, Alarm UK. Their emergence can be viewed as a product of three sets of factors. First, the roads programme, outlined in the 1989 white paper *Roads to Prosperity*, was viewed as both costly and unnecessary. Second, plans to build private-sector 'new towns' in the south to relieve congestion in and around London, and proposals for rail routes to the Channel Tunnel through Kent, caused further concern. Third, changes in socio-economic and political structures created the space for new forms of postmaterialist protest and unorthodox political behaviour to develop. Most of these movements originated in the south, possibly because the recession of the 1980s hit the north harder than the south, generating more concern for jobs in the north even if this meant damage to the environment (Russell *et al.* 1995; Johnston and Pattie, 1990).

The Twyford Down case was at the centre of much controversy in the early 1990s. Although the contentious three-mile M3 extension was eventually built, the Twyford Down protest had a significant impact on other anti-roads campaigns across the UK. In July 1993 the government was forced to back down over a proposal to take the East London river crossing through the 8000-year-old Oxleas Wood in south-east London as a result of the overwhelming opposition of an alliance of up to 3000 people from local, radical and mainstream environmental groups. In autumn 1994, protesters against the construction of an extension to the M11 at Wanstead, East London, barricaded themselves into condemned houses and had to be forcibly removed by police.

Subsequently road protests, deploying many forms of direct action, have become a regular feature of British politics. In particular, movements protesting against construction of the M77 in Glasgow and the Newbury bypass have both attracted massive public support. In addition, more radical groups have started to emerge taking inspiration from North American groups such as Earth First! and the Rainforest Action Group (Rawcliffe, 1995; Young, 1993). In 1994 the anti-roads movement turned its attention towards the role of the private car in society. At a demonstration held on 13 July 1996, 5000 people brought West London traffic to a standstill by staging a party in the middle of the M41.

Protests against exports of live animals have also been a prominent feature of recent years, with many people registering concern about the treatment of British livestock in foreign abattoirs and calling for a limit of eight hours' travelling to be imposed on live exports. The anti-live exports movement has proved successful in reducing the number of ferry companies that deal with live exports.

Finally, a highly effective single-issue pressure group in the late 1990s is Snowdrop. This was established after the Dunblane massacre in March 1996, when Thomas Hamilton shot dead 16 schoolchildren and their teacher before turning his gun on himself. Snowdrop campaigns for the outlawing of all handguns. While the Major government was still in power it prompted the passage of legislation to outlaw the possession of most handguns, despite the strong opposition of many Conservative MPs. One of the first actions of the Blair government in May 1997 was to promise a free vote on further legislation to provide a complete ban. Handguns have now been outlawed in the UK.

New Forms of Political Opportunity Structure

Opportunities for political action may be created in a series of ways. Issue networks which link groups of actors and create new coalitions of interest can be important in mobilizing protest. Examples from the past are the peace (Parkin 1968) and anti-poll tax movements (Butler *et al.*, 1994). The Criminal Justice and Public Order Act 1994 made an equally distinctive contribution to British protest politics in the 1990s. It is a good illustration of an important feature of modern protest politics, the role of the supporters' network.

The issue network which a movement inhabits inevitably includes both supporting and opposing organizations, which give rise to supporters' and opponents' networks. Competition is in fact often greatest between groups which operate within the same issue network (Klandermans, 1990, p. 125). However, because supporter networks provide a movement with resources and political opportunities they are indispensable if a protest is to survive and have an impact.

The provisions of the Criminal Justice and Public Order Bill affected a wide range of groups including animal rights protesters (Hunt Saboteurs Association), ravers (Advance Party), New Age travellers (Friends and Families, Travellers Support Group), squatters (Squatters Action for Secure Homes), trade union pickets (Unison), environmental direct action groups (Road Alert), professional organizations (Kent Law Clinic), co-ordinating groups (Coalition Against the Criminal Justice Bill, Freedom Network), local groups (York for Justice) and other forms of protest including consumer groups (Football Supporters' Association), constitutional reform groups (Charter 88), civil liberties organizations (Liberty) campaigning magazines (*Red Pepper*) and political parties (Green Party, Socialist Workers' Party). A diverse supporters' network emerged from these groups. The existence of overlapping memberships within the network (say Charter 88 and Liberty) was an important source of integration, as well as a crucial source of linkage to other issue networks (such as the constitutional reform supporters' network). This created opportunities to share campaigning resources, protest activities and forms of political access.

Recent research on supporter networks has demonstrated that they are very unlikely to endure. Moreover, the only unconventional political action that achieved consensual approval in a recent study of eight western democracies was signing petitions (Wallace and Jenkins, 1995, pp. 102–3). Such findings lend support to the thesis that the politics of direct action, though increasingly widespread, is likely to remain the preserve of the minority.

An important new opportunity structure for protest movements is the information superhighway (IS), a term used to refer to both information and communications technologies using a broad band system. By the year 2001 around 63 per cent of homes in the UK will be 'passed' by cable with access to the IS. The practical consequence of this development is that individuals and organizations equipped with the necessary hardware, software and subscription services will be able to access a vast bank of information from databases and on-line services worldwide and communicate interactively with others, no matter how far away, both individually and collectively (Percy-Smith, 1996, p. 43). Certain internet facilities for prompting discussion and debate through e-mail and electronic bulletin boards are already available, but the IS will provide even more opportunities.

The IS offers significant opportunities for horizontal networking between groups and individuals in such a way that single-issue groups can easily be mobilized in defence of their interests even when they are spatially dispersed. A further aspect of these systems is that they make it possible for groups to communicate effectively across national boundaries. This is likely to facilitate the emergence of pan-European movements. The IS also presents opportunities for extending local democracy. Amsterdam's Digital City, set up by Amsterdam City Council with support from the Dutch government, provides access to the IS via modem and telephone lines and through provision of free terminals in libraries, hospitals and museums.

There are of course problems associated with these developments which might limit as well as extend democracy. Access to the relevant resources is clearly key to participation in the IS. Moreover, available information may be more susceptible to manipulation by data managers and may not receive the rigorous assessment and evaluation that is possible through face-to-face meetings and discussions. Technological developments can in fact act both as a structural constraint on and as a facilitator of further participation. Communication agencies could impose prohibitively high charges to prevent certain groups from making use of the IS (Richardson, 1994–5, p. 15). At the same time, technological advances, accessible information, reliable sources of information, feelings of political efficacy, and cheap access to facilities could help to generate an exciting new avenue for political participation.

Explaining Changes in Political Participation

There are five interlocking explanations of why these changes in political participation are occurring. *Globalization theories* argue that new political opportunity structures (new foci of decision-making such as the European Commission) and barriers to entry (in this instance the need for EU membership to participate) are the consequence of changes to politics external to the nation-state, such as geopolitics, political integration, the internationalization of capital and global communications (Cerny, 1990). Globalization also affects institutions and processes internal to the nation state. This endogenous process is sometimes referred to as the 'hollowing-out' of the state, a term which infers that the political reach of the British state is being eroded in various ways. Rhodes (1994, pp. 138–9) maintains that there are four key interrelated trends which illustrate the scope of this process: privatization and limitation of public intervention; loss of function by central government departments to alternative service delivery systems (such as agencies); shift of function from the British government to EU institutions; and emergence of limits to the discretion of public servants through the new public management, with its emphasis on managerial accountability and clearer political control created by a sharp distinction between politics and administration. It is argued that this endogenous process has expanded political opportunities for elite participation through forms of governance such as quangos.

The *post-industrialism thesis* argues that a combination of macro-economic, social and demographic changes has loosened traditional social controls and nurtured the development of a new post-materialist political culture. Inglehart's (1977, 1990) work identifies a transformation of value priorities – or 'culture shift' – across western democracies from materialist to post-materialist values. For Inglehart the materialist value system, based on issues of economic and personal security, has been eroded by the increasing importance attached to non-economic, quality of life issues. The post-industrial thesis further argues that growth of the service sector and higher education, an expanded youth cohort, and the coming of the age of affluence have all created broad support for post-material issues (Melucci, 1989). What Inglehart depicted as a 'silent revolution' was reflected in the development of a new style of political action with citizens moving away from traditional modes of representation (political parties, trade unions) to more participatory forms. As a consequence, a proliferation of single-issue protest groups (also known as new social movements) inspired by post-material issues has emerged.

Statist theories hold that the state is central to the study of political participation and that theories of the state provide an important starting point for understanding the politics of social movements (Jenkins, 1995, p. 15). Tarrow (1994, p. 186) argues that unconventional political protest is most likely to emerge when institutional or political changes create new conditions that lower the cost of political action for citizens. Kreisi *et al.* (1995), arguing in a similar vein, categorize Britain as a 'strong state'. They state that the elitist nature of Britain's institutional form makes for executive dominance and allows the state to ignore social movement protest. Hence, the rise in unconventional forms of political protest among single issue movements may partly be attributed to the absence of conventional political opportunities within a 'strong state'. In short, this perspective contends that the institutional form of the state sets the boundaries of conventional and unconventional political action: Britain's first-past-the-post electoral system has provided an enabling context for the British two-party system and has constrained the emergence of new political parties. This perspective also establishes a link between electoral systems based on proportional representation and female political participation (Barkman, 1995, p. 141).

The *new class thesis* contends that changes in the class structure of western democracies have challenged the conventional relationship between people of lower-class positions and political unrest. This perspective insists that protest now emanates from the well-educated and professionally-oriented upper middle class rather than from the industrial working class. This new class, composed of university-educated, salaried professionals, has become the agent for a new form of class struggle and is a major constituent of single-issue reform movements (Berger, 1986).

Dealignment theories focus on changes in the nature of political representation consequent on the decline of political parties. They argue that party dealignment and the transformation of left opposition into centrist opposition has created a more volatile electorate open to the political alternatives that single-issue politics present. Maloney and Jordan (1995, p. 1137) hold that the increase in the number and size of campaigning groups, particularly environmental, has changed the political landscape of Britain over the last 25 years. Dalton (1993, p. 8) writes of citizen groups 'transforming the nature of contemporary democratic politics' by increasing opportunities for, and involvement in, participatory democracy. Some commentators (Dalton, 1994, p. 4; Grant, 1994, pp. 1, 81) now argue that parties have been replaced by groups as vehicles for political participation. In this view participation in such organizations has shifted the channels of politics (from parties to groups), changed the nature of democracy by allowing groups to articulate views more clearly, and turned individuals away from the values that are represented by traditional parties. It does seem clear that single-issue groups have been more successful in articulating post-material views than broad-church political parties, though the doubling of the membership of the Labour Party – to about 400 000 – since the election of Tony Blair as party leader suggests that the political party and the social movement can coexist.

New Labour, New Politics?

The launch of innovative public policy programmes aimed at redressing structural inequalities in society, coupled with the reform of institutions and political processes, can prompt the emergence of new opportunity structures for political participation. New Labour's 'New Deal' on welfare offers an example of the former. If economic resources remain a prerequisite for political participation then a government programme aimed at finding jobs for single mothers, young people aged under 25 and the homeless could help to remove economic impediments to participation. Moreover, New Labour's plans to reform institutions and political processes through constitutional reform promise to create further opportunities for political participation through the devolution of certain policy and administrative functions to Scotland, Wales and the English regions, increased access to information, the development of citizenship rights, and the creation of a 'rights culture' (Chapter 7). Yet for truly radical change in the nature of political participation electoral reform remains imperative. Tony Blair remains not persuaded of the case for proportional representation on the basis that it severs the one-member-one-constituency link. He is, however, more persuaded of the merits of the Alternative Vote system which maintains the single-member constituency system but affords greater representation to smaller parties. Nevertheless, political participation in Britain is clearly experiencing a period of reconstruction. Several conclusions can be drawn about this.

One is that in order to comprehend the nature of political participation it is important to contextualize social and political action. It is crucial to assess whether external processes have an impact (direct or indirect) upon the context and the strategies, intentions and actions of agents actually involved (Hay, 1995). Political opportunity structures can both facilitate and constrain political participation. As such, structures define the range of potential strategies and opportunities available to actors and privilege certain actors over others. Thus structures impose a 'strategic selectivity' on actors, providing resources and opportunities for the powerful, while constraining the powerless. Processes of globalization, such as political integration, can create new channels of political participation for well-resourced sectional groups but erect barriers of entry to poorly-resourced single-issue groups.

A second conclusion is that political participation in Britain is changing. Although working-class protest remains very much alive, new types of political action involving civil disobedience and new groups of actors have emerged (the new class, youth, women, the better educated). Social protest is no longer centred purely on the 'have nots' at the bottom of the class hierarchy, but also on individuals of economic and political standing. This new class is better educated, ideologically sophisticated and more willing to experiment with new forms of political action (Berger, 1986). Social protest has grown in the UK, moving upward in the class hierarchy, building on a new generation, on the expansion of higher education, on change in women's roles in society (Lovenduski and Randall, 1993) and on a post-material value system. Moreover, the criminalization of direct action and the clamp-down on the pursuit of alternative lifestyles appears to have succeeded in bringing more and more young people together and uniting them in a common struggle. The changing nature of group activity has had much to do with the absence of receptive and responsive political institutions. For, as we have seen, it is the institutional form of the state which sets the boundaries of political action.

Third, although the recent upsurge of single-issue groups should enhance participation in the future, effective political participation is linked to educational attainment, political equality and, most significantly, economic resources and political efficacy. Those who are disadvantaged under-participate, or as Parry and Moyser put it 'have not succeeded in compensating for their weak economic position by raising their political voices' (Parry and Moyser, 1994, p. 54). Moreover, while Britain now has a more active citizenry, evidence of successful policy outcomes achieved through 'bottom-up' participation remains rare, while successful participation by elites remains the norm.

Finally, three political phenomena stand out as likely to have a crucial effect on forms of political participation in the first decade of the new millennium: mounting disaffection with government as a consequence of the continued polarization of the workforce within the restructured international economy; the 'opening up' of new political opportunity structures and the 'closing down' of old ones as a result of changes in the nature of governance both internal and external to the nation-state; and the increasing impact of technological change on styles and patterns of political participation.

Part II

7
The Constitution

PATRICK DUNLEAVY

Britain famously has no one founding document, no codified constitution. Instead its modern constitutional arrangements have long been as Burke described them in the late eighteenth century, 'checkered and speckled . . . crossly indented and whimsically dovetailed . . . such a piece of diversified mosaic' (quoted in Mackenzie and Grove, 1957, p. 222). This inherited complexity has seemed to work well enough to both Labour and Tory political elites, who have been its primary modern beneficiaries. So constitutional issues have scarcely ever dominated elections – the last time being in the two 1910 polls focusing on curbing the House of Lords' power. Yet a few days before the formal start of the 1997 election campaign, Labour and the Liberal Democrats issued a report from a joint committee of both parties, pledging concerted action on a wide range of reforms in a new parliament and claiming to give Britain 'a modern constitution fit for the twenty-first century'.

There are, however, two main reasons for being sceptical about this initiative, and about the partial Labour–Liberal realignment which the joint party statement seems to presage. First, the most fundamental guarantee of the established constitutional system, the reason why a common core of institutions in Westminster and Whitehall has survived from Burke's time, has been the 'club ethos' which has always bound together Labour elites with their Conservative counterparts in an agreement to leave the behaviour of ministers and Parliament largely unregulated and the rights of citizens undefined. Instead both major parties' leaderships have preferred to prevent abuses of power by relying on the 'good sense' of politicians, a prudent concern not to over-exploit current government power in case control of the executive should alternate in future, and a shared camaraderie as custodians of a historically venerated and charmingly eccentric system (Harrison, 1996). 'In my view, a two-party system and an unfixed constitution is the highest form of political development yet seen', proclaimed an influential Tory commentator at the end of the 1970s (Gilmour, 1978, p. 226), and his confidence would then have attracted bipartisan agreement. Most British observers, and virtually anyone who obtained Cabinet rank, saw the 'Westminster model' as defining the superior 'flexibility' of a free people, confident in their liberties and representative government.

The key components of the Westminster model gave both major parties' elites so many mutual advantages that they could agree to operate the system unchanged, including:

- An electoral system which strongly protected the Conservatives and Labour from third-party competition and maintained their own internal unity. Dissidents who left the major parties were consigned to the political desert by plurality rule (or 'first-past-the-post') elections.
- A permanent duopoly of control in Parliament operating through the whips systems' 'usual channels', guaranteeing the government passage of its bills, and the main opposition party scope to debate, criticise and question.
- A large freedom of executive action by the government (which the opposition could later enjoy in its turn, creating some self-restraint in how power was used).
- Strong central government controls over all subordinate agencies and local governments within the UK, a potential concentration of executive power unparalleled in any other liberal democracy.
- Extensive protections from judicial interference or controls.
- A capability for the two major party elites to rearrange jointly any aspect of the constitutional order, administrative arrangements, the rights of citizens or the provisions of the law as they wished.

A second reason for scepticism has been the dilemma which has repeatedly tripped up previous proposals for constitutional reforms, the difficult choice for an incumbent government between the following:

- putting through genuinely democratic changes, which may then allow the opposition to capitalize on the enacting government's mid-term unpopularity; or
- using the existing concentration of executive power to try to sustain the government's broader policy programme (for instance, in economic or social policy), which may mean watering down manifesto promises of constitutional reform, a change made more acceptable by the reflection that (after all) constitutional issues matter less to ordinary people than bread-and-butter policies like taxation or the NHS.

Previous Labour governments have always chosen the second course. The Callaghan government in the late 1970s spent years devising feeble and undemocratic devolution proposals for Scotland and Wales which moved few significant powers away from Westminster, and provided for both devolved assemblies to be elected by plurality rule, thereby guaranteeing automatic Labour majorities for both assemblies in perpetuity. And in the late 1960s the Wilson government proposed a 'reform' of the House of Lords which would have made it a completely appointed assembly, controlled by the prime minister of the day. In both cases the reforms failed miserably. The Welsh devolution scheme was rejected by a large majority of voters in a 1979 referendum. Scottish devolution was endorsed by a referendum majority, but with such low turnout that a clause in the Act requiring positive approval from 40 per cent of Scottish voters was not met, and the whole scheme collapsed. The Wilson 'reform' of the Lords was defeated by a cross-party coalition of backbenchers in 1968, appalled at the vast expansion of the prime minister's patronage power which a wholly appointed Lords implied.

These precursors naturally incline seasoned commentators to be cynical about the Blair government's apparently extensive constitutional reform commitments. On this view, Labour in power will quickly cool on any change in the voting system. And when Labour ministers recognize that reforms to limit the power of the executive could mean delivering additional weapons of attack into the Conservative opposition's hands, their enthusiasm will diminish further. Labour ministers will also be advised by Whitehall officials whose every instinct is to centralize power in their own departments. There are also severe practical difficulties in legislating reform. On current parliamentary rules, each 'first class constitutional measure' must have its committee stage on the floor of the House of Commons instead of in a more manageable standing committee. And like all other bills on current rules it must complete its passage in a single parliamentary year. So complex constitutional bills put a severe squeeze on the time available for other legislation. Hence the most likely outcome will be a fudge. Reform proposals will be made the subject of long inquiries, delayed beyond the next election, or just emasculated to remove any initially democratic or decentralizing impetus – so runs the current conventional wisdom.

More optimistic observers argue that Labour has learned important lessons from the past, and from its long period in opposition. It has secured the support of the Liberal Democrats for the bulk of its constitutional programme. Incoming 'New Labour' MPs in 1997 are a different breed from former party stalwarts. And the new government can alter the rules for processing constitutional measures – for example, to allow bills to run on from one parliamentary session to another, or to provide for a new and special committee procedure for constitutional measures. Above all, on this view, the Labour leadership have done enough strategic thinking to realize that unless they want the normal Conservative political hegemony to be restored four or five years down the line, they must have their own long-term project to reweight the political scales in their favour – and in such a project constitutional reforms could play a key role. There are three key battlegrounds, which each lead into their own associated reform agendas and dilemmas:

- The centralization of power in Whitehall, which all parties except the Conservatives now agree must be tackled by devolution more successfully than last time round.
- The collapse of faith in key governing institutions produced by sleaze and perceived abuses or excesses during the long-term Conservative predominance at the centre. Labour and the Liberal Democrats are pledged to combat declining legitimacy by opening up central government, enacting a bill of rights and reform of Parliament.
- Changes in the voting system. Reform efforts here could either grind to a halt completely, or become the key to Labour's long-

term strategy, perhaps in tandem with significant party realignments.

The Centralization of Power

Island Britain has always been a unitary state, with a single domestic source of political power in Westminster, although the British empire was run in a more diversified way. A key reason for the collapse of the 'club ethos' binding Labour leaders to the status quo in the Thatcher years was the radical centralization within the state apparatus, drawing together the threads of power in Downing Street, subordinating all public sector agencies to ministers – particularly the transformation and expansion of quasi-governmental agencies (QGAs) and the suppression of residual local government powers over taxing and local spending (see Chapter 3). The Major government in the 1990s adopted a more consensual 'partnership' approach on issues that remained within local authority competencies, but without restoring any of the lost autonomy in financial decision-making or reversing the transfers of previously municipal functions to QGAs and micro-local agencies (schools, housing estates, contractors).

England has historically been a centralized nation since Tudor times, so here none of this mattered hugely in political terms. In successive rounds of local government elections in the Westminster mid-terms, Conservative councils were almost eliminated and Conservative councillors were reduced to a rump (about a fifth of all councillors, below the Liberal Democrats). But this trend only strengthened ministers' determination to strip away functions from councils now uniformly opposition-controlled. Many of the Tory party faithful displaced from local government were placated with positions on the mushrooming regional or local QGAs (such as hospital trusts, or the governing bodies of further education colleges or grant-maintained schools), thereby maintaining their involvement in 'public life'. By 1994 one estimate put the total number of QGA appointments controlled by ministers at 42 000, more than the numbers of elected local councillors (Weir and Hall, 1994). QGAs controlled budgets of £60 billion by 1996–7, a fifth of all public spending. In London the Thatcher government abolished the Greater London Council and reduced metropolitan government there to a hodge-podge of conflicting and business-dominated QGAs. This step at least created serious and continuing public dissatisfaction with central government's inadequate and uncoordinated direction of the capital's affairs.

In Scotland, and to a lesser extent in Wales, however, 18 years of uninterrupted Conservative rule at Westminster produced major political changes (Chapter 11). The Scottish National Party redefined its central demand as Scottish independence within the European Union, while the Scottish Constitutional Convention (an alliance of Labour, Liberal Democrats, trade unions, local government, voluntary organisations and churches) successfully built up a much wider consensus among all groups which favoured greater Scottish autonomy within the UK. The SCC produced a detailed and workable model of a Scottish Parliament with tax-raising powers elected by proportional representation. In Wales too a much broader consensus of opinion moved to favour a devolved assembly than in the 1970s, with almost unanimity inside Labour's ranks. Both these changes were primarily a reaction to being governed autocratically by 'alien' English ministers, especially under Thatcher. But they also reflected a growing recognition among Scottish and Welsh elites – in business, public administration, the QGAs fostering economic development and academia – that the UK government was not an organizationally appropriate level for developing a coherent industrial policy in the modern economy.

Developments in the European Union gave a great stimulus to this recognition. The Maastricht Treaty set up the Committee of the Regions, and the European Commission insisted that the British representatives should be elected local politicians and not the central government appointees whom Whitehall characteristically planned to instal. The Commission also consistently sought to go past the London ministries and build direct relationships with regional organizations and elites where EU social cohesion money is being spent. Under the Tories Whitehall arguably passed up opportunities for further funding worth millions of ECUs per year in (ultimately vain) attempts to monopolize the representation of British interests in Brussels. The Major government started to mend some of this damage by creating (for the first time since the 1960s) an administrative regionalism in England, in the form of government regional offices combining staff from three departments (Chapter 11). And Whitehall progressively acknowledged the importance of continuing EU regional and urban funding by integrating it with domestic UK spending in the 'single-regeneration budget', run in England out of the new regional offices. But both developments stopped short of any form of political expression for English regions, or any reductions in the unfettered ministerial discretion of the Scottish and Welsh Secretaries. While English public opinion has consistently been sceptical about elected regional authorities, with a opponents fearing that they would be a costly extra tier of government and no consistent public opinion majority for reform, Scottish and Welsh opinion has been steadily favourable to greater autonomy.

In England, however, the Conservatives did suffer in more diffuse ways from the centralization of government, as public responses to surveys showed large majorities feeling powerless and viewing ministers as arrogant. More subtly, the whole political and administrative culture of Whitehall and Westminster changed fundamentally in the 1980s, reflecting the displacement of key industrial, economic, regulatory and 'high-tech' issues from the member state level to the European Union level. The 'drift to Brussels' within the EU highlighted the continued marginalization of Britain as a 'great power' and the end of the Cold War. In the old central government culture, the really important issues were those of 'high politics' – defence, foreign policy, the national economy. But in recent times British political elites (Conservative and Labour alike) have focused their attention more and more on the 'low politics' issues which remain within their unilateral control – especially the organization of the public services (a theme which obsessed the Thatcher and Major administrations alike) and the detailed structure of the welfare state. In effect after 1983 Whitehall *became* a super-local government, determined to wrest detailed control of issues such as education, health care and local service provision from the municipal orbit and vest them instead in more compliant QGAs under its direct control. The opposition parties have more and more copied this focus. Labour's campaigning before the 1997 election focussed on a wide variety of mundane or tiny issues (such as how schools should micro-organize their teaching, or details of law and order policy implementation).

This form of 'centralization', where Whitehall and ministers suck in welfare state issues to compensate for their loss of previous 'high politics' issues, contains within it the seeds of a paradox. As Rhodes (1996) has argued, the low politics issues which now preoccupy ministers and top civil servants characteristically get run by 'policy networks' or policy communities, usually involving powerful professions, local government or QGAs. So ministers' and top officials' ability to get what they want implemented is necessarily more constrained than in 'high politics' issues, such as setting foreign policy or tax levels. Efforts to micro-manage complex policy sectors from the top have often come to grief, notably in the scaling-back of the national curriculum in education (which in its original form was simply unworkable), or in the escalation of managerial and bureaucratic costs inside the NHS following the creation of an 'internal market'. But Rhodes is wrong to argue in a strange hyper-pluralist vein that Britain is now governed by policy communities and policy networks, with ministers reduced to the role of injecting infrequent external stimuli or shocks to the system, and hence incapable of achieving anything more than short-term impacts.

The contemporary prominence of policy communities and networks essentially reflects the British state's decline – the current focusing of domestic politics on the detailed low politics issues which previous generations of ministers and civil servants would have found too dull to be concerned with, but which are now all that is left to them. Nor should we forget the great pathologies of centralization characteristic of Thatcher's attempts to override all policy networks come what may. For instance, more than £4 billion was lost in introducing the poll tax in 1990, only for the Major government to scrap it completely within two years (Butler *et al.*, 1995). Some commentators link the growth of 'policy disasters' in British government decision making to this form of political as well as governmental over-centralization (Dunleavy, 1995).

The Devolution of Power

Analyzing centralization as a pathology is easy, but remedying it effectively in the UK constitutional arrangements is difficult and hazardous. Nevertheless, the Blair government has pronounced itself determined to proceed with a timely and effective programme, focusing first on a bill to create a Scottish Parliament with tax-raising powers, which will be put to a referendum. This process will be followed by a white paper on Wales, and legislation to create a Cardiff assembly with fewer powers than in Scotland, mainly focusing on taking over control of the Welsh Office and of Welsh QGAs. A later bill will provide for consultative 'regional chambers' to be set up immediately in England (indirectly elected via local authorities), which will begin to oversee the government regional offices and develop economic development strategies. This bill will also provide a legal framework for English regional assemblies to be set up on a 'rolling programme' basis, as and when voters in each region have voted in referenda for their creation. A strategic authority for London under a directly elected mayor will be set up as a separate metropolitan body (Chapter 11).

So far so straightforward, but the manner of implementation may not be so simple. Even assuming the legislation could be processed over two sessions and in a special form of committee, there are other major difficulties. In the 1970s ministers and Whitehall insisted on listing in the devolution legislation the specific powers which the Scottish and Welsh assemblies would be allowed to have, with all other powers remaining at Westminster. The new legislation (certainly for Scotland) will adopt a different approach, by listing instead those powers which Westminster will retain, with the new Edinburgh Parliament able to act on any area where it is not specifically precluded from doing so. This approach is certain to produce a need for more joint working between the governments in Westminster and Edinburgh, especially on areas relating to the European Union

Labour has made an important move since the 1970s by conceding the introduction of a proportional representation system (on an AMS model, see below), both for the Edinburgh Parliament and for the Welsh Senedd – although this last change was opposed by the Welsh Labour party until as late as 1996. This shift is an important one because in the 1970s people in the Scottish highlands opposed devolution as extending the dominance of the Labour cities in Scotland's lowland belt. People in north Wales similarly feared that Welsh devolution would entrench the power of the south Wales Labour 'taffia' over them. The form of PR adopted helps the Tories to survive in both Wales and Scotland, and is likely to be welcomed by their supporters there, despite English Tories' opposition to voting system change.

The extent to which the new Parliament and Senedd succeed will depend considerably on their financial resources, which will certainly be closely circumscribed by Westminster and Whitehall, anxious to retain control of public spending totals. Having supplementary tax-raising powers is not a great deal of use to the Scottish Parliament, since extra taxes will be unpopular with voters. Far more important will be the terms under which UK national expenditures are allocated to Edinburgh or Cardiff, and the margins of discretion within which their legislators can allocate spending between priorities. Traditionally the 'secret engine' of the UK union has been the 'Barnett formula' agreed in 1974 under the Labour government, which allocates Scotland, Wales and Northern Ireland a fixed percentage of the public expenditure going into England: 15 per cent for Scotland, 10 per cent for Wales, and 5 for Northern Ireland. This formula was preserved throughout the Thatcher and Major governments, surprisingly because it is very favourable for Scotland and Wales, both strong Labour areas. Originally based on a detailed 'spending needs assessment', the Barnett weightings have not been modernized in over two decades, despite the considerable change in regional fortunes since then. Devolution is bound to trigger an overdue reassessment, not least because Barnett provides no guidance on how to allocate money to English regions if they are set up.

The critical unanswered questions about devolution remain political ones, however. The role of the Secretaries of State for Scotland and for Wales after the reforms are introduced will be scaled back, making their cabinet positions and scale of staffs anachronistic; they might be replaced by a single minister for inter-governmental relations, or abolished altogether. A more pressing and tricky issue for Labour is the so-called 'West Lothian' question, namely how it can be justifiable for Scotland and Wales to be over-represented in the Commons and for their MPs to carry on voting on English legislation covering matters which are devolved to the Edinburgh Parliament or Cardiff Senedd. Labour's dilemma is that in normal times it cannot do without its Scottish and Welsh MPs to assemble a Commons majority, nor does it dare let go either of control across a wide range of important domestic policies in England.

A definitive solution to the West Lothian question would be the 'in and out' option which Gladstone considered for solving the same question over Irish home rule in the 1880s. Essentially some form of English Grand Committee would have to be set up in the Commons to consider legislation affecting only England, from which Scottish and Welsh MPs would be excluded by convention. Labour leaders are confident that even a future Tory government would never countenance this suggestion, since compartmentalizing the Commons in this way would be a further nail in the idea of the UK as a union of nations. It would, however, be very hard to decide what was entirely English legislation, or what bits of laws could not be voted on by Scottish and Welsh MPs.

On broader issues of centralization of control, it is unclear whether the ending of Conservative rule will imply any major change. Greater consultation in the English regions and the reintroduction of elected politics into strategic, London-wide governance will make a difference, especially taken together with the new rhetoric of partnership and 'stakeholding' involving local government. But the 'Brown doctrine' of sticking to Conservative spending plans for two years will ensure that central–local relations have continuing frictions (Chapter 13).

The delays and uncertainties inherent in the 'rolling programme' for English regional devolution also imply that the 'quangoid state' may change little under Blair. Labour has promised a bonfire of QGAs in Wales and Scotland as powers are transferred to the new assemblies. But for England, there are no clear proposals for reform or decentralization, merely the promise that new hands on the patronage tiller will in some vague way democratize the appointments process. Some greater involvement of trades union personnel and Labour-orientated professions in QGA boards, and the displacement of the most obviously contentious Tory appointments, will probably occur, but even then rather incrementally. The Blair government has also proposed a new 'openness' in how QGAs are run.

The Declining Legitimacy of Government

A second long-run consequence of the 1980s was the growth of political 'sleaze', a potent portmanteau label used by the media to describe a wide range of phenomena from sex scandals to corruption, all of them reflecting poorly on Tory governments, especially from 1993 onwards (see Dunleavy *et al.*, 1995). Many of the sleaze problems under the Major government actually related to events in the mid and late 1980s. At that time Tory party hegemony in British politics seemed so complete that the self-restraint which held back previous ministers from abuses of power was clearly breached. This confidence and the centralization of power in Downing Street under Thatcher also created very strong incentives for business interests to invest resources in persuading ministers, Tory MPs and top civil servants to see things their way. There was a large expansion in the lobbying industry at Westminster and big increases in donations by companies and entrepreneurs to Conservative party funds.

The Conservatives also insisted on pushing through what one senior official described as a 'permanent revolution' in public sector organization from 1983 to 1992. These changes additionally opened up scope for the large-scale looting of public sector assets, by destroying historic patterns of administration designed to prevent corruption and to create a distinctive 'public service ethos' of respect for the public interest, legality, and a clear hierarchy of decision-making. In its place the Conservatives encouraged a 'new public management' (NPM) which emphasised the following:

- disaggregation, the splitting up of large, hierarchical units into smaller bodies run by strong entrepreneurial managers.
- competition, with public sector cash following 'customers' to the now disaggregated agencies, as in the schools system or the NHS internal market, and the introduction of private contractors.
- incentivization, dramatic increases in public sector pay inequalities (replacing the previous 'public sector ethos' of lower pay and dedicated professionalism) together with huge privatizations of government-owned assets of all kinds (Hood, 1996; Dunleavy, 1994).

The problems with this approach emerged slowly. Disaggregated agencies (especially QGAs) were vulnerable to being over dominated by their new strong leaders, whose thrusting 'entrepreneurial' styles eroded previous checks and balances, broke down the power of professions and unions, and made their new bodies very top-down organizations. The chairs and boards of most QGAs were dominated by Conservative party allies or business donors, whose roles could easily be seen by critics as 'payback' for their support, especially in the most 'politicized' QGAs, such as the Funding Agency for Schools, set up to run grant-maintained schools which opted out of local authority control (Hall and Weir, 1995). Competition put managers under more pressure to cut corners to succeed, strengthened a tendency to pare jobs to a minimum in public service organizations, and created a 'climate of fear' in which staff protests were stifled. At the same time incentivization dangled larger money prizes in front of managers as the rewards for being successful. Contracting enlarged the scope of business involvement in public services, and with it the potential for corruption or favouritism, with very few additional safeguards put in place. Huge areas of service delivery went to private companies, including virtually all central government computing which went primarily to a single multinational corporation which repeatedly lobbied to take over all income tax and social security administration (Margetts, 1995; Dunleavy, 1994).

Under NPM state decisions had more rather than less impact on private companies. Tiny changes in decisions by supposedly independent regulators could now spell boom or bust for key utility companies, adding or cutting millions from their share prices in a few minutes. A large privatization lobby (merchant banks, management consultants, accountants, legal firms and advertisers) had a direct stake in asset sales. And a rapidly growing contracting industry depended considerably on ministerial decisions. Sales of government assets, ranging from whole industry privatizations, through 'market testing' of blocks of civil service work, to property sales or franchising the national lottery, all proved very hard for ministers and civil servants to get right. A succession of lucky businesses and individuals who were advantaged by mistakes made in the sales process attracted public and media attention. Of course, NPM also included some new forms of counter-weights to try and prevent abuses. Charters for customer care were supposed to preserve the quality of services in the new competition era, but probably had little overall impact. And regulation of privatized public utility industries was supposed to protect customers' interests – none of which stopped their directors in the early 1990s from hugely increasing their remunerations in salaries and share options, the so-called 'fat cats' scandal. Utility profits soared, attracting Labour party proposals for a windfall tax on them.

Although critics warned very early on that the lengthening public/private sector interface along with the destruction of traditional administrative controls, would be bound to cause the growth of near-corruption (what Hood, 1989, termed 'malversation'), the government turned a blind eye (Stewart, 1996). Ministers and top civil servants insisted solemnly that there was no reason to believe that the ethical standards of business people were any lower than those of public sector administrators, and blandly asserted that the British tradition of public life untouched by serious or endemic corruption would continue untouched. And for a time, until Thatcher's fall from power and Major's re-election in 1992, these claims seemed still sustainable. But in the early 1990s they collapsed in a flood of different sleaze allegations, scandals and policy disasters which the Conservatives could do nothing to stem, creating a powerful 'fin-de-siècle' feel to the last days of the Major government.

More general linkages between the Conservatives and business also caused problems. A whole succession of government ministers and senior civil servants moved out of public office to highly paid directorships with firms or industries with which they had previously been dealing, a trait especially clear in the area around privatization but also important in the defence sector. The 1996 Scott report into the breaching of an arms embargo during the Iran–Iraq war, which led to British munitions equipment being shipped to Iraq apparently with the knowledge of ministers and MI6, added an extra flavour of scandal, and showed confusion within Whitehall. In 1996 the Chief Secretary to the Treasury, Jonathan Aitken, also resigned over allegations that he was linked with arms sales to Iran from a firm where he was a director, and that he failed to declare fully all the benefits received from his extensive Middle East contacts. In June 1997 the libel case brought by Aitken against the *Guardian* and *World in Action* collapsed, exposing him as corrupt. The Conservative Party's extremely secretive finances created a series of other disquiets. Throughout the period 1979–92 the chances of receiving prestigious honours (knighthoods and peerages) were much greater amongst firms and individuals who donated large sums of money to the Conservative coffers than amongst those who did not. The party also accepted money anonymously from dubious characters (such as Asil Nadir, who conveniently fled the country before he could be tried) and a series of very large secret donations from overseas business tycoons, with little or no connection with British politics (in one case £2 million, more than a tenth of annual national party finances). And Conservative ministers and MPs repeatedly blocked efforts by Lord Nolan's Committee on Standards in Public Life to widen its inquiries to look into political party finances, or to recommend the establishment of 'disclosure' laws, which are accepted as a bedrock safeguard against corruption in most other established liberal democracies. The UK remained unique amongst western countries in tightly limiting what can be spent by individual parliamentary candidates at local level, but having no limits at all on the amounts that individuals or companies could donate to parties nationally, and no disclosure laws on personal or private company donations.

When these problems finally spread into Parliament in 1994–7, sleaze began seriously to damage the Conservatives' chances of re-election. The most famous instance was the 'cash for questions' scandal in which the owner of Harrods, Mohammed Al-Fayed, claimed to have handed brown envelopes containing wads of cash to two Conservative MPs (Neil Hamilton and Tim Smith) and made similar payments to up to seven others. Additionally Al-Fayed handsomely paid a firm of parliamentary lobbyists to make large contributions to the constituency campaign funds of some 24 MPs, all but three of them also Conservatives. The two MPs at the heart of the scandal resigned ministerial office under pressure, but Hamilton chose to fight (and lose) the 1997 general election in his Tatton constituency. In March 1997 Parliament was prorogued early by Major, starting an unprecedented six-week election campaign, thereby preventing the publication of a Commons select committee report on 'cash for questions'. The opposition parties claimed this move was a deliberate ploy by the Tories, and much of the first week of the election campaign revolved around the sleaze issue. A series of other scandals emerged: of MPs inadequately declaring their interests when speaking in the Commons or on the register of members interests; or putting down motions in the names of fellow MPs to disguise the interest group originating the move; or of Tory whips sitting on or seeking to nobble supposedly independent select committees.

By 1995 over 150 MPs were involved in paid parliamentary lobbying of different kinds, when the Nolan Committee was set up by the Prime Minister to try and head off further scandal. But its report calling for a ban on paid commercial lobbying and a drastic tightening up of the rules governing declaration of interests produced another ugly fracas, with many Conservative MPs objecting to any changes. In the end a reasonably strong and more bi-partisan set of rules was voted through by all the opposition parties with the aid of some disinterested Tory MPs unhappy with their government's line. When MPs went on to vote themselves a hefty pay increase of 26 per cent (in 1996, when public sector pay was frozen and average pay awards were 3 per cent) public cynicism knew few bounds. Opinion poll data suggest that the reputation of Parliament reached an all-time low in the mid 1990s. The proportion of people believing Parliament worked well was 59 per cent in 1991, compared with 16 per cent who said it worked badly, a majority of 43. By 1995 only 43 per cent said it worked well, and 30 per cent said it worked badly, a majority of just 13 (Dunleavy *et al.*, 1995, p. 615).

Rebuilding Faith in Government

Labour's agenda for reforming the central machinery of government stresses some important changes in Whitehall itself, beginning with a Freedom of Information Act, an idea supported by all parties except the Conservatives and by 85 per cent of the public in opinion polls throughout the 1990s. The Major government made a few concessions towards more disclosure, publicizing Cabinet committees' composition in 1992 and issuing an almost completely useless memorandum on open government. Labour will certainly have to fight Whitehall civil servants at every stage to go further, but despite early inaction an information act on lines already pioneered in Canada and Australia seems likely. It would provide for public and media access to government documents with exemptions for national security, commercial confidentiality and personal privacy reasons.

More fundamentally, the Blair government did take early action to incorporate the European Convention on Human Rights (ECHR) into British law, thereby allowing UK citizens to seek ECHR redress in British courts instead. The main importance of the European Convention is that it provides a skeleton framework for a bill of rights which ordinary citizens could use to legally challenge decisions by government ministers and departments infringing their fundamental liberties. Although the UK was one of the earliest signatories of the Convention in the 1950s, the Conservatives and all previous Labour governments have previously agreed that it should not be made part of British law, for fear that it would curb Whitehall's and ministers' powers too much. British citizens have had some redress by appealing to the European Court of Human Rights in Strasbourg and its Commission (neither of which should be confused in any way with the European Union's Brussels institutions, the European Court of Justice or the European Commission: they are completely distinct bodies). But this route was very lengthy, very complex and very costly, so that only a tiny proportion of potential claimants took it. Nonetheless Britain lost many significant cases in the Strasbourg Court, with attendant bad publicity.

Labour's change of heart about incorporation reflects partly their rapprochement with the Liberals on constitutional issues, and partly a recognition that no dramatic changes (with extra costs) are likely to follow. Labour will not now seek to go systematically through previous British laws to bring them into line with ECHR (a procedure known as 'review of law and practice'), but will wait for cases to come through the courts to trigger changes piecemeal. In the near future, the ECHR may anyway become an important part of European Union law, if the member states decide to incorporate it at an inter-governmental conference.

Turning to Parliament, Labour's plans for the Commons include procedural revisions to make it easier to pass constitutional legislation, which will be necessary if a swift devolution timetable is to be adhered to. Yet even Labour MPs may be reluctant to concede to the executive the power to hold bills over from one parliamentary session to the next, without them automatically lapsing as they do at present. If this constraint is successfully removed without any quid pro quo concessions by ministers to backbenchers and the Commons at large, then the balance of power will swing even more firmly towards the executive. And the opposition's ability to pressurize the government by obstruction will be lessened. Some compensating increase of Commons powers is therefore likely, probably in the form of extended powers for select committees to call witnesses and scrutinize the early stages of policy proposals coming forward to legislation. The Labour–Liberal joint commission on the constitution also favoured the use of Special Standing Committees, which could take evidence from interest groups on new legislation. After Labour's sweeping victory, the Blair government needs to find work for the many idle hands on its backbenches, and more powers to select committees could seem a relatively harmless way of giving its 300 MPs outside government something useful to do.

When it comes to the House of Lords, however, Labour will remove hereditary peers' rights to speak and vote (which means an end to their right to attend the Lords at all). It has agreed with the Liberals that:

● cross-benchers with no overt party affiliation will remain a significant element in the reformed chamber, thereby preventing it from becoming just a 'super-QGA' in the prime minister's gift
● the three main parties' shares of the 'political' peers will be adjusted to approximately reflect the distribution of votes at the last general election
● both parties will work to secure a directly elected Lords ('a democratic and representative second chamber') in the longer term – that is, five to 10 years off.

By presenting these changes as incremental ones, on which the electorate has clearly spoken, Labour hopes to defuse the criticism which will certainly follow in the Tory press and the delays threatened by 'backwoods' peers in the upper house itself. Once enacted, though, the removal of hereditary peers could reverberate significantly through British political life, perhaps putting extra pressure on the already troubled status of the monarchy, as its traditional aristocratic underpinning is knocked away.

The Unresponsive Voting System

The necessary and sufficient foundation for the artificial Conservative and Labour dominance of the parliamentary process and of government has always been Britain's electoral system. Popularly known as 'first past the post' the system entails running 659 separate contests in single-seat local constituencies, where each voter marks only their first preference (using an 'X'). When the votes are counted, the candidate with the most support wins, irrespective of whether they got a majority or not. In the 1992 election one close four-way contest in Inverness was won by the candidate with 26 per cent of the vote, so in fact there is no fixed winning 'post' in the system. In 1997 slightly more than 50 per cent of winning MPs obtained more than half the votes locally. The correct label for the British system is 'plurality rule' (a plurality being the largest vote, but not necessarily a majority).

Political scientists have known for half a century with a great deal of certainty that compared with proportional representation systems, plurality rule systems favour the two largest parties, and penalize very heavily third or fourth parties with smaller percentages of the vote, unless their support is regionally concentrated (as it is for the SNP and Plaid Cymru). In addition, the voting system often (but not always) awards an extra 'bonus' of seats to the party that comes first compared with the party which comes second. This so-called 'leader's bias' effect was strongly evident in 1997, with Labour gaining 65 per cent of British seats on 45 per cent of the vote, while the Conservatives were *under*-represented in the Commons. The standard way of measuring how unfairly an election system operates is an index called 'deviation from proportionality'. Table 7.1 shows how it can be calculated for the 1997 election result. For each party you subtract its share of seats from its share of votes, producing a deviation. Then add up the deviations ignoring the plus or minus signs (which would otherwise cancel each other out) to produce a total deviation. The deviation from proportionality score (DV) is just half of this figure, or 21 per cent for 1997.

TABLE 7.1   Deviation from proportionality in the 1997 election

Party	% votes	% seats	%votes minus % seats deviations (ignoring + or – signs)
Conservatives	31.4	25.7	5.7
Labour	44.4	65.4	21.0
Liberal Democrat	17.2	7.2	10.0
Scottish National Party	2.0	0.9	1.1
Plaid Cymru	0.5	0.5	0.1
Referendum Party	2.7	0	2.7
Others	1.7	0.2	1.5
Total	100	100	Total deviations = 42.1

Note: Deviation from proportionality = total deviations/2 = 42/2 = 21.

The DV score can be simply understood as the proportion of MPs in the Commons who would not be sitting there if seats were allocated strictly in proportion to parties' shares of the national vote. In a perfect electoral system it would be 0 per cent, but this level of accuracy is never obtained. In most west European proportional representation systems, DV scores are between 4 and 8 per cent. In Britain (excluding Northern Ireland which has a different party system), DV scores have been two or three times greater than these practical PR levels for more than a quarter of a century, reaching a peak of 23 per cent in the 1983 Tory landslide, when Thatcher benefited hugely from leader's bias. Because third and fourth parties now receive so consistently large a share of the vote in Britain, we have one of the most disproportional electoral systems anywhere in the western world. (This situation is very different from the world's largest plurality rule system, the USA, where there is strictly two-party competition and DV scores are as low as they are in PR systems.)

What is more the national DV scores in Britain greatly *understate* the amount that the system distorts people's votes on the ground, because Labour's over-representation in the industrial north and in Scotland to some degree offset the Tories' normally huge over-representation in south-east England. In this region (outside London), the Conservatives won 97 per cent of seats in 1992 on the basis of 55 per cent of votes, giving a regional DV score for the south-east of 41 per cent – just about as unrepresentative as it is possible for a voting system to become and still count as 'democratic'. A similar result was gained by Labour in the Glasgow region. By contrast, in 1997, Labour's advances made the South East more diverse, but increased DV scores to over 30 per cent across all northern and urban regions. There is no doubt that running multi-party elections exclusively in single-member constituency contests is the source of the British system's high DV score. Unless people revert to two-party loyalties (as in the USA), British elections could only be made more proportional by introducing either large multi-member constituencies (with at least four MPs being elected in each constituency area), or a system of 'top-up' seats which could be allocated to parties which are under-represented in local constituency contests (the system used in Germany). Both these possible solutions could undermine the mystic bond which all MPs in the Commons believe binds them to serve the interests of their constituency – a strong form of accountability which most British voters undoubtedly do value. The key objection of traditionalists is that introducing a system with lower DV scores would lose the 'exaggerative' power of the present system, preventing the formation of single-party majority governments. On voting trends in the last 25 years it would usher in permanent coalition governments with the Liberal Democrats permanently holding the balance of power, an outcome which would be anathema for both major party leaderships.

Not surprisingly, both Tory and Labour leaders were perfectly happy to collude to keep the existing voting system completely unchanged throughout the post-war period, until the early 1990s when Labour leaders began to have disquieting second thoughts. Neil Kinnock set up an internal Labour party commission, the Plant Report, which recommended a minimal change to the system called 'supplementary vote' (see below). Kinnock's successor as Labour leader, John Smith, at first tried to persuade the Plant Commission to endorse the status quo, and then stopped their recommendation from creating potentially acrimonious debate in Labour's ranks by promising to hold a referendum on electoral reform. Tony Blair has maintained a public stance of being 'unpersuaded' of the need for reform (because of the threat to constituency links and fear of giving too much power to 'small' parties), but he unexpectedly maintained Smith's referendum pledge. After Labour's electoral landslide the status and timing of the voting referendum remained in doubt. On Labour and Liberal plans a commission would have to be set up to draw up one agreed PR system, to be offered as the single alternative to the status quo.

The Future of Electoral Reform

The new Labour government will certainly usher in a period of decisive change in the ways that many British citizens vote. One possibility is that a new PR system of voting may be used for the 1999 European elections, where Labour's current large majority of MEPs (elected under plurality rule) would be endangered by a mid-term swing against the new government – unless PR was introduced to limit the damage substantially. However, the time-table for this change to take place was very tight by 1997. But as long as devolution proceeds, new voting systems will definitely be used to elect the Scottish Parliament and the Welsh Senedd. Both of them are variants of the Additional Member System (AMS), used in Germany since the 1950s and now in New Zealand, following a 1993 referendum victory for electoral reform there. In both countries some MPs are elected in local constituencies by plurality rule, and then a set of top-up MPs are elected at either a regional or national level. Parties which have gained many constituency seats get fewer top-up MPs, and parties which have piled up votes but not won many constituency seats get more seats at the top-up stage. This process ensures that each party ends up with same percentage share of seats as they have votes, a fully proportional outcome – except that very small parties which win no local seats and also less than 5 per cent of the national vote do not gain representation at all, a 'threshold' barrier designed to deter the over-fragmentation of parties.

In Germany and New Zealand half of MPs are elected in constituencies and half at the top-up stage, but there is nothing sacred about these ratios. In the UK a Hansard Commission report in the 1970s suggested an AMS system for the Commons based on 75 per cent constituency MPs and only 25 per cent top-up MPs, which would be unlikely to be fully proportional. In both Scotland and Wales the current proposals are to elect one member of the devolved assemblies for each Westminster constituency (which saves on drawing up new boundaries and is less confusing for voters), and then to have seven top-up members for each Euro-constituency in Scotland and five top-up members for each Euro-constituency in Wales, giving the following overall distribution:

	Constituency members	Top-up members
Scottish Parliament	73	56 (43%)
Welsh Senedd	40	20 (33%)

If both these assemblies are enacted, approved by referenda and up and running by 1999 or the year 2000, these models are likely to have a big influence on thinking about the one proportional system which will be put to UK voters as an alternative for Westminster elections. An AMS system with a large majority of constituency MPs and a minority of top-up MPs looks certain to be the front-runner for inclusion in the referendum as the alternative to plurality rule. The top-up MPs would almost certainly be organized at regional level, and they would not be chosen from party lists that could be controlled by the party leadership. Instead a party's top-up MPs would come from its 'best losers' in the constituency contests in that region, thereby ensuring that all winning candidates had to stand for election in some specific constituency.

But the whole timetable of a commission, referendum, legislation and then boundary redrawing looks too tight for any new electoral system to come into place for the next general election. Once Labour is in office there may well be pressures to put off the voting systems referendum until very late in the new parliament. Finally, of course, there remain huge problems of whether the electorate would accept electoral reform in the referendum. Labour opponents of change, such as Jack Straw, have publicly proclaimed their desire to see a quick referendum with the Labour and Tory leaderships united in their desire to kill off all talk of proportional representation for decades to come by assembling a sweeping majority for the status quo. But Tony Blair may yet change sides, being persuaded of the need for reform by the commission's report or by pressure from new Labour MPs facing defeat after only a single term of office.

Electoral reformers themselves look badly prepared for a referendum. Many continue to propose a great range of different electoral systems, and still do not accept the inevitable emergence of AMS as the referendum choice. In the past the Liberal Democrats (and the amazingly sectarian Electoral Reform Society) have always held out for the introduction in the UK of the Irish electoral system, called the Single Transferable Vote (STV). Here voters elect multiple MPs in large constituencies (perhaps five times as big as current constituencies) and can pick and mix their own slate of candidates drawn from different parties. STV is a proportional system but critics argue that it is hard to explain how it works and it tends to erode party discipline. There is zero chance that Labour will ever accept this system in the UK, and it was ruled completely unacceptable by the party's Plant Commission. So the Liberal Democrats are likely to accept AMS as the best available alternative.

The other two systems which have been much discussed in the UK entail only small modifications to plurality rule, keeping the existing 659 local constituencies intact, but altering the voting papers that citizens use to allow people to express multiple preferences instead of just one, so that every MP would be elected by a majority in each constituency. There are two ways of doing this. In the Supplementary Vote (SV) system, voters put an X by their first choice candidate in one column of their ballot paper, and another X by a different candidate in their second choice column. The first preferences are counted and if one candidate has a clear majority he or she is elected. If no one has a clear majority, the top two candidates stay in the race, but all the other candidates are eliminated and their voters' second preferences are inspected, to see if any can be added to the top two candidates' piles. At the end of this process, whoever leads wins. The Supplementary Vote was only invented in 1990 (by D. Campbell Savors, J. Mahon and P. Dunleavy), but it was recommended as a compromise choice by the Plant Commission in 1992. Its great appeal is that it helps Labour win a few seats and the Liberal Democrats quite a few more, all at the expense of the Tories. It also safeguards Labour against ever losing out to third-placed candidates (an important threat in Scotland and parts of Wales which are four-party systems now). And it retains ultra-simple 'X' voting to which British voters are said to be attached. The other non-proportional possibility for Labour is the Alternative Vote (AV). Here voters must number candidates, 1, 2, 3 in order of preference. If one candidate has a majority on first preferences he or she is elected, but if no one has then the bottom-placed candidate is eliminated and those voters' second choices are redistributed over remaining candidates. If still no one has a majority, the new bottom candidate is eliminated and another redistribution is made. This process continues until either someone gets a majority, or there are only two candidates left in the race, when the leading person wins. The AV system has been used for a long time in the Australian lower house and so is widely known, but it is not used anywhere else in the world. Its effects are the same as the Supplementary Vote, but it is much more difficult for voters to understand how votes are counted. Critics argue that in a tight contest, the winner may end up being selected on the basis of some voters' third or fourth preferences, which may not be 'real' preferences.

A final aspect of change in the British constitution is the apparent advent of 'government by referendum'. Referenda will be held in Scotland and Wales on devolution, in London and perhaps in some English regions too. If the government decides to join the European single currency, a referendum on entry to EMU will be unavoidable – all three major parties promised to hold one in their 1997 manifestos. And Labour and the Liberal Democrats have pledged a voting systems referendum as well. This rash of referenda introduces some new problems into British public life. First the vital question wordings on which people must decide have to be drafted, and perhaps not by the government alone (as in the past) but by some bipartisan commission. Second, there are no laws in Britain currently limiting campaign spending by either side in referenda, although official government spending or public contributions can obviously be limited. Will referenda thus benefit the side with the deepest pockets? Third, all of the new proposed questions are very difficult ones to decide. For voters to make informed and intelligent choices some extended public information campaigns would be needed. How many people will vote may also be problematic. But the experience will certainly be an unusual one for British citizens, unused to the idea of direct democracy.

Conclusions

On constitutional issues politicians are always constrained to talk in ethical and disinterested terms, but their underlying propensity is to think strategically, in terms of party interests. The Labour–Liberal concordat on a wide range of reforms could be a decisive breach in the 'club ethos' which has hitherto bound Tory and Labour leaderships together in defence of the status quo. It may open up a realistic prospect for the first time in the post-war period of a wide-ranging series of changes, agreed by parties who between them command the support of a convincing majority of voters. But ambitions for a great reform Parliament can all too easily come to grief, as ministers succumb to conservative White-hall briefings, constitutional changes are squeezed out by more immediate policy exigencies, the balance of parties' popularity changes, and good intentions fade in the face of the natural desire of governments to husband power for their own protection. Nonetheless, in what looks likely to be a low-key government, constitutional reforms could still provide a grand theme for change.

8
Parliamentary Oversight

PHILIP NORTON

Parliaments are to be found in most countries of the world. Their very existence suggests they serve some purpose. But do they? In the United Kingdom, critics suggest that the House of Commons is a marginal political institution, dominated usually by a single party and having no appreciable impact on policy making. Policy proposals are initiated elsewhere and then drawn up and agreed within government. Only then are they placed before Parliament for approval, which it is known in advance will be given. According to two leading students of British politics, 'the significance of Parliament . . . is its very insignificance' (Richardson and Jordan, 1979, p. 121).

Such criticism of the national parliament is not peculiar to the United Kingdom. Similar criticism is levelled at parliaments in other West European countries and also within the European Union. The European Parliament has been accused of 'lacking true legislative capabilities' (Thomas, 1992, p. 4). Until 1987, the Parliament was an advisory body and the powers it has acquired since in the law-making process only apply in certain cases. In so far as it has extended its powers, it has – according to some observers – done so at the expense of national parliaments. On this view, legislative power is a zero-sum game: what power is acquired by one legislature is at the expense of the other. And that power anyway is seen as being very limited. Public policy is determined at EU level by the Commission and the Council of Ministers, and at the national level – certainly in the United Kingdom – by the national government. The Parliament operates very much at the margins: in the words of Labour MP Austin Mitchell, in the United Kingdom 'the executive drives a legislative steamroller . . . opposition MPs can heckle . . . they can neither stop nor detour it' (Mitchell, 1995, p. 196). Europe, on this line of argument, is filled with executive steamrollers. Other scholars argue that parliaments are not so marginal as these critics suggest. Rather, they argue, parliaments do matter. They do so for two reasons. First, parliaments have several consequences for their respective political systems (Packenham, 1970). These include a 'safety valve' function (providing an outlet for different views in society) and 'errand running' (undertaking tasks on behalf of constituents). In the case of the British Parliament, there are two other functions that make it particularly important. One is as a law-effecting body. The outputs of Parliament – Acts of Parliament – are binding and, under the doctrine of parliamentary sovereignty, can be set aside by no body other than Parliament itself. Who controls Parliament can thus determine the law of the land. In the words of Ralph Miliband, the elected nature of the House of Commons renders illegitimate any radical alternative, 'for it suggests that what is required above all else to bring about fundamental change is a majority in the House of Commons' (Miliband, 1984, p. 20). In terms of constituting the core law-effecting body, Parliament has always been important, indeed at the heart of the constitution (see Judge, 1992). The other function is that of being the principal recruiting and training agency for government office (Norton, 1993). For anyone wanting to be in government, the route to office is through Parliament. In the United States, in contrast, there are multiple routes to the top. Candidates for the presidency are not necessarily drawn from Congress. In Britain, those wanting to be ministers have to enter Parliament and make their mark there. The House of Commons provides an important training, or rather testing, ground for prospective office holders.

Second, most parliaments have *some* impact on public policy. In terms of policy effect, three types of legislature have been identified (Table 8.1). The US Congress stands as a rare example of a policy making legislature. The British Parliament nestles among a large number that fall within the category of policy-influencing legislatures. It is a category occupied by most parliaments in western Europe (Norton 1991a). The third category, legislatures with little or no policy effect, comprises essentially legislatures in

TABLE 8.1   Types of Legislatures

Policy-making legislatures
Legislatures which can modify or reject measures brought forward by the
government and can formulate and substitute policies of their own

Policy-influencing legislatures
Legislatures which can modify or reject measures brought forward by the
government but cannot formulate and substitute policies of their own

Legislatures with little or no policy effect
Legislatures which can neither modify nor reject measures brought forward
by the government nor formulate and substitute policies of their own

---

Source: Norton (1984).

communist and one-party states elsewhere and, given the collapse
of communist regimes in central and eastern Europe, is a diminishing category.

Historically, Parliament has been a reactive or policy-influencing body, looking to the executive to formulate and bring
forward measures of public policy. Parliament has then scrutinized those measures before giving (or withholding) assent to
them. Parliament has never really been a law-making or policy
making body on any continuous basis. Its principal task in terms
of proposals for public policy, as well as the conduct of government, has been one of scrutiny. This reactive role has always been
of some importance. The fact that government needs Parliament
to give assent to measures and its request for money means that
Parliament has some leverage which, on occasion – sometimes
more frequently than at other times – it has been prepared to use.
The impact of the British Parliament today, as in the past, might
not be great but it can and does have some effect on public policy.

There is a problem in that this impact might not always be
observable. Governments may be put under pressure at private
party meetings by their own supporters either to introduce or to
drop measures (see, for example, Butt, 1967; Lynskey, 1970,
1973). Influence may be exerted even without a meeting taking
place: government ministers may anticipate a negative reaction
from their own party in the House and decide not to bring a
proposal forward. Such non-decision making is not amenable to
measurement. However, various occasions have been identified

when government does change policy following overt pressure from MPs (see Jackson, 1968) and these have occurred on a sufficient number of occasions for Parliament to be classified as a policy-influencing legislature. We thus have a *prima facie* case for asserting that parliaments do matter. The question that then arises is: will they continue to matter? Two competing hypotheses can be advanced. The first is the *marginalization* thesis. This hypothesizes that parliaments will become increasingly marginalized as policy making power becomes more concentrated in executives. Even if they were not irrelevant in the past, parliaments will become close to irrelevant in the future, reduced to marginal tasks such as errand running for constituents. The second is the *assertiveness* thesis. This argues that parliaments will respond to a greater concentration of power in executives by being more assertive. Members of parliament will be driven to act by the demands of citizens or by their own desire to affect outcomes. This assertiveness will manifest itself through changes in behaviour and in the powers and structures of the institution. Which is the more plausible hypothesis?

Marginalization?

The basis for the marginalization thesis is clear. Post-war years have seen a significant increase in the size and responsibilities of government. The change has been qualitative as well as quantitative. Governments are called upon to engage in activities that are not only more extensive than before but also more complex. This is reflected in the UK in two ways. One is in the volume and detail of legislation laid before Parliament. Government bills are not necessarily more numerous than in earlier decades, but they are greater in volume than before. Excluding Consolidation Bills (which do not create new law), more than 2000 pages of legislation are passed each year, more than three times the volume enacted in the 1950s (Hansard Society, 1992, pp. 11–12). The measures embody often extensive detail, especially where some form of regulation is involved, as with the annual Finance Bill. The second way in which it is manifested is in the volume of delegated legislation: detailed regulations that are made under the authority of the parent Acts of Parliament. The number of such regulations, known as statutory instruments, increased dramatically in post-war years (Hansard Society 1992, pp. 401–2) and there are now usually more than 2000 statutory instruments promulgated each year (in 1992 and 1993 there were more than 3000), occupying more than 9000 pages. Parliament has neither the time nor the resources to formulate legislation nor to subject government legislation, and delegated legislation, to extensive and detailed scrutiny. Nor, it is argued, does it have the political will, a prerequisite for effective scrutiny, and the larger the government's majority – as with the Conservative government of 1983–7 (overall majority 144) and the Labour government elected in 1997 (overall majority 179) – the less amenable is government to parliamentary scrutiny.

As demands on government continue to grow and as its international obligations increase, not least as a consequence of membership of the European Union, then government will spend most of its time in talks with representatives of organized interests and EU officials. Parliament will not figure in those activities. Instead, government will bring agreed measures forward for approval and use its majority to ensure their approval. Despite isolated mutterings, government will be successful in getting its way.

A similar line of reasoning applies in the case of the European Parliament. Though it has been given the title of a parliament and some role in certain law-making processes under the European treaties, it has not been able to keep pace with the power accumulation of the Commission and the Council of Ministers. The Commission is the power house of the European Union, vested with certain original powers and increasingly powerful as a consequence of the implementation of the Single European Act (1987) and the Treaty on European Union (1993). As the competence of the European Community has been extended, then so too has the power of the body at the heart of that community. The European Parliament has no power of initiation and can only react to measures proposed by the Commission. Given the extent of activity necessary to achieve and police a single market, then the Parliament has a limited capacity to keep track of what is happening and a limited formal capacity, in any event, to affect outcomes. Proposals brought before the Parliament are subject to different processes, depending on the treaty provisions – there are 16 different voting procedures – and in most cases the Parliament lacks the power to resist the will of a unanimous Council of Ministers.

Furthermore, the Parliament has to compete with other bodies that have to be consulted by the Commission, principally the Economic and Social Committee and the Committee of the Regions. The Parliament also sees its position threatened by demands for a greater role in European law making by national parliaments and by calls, especially by some French and British politicians, for it to be supplemented by a second chamber (for example, Heseltine, 1989, p. 35) or a Committee of Parliaments (Brittan, 1994, p. 226). The Parliament thus sees itself squeezed between a powerful unelected European body, the European Commission, and the national institutions represented especially through ministers in the Council of Ministers.

The Parliament itself is not a recruiting body for office holders (members of the Commission are not drawn from MEPs) and, in the words of Martin Westlake, 'the only way up is out' (Westlake, 1994a, p. 6). Membership of national parliaments is still seen, certainly in the UK, as more prestigious than membership of the European Parliament. Even if well-known figures are elected, they often have other interests to attend to and are infrequent attenders. Ensuring a good attendance at plenary sessions, especially for business that requires an absolute majority of members to vote yes, is a notably difficult task. Parliaments thus appear prone to marginalization in a policy making process that is increasingly and necessarily executive-oriented. There appears little likelihood of that trend being reversed.

Assertiveness?

What, then, is the line of reasoning of the assertiveness hypothesis? There are a number of developments of recent years which have strengthened the British and European Parliaments. If we take power as having two components – coercion (A having the capacity to get B to do what A wants regardless of B's wishes) and persuasion (A getting B to do that which B may not otherwise do) – then both have become relatively more powerful in recent years. Parliament in the UK has the formal power to vote against the government but has rarely used that power. The past quarter-century has seen a greater willingness (albeit at most times modest) to use this coercive power. More significantly in relation to the executive, it has also expanded its persuasive powers through major changes in its own structures and procedures. It has become a more specialized body of scrutiny. The European Parliament has acquired greater coercive powers and has proved willing to use them. These powers underpin its capacity to exercise scrutiny of the Commission.

Parliamentary Scrutiny in the UK

Both Houses of Parliament have seen changes in the 1990s. Though the House of Lords has seen some modest development in the use of committees, the most significant changes, which will form the basis of this chapter, have taken place in the House of Commons. The House has seen two broad trends in its development. One concerns members, the other the institution in terms of its structures and processes. Members have become more independent in their behaviour and more regulated in their conduct. The institution has become more specialized, with a shift in emphasis from the chamber to committees. In combination, they make for an institution in a better position than before to scrutinize government and to influence public policy.

For most of this century, MPs have been highly cohesive in their voting behaviour. They have voted loyally with their parties (see Lowell, 1924, Beer, 1965). In the years from 1945 to 1970, the occasions when MPs voted against their own side were few and far between and never on a scale that threatened the government's majority. The years since then have seen a notable increase in the willingness of MPs to vote against their own side. There was a significant change in behaviour in the 1970s. MPs in the 1990s have maintained a level of independence comparable to the 1970s. The willingness of MPs to vote against their own side is notable for its breadth (the number of times it occurs) and depth (the number of MPs involved on each occasion). The significance of such behaviour has been more variable.

Table 8.2 shows the percentage of divisions in the House of Commons from 1945 to 1997 in which one or more MPs cast votes against their parties. As is clear from the table, the occasions were

TABLE 8.2   Divisions witnessing dissenting votes, 1945–97

Parliament (number of sessions in parenthesis)	Number of divisions witnessing dissenting votes Lab.	Con.	Number of divisions witnessing dissenting votes expressed as % of all divisions
1945–50(4)	79	27	7.0
1950–51 (2)	5	2	2.5
1951–55 (4)	17	11	3.0
1955–59 (4)	10	12	2.0
1959–64 (5)	26	120	13.5
1964–66 (2)	1	1	0.5
1966–70 (4)	109	41	9.5
1970–74 (4)	34	204	20
1974 (1)	8	21	23
1974–79 (5)	309	240	28
1979–83 (4)	161	158	19
1983–87 (4)	83	202	22
1987–92 (5)	137	199	19
1992–97 (5)	143	170	20.5

Source: Norton (1996a), updated by author.

few and far between in the period before 1970, and at their most numerous in parliaments in which the government had a large overall majority. Since 1970, the number has increased and the level achieved in the 1970s has been maintained at a similar level in the 1980s and 1990s. When Conservative MPs have voted against their own side, they have done so in greater numbers than before. They thus join Labour MPs who have always tended to 'hunt in packs'. Of the occasions when Labour MPs voted against the whip in the 1992–7 Parliament, 62 per cent involved 10 or more Labour MPs. On six occasions, 60 or more Labour MPs voted against the leadership.

MPs, then, are more willing to vote against their own side on more occasions and do so in greater numbers than before. There remains a difference between the parties. Labour MPs are less likely than Conservative rebels to vote in the whipped lobby of their opponents. They tend to vote against the whips either when their own party is abstaining from voting or when it is supporting the Conservatives in the lobbies (Norton, 1996a). In the 1992–7 Parliament, for example, Labour rebels hardly ever entered the

Conservative lobby. This distinction has relevance for the third measurement, that of significance.

Significance is defined in terms of government backbenchers voting in the Opposition lobby and doing so in sufficient numbers to threaten the government's majority. Significant votes were virtually non-existent in the years up to 1970, frequent in the parliaments of 1970–4 and 1974–9 and rare in parliaments from 1979 to 1992. In the 25 years from 1945 to 1970, only one vote qualified for the category and even that did not result in a defeat for the government. In the period from 1970 to 1979 no fewer than 112 occasions qualified. Not all resulted in government defeats: the Conservative government of 1970–4 suffered six defeats and had various narrow escapes. The Labour government in the 1974–9 Parliament suffered 23 defeats because its own supporters voted with the opposition (Norton, 1980, pp. 491–3). In the period between 1979 and 1992, only three votes qualified – one in each Parliament (Norton 1996a). This figure slightly masks the vulnerability of government, since on a number of occasions its majority was threatened by backbenchers abstaining from voting rather than actually voting with the opposition. The government suffered one defeat in each Parliament. In the Parliament of 1992–7, the number of significant votes increased and resembled the 1970–4 Parliament in that there were several votes that qualified (more than 36) although the government suffered only four defeats (Cowley, 1996), the government being saved by minor parties either not voting or voting in the government lobby.

Describing these changes is less problematic than identifying their causes and assessing their consequences. Three hypotheses have been advanced to explain the change in behaviour:

- *poor leadership*, Edward Heath's style of prime ministerial leadership triggering cross-voting by government backbenchers (Norton, 1978)
- *the end of the '100 per cent rule'*, Labour backbenchers in the 1970s realizing that government defeats did not entail government resignation (Schwarz, 1980)
- *a 'new breed' of MP*, MPs entering the House with a stronger desire than their predecessors to influence policy (see Mellors, 1978; Evans and Taylor, 1996, p. 268).

These explanations have been the subject of academic controversy. The 100 per cent rule thesis has found little or no support (Franklin *et al.*, 1987) and no study has found empirical evidence to support the new breed thesis (Norton, 1978, pp. 218–20; Franklin *et al.*, 1987). This writer has continued to advance the poor leadership thesis (Norton, 1987, 1995), which has not yet been successfully disproved.

What generalizations can be drawn from the changes that have taken place? On the one hand, MPs still rarely vote against their own side (Rose, 1983; Cowley, 1996) and when they do so – even though the occasions are more frequent and more MPs take part – they rarely cause serious problems for government. On the other hand, the changes have made some difference. Some policies have been dropped or changed as a result of defeat or because of the political embarrassment flowing from dissent. The most obvious instance came in 1986 when 72 Conservative MPs voted with the opposition to defeat the Second Reading of the Shop Bills (to deregulate Sunday trading). More pervasively, it has been argued that there has been a change in the relationship between government and Parliament in that the government knows it can no longer take the House for granted. It will usually get its way but is not guaranteed that it will on every occasion. Consequently, it anticipates parliamentary reaction in a way it did not do previously and modifies policies if it believes they will encounter problems on the backbenches. This was perceptibly the case with certain policies during the 1992–7 Parliament (as over post office privatization in 1994), when the government had a slim overall majority. However, even during the 1983–7 Parliament, when the Conservative government had its biggest overall majority since 1935, the Government Chief Whip, John Wakeham, saw his role as that of a 'fixer', seeking to arrange deals between ministers and backbenchers (see Norton 1985, pp. 33–5). On this line of argument, the House under the Labour government of Tony Blair has the potential to have at least some impact.

A More Professional House

The other features of the House – the greater regulation of MPs' conduct and the development of more specialized structured for scrutiny – can be subsumed under the heading of a more professional House. MPs are now required to adopt stricter codes of conduct than before, especially in terms of outside remuneration, and have fairly specialized means for scrutinizing government. The latter development preceded the former.

Specialization. For most decades of this century, the emphasis in the House of Commons has been on the chamber. Standing committees, for scrutinizing the detail of bills, were introduced as standard in 1907 but these constituted, and still constitute, committees appointed on an ad hoc basis, and serve to benefit government: they facilitate the passage of bills (several standing committees can meet at the same time, whereas there is only one chamber) and government bills have priority in all but one committee. Two investigative select committees existed in the form of the Estimates Committee (looking at how policies could be carried out more cost-efficiently) and the Public Accounts Committee (checking that money had been spent for the purposes allocated), but they were the exceptions. These committees apart, MPs had few opportunities other than those offered by the chamber to scrutinize the actions and the legislative proposals of government. There were debates on the floor of the House and there was Question Time. Government dominated the timetable and debates were generally set-piece affairs, each speaker delivering a prepared speech. Question Time became increasingly popular, but the more questions that were asked (within the limited time set aside for it) the less time there was to pursue any one question in depth. Many MPs were sceptical about the value it served (see Barker and Rush, 1970). Backbench dissatisfaction led to some experimentation with select committees but did not prove overly successful. The committees were overly dependent on government support. Growing dissatisfaction resulted in more pressure for change in the 1970s, and in 1979 14 new departmental select committees were appointed. Their appointment was the most radical change in parliamentary procedure this century. The committees were appointed 'to examine the expenditure, administration and policy in the principal government departments . . . and associated public bodies'.

The departmental committees proved to be active bodies, especially in taking evidence from ministers, civil servants and representatives of a range of outside bodies, and in publishing reports embodying recommendations for government action (see, for example, Drewry, 1989). In the first twelve years of their existence, they issued just over 900 reports (Norton, 1993, p. 101). The committees have since been increased in number to 17 and are now comprehensive in their coverage of government departments and sectors of government responsibility. The committees have been credited with providing detailed scrutiny of some government policy, doing so in a relatively non-partisan environment (ministers are not appointed to the committees and reports are usually agreed unanimously), raising issues and on occasion persuading government to act. On the debit side, they lack extensive resources to commission or undertake research, have no sanction against the government if it ignores their recommendations (the record here is patchy, see Drewry, 1989; Dawes, 1993), and have difficulty at times in ensuring a committed and knowledgeable membership (Norton, 1994). Questioning of witnesses may not be exactly forensic and some witnesses are adept at side-stepping difficult questions. The committees do, though, mark a remarkable advance in terms of parliamentary scrutiny, certainly relative to what existed before. Furthermore, the 1990s have seen incremental changes which, in combination, mark a notable shift in emphasis from the chamber to the committee room.

On one side of the coin, the departmental select committees have increased in number. To their number has been added a number of others. European documents recommended for debate are now sent for debate not in the chamber but in one of two European standing committees. A Select Committee on Deregulation has been appointed. A committee on the security services has been created which, though set up by statute rather than parliamentary motion, comprises senior parliamentarians. There is a new Committee on Standards and Privileges. In a slightly different context, the Scottish Grand Committee, which considers matters affecting Scotland, has had its powers increased so that it can question ministers other than Scottish Office ministers. Each of these changes is not in itself of great import but in combination they show a greater propensity on the part of the House to resort to committees for the task of scrutiny.

On the other side of the coin, there is less emphasis on the floor. Following widespread dissatisfaction among MPs with hours of sitting and working practices, a special committee was appointed in 1991 and reported in 1992 (Select Committee on Sittings of the House 1992). Its recommendations were debated and accepted by the House in 1994. As a result, late and all-night sittings have been reduced substantially in number. Also, 10 Fridays are designated as non-sitting Fridays (private members' motions – previously taken on a Friday – now being taken during new Wednesday morning sittings), and business on Thursday evenings organized usually so MPs can get away early. Indeed, such was the effect of the changes, coupled initially with fairly light sessions in terms of the business to be transacted, that some MPs in 1996 began to complain that very little serious business was now transacted in the chamber.

The effect of these disparate changes has been to produce a House of Commons that resembles more its continental counterparts, such as the German Bundestag, where the emphasis has traditionally been on scrutiny by committee rather than through chamber debate. Greater specialization, it is argued, allows for more detailed and systematic scrutiny, as well as getting rid of some of the partisanship that pervades the chamber. As such, the House has become a somewhat more professional scrutinizing body. Though committees remain limited in what they can do, they mark an advance on what existed before.

Regulation. There is another dimension to a more 'professional' House in that the conduct of MPs has also become more regulated. Various pressures have led to MPs being subject to a professional code of conduct. The period since 1979 has seen a growth in the number of professional political lobbyists (Grantham and Seymour-Ure, 1990). The arms-length stance towards groups adopted by a Conservative government in the 1980s, coupled with the growth of select committees and some measure of more independent behaviour, made Parliament more attractive to organized interests (Norton, 1991b) and lobbying has become a notable feature of Westminster life. A number of MPs have variously been retained as advisers or consultants by lobbying firms. Other MPs have hired themselves out as consultants to bodies wanting to influence the political process (see Hollingsworth, 1991). An analysis of the 1995 Register of Members' Interests revealed that 168 MPs held between them 356 consultancies (Committee on Standards in Public Life 1995, p. 22).

This development coincided in the 1980s and early 1990s with greater interest in the activities of politicians by the mass media. A number of MPs were caught up in various scandals, some sexual and some financial. The extent to which MPs were available for hire by organized interests variously made the headlines. In 1994, two Conservative MPs failed to turn down immediately the offer of money (made surreptitiously by a journalist) to table parliamentary questions and the resulting publicity about 'cash for questions' led to the appointment of a committee to enquire into standards in public life. The committee, chaired by a judge (Lord Nolan), reported in 1995 and recommended a code of conduct for MPs, the disclosure of income from parliamentary consultancies, the appointment of a Commissioner for Standards to oversee the rules and investigate complaints, and a ban on MPs working as consultants to lobbyists with multiple clients.

The recommendations proved controversial, some Conservative MPs attacking them on the grounds they would force some MPs to give up parliamentary life. However, after two major debates and two reports from a select committee appointed to make recommendations on the report, the House eventually decided (some Conservative MPs joining with Labour MPs to form a majority) to go even further than the Nolan Committee recommended. Not only did it vote for a Code of Conduct, the appointment of a Parliamentary Commissioner for Standards (plus a new Select Committee on Standards on Privileges, superseding the old Privileges Committee) and the disclosure of income derived from services offered as parliamentarians (for example, advising a firm on how to make its case to ministers), it also voted to ban all paid advocacy by MPs. Members were thus prohibited from advocating a particular cause in return for money.

These changes were prompted by the need to meet public concern. A Gallup poll in 1985 found that 46 per cent of those asked believed 'Most MPs make a lot of money by using public office improperly'. In 1994, 64 per cent gave the same response. Though most MPs were not using public office improperly to make money, the public perception that they were had to be countered. The consequence of the response by the House was a more regulated membership, subject to a code and practices that existed in many professional organizations and in a number of legislatures elsewhere.

Membership

The House has also seen a change in the nature of its membership, a change that encourages specialization. Over time, members have tended to serve in the House for longer than before. There has been a growth of what has been termed 'career politicians', that is, people who devote themselves to politics. They serve in some political post (a researcher or ministerial adviser, for example) and then enter Parliament relatively young and regularly seek re-election. They often throw themselves into political activity, utilizing committees as a way of gaining knowledge and experience.

The increase in the number of career politicians is viewed by some as detrimental to the House of Commons, limiting the range of experience of its members. On the other hand, the backgrounds of MPs may be argued to facilitate greater specialization. There has been a notable increase in the number of MPs with a university education. Of new Labour MPs elected in 1997, 75 per cent were university educated. The figure for new Conservative MPs was 90 per cent. (In the preceding Parliament, 61 per cent of Labour MPs and 73 per cent of Conservatives were university educated.) The 1997 election also saw a large number of new MPs elected who had served as councillors. Almost two-thirds of new Labour MPs (64 per cent) had served as councillors (as had no less than 70 per cent of new Liberal Democrat MPs and 25 per cent of new Conservative Members). Councillors are used to a political process that is based on committee work.

One other feature that may affect attitudes towards specialization is the greater number of women MPs in the House of Commons. A record number was elected in 1997: a total of 120 (101 of them Labour), comprising 18 per cent of the House. In the outgoing Parliament, the figure had been 63, just under 10 per cent of MPs. Many women previously in the House had criticized the chamber, apparently preferring committee work to the partisan environment of the chamber. If that attitude proves prevalent among women MPs, it may act as a further stimulus to specialization.

Where to from here?

Exponents of the marginalization thesis would argue that the changes of recent years have done little to affect the basic relationship of Parliament to government. Many who want to see a strong Parliament, something more akin to a policy making legislature, are advocates of radical constitutional reform. (In its most extreme form, this would entail a separation of powers, but proponents tend to argue instead for a new electoral system.) Those who adhere to the assertiveness thesis concede that it could be strengthened as a policy-influencing legislature. Various proposals have been put forward in recent years to reform the structures and procedures of the House. In May 1997 Tony Blair reformed Prime Minister's Question Time, including a single half-hour session each week instead of two fifteen-minute sessions. This change is very much at the margins in terms of having much effect on parliamentary scrutiny. Other bodies, such as the Hansard Society Commission on the Legislative Process and the reform movement Charter 88 – have put forward more radical proposals for reform (see Norton in Hansard Society 1992 and Norton 1997). Among the more substantial proposals are the following:

- Introducing pre-legislative committees, so that MPs can discuss possible bills before the government has committed itself to the measures.
- Getting rid of the sessional cut-off, under which bills fall at the end of the parliamentary session if they have not completed all their stages. Allowing bills to carry over from one year to the next would give the House more time to consider them and for bills to be introduced across the year rather than all at the beginning.
- Using special standing committees to scrutinize bills. These committees, unlike the normal standing committees, can take evidence from witnesses. The procedure can produce better-informed committees.
- Subjecting bills to a compulsory timetable, thus ensuring that each part of a bill gets some scrutiny. Voluntary timetabling was introduced in 1994 and has proved successful: many MPs want it to be a permanent fixture.

- Making standing committees live up to their name and actually having a fixed or core membership, so that they can build up the specialization and ethos associated with the permanent select committees.
- Giving select committees greater resources to undertake or commission research. One proposal is to give each committee a budget of £2 million a year to commission independent research (Banham, 1994). Another is to allow the committees to utilize the staff of the National Audit Office (NAO). At present, NAO work is conducted and reported only to the Public Accounts Committee.
- Giving select committees greater powers, including power to confirm public appointments and to compel the attendance of ministers.

A much more radical proposal is to reduce the size of the House of Commons, thus freeing resources for redistribution to the MPs that remain. In combination, it is argued, these various changes will make a difference to the quality of parliamentary scrutiny. Legislation will receive more detailed, informed and extended scrutiny. Ministers will be subject to more informed questioning, from which they cannot escape. By being seen to subject government to more rigorous scrutiny, the hope and intention is that it will also restore public faith in the institution.

Do Parties Matter?

In terms of achieving reform, will it make a difference which party is in power? In terms of *constitutional* reform, it is certain to make a difference (the Labour government elected in 1997 has a substantial reform agenda), though not necessarily as much as some proponents of change may believe: there is limited time within a Parliament to get major constitutional reform bills through.

In terms of *parliamentary reform*, there is little evidence that it will make much of a difference. We have noted some behavioural differences between the parties and the Labour Party has usually a greater disposition towards change than the Conservative Party. However, a desire for change spans the parties. Some Conservative MPs have been more ardent advocates of change than Labour MPs. (At the beginning of the 1992–7 Parliament, some of the strongest opponents of change were to be found in the Labour whips' office.) As for the party leaderships, the important consideration is not party as such but rather whether the party is in government or opposition. In opposition, a party tends to be a proponent of significant parliamentary reform. When in government, it tends to look less favourably on proposals designed to subject it to more rigorous and critical scrutiny. In 1996, the Labour Party published some modest proposals for parliamentary reform, emphasizing a strengthening of select committees and a reform of prime minister's question time. At the end of the year, the Parliamentary Labour Party agreed changes proposed by the leadership designed to impose tighter discipline on Labour MPs in return for greater consultation. As an opposition, the leadership wanted to strengthen parliamentary scrutiny. As the alternative government, it wanted to avoid a situation in government where it might be subject to defeat by its own side.

What is important for achieving change is not necessarily which party is in power, but rather a combination of three variables: (1) the political will on the part of MPs to achieve change, (2) a reform-minded Leader of the House of Commons (the minister who will lay the proposals before the House), and (3) a coherent set of proposals behind which MPs can rally. There is often a limited window of opportunity for achieving change, normally at the beginning of a Parliament before MPs get bogged down in other business. That window of opportunity was exploited at the beginning of the 1979 Parliament. In 1997, the incoming Labour government was committed to proposing a special committee on reform, to make recommendations to the House for changes in procedure. The ball was put in Parliament's court.

Scrutiny by the European Parliament

The European Parliament (EP) started life as an assembly. It was established under the original treaties (of Paris and Rome) as an advisory body. Though it titled itself a parliament from 1962 onwards it remained an advisory body as well as an unelected one. Its members were drawn from members of the parliaments of the member states. It has grown in power and prominence since. An act signed in 1976, though not ratified until 1978, provided the legal basis for direct elections to the Parliament. Since 1979, the EP has been directly elected, giving it a democratic legitimacy of its own and separating it from the national parliaments. The EP has also acquired power in the law-making process as a result of three developments:

- *The Isolucose case.* The first was the decision of the European Court of Justice in the *Isolucose* case in 1980. This held that, though the opinion of the EP was advisory only, its opinion nonetheless had to be received before a measure of European law could be agreed and enacted.
- *The Single European Act.* The Single European Act took effect in 1987. It extended the competence of the European Community to various sectors not previously covered by the treaties and introduced *the co-operation procedure* for measures necessary to achieve the single market. The co-operation procedure provided for qualified majority voting in the Council of Ministers (replacing the normal practice of requiring unanimity) and for a greater role for the EP.

  Under the co-operation procedure, the normal practice is followed in which the opinion of the Parliament is sought, after which the Council adopts a 'common position' and the EP – at this second reading stage – considers it and accepts, amends or rejects it. The Commission then looks at the proposal again, taking into account the stance of the EP. It then resubmits it to the Council and the Council can adopt it, but it has to adopt it by a unanimous vote if it has been rejected by the EP. Of the 259 acts adopted under this procedure between 1987 and 1992, the Council accepted 44 per cent of the EP's first reading amendments and 26 per cent of its second reading amendments.

  The Single European Act also conferred other powers on the EP, including the power to approve the accession of new members to the European Community. The act also gave it the formal title of a parliament.
- *The Treaty on European Union.* The Treaty on European Union (the Maastricht Treaty) came into force in November 1993. Among its various provisions, it introduced a *co-decision procedure*. This strengthens the position of the EP. Under measures subject to this procedure, the Council and the EP have to agree

a common position before legislating. The EP cannot force the Council to adopt a measure it does not wish to adopt, but it can block the measure. Measures under 15 treaty articles, including most internal market legislation, fall within the scope of the procedure. The treaty also gave the EP the power to request the Commission to submit proposals on matters which it considered necessary for the purpose of treaty implementation. Though still short of having the power to initiate measures, the EP is able to use the provision to push for the introduction of its 'own-initiative' reports.

The EP has thus changed remarkably in less than two decades. It has acquired a role in European law making far in excess of that which it previously had. It operates extensively through 19 fairly large committees (see Westlake, 1994b; Judge and Earnshaw, 1994) – it meets in plenary session for only one week each month – and increasingly is taken seriously not only by other EU institutions but also by bodies seeking to influence outcomes at EU level. Lobbying of the EP is now extensive (Dinan, 1994, p. 278; see also Mazey and Richardson, 1993). There are believed to be between 2000 and 5000 lobbyists in Brussels. Of passes issued each day to individual visitors to the EP, about three-quarters are thought to be given to lobbyists (Jacobs and Corbett, 1990, p. 235). There is clearly a belief that the EP matters.

Where to from here?

However, there is an intense debate as to what extent the EP will, and should, matter in the future. Members of the Parliament, as well as most national governments in the EU, want to strengthen it. Members are keen to exploit existing powers to give them greater leverage in their relationship with the Commission and Council of Ministers. They also want to see its powers further increased. Among changes demanded are (1) the power to initiate measures, (2) greater power over the budget, and (3) the extension of the co-decision procedure to all measures subject to qualified majority voting in the Council of Ministers (see David, 1995, p. 5). Only when such powers are granted, it is argued, will the EP constitute a real parliament, enjoying formal powers similar to those of national parliaments.

The argument in favour of strengthening the EP is that it is the directly-elected assembly of the citizens of the EU and should therefore be the body principally (or, in the view of some, exclusively) responsible for the scrutiny and approval of European law. Those who advocate this approach are generally hostile to national parliaments playing a role in the process at the level of EU institutions. Rather, they argue, there should be a dual approach, the EP gaining greater powers at the EU level and national parliaments being strengthened in relation to national governments, ensuring that proposals are properly scrutinized before the appropriate minister departs for the Council of Ministers.

This view is not necessarily shared by all members of national parliaments, especially in Britain and France. Critics of European integration, such as Eurosceptic MPs in the House of Commons, want national parliaments to play a more central role in European law making. They object to the growing powers of the EP and variously criticize the exercise of those powers. The investigation by an EP committee of how the British government handled the BSE ('mad cow' disease) crisis incurred the wrath of some Conservative MPs when it was revealed early in 1997 that the committee was likely to issue a highly critical report accusing the government of a 'cover up'. To the MPs, the EP was moving into territory that was none of its business. Some British MPs want to renegotiate the UK's terms of membership, or amend the 1972 European Communities Act, in order to empower the British Parliament to refuse assent to EU measures. Others, a category not confined to Eurosceptics, have suggested strengthening national parliaments collectively through the creation of an EP second chamber, composed of members drawn from national parliaments. A lack of agreement militates against achieving a greater formal role for the EP in the process by which European law is made (see Norton, 1996c). Members of national parliaments and the members of the EP often adopt a critical stance towards one another. Though some co-operation takes place in a number of EU countries, members of parliament and MEPs typically operate with little regular contact between them. Consequently, developments within national parliaments and the European Parliament are essentially discrete rather than inter-linking and reinforcing.

Conclusion

The evidence of recent years can be used to bolster both the marginalization and the assertiveness hypotheses. Policy making is executive-centred. Legislatures are not central to the 'making' of public policy. The greater the powers vested in executives, especially now at European level, the more difficult it is for legislatures to keep abreast of what is happening and to have any meaningful impact on outcomes. For proponents of the marginalization thesis, the executive steamroller rolls on, picking up steam.

Proponents of the assertiveness hypothesis can call in aid the greater willingness of members of parliaments to be involved in the scrutiny of legislative proposals – and of executive actions – and of the acquisition of the tools necessary to undertake continuous and structured scrutiny. Whereas voting against the government in the division lobbies is negative and reactive, select committees allow for scrutiny that is both consistent and constructive. Furthermore, it can be argued that as more policy competence flows to the institutions of the EU, the greater the role that should be played, and is being played, by the European Parliament. The EP is not constrained by the same partisan influences that operate at national level and is keen to see its scrutinizing role extended. The task of national parliaments thus becomes one of subjecting national governments to scrutiny. Within that context, it can be argued that the British Parliament does a somewhat better job now than before. However, it has the capacity to develop it much further.

9
The Central Executive

CHRISTOPHER HOOD AND OLIVER JAMES

How different is the central government machine that Labour has inherited in 1997 from the one it bequeathed to the Conservatives in 1979? What forces are shaping its development? We begin by looking briefly at recent developments in the three main parts of UK central executive – the core executive, the civil service and the 'quango state' – since they provide recognizable landmarks for discussion. But of more fundamental concern in this chapter are some of the underlying mechanisms which regulate changes across the government machine – as politicians, governments and thousands of public managers respond to a constant pressure to do more with scarce resources, and adapt to the opportunities provided by new technologies and the demands of new social problems. Our theme is that despite the importance of change, there are only a few basic options for designing central governance arrangements – and most reforms and reorganizations can be seen as combinations of these options.

Recent Changes

The middle 1990s have been a period of stabilization in central governance arrangements, mirroring in many ways the more general impact of the Major government in slowing down and moderating the hectic pace of policy changes under the Thatcher governments. Major proved to be a very different leader from his predecessor, but his strategies continued to shape central government in a 'new public management' vein.

The 'Core Executive'

The full array of coordinating and arbitrating mechanisms at the heart of central government was often neglected in previous discussions of prime ministerial and cabinet government, so the term 'core executive' was invented as a shorthand term for this complex apparatus (Dunleavy and Rhodes, 1990; Rhodes, 1995). As shown in Figure 9.1, the core executive includes the PM and Cabinet, security and intelligence services, central agencies (notably the Treasury, Cabinet Office, Foreign and Commonwealth Office) and key individuals including the law officers. At the centre is the Cabinet and its network of overlapping committees (shading into official committees) where Ministers wrangle over policy.

The core executive is a small community. In May 1997 there were 22 Cabinet members, just over 110 members of the government in total, and 26 top civil servants (Grade 1 and 1A officials, comprising heads of Whitehall departments, and the Head of the Civil Service and Secretary to the Cabinet, a civil servant who bridges the bureaucratic and political sides of central government). Concentrated in half a square mile of central London, this apparatus is no 'government of strangers'. It is a 'village' small enough for everyone to know each other well and to be preoccupied with pursuing and maintaining their reputation.

The EU Commission and Council, together with the EU committee network, form another set of 'colleges', interacting with the domestic Cabinet committee structure. Indeed, at the political centre of government, the Cabinet Office is often said to have gained power relative to the Treasury because it is the conduit for EU business, with its European lawyers and European Secretariat. Within Whitehall, the management of public spending forms another 'community' of departments interacting with the Treasury. The political management of the UK is likely to figure larger in core executive concerns than before – with the prospect of a devolved parliament for Scotland and an assembly for Wales, as well as continuing political negotiations for a peace settlement to reshape the government of Northern Ireland.

How this system of interlocking circles of influence operates has been much debated over the years. Especially during Margaret Thatcher's period of office, it was often claimed that the elements

FIGURE 9.1 Central government and the 'core executive'

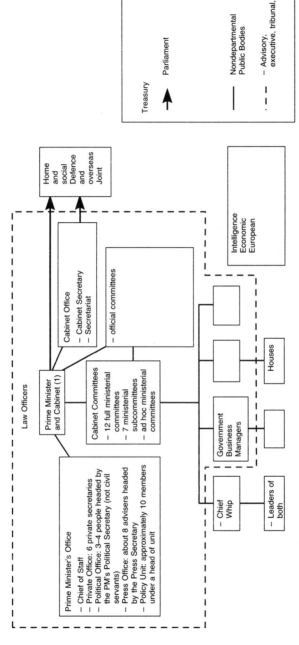

other (usually report to a department)

of 'collegiality' inside the core executive (summed up in the normative ideal of the collective responsibility of ministers and 'cabinet government') were weakening. Instead prime ministers were said to be acquiring a quasi-presidential power to pursue policy contrary to the wishes of Cabinet colleagues (Foley, 1993). For this school of thought, we might expect to see a 'Blair presidency', modelled on the 'iron lady' stereotype of Margaret Thatcher's leadership.

However, the claim that there is a long-term trend away from checks on prime ministers is contested. Observers like Jones (1995) stress the continuing constraints placed by cabinet and party colleagues on prime ministerial power. Recent British PMs have frequently been at odds with their Chancellors and Foreign Secretaries, particularly over Europe, and a Chancellor–Foreign Secretary coalition can undermine the PM's policy position, as in the case of the UK's entry into the European Exchange Rate Mechanism (Jones, 1995, p. 96; Burch and Holliday, 1996, pp. 220–6). Indeed, if the recent Conservative record is anything to go by, contemporary prime ministers are just as vulnerable to leadership challenges from their colleagues as in the past, if not more so. Margaret Thatcher's downfall in 1990 (following an unsuccessful challenge by a 'stalking horse' the previous year) is the only twentieth-century case of a sitting PM in good health being removed from office in peacetime by a leadership challenge from within her own party. (Lloyd George's ouster in 1922 is the closest parallel, but he led a coalition government.) Thatcher's successor, John Major, faced a similar threat to his position in 1995, driving him to a pre-emptive summer resignation to forestall an autumn contest, to fight off a challenge from a Cabinet colleague. Such developments seem to sit ill with the 'Presidential politics' view that the PM's power is steadily growing.

We have no ready indicators of long term changes in levels of Cabinet activity or 'collegiality'. Cabinet committee data have been released for too short a period (since 1992) to permit firm conclusions about general trends, and in any case they do not record the large penumbra of official and ad hoc groups surrounding the main Cabinet committees (see Hennessy, 1986, p. 26). According to Burch and Holliday (1996, p. 45), Thatcher cut Cabinet committee meetings (both ministerial and official) by a third between 1979 and 1990, preferring to work through informal 'inner cabinets' and bilateral meetings with ministers. Such informal practices make it difficult to assess how collegially the core executive was operating from official listings of committees and their membership. The official records show that the number of formal Cabinet committees fell slightly between 1992 (when committee data was first published) and 1996, from 26 to 19, but this fall does not necessarily denote declining control by ministers as a whole. To the extent that the Cabinet committees which remained were more inclusive, it might even suggest the opposite. The 19 Cabinet committees as of June 1997 with details of chair and number of members are given in Table 9.1, although additional ministers may attend from time to time.

Some important regular meetings are not official Cabinet committees and are not included on this list. There are regular strategy meetings between the Prime Minister, Deputy Prime Minister, Chancellor of the Exchequer and Foreign Secretary. The Minister without Portfolio in the Cabinet Office, Peter Mandelson, has acknowledged (letter, *The Times*, 4 June 1997) that he chairs a daily meeting similar to the previous government's Cabinet Committee on Co-ordination and Presentation of Government Policy which was chaired by the Deputy Prime Minister, Michael Heseltine.

The main external way of regulating the executive is formally by Parliament. But apart from the work of the Commons' professional investigators (the National Audit Office and to a lesser extent the Parliamentary Commissioner for Administration), the system of select committees to oversee different domains of policy has well-known weaknesses, in terms of limited resources and authority, particularly in dealing with ministers (see Chapter 8). The 1996 Scott report on the export of arms to Iraq highlighted the limits of Parliamentary supervision in sensitive policy areas. Ministers were able to alter controls on arms exports to a potentially hostile country with little attention from Parliament (Scott, 1996, p. 1759), and according to Scott, failed to inform Parliament fully, ignoring the duties set out in *Questions of Procedure for Ministers*, the rule-book drawn up by prime ministers and top officials to govern ministerial conduct (Scott, 1996, pp. 1799–1806). Continuing media and public concerns about 'sleaze' – improper conduct of public business or abuse of public office – have been an important part of the backdrop to politics in

TABLE 9.1   Ministerial standing committees of the cabinet in June 1997

Chair	Committees: Policy Area (and Designation), Number of Members
Prime Minister	Defence and Overseas Policy (DOP), 6 Constitutional Reform Policy (CRP), 13 Intelligence Services (IS), 6 Northern Ireland (IN), 6
Deputy Prime Minister and Secretary of State for the Environment, Transport and the Regions	Home and Social Affairs (HS), 20 Environment (ENV), 18 Local Government (GL), 19 Sub-committee on London (GL(L)), 12
Chancellor of the Exchequer	Economic Affairs (EA), 18 Public Expenditure (PX), 9 Sub-committee on Welfare to Work (EA(WW)), 13
Lord Chancellor	Queen's Speeches and Future Legislation (QFL), 11 Devolution to Scotland and Wales and the English Regions (DSWR), 19 Sub-committee on Incorporation of the European Convention on Human Rights (CRP(EC)), 17
President of the Council and Leader of the House	Legislation (LEG), 14 Sub-committee on Drug Misuse (HS(D)), 12 Sub-committee on Health Strategy (HS(H)), 15
Other Ministers (Chair indicated)	Sub-committee on European Issues ((E)DOP), Chair: Secretary of State for Foreign and Commonwealth Affairs, 19 Sub-committee on Women's Issues (HS(W)), Chair: Secretary of State for Social Security, 14

the 1990s, not just in the UK but in other wealthy democracies too. The executive up to now has responded to this concern only by a modest expansion of 'sleaze policing' and explication of (non-statutory) codes of conduct for ministers and civil servants.

By contrast, oversight of the executive by the judiciary seems to have strengthened as a result of increasing judicial activism, both within the UK and also by the European Court of Justice. Annual applications for leave for judicial review of administration in England and Wales rose over sixfold, from 533 in 1981 to 3208 in 1994 (Bridges, Meszaros and Sunkin, 1996, p. 7), and many observers claim judicial review has grown in qualitative as well as quantitative importance. Other forms of oversight have developed too: after the early 1990s' preoccupation with political 'sleaze' (Ridley and Doig, 1995), rules of behaviour for Ministers and MPs were spelt out and to some extent tightened. New rules on declaration of MPs' financial interests were adopted in 1995, and after the report of the Nolan Committee on Standards in Public Life in 1994, a Parliamentary Commissioner for Standards was set up and a Public Appointments Commissioner was established to oversee the 'merit' principle in appointments to non-departmental public bodies.

The Civil Service

The last time the Labour party won government after a long period in opposition (in 1964) there was much discussion of the political reliability of top civil servants in terms of their ability to adapt to a new party-political agenda. As Conservative political fortunes waned in the 1990s, senior civil servants were at pains to stress the bipartisan nature of reforms in the public service (see Sir Peter Kemp, reported in Treasury and Civil Service Committee, 1990, p. xxii). But even if (as seems likely) the 'loyalty problem' is not widespread, the long Conservative incumbency may have left its stamp on ways of working within Whitehall. For instance, Foster and Plowden (1996), commenting on the Scott report on arms sales to Iraq before 1990, suggest that a long period of emphasis on civil servants' role as policy implementors rather than policy makers has downgraded one of the major contributions to policymaking by civil servants, namely the drafting of policy statements. The consequence may be reduced accountability to Parliament, since without authoritative statements of policy it is difficult to tell whether the executive is following its own guidelines, and very hard to identify who is responsible for violations. Whether a new government, or an opposition with more experience of government, will cause civil servants' responsibility for spelling out policy to be re-emphasized remains to be seen.

The civil service the Blair government inherits is different from that of a generation ago in many other ways. Apart from having

been heavily 'downsized', 'market tested', 'outsourced', and 'delayered', it has been 'corporatized' into over 120 separate 'businesses' (known as executive agencies). This change has greatly increased the role that ministers play in senior civil service appointments and produced a twin-track civil service at the top. Most agency chief executives still come from the civil service. But few come from the standard 'generalist' mandarin background, and over a quarter of the 129 agency chief executives in post in 1996 had been appointed from outside (Cabinet Office, 1996b, p. 11). Similarly, the 'career service' feature of the civil service has been weakened to some extent. Instead of being an organization in which top posts were exclusively filled by those who entered as young bureaucrats in their early twenties, an increased number of top civil service appointments are now publicly advertized and filled by 'outsiders'.

Tables 9.2 and 9.3 summarize the legacy of Conservative rule, cataloguing respectively the main civil service and other public service reforms introduced since the last Labour government. There has been a notable retreat of the traditional 'public bureaucracy state' of high public employment, with more than one civil servant in five disappearing from the public payroll and over 1 million public enterprise jobs passing into the private sector. There is no prospect of the Blair government being able to reverse most of those changes even if it wanted to. But that still leaves Labour ministers with plenty of scope for selective unpicking and re-engineering of the machinery of government to achieve different emphases. How far a new government can realistically expect to do things differently is a main theme of the second part of this chapter.

The 'Quango State'

Outside the civil service and local government is a burgeoning set of organizations which deliver public services, advise, adjudicate, regulate and allocate public money. Taken together they amount to a sizeable domain of ministerial patronage, with ministers appointing over 40 000 people each year to the boards of the remaining nationalized industries, NHS bodies and 'Non Departmental Public Bodies' (Hogwood, 1995, p. 41). The exercise of such patronage was entirely unfettered until 1995, but since then some attempt has been made to extend the 'merit' principle from civil service appointments (overseen for over 100 years by the Civil Service Commission) to 'quango' appointments, in the form of a Commissioner for Public Appointments, who now scrutinizes ministerial appointments to about 1000 non-departmental public bodies.

However, even beyond this set of semi-regulated organizations is another group of bodies, providing local public services, which are almost wholly funded from central government and are supervised by ministers or executive bodies under ministerial control. Ministers tend not to be involved in appointments for such organizations, and these bodies are not centrally listed in the same way as the 1194 central-level 'non departmental public bodies', though they are of major and growing importance. The number of nationally funded local bodies of this type has been put at over 4500 (Weir and Hall, 1994, pp. 8–10) and they took on important functions in the 1980s and 1990s as government aimed to reshape public services formerly provided by local authorities. Key examples were centrally-funded housing associations, City Technology Colleges and grant-maintained schools which had 'opted out' of local authority control. Although the Conservatives came into office in 1979 pledged to prune the 'quango state', such organizations have not declined in importance, and indeed many new players have been added. The Labour Party, which was highly critical of the 'quangocracy' in its long period in opposition, now faces an even greater challenge in pruning or managing this sector than did Margaret Thatcher in 1979.

Four Fundamental Control Mechanisms in Central Governance

In any liberal democracy steering or controlling the central executive involves creating and maintaining a system of checks and balances, to ensure that concentrations of power in the hands of central state actors can both be politically controlled but also operated within clear limits. Of course different countries have evolved a very wide range of institutional arrangements for accomplishing this difficult task, and the British system we have reviewed briefly so far is no more special or eccentric than any

TABLE 9.2   Major Conservative civil service changes

Date	Name of programme	What it involved
1979	Efficiency scrutinies	At first, one-off scrutinies in depts., later more emphasis on issues linking depts.
1982	Financial Management Initiative	Identification of dept. aims, costs and performance indicators; move to 'cost centres' and management inf. systems
1985	Pay Linked to Performance	At first for CS grades 3–7, Grade 2 added in 1987, with discretionary pay for the highest grades
1989	Next Steps programme	Creation of c.100 'executive agencies' under CEOs, with missions defined by framework documents agreed with Ministers
1991	Market Testing	Opening up CS work to outside contractors, requiring govt. depts to identify 30 per cent of their work for market testing. £2bn. of activity market-tested between 1992 and 1994
1991	Pay and grading delegation, begun in 1991 and completed in 1996	Responsibility for pay and grading below senior levels delegated to depts and agencies
1993	Fundamental Expenditure Reviews	Value-for-money assessment of dept. running costs and consideration of alternative ways of policy delivery
1996	Senior Civil Service	SES-type measure, involving all CS grades 5 and above as part of a common elite corps, with written contracts and individually determined pay
1998	Resource Accounting and Budgeting	By 1998 all depts to introduce accrual accounting techniques, which integrate capital and current spending. (To be applied to public spending as a whole by 2000)

Comment	How linked with types of regulation
Response to perceived failure of large-scale top-down CS reforms of 1960s and 1970s	Competition (by ambitious CS for Cabinet attention) mixed with review from Efficiency Unit
Development from DOE MINIS program and Efficiency Scrutiny program	Mix of review (by extra information held by the top/centre) and competition (by cost centres able to be league-tabled)
Possible response to 1981 CS pay strike; return to proposals of 1968 Fulton Report on CS	Aimed to increase competition by CS for pay as well as for promotion to higher grades
Seen variously as response to FMI failure or success (see Jordan, 1992, p. 3); return to 'buried' proposals of 1968 Fulton Report on CS	Increase in formal oversight through explication of framework documents and regulatory frameworks
Application to central govt of 1980s CCT procedures developed in local govt and NHS. Superseded by efficiency plans in 1994 after low take-up by Depts	Aimed to increase competition (public and private) for public service provision
Part of Treasury shift away from detailed oversight of CS management	Replacement of specific pay oversight by overall running costs regimes; move away from contrived randomness in Treasury style
Linked with 'delayering' of senior CS, esp. in 1994 Treasury FER (shedding 25% of Grades 1–3)	Selective review, with competition element akin to 1979 efficiency scrutinies
Introduced in 1994 *Continuity and Change* Civil Service White Paper, as an attempt to buttress career senior CS with common mores	Attempt to restore elements of 'Whitehall village' mutuality
Move away from traditional cash accounting systems, following experiments in early 1990s and in part copying NZ experience	Arguably neutral among basic control modes

TABLE 9.3   Other major Conservative public service changes

Date	Name of programme	What it involved
1979	Privatization and regulation programme	Shift of public enterprise to private owners and creation of 'light rein' regulators for utilities from 1984
1980	Compulsory competitive tendering	LAs required to put out defined services to competitive tender, starting with 1980 LG Planning and Land Act, extended by legislation in 1988 and 1992
1991	Citizen's Charter	A 'consumerist' program for clearer published service across the whole PS, and coherent redress, compensation and complaint methods
1992	Private Finance Initiative	Use of private sector to provide public sector infrastructure using private capital in exchange for a flow of payments

other. But underlying the surface dissimilarities between countries, it is possible to argue that in any particular central executive four fundamental control mechanisms operate – which can be termed competition, oversight, mutuality and contrived randomness (see Hood, 1996).

● 'Competition' denotes the way politicians, bureaucrats and other key actors are controlled through rivalry. Competition for votes and office is pervasive in democratic politics, but competition is also an important way of keeping bureaucracies under control (see Horn, 1995). For example in 1995 over 50 would-be civil service mandarins contended for every 'fast stream' Grade 7 vacancy in the British civil service. Those individuals who succeeded would compete thereafter for promotion, ministerial attention, titles, honours – even for plum jobs in business on retirement. Indeed, the number of civil servants in the 'middle' policy grades (Grades 4–6 inclusive) for

Comment	How linked to types of regulation
Extension of programme from a modest initial base as experience developed; regulatory model cloned from OFT	Oversight and review (through development of more explicit regulation) mixed with extension of competition in some areas
Extension of LG programme from a narrow base over the 1980s (with 'pioneering' LAs used as a model), extended to NHS (1983), white-collar LG work (1992) and CS (1991)	Aimed to increase competition by making bureaucrats compete for their own jobs against the private sector
Response to early 1980s cost-cutting style; adoption of model used by some Labour local authorities (e.g. York, Lewisham)	Mainly oversight and review, through inspection, explication of standards and grievance mechanisms
Reaction to traditional public finance principle of govt. borrowing wholesale and itself managing capital spending contracts	Ostensibly aimed to increase competition by competitive tendering to choose private sector suppliers

each top job (Grades 1–3 inclusive) is in fact more than the number of backbench MPs for each paid ministerial office, suggesting that bureaucrats have to compete more fiercely for promotion than MPs.

- 'Oversight' denotes the way politicians and bureaucrats are controlled by formal review, audit or inspection by external agents. Such processes are widespread throughout government. In constitutional theory, we have already noted that Parliament oversees the operations of the executive as a whole, especially the behaviour of ministers and top civil servants. And under Parliamentary approval, public servants down the line are subject to an army of further overseers who monitor standards and champion values like equal opportunities, quality, efficiency, value-for-money, privacy, security, safety and legality. Government actions are subject to judicial review (by domestic courts and the European Court of Justice) and to review by 60 or so specialized tribunals and around 17 ombudsmen. Audit offices – including the National Audit Office, Audit Commission and European Court of Audit – examine government spending for efficiency and legality. In fact, UK central government seems to devote several times as much money to overseeing the public services as it does to regulating the much-discussed privatized utilities. Total public spending on a core set of central government 'regulators', including the NAO, central agency oversight units, inspectorates and reviewers, and the various ombudsmen, was about £139m in 1994–5, compared to about £33m spent on the privatized utility regulators.

• 'Mutuality' denotes the way that individuals are controlled by group pressures within organizations, from peer-group or other reciprocal patterns. Mutuality works in the opposite way from oversight, since the control comes from inside a group, from socialization into particular ways of working and the internalization of common values. Individual behaviour is checked through collective reasoning and debate, or by informal expectations and values built up in interactions with colleagues over long periods of time. We have already noted the importance of collegiality and collective responsibility as guiding ideas in the traditional descriptions of the apex of British cabinet government. But 'government by committee' (Wheare, 1955) is a way of life throughout the whole of UK central government. The Cabinet structure works through a network of committees, and within the bureaucracy too much business has traditionally been conducted through a 'meetings culture' of committees within and across departments. The same pattern extends at official level to the EU policy circuit. In addition, many Cabinet Office staff, as well as all the civil servants attached to the PM's unit at 10 Downing Street, are seconded from other departments, which also serves to heighten mutuality within the senior civil service (Dowding, 1995, p. 181). Two decades ago, Heclo and Wildavsky (1974, pp. 14–15) argued that mutuality rather than outside oversight was the strongest force regulating the few hundred people in the senior UK civil service, through a culture of mutual rating.

• 'Contrived randomness' is the last approach, a system of control which works by making life unpredictable for politicians and bureaucrats, like random breath testing of motorists. If you cannot predict your future, in the sense of which organization you will work in, who your colleagues will be, and where surveillance or questions will come from, then corrupt conspiracies or illegitimate elite collusions are harder to organize than in a more predictable world (Rose-Ackerman, 1978, pp. 183–6; Bentham, 1983, p. 281; Burnheim, 1985, p. 167). Less commonly discussed than the other forms of regulation, contrived randomness can be an important source of control in and over government. Politicians and bureaucrats often complain that they are exposed to 'random agenda selection' (Breyer, 1993, pp. 19–20), with their fates being determined on the roulette wheel of media and public attention. But while such processes are often deplored as undermining policy rationality, they can also serve to control politicians by making their environment hard for them to predict. Nor is contrived randomness just a feature of politics. Just as multinational corporations often post key employees unpredictably around the globe (to prevent them 'going native'), so career patterns in top civil service ranks have often made it hard for rising bureaucrats to predict where they will next work and with whom. Senior civil servants rarely serve for more than three years in any one position. And career bureaucrats rising to be permanent secretaries of departments have rarely ended up presiding over the bit of Whitehall in which they spent most of their working lives. Taken to extremes, such practices turn bureaucracies into a sort of gaming machine, with no one able to predict just where the chips will fall the next time the wheel is spun (see Hood, 1976, pp. 160–3).

These four mechanisms are to some extent in tension, pulling against one another at the margin. Mixes and matches are possible too. Figure 9.2 also shows that by combining any two mechanisms it is possible to produce hybrid forms of control mechanisms, some of which have been extremely influential in recent public service changes in Britain. Combining competition with strong regulatory oversight, for example, produces the 'quasi-market' form of control, which Conservative governments developed for almost a decade from 1988 as the key mechanism for managing the National Health Service. We apply these ideas in a little more detail by looking at the restructuring of the public

FIGURE 9.2   Four fundamental ways of regulating the executive (and
some intermediate types)

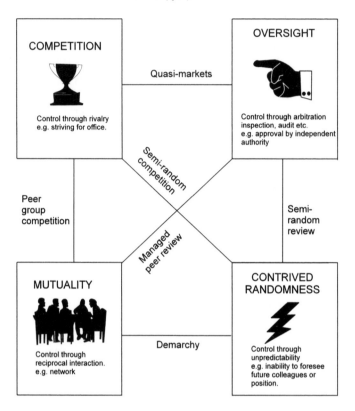

service in Britain carried out by successive Conservative governments since Labour last held power in Westminster and Whitehall. None of the basic forms of regulation seems to have
disappeared; but the balance and style has changed with the
advent of new types of competition and new or revamped oversight systems.

Assessing Public Service Change

A constant theme of Tory rhetoric for over a decade has been the
need to introduce more 'competition' into the way that the British

state carries out its tasks. However, along with changes weakening central direction and increasing competition came new forms of oversight. The ostensible separation of service-delivery from 'policy', and the delegation of responsibility for resource use in public management, was accompanied by an enhancement of formal oversight of public services in other forms. So the changes ostensibly designed to produce more competition, seem to have been accompanied by a 'mirror image' development in the form of a growth of more and more formal oversight systems. As a result the overall style of regulation over the public service seems to have been changing towards both the competition and the oversight processes shown at the top of Figure 9.2, and away from the traditional processes shown at the bottom – where the civil service (and other public service professions) was regulated both by informal 'club-like' mutuality processes at senior levels and by elements of contrived randomness in lower ranks. Most of the public service changes summarized in Tables 9.2 and 9.3 are compatible with this hypothesis.

Competition

The extent to which the public service reforms added up to a coherent package has been much debated, but to the extent they did competition was clearly the most publicly emphasized unifying theme in the late 1980s and early 1990s. Allied with a more 'business-management' style, competition was trumpeted as an all-purpose remedy for the alleged ills of government bureaucracy. This doctrine served to justify the sudden accentuation in the 1980s and 1990s of several long-term trends, including:

- the use of quangos rather than government departments for many functions, a trend going back at least to the 1920s;
- the outsourcing of work once performed by 'industrial' civil servants, a trend going back to the 1950s; and
- increased delegation to departments of matters once requiring central agency authorization, notably accelerating delegation of Treasury financial approvals (a trend since the 1950s) and the withdrawal of the Civil Service Commissioners from a direct role in civil service recruitment (which began in the 1960s).

On top of those existing trends were added:

- the creation of executive agencies within the civil service, an idea going back to the 1960s and falteringly attempted in the early 1970s, but now implemented vigorously across the civil service since 1988;
- the growth of 'cost centres' designed to increase managerial responsibility and initiative; and
- the complete replacement of central prescription of pay scales and grades by Treasury oversight of overall departmental running costs.

At the same time traditional forms of civil service competition – rivalry for recruitment and promotion – do not seem to have weakened greatly in the recent past. Table 9.4 indicates levels of competition for 'fast stream' places (the fast-track recruitment route for aspiring top mandarins) from 1980 to 1995. It also indicates the degree of competition for promotion to top positions by showing the ratio of top to middle positions (in the 'policy' grades), taking 'top' as the highest three civil service grades (1–3) and 'middle' as Grades 4–6. It shows that there were 7 to 10 'middle' grades for every 'top' position over 1980–95 (or 25 to 30

TABLE 9.4　Competition amongst civil servants for top posts, 1980–95

Year	Competition for civil service promotion			Competition for selection as a civil servant		
	Top grade jobs (G1–3)	Middle grade jobs (G4–6)	Ratio of top to middle grades	Fast Stream places	FS applicants	Ratio of applicants to FS places
1980	813	5512	1:7	183	5 052	28:1
1985	670	5573	1:8	205	11 954	58:1
1990	668	6816	1:10	340	5 510	16:1
1995	593	5389	1:9	246	12 571	51:1

Source:　*Civil Service Statistics* and figures from CS Commission
Note:　FTE staff numbers at 1 April 1986–95 and 1 January for 1979–85. The FTEs count altered slightly in 1995, and for 1980–3 equivalents to Grades 4–6 are used. 'Fast stream' means posts included in the 1995 FS and equivalents for previous years.

if we count Grade 7s as 'middle'), suggesting that competition for promotion – a central mechanism of control over bureaucracies – seems to have slightly increased over the whole period.

But in addition to traditional forms of rivalry, three newer forms of competition have developed strongly inside the public services, some of them 'hybrid'. One is the development since 1984 of merit pay to replace relatively fixed and published classified pay scales. The 'Senior Civil Service' created in 1996 replaced the old central grading structure with 10 broad pay bands. At the top, Permanent Secretaries' pay is set individually by a remuneration committee including members of the Senior Salaries Review Body. Permanent Secretaries in turn set the pay of their departmental SCS subordinates in the lower nine bands (PM *et al.*, 1995, pp. 35–45; Review Body on Senior Salaries, 1996, p. iii). The move carries the previous development of merit pay to a greater (and more opaque) level of individualization. Whether it will make it politically easier for the new government to handle top public service pay (always a sensitive issue for Labour governments) remains to be seen.

Second, competition increased through increasing 'lateral entry' for top bureaucratic jobs (Permanent Secretaries and agency Chief Executives). By the mid-1990s just under a third of all Grade 1–3 vacancies were open to external competition, leading to an outside appointment in about half the cases (CS Commissioners, 1996, p. 6). If this trend continues, external appointees will soon comprise about 15 per cent of senior grades, heightening the competition faced by middle-level civil servants aiming for the top. However, over 50 per cent of external Grade 1–3 appointments between 1993 and 1996 were 'managerial' positions (agency heads and NHS executive senior managers), with less than 10 per cent in departmental headships or deputy headships, suggesting traditional 'mandarins' retain a powerful hold over those positions.

A third attempt to increase competition was the introduction of 'market testing' (in the 1991 *Competing for Quality* White Paper), by which departments were obliged to tender against other suppliers for defined blocks of work. But market testing came late to Whitehall (a decade or so after compulsory competitive tendering in local government), and the sluggish pace of market testing in central government contrasted sharply with the runaway implementation of reforms like 'Next Steps' agencies or the Citizen's Charter. The program lagged behind its targets, and those targets were abandoned in 1994 (replaced by a requirement on departments to produce 'efficiency plans', in which market testing might or might not figure). Moreover, Whitehall departments have been little exposed to the competitive force of the rating systems or league tables developed for schools, hospitals, universities and local authority services, although executive agencies have been increasingly exposed to comparison on key indicators in annual reviews (*Next Steps Review 1994*, Cm 2750, 1994, Annex A, pp. vi–viii).

In principle outsourcing services once provided directly by state bureaucracies may step up competitive pressures. But market testing – as far as it went – only tested the state against the market, not markets against the state (in fact competition in commercial markets by departments and agencies was forbidden). And whether outsourcing in fact always clearly increased the competitiveness of public service provision is debatable. Many outsourcing deals like the contract with the multi-national company EDS for all Inland Revenue computer work in 1994 set up long-term relationships with dominant suppliers. Such a firm's position might well be hard to shake when the time came for contract renewal, since the British government's own capacity to do the work would by then have disappeared. The Private Finance Initiative, introduced in 1992, was likewise associated with long-term franchises running into decades and therefore representing a long-term inheritance for subsequent governments for the provision of capital facilities. The PFI also replaced the traditional system for providing capital facilities in the public service, where central government used its leverage in the capital market to borrow funds and then directly managed contractors to provide the facilities. For selective projects, PFI substituted a system of deals in which private entrepreneurs provided public facilities at their own expense, in exchange for long-term income payments or franchising rights.

Oversight and Review

Along with attempts to increase competition have come new forms of oversight over the public service. In addition to growing judicial review, systems of inspection, audit, complaint-handling and standard-setting have been reconfigured in what some have dubbed an 'audit explosion' (Power, 1994), although the term 'compliance explosion' might be more accurate. Public audit was greatly expanded and reshaped in 1982–3, with the creation of the Audit Commission to incorporate the former District Audit Service and the revamping of the Exchequer and Audit Office into the National Audit Office. Subsequent changes in audit practice have extended the scope of audit from the traditional checking of the 'regularity' of payments into a form of policy evaluation. The independence of public audit bodies has increased, helping them to mount more high-profile challenges over policy and practice in central government, the NHS and local authorities. There seems to have been a long-term shift in central government audit away from the old process in which 'little people' in the audit office challenged lapses by other 'little people' in departments, with top officials becoming involved only as spokespeople when the issues 'ricocheted' up to the Public Accounts Committee. In the emerging system, public auditors have increasingly criticized senior public officials for policy decisions for which they were directly responsible, as in the NAO's 1992 report on the Pergau dam affair which caused a media storm and led the Malaysian government to suspend government contracts with the UK. In this case the British government financed a dam project in Malaysia under the heading of development assistance, but apparently as a *quid pro quo* for Malaysian purchases of British arms. The high profile deal was promised by Margaret Thatcher in 1989 and approved by the Foreign Secretary in 1991, despite civil service objections about poor value for money in the dam project – which was controversial on environmental grounds and for its adverse impacts on local residents. Since Labour came into office pledged to increase the scope of the NAO, there seems little prospect of this process being reversed.

Another shift in public service oversight was the response to demands from the House of Commons' Treasury and Civil Service Committee (later the Public Services Committee) for a formalization of rules governing civil service ethics and conduct. Codification has taken several forms. The 1993 Civil Service Management Code replaced a set of other guides, circulars and codes, to establish general guidelines instead of the previous regime of detailed approvals (there are parallels with what has happened to Treasury expenditure control). In 1996 a non-statutory Civil Service Code (replacing an earlier more *ad hoc* document, the 1985 'Armstrong Memorandum') spelt out civil servants' duties and the standards of conduct expected of them, with appeals to be heard by the Civil Service Commissioners. The code prohibited officials carrying out acts specified as illegal, improper or unethical, those breaching constitutional convention and those involving maladministration (Civil Service Commissioners, 1996, pp. 23–4), but the Code restated the doctrine that civil servants owe their primary loyalty to ministers rather than to any wider public interest or to Parliament as a whole.

A third development in oversight has been more emphasis on grievance-handling bodies, including the creation of a Prisons 'Ombudsman', a range of other complaints adjudicators encouraged by the 1991 Citizen's Charter, and the Commissioner for the Security Services, which were put onto a statutory basis in 1992 after the end of the Cold War. In addition, the role of some standard-setting bodies has been markedly expanded, notably the schools inspectorates. Since 1992 Ofsted and its counterpart in Wales have been formally independent of the English and Welsh education ministries (no such change has occurred in Scotland) and at the same time have radically changed their operating style, moving away from direct employment of inspectors towards franchising schools inspection functions to outside teams of contractors, expanding and formalizing the inspection process, and (in England at least) adopting a much higher media profile. The 1991 Citizen's Charter, embracing the development of performance standards across the public service, was also associated with an emphasis on independent inspection and grievance-handling as a key to good government. Whatever happens to nomenclature and particular initiatives, this general trend for more oversight seems unlikely to be reversed in the near future.

Mutuality

To what extent did rising emphasis on competition and formal oversight involve a relative weakening of the controls at the bottom of Figure 9.2 – mutuality and contrived randomness? Such a shift is less obvious inside the core executive than in the outer reaches of the public service. For instance, market reforms in health care were clearly intended to weaken professional collegiality and self-regulation, and instead to enhance the power of hospital general managers. And the competition for high ratings in inspections was designed to have a similar effect in education. But the impact of the new oversight systems on the importance of 'mutuality' processes in the top civil service is unclear. Some forms of mutuality may even have increased. The development in 1996 of a Senior Civil Service for Grades 1–5 (as noted in Table 9.2) was an attempt to preserve or augment a small cohesive corps at the top of Whitehall. And working with European institutions also introduces a new dimension of mutuality with EU counterparts. Team working has been strengthened in the senior civil service to some degree, with the introduction of management boards in many Whitehall departments. And the overall 'mutual ratings' culture of the civil service (as noted earlier) has evidently not changed overnight.

However, four factors seem to be working in the opposite direction, weakening the scope for mutuality at the top. One is the apparent reduction in the number of meetings of civil servants within the Cabinet committee structure, as mentioned earlier. A second is the extension of formal oversight in forms such as the Civil Service Code, the changed powers of the CS Commissioners, or the 1993 'open government' White Paper (with the Parliamentary Ombudsman responsible for overseeing compliance). A third factor has been the radical 'delayering' of senior staff, with 25 per cent of the top grade jobs removed from some departments since 1994. In principle this change might enhance a 'mutuality' style (since it makes Whitehall's 'village world' even smaller), but it also reduces the density of mutual surveillance over policy development. Moreover, the effect of delayering on mutuality may be shaped by a fourth element, the weakening of the career civil service tradition, with more outside appointments to the senior ranks than in the recent past. Changes of this kind are even more notable at the level of executive agencies, and seem likely to mean that part of the mutual 'rating game' played out among a relatively fixed cast of Whitehall characters over decades, has been weakened.

Contrived Randomness

Assessing the effects of changes in the public service on contrived randomness as a form of control is also difficult, since nothing approaching hard data is available, but recent changes again seem likely to have weakened this form of control. Contrived randomness works by posting people in unpredictable ways around large ramified organizations, which themselves operate through collegial or 'dual key' decision systems requiring two or more individuals to 'open the lock'. In organizations designed in this fashion the handling of money, contracts or staff cannot be monopolized by any one individual. Downsizing a public bureaucracy makes it less likely that any two or more individuals within the organization will be strangers to one another and reduces the scope for unpredictable postings. Delayering is likely to have a similar effect and reduces the likelihood of unpredictable surveillance interventions from higher grades.

In addition, the Treasury's Fundamental Expenditure Review (FER) introduced in the mid-1990s may signify a further shift away from 'contrived randomness' as a method of controlling spending. The old system started with requests by departments for spending permission to undertake specific actions, which then elicited (by a semi-random process) a series of Treasury questions about departmental policy and management. This random spotlight on departmental activity under traditional Treasury oversight procedures has been replaced by more generalized illumination, since the FER heralded a move towards 'strategic' target-setting linked with the devolution of detailed spending controls to departments (HM Treasury, 1994). But such shifts do not seem to have been accompanied by any marked increase in random checking procedures over the civil service.

Nevertheless, there may be some countervailing processes introducing new elements of randomness. One is the creation of a more complex structure of public sector organization, which may increase unpredictability as those organizations increasingly have to combine if policy delivery is to be effective. A second change is the increase in lateral entry, noted earlier, which in principle increases the chance factor in interactions over a lifetime civil service career. A third has been the attempt to create a Senior Civil Service for Grades 1–5 (as noted earlier), which in principle might increase the scope for unexpected postings around the system at short notice. Lateral entry may well introduce a new form of contrived randomness, but it seems doubtful if the other two developments are likely to compensate fully for the decline in randomness brought about by other changes. The experience of senior executive systems in other countries suggests that it may not be easy to develop a truly go-anywhere corps of top officials, particularly if pressures for delayering and lateral entry rise.

Hybrid Forms of Regulation

Some new forms of regulation in the public service have been 'hybrid' combinations of the four main types in Figure 9.2, but most of these compounds have been applied *by* the core executive to other parts of the public service (rather than inside the core executive itself). The commonest hybrids seem to be quasi-markets, peer-group review and peer-group competition. Quasi-markets link competition and oversight (Le Grand and Bartlett, 1993), so that competition occurs in a framework governed by administrative regulation rather than just under contract law (indeed, litigation over 'contracts' amongst public agencies involved is often forbidden). But this hybrid, a marked feature of institutional reforms in health care and education, has been markedly absent from the core departments of Whitehall.

The same applies to peer-group review, a combination of mutuality and oversight, which is perhaps epitomized by the NHS 'clinical audits', in which doctors, nurses and other health care professionals systematically review clinical practice, a process formalized and emphasized in the 1989 White Paper *Working for Patients*. Suggestions for a similar process to assess the quality of policy advice by senior civil servants in Whitehall have been firmly resisted to date. But peer-group review was an important part of the formula used for the 'Rayner scrutinies' – the programme of investigations into discrete areas of departmental activities introduced by Margaret Thatcher's first efficiency adviser, Lord Rayner, in the early 1980s. These assessments were made by departmental civil servants themselves, eager to prove their mettle to Lord Rayner and the Cabinet.

There is a fine line between peer-group review and peer group competition, but peer-group competition too has been extensively used by the core executive, particularly to regulate previously autonomous professionals. Its most dramatic application has been to the publicly funded universities, which have had to compete for research ratings (since 1988) and teaching ratings (since 1992) awarded by committees of academics, the result of the rating assessments affecting each university's grant funding. The closest the core executive has come to increased application of peer-group competition to its own activities is in the 'PX' public spending regime introduced as 'EDX' in 1992 by the Major administration. The PX cabinet committee is in effect a revamped form of Treasury Board. In the old system spending negotiations between the Treasury and the departments worked through 'bilaterals', with a ministerial committee (the so-called 'Star Chamber') operating as a court of appeal rather than a forum for discussion. The new process specifies a global spending total in advance, meaning that ministers have to compete for shares of a fixed total sum, rather than log-rolling to push up the overall total.

But the 1990s generation of reforms seems to involve little conscious use of any of the three hybrids forms involving randomness. In an age when 'new right' ideas are widely seen as influential, it is noticeable that Niskanen's (1971, pp. 219–20) advocacy of random oversight of bureaucracies and programs has been ignored, while other features of his recipe have been enthusiastically adopted, such as outsourcing and performance pay. In those public services formerly dominated by strong professional groups with an ideology of collegial control (such as medicine and education), the reduced reliance on pure forms of mutuality has lead to wider use of more hybrid forms of mutuality. But there does not seem to have been any corresponding development of hybrids involving randomness.

Conclusion

The new Labour government will put its own spin on the 'new public management' – a convenient but imprecise label for a family of linked institutional reforms aiming to impose new forms of discipline on public service providers. The names of bodies may change. Administrative furniture will be rearranged. A Freedom of Information Act is promised to replace the current non-statutory arrangements. And the prospect of constitutional changes such as devolution may have considerable implications for the future operations of Whitehall and for the 'quango state' (see Chapter 7). A 'maximal' devolution settlement, including regional assemblies in England, could bring the 'quango state' under more democratic control and even offer a different way of organizing the national-scale executive agencies into which the Conservatives 'corporatized' the civil service. But this prospect seems remote at the time of writing. And even in Scotland and Wales a devolution settlement might be expected to lead to the creation of some new quangos, as well as putting the spotlight on judicial routes for handling intergovernmental conflicts.

However, there seems little possibility of any general return to the 'public bureaucracy state' of two decades ago, and some of the underlying trends towards re-regulation of the public services seem as likely to increase as to be reversed. Discussion of 'new public management' has focused on claims that 'reinventing government' on modern corporate-management lines will liberate public managers from stultifying systems of rules, and instead develop a more entrepreneurial, consumer-driven and strong leadership public service style controlled more by competition than by 'command and control' from the top. But the analysis here suggests that conventional interpretation captures only one part of the picture. Certainly, new forms of competition have been introduced in the public services to supplement traditional types, although whether that competition will prove durable is debatable. However, along with attempts to 'managerialize' and 'entrepreneurialize' public services has gone a marked extension and development of oversight – a growth of audit, inspection, grievance-handling and judicial review which introduce copious new bodies of rules and standard operating requirements.

This trend seems most unlikely to be reversed. Devolution may well add a new set of auditors and grievance-chasers, as well as 'probity police' attached to any new assemblies. And the general pressures for enhanced public audit and public service standard-setting (for example, across public education) seem unlikely to die down. Even for the political executive there have been signs of a development towards more formal oversight, not just in the growth of judicial review but also in changing arrangements for senior civil service appointments, quango appointments and the development of more formal codes of conduct for politicians. It is of course possible that the 1990s media and public concern about 'sleaze' may die down with the advent of a new government (as happened to some extent when Labour replaced the Conservatives in the mid-1960s after a long period in opposition). But it is equally possible that Labour's promise in opposition of enhanced emphasis on 'sleazebusting' machinery may herald the onset of the American syndrome of a self-fuelling anti-corruption industry which may or may not succeed in making government more honest but certainly imposes ever-more-stringent procedural and bureaucratic requirements on it, with steadily widening definitions of what counts as corruption and impropriety (see Anechiarico and Jacobs, 1996).

More generally, if the new regulatory configuration (of increased competition linked with increased oversight) continues to develop in UK government, costs as well as benefits can be expected. De-emphasizing two traditional recipes for control over bureaucracy – namely mutuality and contrived randomness – may have its downside. Among the potential costs of de-emphasizing mutuality is a further fragmentation of communication structures, emphasizing a weakness at the heart of most bureaucratic systems and possibly risking an increased incidence of the administrative disasters and policy fiascoes which Dunleavy (1995) claims to be characteristic of UK government (contrast Gray, 1996). Similarly, the lack of attention to randomness in regulating administration may produce controls that are too predictable to be effective. Whether such costs can be avoided by hybrid regulatory forms, intended to combine the best of all worlds, remains to be seen. Administrative reforms often produce unintended side-effects and reverse effects (Sieber, 1981), and there is no reason to suppose that 'new public management' will be an exception.

10

The Regulatory State

MARTIN LOUGHLIN AND COLIN SCOTT

Recently, there has been a discernible shift towards a regulatory mode of governance. This innovation has inspired commentators to talk of the emergence of 'the regulatory state', a distinctive style of governance which they see evolving throughout the industrialized world (Majone, 1994; Majone, 1996; McGowan and Wallace, 1996). In examining this trend, we must first try to identify this phenomenon. By 'regulation' we mean the attempt to modify the socially-valued behaviour of others by the promulgation and enforcement of systems of rules, typically by establishing an institutionally distinct regulator (Selznick, 1985; Ogus, 1994; Daintith, 1989). The increasing use of regulation as a formal instrument of government may thus arise because of the growing need to 'steer' the behaviour of a variety of actors – both public and private – who operate at some remove from the central state (Osborne and Gaebler, 1993). This certainly has occurred in the UK and the trend seems to be a consequence of certain basic changes in the role and structure of government.

One basic change which has occurred in government has been the separation of provision from production, or policy making from operational tasks. The most obvious examples of this phenomenon in the UK are found in the commercial sphere where the operational tasks associated with the production of utility services have been progressively privatized, while responsibility for policy over the provision of these services has been assigned both to new regulatory agencies, such as the Office of Telecommunications, and to sponsoring departments, such as the DTI. This movement, however, is simply illustrative of a more general shift visible throughout government: many of the operational tasks of central government have been hived off to 'Next Steps' or executive agencies, leaving policy making with the parent departments; through a series of reforms, most notably the regime of compulsory competitive tendering (CCT), local authorities have been obliged to differentiate their responsibility for the provision of a service from its production; and, within the National Health Service, hospital trusts, the producers of services, have been separated from health authorities who use purchasing responsibilities to regulate the supply and price of such services. It is as a consequence of such basic reforms that we see the emergence of the regulatory mode of governance. Consequently, although the state has long been involved in regulating business activity (Finer, 1932; Macdonagh, 1961; Parris, 1969), recent changes affecting both public and private sectors have meant that regulation, in our formal, institutionally-focused sense, is now emerging as a key mode of governance.

The shift towards the regulatory mode of governance in the UK may be viewed as a displacement of the welfare state model of government. Under the welfare state model, government functioned through relatively homogeneous units of public servants who constituted a permanent corps of officials employed on standard terms and conditions. The welfare state was a service-delivery state, in which government assumed responsibility not only for the provision of a wide range of services but also for their production. Relations within and between the various public sector bodies were relatively informal and opaque to the outsider. Relations between the welfare state and citizens were characterized by high levels of discretion. The breakdown of monolithic welfare state institutions through the separation of operations from policy making is nevertheless only one feature of the newly emergent regulatory mode of governance.

A second characteristic is the trend towards the creation of free-standing regulators. The regulatory offices in the utilities sectors are obvious examples, but the growing importance of regulators within government to oversee the public sector should not be under-estimated. Prominent examples include the National Audit Office and the Audit Commission, the new or reformed inspectorates such as those for prisons (1981) and schools (the Office for Standards in Education (Ofsted) 1992) and various new independent grievance handlers such as the Revenue Adjudicator (1992) and the Prisons Ombudsman (1994).

A third aspect of the regulatory mode of governance is a much greater formality than existed in the old bureaucratic arrangements which the regulatory mode partly replaces. This is evident in the increasing use of formal rules as instruments of guidance, whether in the licences of utility companies, the contracts for provision of local services or the Framework Documents governing relations between executive agencies and their sponsoring departments. Notwithstanding government attempts to the contrary, this may lead to lawyers becoming more centrally involved in regulating the governmental processes. Although in certain respects the regulatory mode allows greater discretion, for example in relation to pay and conditions of employees, in other respects there is less, as obligations and rights become more tightly defined. One general consequence, arguably, has been to render government arrangements more transparent.

The reasons for the shift towards the regulatory mode of governance seem to be primarily a response to the phenomenon of fiscal stress (Foster and Plowden, 1996) and are only partly ideological. The distrust of government bureaucracies which has characterized New Right governments in Britain and elsewhere can be rationalized as the product of the failure of government to deliver public services efficiently and effectively. It is thus not surprising to find that, as public bureaucracies have been broken down, new arrangements have been put in place which attempt to maintain government control (Hood and Scott, 1996). This trend towards instituting new mechanisms of oversight has been reinforced by a related ability of professional associations in such sectors as education, health and financial services to undertake self-regulation. New Right concerns with reduction of public expenditure, which provided part of the rationale for privatization, seem today to be equally important to left-leaning parties and governments. A final factor in the shift towards the regulatory mode of governance in the UK is membership of the European Union, with its new regulatory institutions and new systems of rules aimed at securing a level playing field for trade and more general European integration.

The new Labour government has already set about consolidating many of the reforms which contribute towards the regulatory state. Indeed, given the fiscal constraints which Labour has placed on itself, changing regulatory arrangements or providing new regulation may be attractive, as it has few expenditure implications. A number of themes of such change are emerging. First, the removal of some operational tasks from direct ministerial control is balanced by greater centralization in respect of other powers. For example, new legislation has transferred control over interest rates from the Chancellor of the Exchequer, Gordon Brown, to the Governor of the Bank of England (in a collegiate regime involving a new advisory board) (Chapter 14) and created a Food Standards Agency independent of the Ministry of Agriculture, Fisheries and Food (Chapter 17). But the role of the Cabinet Office in coordinating and regulating Whitehall has been enhanced, the Home Secretary, Jack Straw has reassumed parliamentary accountability for the operational aspects of prisons, and David Blunkett, the Education Secretary, has indicated a willingness to make greater use of his powers to close or take over failing schools. A second theme concerns the adoption of symbolic changes in regimes established by the Thatcher/Major administrations. While it is difficult confidently to separate substantial change from the merely symbolic, it is likely that new legislation to prioritize consumer protection in utilities legislation (being piloted by John Battle, the new utilities minister at the DTI), and to abolish the internal market in the National Health Service are in the latter category. On the other hand, institutional reforms in respect of utilities regulation, which may include creating a single Office of Communications (Murroni *et al.*, 1996) and a single energy regulator, are regarded as long overdue, and the one-off 'windfall tax' levied on utility companies will provide a substantial contribution to Chancellor Brown's first budget. A third theme of the new Labour government is a greater commitment to European norms, reflected in the Foreign Secretary, Robin Cook, seeking to expedite the UK's accession to the Social Chapter of the Maastricht Treaty (which will bring with it new regulatory requirements in respect of employment) and promising legislation to incorporate the European Convention on Human Rights into English law. This latter change will significantly extend the rights of individuals *vis-à-vis* government in the domestic courts.

Privatization and Regulation

Although the British state has been involved in regulating business for many centuries, the privatization of the utilities sectors in the 1980s and 1990s has given such regulatory activity a discrete institutional focus in the new regulatory offices which were modelled on the Office of Fair Trading (established in 1973). The privatization programme reflected a distrust in the public operation of services, which was rooted in a perception of inefficiency. This programme also delivered certain opportunistic benefits to the Thatcher governments, such as reducing public expenditure, widening share ownership and reducing the power of public sector trade unions.

Within the British political system the power of government to decide policy and implement it through legislation is virtually unqualified. Certainly there are few real political checks and, in contrast with France or the United States, no constitutional restrictions (Prosser and Graham, 1991). Consequently, consultation on the privatization programme was very limited and government was able to maximize benefits to itself, such as widening share ownership. This was achieved by privatizing the service providers in telecommunications (1984) and gas (1986) as virtual monopolies, rather than following the prescription of economists that they should have been broken up (as occurred in the United States with the private AT&T telephone company). Only in the later privatizations of electricity (1989) and rail (1993) was some degree of restructuring achieved (Scott, 1993), and only in the case of national (1980) and local (except London) buses (1985) was liberalization introduced on privatization (AMA, 1992).

The new regulatory arrangements for the privatized sectors also reflected the tradition of strong executive power. Notwithstanding the establishment of new regulatory offices, many key powers over the sector were retained by ministers through statutory powers to issue licences/authorizations, through the holding by government of 'golden shares' and rights to appoint directors to privatized firms, and certain rights to issues directions or guidance to the regulators. Further, the new regulatory offices (Oftel, 1984; Ofgas, 1986; Offer, 1989; Ofwat, 1990) were given virtually no powers to make regulatory rules. Consequently, although being given very demanding responsibilities, the regulators often found that, because of the failure to restructure the industries, they lacked the tools to carry out their tasks. And when regulators have made imaginative use of their limited powers to modify licences, regulated firms have complained vigorously that the actions are illegitimate and have mounted legal challenges (Graham, 1995).

Although the effectiveness of the new regulatory instruments associated with privatization has been constrained by the British state tradition, there is also evidence to suggest that this tradition is being changed by activity within these newly-regulated sectors. Consistent with tradition, they have little in the way of duties to consult formally over how they exercise their powers. Nevertheless, the separation of regulation from operation on privatization has, of itself, increased transparency (McEldowney, 1995) and the regulatory offices have sought to enhance their legitimacy by engaging in broader public discussion of their tasks than the legislation requires (National Audit Office, 1996). There is also some evidence of greater formalization in enforcement procedures, thereby challenging the general tradition in British regulation of closed and highly discretionary enforcement systems. These changes are likely to result in the emergence of a new and important body of regulatory law (McEldowney, 1995).

Deregulation and Self-Regulation

Alongside the new regulatory instruments associated with privatization, successive Conservative governments have promoted a policy of deregulation – defined as reducing unnecessary and over-intrusive regulatory requirements on business. This has been achieved, somewhat paradoxically, by providing for greater co-ordination of regulatory responsibilities by government departments. The Enterprise and Deregulation Unit (established in 1985) initially policed new government regulations and required every department to measure the costs to business of complying with new laws. However, since such compliance cost assessment did not balance costs against the social and economic benefits which might be derived, it is arguable that the deregulation policy effectively created a presumption against new regulation (Froud and Ogus, 1996).

A second plank to that deregulation initiative, the review of existing legislation, failed initially and was relaunched only in 1992 under the guidance of Michael Heseltine, then President of the Board of Trade, who promised a 'bonfire of red tape'. This was to be achieved through the Deregulation and Contracting Out Act 1994, which empowered ministers to amend primary legislation through statutory instruments whenever such modification reduced unnecessary regulatory burdens. Under the terms of this legislation, wide-ranging departmental reviews have been carried out and much legislation has been modified.

Consistent with a policy of pursuing the least burdensome means whenever some regulation is deemed to be necessary, government has also encouraged forms of self-regulation. Sometimes self-regulation has been mandated by statute (as with the Financial Services Act 1986); elsewhere, it has been encouraged by the threat of legislation (as with the Advertising Standards Authority and the Press Complaints Commission); and in a third set of cases, it has been established through the administrative scrutiny and approval of self-regulatory codes which meet certain minimum criteria (as with the codes approved by the Director General of Fair Trading under the Fair Trading Act 1973) (Black, 1996). The Blair government is exhibiting some scepticism about self-regulation, and in May 1997 announced the replacement of self-regulation of financial services with agency regulation by an enhanced Securities and Investment Board.

Euro-Regulation

Membership of the EC has produced both an important new source of regulatory rules for the UK and the establishment of new regulatory institutions at Community level (for example, in relation to competition and medicines). The EC has favoured regulation as a key instrument of European integration primarily because it possesses a very limited budget; though it has made use of expenditure programmes, as with the Common Agricultural Policy and Regional Policy, requiring member states to implement new common regulatory rules is likely to be a more cost-effective strategy. Although the setting of Community standards is increasingly being delegated to standard-setting institutions at Community (for example, CEN, CENELEC) and national (for example, DIN, AFNOR and the BSI) level (Scott, 1995, pp. 152–4), the UK government, in order to be able to demonstrate compliance, has generally sought to formalize and centralize the enforcement of Community norms (McGowan, 1995, p. 246). While the UK government has publicly expressed concern about the loss of sovereignty associated with EC membership, it has in fact been among the most assiduous of member states in adapting regulatory structures to meet Community obligations (Daintith, 1995).

The contemporary agenda for Community regulation is over-shadowed by twin concerns with legitimacy and effectiveness. Central to this discussion has been the issue of determining the appropriate level for regulation (Ogus, 1994, pp. 101–3). The development of new Community regulatory institutions, especially within the field of competition, is an important item on the agenda of the 1997 Inter-Governmental Conference which will determine Treaty amendments needed for the realization of the Community's continuing mission. At the previous IGC which led to the Maastricht Treaty (1992), the issues were partly resolved through Treaty amendments to incorporate a principle that regulation (and other tasks) within the Community be pursued at the lowest appropriate level for effectiveness (the principle of subsidiarity). The subsequent Commission review has resulted in certain Community standard-setting activities being abandoned (Maher, 1995). Consequently, the institutionalization of the principle of subsidiarity is likely to reduce the pace at which British regulatory regimes will have to change to meet Community obligations. In any case, the main instrument of Community legislation, the Directive, has permitted member states to adapt existing domestic regulatory regimes to incorporate new Community norms. Consequently, disruption of existing regulatory practice in the UK arising out of Community membership has been less than it would have been had completely external regulatory regimes been imposed (Maher, 1996).

Regulating the Public Sector

Thus far we have examined those aspects of the regulatory state associated with regulation of the private sector. In certain respects, however, the impact of this shift in style of governance has been more marked within the public sector, which has seen a greater degree of formalism, institutional differentiation and service specification. The separation of policy making from operational functions has been at the heart of a set of public sector reforms commonly referred to as the New Public Management (see Chapter 9). The governance of relations between these policy and operational units constitutes one of the most important challenges within the regulatory state (Foster and Plowden, 1996). A significant feature has been a greater formalization in intragovernmental relations, commonly expressed through documents with contractual or quasi-contractual status. Given the tradition of informality within British government, this often means in practice that relationships which are apparently designed to be governed by formal contractual documents are in fact managed by a mixture between contractual and traditional bureaucratic or hierarchical relations. Given that even within wholly private contractual relations there is often a hierarchical element which owes more to the relative power of the parties than to the terms of the contract, this feature of the new public management is not altogether surprising.

Regulation by Contract

Government has often used its power of procurement to require its suppliers to comply with certain policy objectives, for example in relation to paying employees fair wages (Daintith, 1979). The use of contracts as regulatory instruments in this manner has increasingly been rendered illegitimate by rules imposed on local government that 'non-commercial considerations' may not be taken into account in the selection of contractors (Radford, 1988), and by European Community procurement rules which attempt to prevent public authorities from favouring national suppliers over other suppliers from other member states (Fernandez-Martin, 1996). However, with the separation of operations from policy activity, regulation by contract has become an important part of intra-governmental relations (Harden, 1992). Problems arise for two main reasons: first, because the 'purchaser' is generally not the ultimate consumer of services which the operational unit is supplying and, secondly, because it may be very difficult to specify with precision what is being supplied. These problems, together with the difficulty of eradicating traditional practices rooted in bureaucratic or hierarchical relations, have caused considerable difficulties in practice. Take, for example, Next Steps agencies. Relations between sponsoring department and agency are supposed to be governed by a Framework Document, a form of non-enforceable contract which specifies the objectives and targets of the agencies. One set of problems arises where there are political aspects to the agency's task. To some extent these may be overcome by specifying in the Framework Document that certain classes of decision are to be reported to the sponsoring department; but this carries with it the expectation that ministers may intervene where matters are not to their liking. This is exemplified by the relationship between the Prison Service executive agency and the Home Office, where the routine and day-to-day intervention of ministers seems to have wholly undermined the policy/operations divide (Learmont Review, 1995, paras 3.83–86). Derek Lewis, the first director general of the Prison Service, has suggested that former Home Secretary Michael Howard redefined policy matters as those which are successful and operational matters as action in which the Prison Service fails. Thus, following a breakout from Parkhurst Prison, Howard was able to intervene to remove the governor of Parkhurst Prison (and in one commentator's view this fell outside the range of 'normal' operational decisions: Kemp, 1996) while at the same time still evading responsibility for the allegedly operational failures which led to the breakout and which ultimately resulted in the dismissal of the director general. The new Home Secretary, Jack Straw, has already responded to the deficiencies in the relationship by reassuming parliamentary accountability for the operational activities of the Prison Service. Thus, it is an openly hybrid arrangement, rather than an arm's-length relationship governed by quasi-contract, which falls to be evaluated.

Franchising

Related to the technique of regulation by contract is that of franchising. A franchise is a concession carved out of someone's right to own or operate some form of service, under which the franchisee is granted the right to operate that service for a certain period and on certain terms specified in the franchise contract.

Franchises are widely used in the private sector to allow companies such as McDonald's and Benetton to expand their operations and spread their brand without assuming the risks associated with owning and operating shops themselves. They supply the brand name and production or marketing methods to the franchisee in return for a fee. Franchisees have obligations to maintain the quality of the brand. Franchises have been used by government to allocate certain monopoly rights (for example, in relation to commercial broadcasting) and both to regulate service provision and to provide transparent methods of providing subsidies (as in the case of railways). In practice franchise contracts in the public sector have generally proved more interventionist than intended, as government invariably reserves the right to intervene and often has incentive to do so (Baldwin and Cave, 1996).

The franchise contracts allocated for the operation of railway services specify the obligations of the service-provider in terms of minimum service quality and the amount the franchisee should pay the government (in the case of a profitable line) or the amount of subsidy which the franchise attracts (in the case of an unprofitable line). But matters which are not relevant to the performance of the public task (such as the pay and conditions of employees) should in theory be left outside the terms of the contract. The tasks of allocating franchises and monitoring compliance have been allocated by government to the Office of Passenger Rail Franchising (Opraf, established 1993). It is clear, however, that there remain important political issues in which the minister will take an interest, notwithstanding the existence of the new arrangements. This is reflected in the power in the Railways Act 1993 for the minister to issue guidance to Opraf. Although in theory the new arrangements for franchising of the railways should remain free from political interference, the minister has used this power to issue directions that service frequency requirements in franchises should be based on the old British Rail timetable. This direction was issued so the minister could avoid the adverse political consequences involved in a drastic reduction in service frequency. When Opraf sought to award franchises giving wider market-based discretion to franchisees than the directions apparently permitted, the award of the franchise contracts was successfully challenged (*R* v *Secretary of State ex parte Save Our Railways*, 1995, Court of Appeal, unreported). The courts thus support the reality of the new arrangements, which constitute a hybrid of traditional hierarchical relations and contract over the new pure contractual model.

Audit and Charterism

Public sector reform since the 1980s raises important new issues of control and accountability. Many of the reforms have the effect of delegating managerial responsibilities that once were within the direct control of ministers. Since central government retains a profound interest in the financial control of new agencies and bodies (insofar as they remain responsible for public expenditure), they have developed new techniques and institutions of financial regulation to operate in conjunction with the new regulatory bodies (Hood and Scott 1996). Novel accountability issues arise primarily because of the greater distance between these new decision-making bodies and ministers, and this weakens the traditional practice of parliamentary accountability. Nevertheless, serious concerns have also been expressed about the tendency of the government to stock this growing range of non-departmental public bodies with its own supporters (Weir and Hall 1994) and during the 1990s the issue of 'Standards in Public Life' has rarely been far from the front pages of the press (Nolan Report, 1995).

New institutions for regulating public sector activities range from bodies operated and managed within central government, often having a brief to regulate across the whole of Whitehall (for example, the Citizen's Charter Unit and the Efficiency Unit) to bodies with a more discrete institutional existence and with greater independence to determine their direction and methods (for example, the Audit Commission and the National Audit Office). In between, there is a group of middle-range inspection bodies such as the Office for Standards in Education (Ofsted), the Inspectorate of Constabulary and the Prisons Inspectorate. What all these bodies have in common is a basic shift in orientation in which the traditional oversight values of probity and professionalism are being supplemented or displaced by concerns with efficiency and value for money (VFM) (Loughlin, 1992, ch. 4).

This trend is most clearly seen in the development of public audit. The Audit Commission was established in 1982 to provide a centrally co-ordinated oversight of local public expenditure (extended to health in 1990) and to extend the range of audit values from probity to VFM. The central government auditor, the National Audit Office, established in 1983, replaced the old Exchequer and Audit Department to provide a greater degree of independence from Parliament (to whom the NAO still reports) and to extend its values to include VFM. This broadening of the auditor's remit has resulted in a much greater emphasis on performance indicators, and thus a shift in focus from the traditional concerns with inputs (for example, pupil–teacher ratios) towards the output of public bodies (for example, school league tables based on exam performance). Key performance indicators have been those concerned with the relationship between costs and resources (*economy*), between resources and outputs (*efficiency*), and between outputs and outcomes (*effectiveness*). The growing use of such mechanisms has caused some to identify an 'audit explosion' in government (Power, 1994).

Accountability and contractualization were linked within the Conservative government's Citizen's Charter programme, which has been designed to raise the quality of public service through greater use of standards, openness, information, choice and new redress mechanisms. This programme is overseen by the Citizen's Charter Unit within the Cabinet Office. All departments are required to show how, in provision of services to the public, they have implemented the principles. Good performance is rewarded by the bestowal of Chartermark awards, which thus provide incentives to privatized utilities, local authority service providers and central government departments. Most of the principles underpinning the Citizen's Charter programme are culled directly from approaches to service quality in the private sector. In the use of such private sector ideas and the reliance on contractual or quasi-contractual instruments as the chief means of accountability for public service provision, government neglects the difference between public and private services and their providers. The notion of citizenship as a distinctly political relationship seems to have been abandoned in favour of a repackaging of the citizen as consumer (Barron and Scott, 1992).

Conclusion

The problems associated with the emergence of the regulatory state are not essentially political in any party political sense. Rather, the shift presents a more fundamental set of issues concerning the British state tradition. The basic difficulties we are experiencing in accommodating the regulatory mode of governance within the British tradition of parliamentary government may in fact cause us to question whether a distinctive 'regulatory state' has yet emerged in Britain, and it may be the case that, for some time to come, our arrangements will best be expressed as some form of hybrid. That is, notwithstanding the fact that the state apparatus has been transformed during 18 years of Conservative rule, those aspects of our state tradition which are inconsistent with the idea of the regulatory state still exert a major influence over contemporary practices.

Two problems evident in the new arrangements may be highlighted. First, there has been a strong tradition within the British system of vesting public power in ministers and, within the welfare state model which is being eclipsed, government departments are accustomed to being the pivotal institutions. The regulatory state model suggests that departments need to relinquish control over much day-to-day detail, whether in relation to social security payments, prisons, health care or the utilities sectors. The reluctance of ministers to give up control has meant that in some cases regulators have not been given the powers which they need to fulfil their responsibilities, and that when they do attempt to wield real power their legitimacy is threatened. In other instances ministers constantly intervene in matters which are supposed to be operational matters. At best, the tradition of ministerial power suggests that the regulatory state model can never be fully achieved and at worst the claimed benefits of the new administrative arrangements may be comprehensively undermined.

The second problem of the British state tradition is that it is rooted in informality. One consequence of this is that we have an underdeveloped system of administrative law and no general framework within which administrative agencies operate. The risks which are run here are either that the state rushes towards the over-legalization or juridification of matters where legal rules and procedure are unlikely to be conducive to good government (Stewart, 1985, Teubner, 1987, Loughlin, 1996, ch. 7), or that our failure to develop an adequate legal framework may damage the credibility of both the existing legal system and the new administrative arrangements.

11
Territorial Politics

IAN HOLLIDAY

At the centre of the Blair government's programme is a set of policies designed to reshape Britain's institutions of sub-central government and to redistribute powers between them and the Westminster Parliament in which governing authority – or sovereignty – has historically been concentrated. The key policies are creation of:

- a 129-member Scottish Parliament elected by the additional member scheme and having limited tax-raising powers, to be in place by 1999
- a 60-member Welsh Senedd also to be elected by the additional member system but not having tax-raising powers, to be in place by 1999
- a strategic authority for London covering the same territory as the old Greater London Council (which was abolished in 1986) but having wider powers and, more importantly, a directly-elected mayor, to be in place by 2000
- Regional Development Agencies in the rest of England, to be in place by 1999; in the more distant future, indirectly- and then directly-elected regional assemblies.

All the elected elements in this programme are subject to popular approval in a referendum.

This is an ambitious programme of change in a policy area marked by important issues of culture and identity, of sovereignty and subsidiarity, and of often significant technical detail. In this policy area many previous governments have come to grief. The mainly minority Labour governments of 1974–9, led by Harold Wilson and James Callaghan, struggled for years with the issue of devolution before being brought down by it. However, if the Blair government can effect real change here it will have a substantial impact on British politics, for what has traditionally been a London-centric system will be subject to real centrifugal pressures and will start to function in novel ways.

Territorial Politics in the UK

The territorial politics of the British state are odd. The very terminology is highly confusing, as use of the term 'British' (in, for example, the title of this book) properly refers only to the UK sub-nations of England, Scotland and Wales, and omits Northern Ireland. This usage reflects a gradual stitching together of the UK over many centuries, and also the very ambiguous place which first Ireland and then Northern Ireland have occupied in the Union. In this book a separate chapter (Chapter 12) is devoted to the politics of Northern Ireland.

The UK developed essentially through English conquest of Wales in 1536, union with Scotland in 1603 (crowns) and 1707 (parliaments), and domination of Ireland for much of the past millennium. The Act of Union 1801 which saw Ireland formally incorporated into the UK had to be revised following civil war in Ireland in 1916. Partition and creation of a free Irish state followed in 1921. Through each of these changes in the boundaries of the British state one territorial principle – that of the unitary state – became central. The great Victorian constitutionalist A. V. Dicey argued that the British constitution was dominated by the doctrine of parliamentary sovereignty, which states that whatever (the crown in) Parliament decrees is law (Dicey, 1915). Even at the end of the twentieth century, this doctrine retains an unchallenged primacy within the British constitution (Bogdanor, 1996).

Its consequence for territorial politics is that the UK has never had a formal and entrenched division of powers such as is found in federal systems (like the USA or Germany). Although it has had subordinate assemblies – in, for example, Scotland in the seventeenth century and Northern Ireland in the twentieth – they have not had any constitutional significance or protection. The powers of Stormont, which was created as Northern Ireland's Parliament in 1921, were simply abrogated by Edward Heath's government in 1972 and transferred to a Secretary of State.

This was, however, entirely characteristic of the British way of handling territorial politics, which has been by political centralization in Westminster and Whitehall and some measure of administrative decentralization in the UK sub-nations. The main form of political representation for territorial interests has always been through the Westminster Parliament, where all sub-nations except England are now over-represented. Scotland, for example, elects 72 MPs, which is some 14 or 15 more than is justified on the basis of its population. Additionally, each sub-nation except England now has its own territorial office, headed by a cabinet minister with a small office in London and substantial offices in the leading city (Edinburgh, Cardiff and Belfast) of the relevant sub-nation. The Scottish Office was established in 1885, the Welsh Office in 1964 and the Northern Ireland Office in 1972. In different ways these offices replicate the structure of the British state itself and generate a situation in which a quasi-prime ministerial figure exists within each of the UK sub-nations. Crucially, however, that figure is but one member of a cabinet of 20 or more members, and is thereby constrained in significant ways. In England, there is no equivalent structure. In recent years important changes have however been made to English administration. These reforms were flagged up in the Conservatives' 1992 manifesto, spelt out in detail by Environment Secretary John Gummer in November 1993, and put into effect in April 1994. They comprised creation of integrated regional offices and institution of a single regeneration budget (SRB). Central to this change was harmonization of previously distinct regional boundaries employed by government departments such as Environment, Trade and Industry, and Transport (Hogwood, 1995, p. 272). Linked to it was the SRB, presided over by EDR, a cabinet committee on regeneration chaired by the Environment Secretary. In July 1995 this committee was fused with several others to form EDC, a very large cabinet committee on competitiveness chaired by Deputy Prime Minister Michael Heseltine (Burch and Holliday, 1996, p. 85). The intention was to generate increased coherence and effectiveness in English sub-central administration (Chapter 10). The new government office regions are shown in Table 11.1.

TABLE 11.1   British government office regions since April 1994

Region	Population (m)	Region	Population (m)
North East	2.5	London	6.8
North West	5.3	South East	7.5
Merseyside	1.4	South West	4.6
Yorks/Humberside	4.8	West Midlands	5.2
East Midlands	4.0	Scotland	5.0
Eastern	5.1	Wales	2.8

Source: Hogwood (1995, p. 274).

Territorial Politics and the 1997 General Election

The 1997 general election, like each of its predecessors for three decades, showed that a clear territorial dimension also exists in British electoral politics (Table 11.2). Labour won an absolute majority of votes in Wales and the three northernmost regions of England. It came close to winning a majority of votes in London, the East and West Midlands and Scotland. The Conservatives fared badly in all these regions, securing no seats at all in Scotland and Wales. In the South East (outside London), however, the Conservatives won a plurality of votes and more than twice as many seats as Labour. More than half of all Conservative MPs now hold seats in London and the South East. In the South West Labour was pushed into third place behind the Conservatives and the Liberal Democrats. Beyond the three main parties, nationalist parties made significant showings in Scotland (where the Scottish National Party (SNP) won 22 per cent of the vote and six seats) and Wales (where Plaid Cymru won 10 per cent of the vote and 4 seats). The sectarian parties which triumphed in Northern Ireland were entirely different from those which fought the election on the mainland.

The Labour Party actually won in 1997, having lost four successive general elections prior to that, by significantly increasing its vote in England. By taking its share of the English vote from 34 per cent in 1992 to 44 per cent in 1997, Labour raised its number of English seats from 196 to 329. Its largest gains were in

TABLE 11.2   Regional distribution of UK seats and votes for the three
main parties at the 1997 general election

	% vote			MPs elected		
	Lab	Con	Lib Dem	Lab	Con	Lib Dem
Wales	55	20	12	34	0	2
Scotland	46	18	13	56	0	10
England	44	34	18	329	165	34
North	61	22	13	32	3	1
North West	54	27	14	60	7	2
Yorks/Humberside	52	28	16	46	7	2
London	49	31	15	57	11	6
East Midlands	48	34	13	31	14	0
West Midlands	48	34	14	44	14	1
East Anglia	38	39	18	8	14	0
South East	32	41	21	36	73	8
South West	26	37	31	15	22	14

the South East (31) and London (25). However, Labour retains a
higher and more loyal following in Scotland and Wales, and is
expected by its long-suffering supporters to deliver on territorial
political promises made in the years of opposition from 1979 to
1997. This is one key reason why territorial issues figure so
prominently on the Blair government's agenda.

Territorial diversity in British electoral outcomes is by no means
unprecedented. In the nineteenth century Scotland and Wales
were both bastions of Liberalism. In the twentieth, Wales moved
strongly towards Labourism whereas Scotland experienced brief
Conservative dominance in mid-century before also becoming
strongly Labourist (Midwinter *et al.*, 1991). Since its creation at
the start of the 1920s Northern Ireland has been fiercely unionist,
but not always supportive of the Conservative (and Unionist)
party. England has always tended towards Conservatism, though
it too has experienced significant regional variations on this
theme.

Despite this, there was a period after the second world war
when Britain's multinational character was thought to be largely
irrelevant to its political system. Peter Pulzer famously wrote in
1967 that 'Class is the basis of British party politics; all else is
embellishment and detail' (Pulzer, 1967, p. 98). His timing could

not have been more unfortunate. In the very years in which these words were written and published, the 'embellishment and detail' which Pulzer dismissed began to reassert themselves as key bases for British party politics. In July 1966, Plaid Cymru won a parliamentary seat from Labour at a by-election in Carmarthen. In November 1967, the SNP also secured a by-election victory over Labour in Hamilton. In October 1968, civil strife erupted on the streets of Northern Ireland. Ever since, British party politics has had an important territorial dimension.

Territorial Politics in the Conservative Years

In recent years almost all political parties have reacted to the oddity of Britain's territorial arrangements and the territorial dimension in voting patterns by proposing some form of constitutional change. In April 1995 a Constitution Unit was also established in London to sponsor independent inquiry into constitutional change. It published three authoritative reports on devolution in June 1996 (Constitution Unit, 1996a, 1996c, 1996d). Proposals for change have often been widely supported, and with good reason. Scots and Welsh did not wholly appreciate voting Labour but ending up with Conservative governments for four successive general elections. The policy fiasco of early introduction of the community charge (or poll tax) in Scotland merely compounded this problem (Butler *et al.*, 1994). Irish and continental European experience also appears to show that decentralized structures are necessary to regional economic coherence (Rhodes, 1996), and it is certainly the case that regional political institutions have developed in many west European countries in recent years (Sharpe, 1993). Furthermore, some hold that British exceptionalism within the EU is increasing and needs to be addressed (Keating and Jones, 1995). This has been exposed chiefly by EU procedures for distribution of structural funds, which require that bids be developed and submitted on a regional basis. It has also been revealed by creation of the Committee of the Regions (under Article 198 of the Maastricht Treaty on European Union), to which Britain is unique among major member states in sending no elected regional representatives. On top of all this, there are many cultural and emotional arguments for change.

The single significant exception to the party political consensus that major reform is needed is the Conservative party. Thus pressure for territorial change has not swept the entire political landscape in the way that was managed by, say, Keynesian economic orthodoxy in the years after the Second World War. Under both Margaret Thatcher and John Major, the Conservative party was deeply committed to the formal status quo (Holliday, 1997). In this statement the chief stress falls on 'formal', for in the years of Conservative government from 1979 to 1997 substantial changes to territorial political arrangements were in fact made. Most importantly, these comprised the stripping of local government functions and indeed the disintegration of local governance which has been extensively documented by many commentators (Chapter 13). Powers that had been exercized by local councils moved in a series of directions: to local people, to non-elected quangos operating locally, regionally and nationally, and to central government. Very few new powers were conferred on local government itself by the Thatcher and Major governments. In addition, Conservative governments after 1979 undermined many regional policy structures developed in the 1960s and 1970s. In 1979, regional economic planning councils were abolished (except in Scotland, where a Scottish Economic Council continued to function), and cash was diverted away from regional policy. In the 1980s, the privatization drive removed important regionalized bodies from the public sector (Hogwood, 1995, pp. 267–8). In the 1990s, reforms in the NHS shifted control away from regional structures to the NHS Executive in Leeds (Holliday, 1995). However, not all Conservative initiative was negative and centralizing. In a series of ways – economic, political, cultural and administrative – the Conservatives sought to make a positive case for the Union and to sustain themselves in increasingly adverse circumstances.

The economic case had many dimensions, some of which were related to the Scots' 'tartan tax' debate which is discussed later. Central to it was, however, the contention that the inward investment secured by Britain's sub-nations and regions in the 1980s and 1990s could be seriously jeopardized by reform. This was, in fact, the precise opposite of the argument advanced by nationalist and regionalist groups (Burch and Holliday, 1993; Hutton, 1995). Moreover, here the stakes were high. When, in July 1996, Wales beat Scotland to secure inward investment of £1.7 billion by the LG Group of Korea, it set a new EU record. In overall terms, Britain is the leading recipient of inward investment in the EU (*Economist*, 13 July 1996, p. 24).

Politically, the Conservatives insisted to Scots and Welsh that both domestically and within the EU their best representation was to be gained through a Secretary of State with full membership of cabinet, rather than through a subnational parliament or assembly. This argument did not have a clear English equivalent, though to consider the concerns of Londoners the Conservatives did create EDL(L), a cabinet committee for London chaired by the Environment Secretary. The Conservatives also made a series of small changes designed to undermine more radical reformist plans. In Scotland, for example, they transferred Grand Committee meetings to Edinburgh in an attempt to give Scotland more voice in its own government.

Culturally, the Conservatives made changes which were viewed by many as pure tokenism, but which were nevertheless key parts of their resistance to reform. Among the more notable was Major's return of the historic Stone of Scone, held in England for some 700 years, to Scotland at the end of 1996. It was accompanied by small increases in funding for Scottish historical scholarship and related matters. No equivalent gesture was made to the Welsh, and none was envisaged for the English regions. Here, however, the Conservative cultural strategy was different, comprising only an attempt to stress the unity of the nation and the dangers inherent in any policy which might divide it.

The Conservatives' most important (and often least noticed) initiatives were administrative. In Scotland and Wales they radically altered the local government structure, creating a set of unitary authorities which could be claimed to make a further strategic tier unnecessary on strict efficiency grounds (Chapter 13). They also made changes within the structure of the state, establishing distinct government agencies in Scotland in particular. In April 1989, Scottish Homes and Housing for Wales were set up. In April 1991 Scottish Enterprise (and Highlands and Islands Enterprise) were established. In April 1992, Scottish Natural Heritage was created. In April 1993, separate Scottish and Welsh Higher Education Funding Councils were set up. More generally, the 'taking stock' of administrative arrangements in Scotland and Wales which John Major promised in the run up to the 1992 general election had some positive effects with, for example, responsibility for the arts in Scotland being transferred to the Scottish Office (Hogwood, 1995, p. 288–9). Administrative changes (mentioned above) were also made to the government of England.

The net effect of the Conservative reforms was to streamline the regional profile of the British state. The reforms were not comprehensive, and many incoherences remain. Even in departments which have adopted the new English regional boundaries, some agencies – such as the Highways Agency in the Department of Transport – use different ones (Hogwood, 1995, p. 276). However, at the end of the Conservative years there was a more authoritative regional division of England than the chaos of regional boundaries which had previously existed, and there was more administrative decentralization.

None of this was viewed as enough by any of the Conservatives' critics. Perhaps most important in building a coalition for change was the Scottish Constitutional Convention (SCC), which first met on 30 March 1989 and brought together a very wide spectrum of Scottish interests, ranging from political parties to organized interests (like local government and trade unions) and voluntary organizations (like churches and charities). Indeed, only the Conservative party and (for odd reasons which will be analyzed later) the SNP were not formally represented at the SCC. Most of the Convention package was presented to the Scottish people on St Andrew's Day, 30 November 1990. Its central elements were a Scottish parliament with tax-raising powers elected by proportional representation and a Scottish bill of rights (Marr, 1992, pp. 205–8). In Wales too a broad consensus of opinion developed in favour of a devolved assembly, with virtually unanimous support in Labour ranks. Both changes revealed a dislike of sometimes autocratic government by 'alien' English ministers, especially under Thatcher. They also reflected a growing recognition among Scottish and Welsh elites – in both the public and private sectors – that national government was not an appropriate organizational level for managing industrial policy in an emergent 'Europe of the regions'.

Implementing Labour's Programme

The Blair government's initiatives build on this activity. They form a rolling programme of devolution in two senses. On the one hand, more powers will be transferred sooner to Scotland than to Wales, which in turn will be ahead of any of the English regions (except London). On the other, the powers that are transferred in the initial phase of activity can be expected to be just the first step in a series of sovereignty transfers which will progressively reshape the British state. In England the first stage of Regional Development Agencies and a programme of regional consultation is expected to be followed by indirectly-elected assemblies and eventually directly-elected assemblies. It is however possible that some regions could progress more rapidly through this series of stages than others.

Initially, the most important individuals in implementing Labour's programme are ministers and officials at the centre of the state which is about to be decentralized. Here the key ministerial figures are:

• Prime Minister Tony Blair, who chairs the cabinet committee on Constitutional Reform Policy, CRP, with a membership of 13.
• Lord Chancellor Lord Irvine, who is known to be personally very close to Blair and who chairs the cabinet committee on Devolution to Scotland and Wales and the English Regions, DSWR, with a membership of 19.
• Scottish Secretary Donald Dewar and Welsh Secretary Ron Davies who take creation of national assemblies to be their primary responsibility.
• Deputy Prime Minister John Prescott who is also Secretary of State for the Environment, Transport and the Regions and who is overseeing all aspects of English regionalization; Prescott chairs the cabinet sub-committee on London, GL(L), with a membership of 12; his Minister for London is Nick Raynsford.

In each case, the government's approach involves securing parliamentary consent for a precise question on devolution to be put to the people in a referendum, publishing its proposals in detailed form by means of a white or green paper, and leading the campaign for a 'Yes' vote in the relevant areas of Britain. It also comprises planning for transfers of powers to devolved assemblies.

Labour's huge majority in the House of Commons, reinforced by the very poor showing of the anti-devolution Conservative party in the 1997 general election, provides it with ample political resources for each of these stages of activity. On the results of the 1997 general election, however, Labour on its own would not secure a governing majority in the Scottish Parliament, though it would in a Welsh Senedd. Both are to be elected on a system of proportional representation. For this and other reasons, there are therefore tensions within all British political parties which could affect the course of events in this sphere.

Territorial Politics and the British Party System

Party political positions on reform sometimes alter and are often internally contested and divisive. It is clear that proposals for change cannot be placed on a simple left–right axis, with the left being pro change and the right anti (Holliday, 1994). Instead, the politics of power distribution within the state must be viewed as separate from the politics of resource distribution within society, and generate a two-by-two matrix which places a centralization-decentralization axis across the standard left-right axis. The resultant four quadrants are (a) old left committed to nationalization and centralization, (b) authoritarian right committed to parliamentary sovereignty, (c) new left committed to decentralization and empowerment and (d) enabling right committed to local distinctiveness (Figure 11.1).

FIGURE 11.1 Matrix of positions on resource distributions within society and power distributions within the state

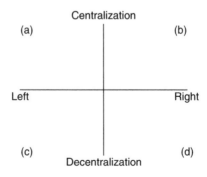

Labour

In contrast to its present position, the Labour Party has been essentially centralist for much of its history. In 1945 the Attlee administration sought to implement a series of reforms which was both socialist and centralist. In 1956 party leader Hugh Gaitskell told the Scottish party that Labour was officially unionist (Marr, 1992, p. 106). This strand of thinking was still prominent in the Labour Party during the devolution debates of the 1970s, when left-wing Labour MPs expressed deep hostility to reform. Prominent among them was Neil Kinnock, who held devolution to be a betrayal of class politics (Marr, 1992, p. 142). For many years, then, many Labour activists could be placed in quadrant (a) of Figure 11.1.

Today much of the Labour Party is located in quadrant (c): the days of statist solutions to economic and social problems are long gone and the party is officially committed to real measures of decentralization. The reasons for this shift are many. At an ideological level the party now has a much weaker commitment to egalitarianism than was once the case, and has thus lost the key rationale for its earlier centralism. Structurally, Labour is a strongly non-metropolitan party, and the fact that its MPs, local councillors and activists come predominantly from outside London and the home counties has been an important element in its support for territorial change. In terms of party competition the party has had to espouse some form of nationalism to protect its crucial Scottish and Welsh votes from the SNP and Plaid Cymru. In terms of political experience the party spent so long on the political sidelines in the 1980s and 1990s that it was almost bound to develop a critique of the centralized state. However, Labour is by no means unified on territorial issues. Even within the Scottish and Welsh Labour parties there have been important sectarian splits over issues such as a PR base for devolved assemblies (to which Labour is now committed). In Wales in particular this has been deeply divisive, with many Labour activists retaining a commitment to majoritarianism even though this is patently unworkable as a way forward.

It now seems likely that the main pressures the government will face from within the Labour Party will be for more rather than less decentralization. Those pressures could, however, be contradictory. In parts of England like the North East, where regional identity is comparatively strong and regional activism has been evident for some years in coalitions of political and business leaders, pressure from the regional Labour elite to speed the process of change is likely to be very strong. The fact that the North East borders Scotland has always made it very conscious of developments there, and the creation of a Scottish Parliament could have substantial knock-on effects. However in the North West, which also borders Scotland, pressures for a single regional authority could be less great because in the region's two main cities, Liverpool and Manchester, Labour activists are often more interested in developing city regions than an over-arching regional authority. This sort of conflict could also be witnessed in other parts of England where regional boundaries are contested and no clear regional capital exists. The current South West region stretches from Cornwall to Wiltshire and has very little sense of identity. The process of English regionalization could therefore be long and complex.

Conservative

The Conservative Party was so marginalized in the 1997 general election, and its stance on devolution was so manifestly rejected by the voters, that it might be considered irrelevant to change in this sphere. However, as the major opposition party to Labour, and as the UK's historic governing party, the Conservative Party should not be overlooked as Britain strives to develop a territorial distribution of power which can secure all-party support.

The Conservative Party has historically been unionist to the extent that it even incorporates this term in its full title. It is a quintessentially English party, with its tone being set chiefly by MPs, councillors (few in number though they have been in recent years) and activists drawn from London and the home counties. Only rarely has the Conservative Party been a proponent of territorial political change. Under Edward Heath, whose 'Perth pledge' of May 1968 committed a Conservative government to creating an elected Scottish assembly, the party spent an uncomfortable few years being officially devolutionist (Bogdanor, 1980). At this time it just moved into the bottom half of Figure 11.1, locating itself near the top of quadrant (d). However, even when devolution was party doctrine many Conservatives retained the centralist unionism which has long been an important part of party identity, and under the leaderships of Thatcher and Major – both of whom were instinctive unionists and centralists – the party returned to the position of fierce unionism with which most Conservative activists are most happy.

Under William Hague's leadership, much of the Conservative Party is thus located in quadrant (b). Their case has a series of dimensions. Often it develops into a form of constitutional romanticism which holds that the British constitution has evolved into something so very close to perfection that it should now bring many centuries of change to a halt. It is hard to find a rationale for this argument. Sometimes it contends that institutional re-engineering is merely the latest refuge of an intellectually bankrupt left (Willetts, 1992, p. 152). The implication of this charge is twofold: that here, as in the economic sphere in the 1960s and 1970s, the left will find that political reality confounds its neat schemes; and that, as in the economic sphere in the 1980s and 1990s, the right will again secure an intellectual victory. Although there may be something in this, it is hardly adequate as a response to the many pressures for change which have emerged in recent years. Often it takes the line advanced most forcefully by Major, that the Union will collapse if its delicate balance is tinkered with.

At the heart of much of the Conservative case against reform has been the 'tartan tax' debate. By raising the spectre of the tartan tax, Major's last Scottish Secretary Michael Forsyth sought to convince Scots that they would suffer direct material loss if they were to vote for a Scottish Parliament. In fact, the financial freedom proposed for that parliament by the Labour Party is so feeble that the most tax it could levy on any Scot in a single year is a mere £648 (*Economist*, 13 July 1996, p. 31). Nevertheless, the effectiveness of the 'tax bombshell' campaign in the 1992 general election made this a potent argument which caused Labour strategists much concern.

The extent of the 1997 electoral disaster has however made it clear to much of the Conservative Party and elite that they must now take decentralization plans seriously and play a meaningful part in debates about subnational assemblies. The Scottish party is particularly divided over this issue, with pro-devolution activists who were marginalized during the Major years arguing that the only way in which Conservatives can hope both to rebuild their electoral strength and to influence the course of debate is by making a positive commitment to devolution. In doing so, Conservatives can readily draw on a series of traditional party principles. These include a commitment to the decentralization of power, a belief in the vitality and integrity of local communities, a suspicion of the central state, a faith in the diversity of those elements which have been brought together to form the UK, and a recognition that the British constitution is in a permanent state of evolutionary change (Burch and Holliday, 1992). Following the centralist politics of the Thatcher years in particular, many Conservatives may now seek to recover their decentralist heritage so that the party can compete both nationally and within the regional electoral systems which are in the process of being created.

Scottish National

The SNP was formed in 1934 from a merger of the National Party of Scotland (formed in 1928) and the Scottish Party (formed in 1932). Although it won a Westminster seat at a by-election in April 1945, it quickly lost it at the general election of July 1945 and did not have further such success until 1967. It has since been an important, but never quite central, force in Scottish politics. Throughout its existence, the SNP has obviously been positioned in the bottom half of Figure 11.1.

The party has, however, had important internal debates about its precise placement in that part of the matrix. Indeed, for much of the 1970s and early 1980s, the relationship between nationalism and socialism was a key area of debate. Under the Callaghan government of 1976–9, Jim Sillars led a group which broke away from the Labour Party to form the Scottish Labour Party (SLP). The SLP was explicit in its attempt to fuse socialism and nationalism, and generated support within the SNP to the extent that it was eventually incorporated within it. However, other members of the SNP were deeply hostile to any prioritization of socialism (and to Sillars personally), arguing that the nationalist aim should be absolutely core. Although the SNP retains a left-wing orientation, this view has tended to prevail in the 1990s under the leadership of Alex Salmond.

At the same time, a debate about the SNP's position on the centralization–decentralization axis has developed. Few in the SNP seek anything other than Scottish independence. However, the tactics appropriate to attainment of this goal have become a central issue for the party in recent years. The position taken by it during the 1987–92 Parliament, when the SCC was formed, was absolutist and extremist, and resulted in its non-participation in the Convention. Similarly, in the 1992 general election campaign the party sought immediate separation from the UK under the slogan 'Free by '93'. The result was a rather disappointing poll of 22 per cent and election of only three MPs. Largely in consequence, the party has subsequently altered its strategy so that now, although it continues to seek independence as an ultimate goal, it is prepared to take something of a gradualist route to it. This means that it proposes to participate in the Scottish Parliament which the Labour government wants to set up, believing that this can be used as a stepping stone to independence. It now has a very strong tactical position, being well placed to benefit from whatever befalls the Scottish Parliament. Success can be interpreted as evidence that Scotland needs to take more control of its own affairs. Failure can be put down to the hamstrung nature of the parliament and would thus be equally useful as an argument for further change.

Plaid Cymru

In Wales Plaid Cymru similarly operates in the bottom half of Figure 11.1, and is committed to independence for Wales. It is, however, a more marginal party than the SNP, being strong in north and west Wales but very weak in the more populous southern parts of the country.

Plaid was formed in 1925, and registered the first nationalist success of the new wave of mobilization which began to sweep the British polity in the mid-1960s. It has, however, never been a central force even in Welsh politics, and since 1979 has not polled more than 10 per cent of the Welsh vote in a general election. For much of its history the party has been divided between cultural and economic/social nationalists. In the 1980s it became quite socialist as the latter group gained an upper hand. In the 1990s, by contrast, it has been more interested in cultural and environmental concerns, and has developed electoral alliances with the Greens (Lynch, 1995). In the 1992 general election one MP was elected by this alliance.

Liberal Democrat

The Liberal Democrats and their predecessor parties have a long and distinguished history of operation in the bottom half of Figure 11.1: in either quadrant (c) or quadrant (d). Indeed, what has long been most distinctive about British Liberalism has been not its placement on the left–right axis but its placement on the centralization–decentralization axis. In the home rule debates of the late nineteenth and early twentieth centuries the Liberal Party was a leading proponent of reform, advocating 'home rule all round' on the eve of the first world war. In the years of its political marginalization which followed that war the party continued to be strongly decentralist in orientation. In part, this reflects its strength in the Gaelic fringe of British politics: parts of Scotland, Wales and the English South West.

Today, Liberal Democrats are strongly in favour of a decentralization of power to sub-national and regional assemblies, and tend to operate very much at the bottom of Figure 11.1 on the border between quadrants (c) and (d). Much of their inspiration is now European, and they contend that in this sphere (as in many others), the UK has moved too far from the EU mainstream.

Managing Territorial Political Change

A key Conservative charge has been that Labour's territorial plans represent dangerous constitutional innovation. This is, in fact, hard to square with the historical record which contains clear evidence of territorial assemblies and other change in territorial structures (Mount, 1992). Indeed, creation of a domestic variant of the variable geometry which is emerging within the EU could easily be said to build on constitutional practice from Britain's past. This is not, however, to say that territorial political change presents no potential problems. Indeed, it is quite possible that the Blair government could find itself facing serious difficulties in this sphere.

Within British sub-nations, the basis on which decentralized assemblies will operate is a potentially substantial problem. Labour has attempted to address part of it by holding a separate referendum question on the 'tartan tax' issue. It has also adopted a very minimalist position on the question of decentralized assembly resources, proposing little freedom of financial manoeuvre for a Scottish Parliament and even less for other bodies. It seems unlikely that this kind of stance will satisfy the majority of local opinion in areas which are allowed their own assembly. However, there is also the real possibility that majority opinion outside regional assemblies' terrain will object to any significant decentralization of power. In this respect, the argument really is in the detail. Relations with the Westminster Parliament raise a series of questions. Central to them is of course the division of responsibilities between the central and local assemblies.

The knock-on effects which could develop in this sphere have long been the spectre at this particular feast. To put it at its most succinct, is the break-up of Britain the logical consequence of any real decentralization of power to national and regional assemblies (Nairn, 1977)? The Conservative Party, with its long and sustained tradition of unionism, argues that it could be. Others argue that it is not, and that in fact Britain can only be held together if some power concentrations at the centre are dispersed. It is possible that the Labour government's policy of referenda all round is the perfect answer to this problem. Unless majority popular support can be secured for the idea of a particular assembly, it is unlikely to develop a popular base. This should mean that assemblies only emerge where there is real popular support for them: certainly in Scotland and London, probably in Wales and the North East of England, possibly nowhere else. However, there is a chance that the Spanish experience will be replicated in the UK. This is that the process of regionalization establishes a kind of regional virility test in which very few regions are willing to settle for less than the very best on offer. But maybe this chance is limited in tax-resistant Britain where arguments of potential cost will always prove forceful elements in any 'No' campaign. The limited nature of English regional identity is also likely to undermine full-blown regionalism, though it may have little impact on the emergence of Regional Development Agencies with a quasi-democratic underpinning.

At Westminster the core long-term problem relates to the 'West Lothian' question, named after Tam Dalyell's constituency. Central to this question are the rights of Scottish MPs in the House of Commons. Will they, for example, have the right to vote on English legislation governing matters which in Scotland had been devolved to a Scottish Parliament? There is, however, a wider question relating to the security that decentralized assemblies could enjoy in the absence of a written constitution. Enoch Powell, a trenchant opponent of change, is clear that there is none (Marr, 1992, p. 122). It is also evident that a written constitution would be a major constitutional innovation for the British. Are relations between the Westminster parliament and decentralized assemblies therefore likely to be condemned to substantial conflict and instability? Many fear that the answer to this question is yes.

Additionally, there is the question of representation at Westminster and Whitehall. When, for example, a Scottish Parliament is established, will Scots be entitled to over-representation at Westminster? What, moreover, will become of the Secretaries of State for Scotland and Wales in the event of real decentralization? These are key questions to which the Labour government does not as yet have clear answers. Any attempt to fudge them could have negative consequences in the long run.

The Future

This policy area is fraught with problems. It taps into issues of culture and identity which have been found not only in other parts of the world but also within the UK (in Northern Ireland) to be only marginally susceptible to negotiation and compromise. As it happens, territorial debate in England, Scotland and Wales has been very peaceful to date, but that should not be allowed to obscure the depth and sensitivity of some of the issues involved here. In addition, this whole area links into issues of sovereignty and subsidiarity which have been so contentious for Britain in the EU that no government is going to be anything other than extremely wary about them domestically. Furthermore, it raises the technical issues which have already been discussed.

The Labour Party – in opposition and now government – has been so cautious in pursuing this agenda that the main danger which faces it is of failing to deliver on widely-held expectations. Its policy of referenda all round actually makes a lot of sense, but the dual referenda policy in Scotland won it few friends and suggested to many that Labour could fail to deliver on large parts of the agenda for change. The key question is whether it would matter if this turned out to be the case.

Some would of course argue that this was positively a good thing. This continues to be the official Conservative position, and would certainly be welcome to many in the party's ranks. However, given the sustained campaign for change in Scotland in particular it is hard to believe that this position is really sustainable. Soon the Conservative Party must resuscitate the decentralist elements of its tradition and seek to play a positive part in reform debates (Burch and Holliday, 1992). Then there is a chance that real decentralization will take place and have a secure place in the British political system.

The likely impact of such a change is hand to assess. The possible benefits of change can certainly be overstated. The vaunted economic and political importance of German regions is unlikely to be replicated in the UK because it derives from pre-existing economic patterns and constitutional arrangements at the centre of the state (Minns and Tomaney, 1995). On the one hand, the German economy has no single dominant region, whereas in Britain the London and the South East are very dominant and could easily remain so. On the other, German regions have a voice at the very centre of the German state through representation in the upper house of parliament (the *Bundesrat*) and an entrenched place in the policy process, neither of which currently features in British government plans. Similarly, the possible downside of change can also be exaggerated. The apocalyptic view which sees a break-up of Britain further down this particular road ignores the fact that the British state has changed its territorial arrangements at many points in its history without disintegrating. Indeed, a break-up of Britain is more likely to be averted than promoted by change which meets the clear desires of Scots in particular.

It is in fact likely that the most important impact of decentralization on British politics will be the change it makes to the

functioning of the system. The British state has been focused on London for so long that even Labour's programme of incremental reform will come as something of a shock. It will oblige politicians and civil servants – who have always looked to the centre – to start looking to some of the peripheries in some policy making. It will also change the political loyalties and possibly even the identities of voters. It will require political coalitions to be built on explicitly territorial bases. As such, it could set in train an important process of political reorientation, away from the hitherto dominant Westminster and Whitehall and towards regional capitals in key parts of Britain.

12
Northern Ireland

ARTHUR AUGHEY

Northern Ireland policy is the encounter of imaginative official enterprises (wise or not) with the prevailing and predictable dogmatic style of local politics (wise or not). This chapter examines the continuing process of policy initiatives undertaken by the British government, often in co-operation with the Irish government, and outlines the likely limitations of such enterprises when they confront the traditional concerns of Northern Ireland's political actors.

The Downing Street Declaration

In 1993, British government policy on Northern Ireland changed tack. Hitherto, the purpose of official policy had been to marginalize the terrorists and their political advocates, in particular, Sinn Fein and the IRA. The Anglo-Irish Agreement of 1985 had been based explicitly on that policy and Margaret Thatcher had hoped to recruit the Irish government to that task. Political agreement between constitutional parties, it was believed, would have to come first and such agreement would be the essential condition for ending the violence. In the summer of 1993 this policy emphasis was reversed. The common purpose of the British and Irish governments became the search for an agreement which would enable the *inclusion* of those formerly designated the enemies of democracy. The achievement of peace was now understood to be the necessary condition for that agreement between the constitutional parties which had so far proved elusive. The endeavour embarked upon in 1993 was to find a form of words which would permit the IRA to stop its campaign and which would permit Sinn Fein to abandon its overt support for 'armed struggle'. A similar opportunity would also exist for loyalist

241

paramilitaries, and those parties associated with them, to enter mainstream politics. The result of this new emphasis was the Downing Street Declaration of 15 December 1993. Its meaning was ambiguous.

As the then Prime Minister, John Major admitted, the Declaration's objective was one 'which was obvious, simple, yet extremely difficult to accomplish – that we bring together the positions of the British and Irish governments in a single statement to demonstrate that there is no excuse, no justification and no future for the use of violence in Northern Ireland' (*Irish Times*, 16 December 1993). That extreme difficulty was reflected in the Declaration's labyrinthine language. The British government agreed that 'it is for the people of the island of Ireland alone, by agreement between the two parts respectively, to exercise their right of self-determination on the basis of consent, freely and concurrently given, North and South, to bring about a united Ireland, if that is their wish'; while the Irish government accepted that 'the democratic right of self-determination by the people of Ireland as a whole must be exercised with, and subject to the agreement and consent of a majority of the people of Northern Ireland'. That joint formula confirmed the view of the Irish Foreign Minister, Dick Spring, that the enterprise of constructing the Declaration was akin to squaring the political circle.

It took eight months of debate within republicanism, as well as pressure from without, before the IRA, on 31 August 1994, declared its ceasefire. On October 13 the loyalist paramilitaries followed suit (Rowan, 1995, p. 85).

Reaction to the Ceasefires

Underlying the overwhelming support for the end to sectarian violence and the official optimism about economic development and social improvement was the old ambiguity about Northern Ireland's political future. Within a week of the ceasefire, the Prime Minister of the Irish Republic, Albert Reynolds, met John Hume, leader of the SDLP, and Gerry Adams, president of Sinn Fein, in a public demonstration of reconciliation amongst the nationalist 'family'. That was an important psychological boost for northern nationalists. It seemed to confirm that nationalism had become substantially stronger while unionism had become correspondingly weaker. The politics of the peace process had become already the politics of communal assertion despite the public rhetoric of reconciliation between the traditions. There were good reasons for nationalist self-confidence beyond republican hubris and calculations of political leverage. The 1991 census had revealed that the Catholic population of Northern Ireland was above 40 per cent and possibly as high as 42 per cent. This sense of demographic strength was encouraged by the condition of the ceasefires. There is evidence to suggest that the peace process helped to polarize northern Catholic opinion in favour of Irish unity because that option now seemed more attainable than before – despite all the public statements by nationalist Ireland that an agreed Ireland does *not* mean a united Ireland. A change in the means *ought* to have meant a change in the end to be attained. Yet the social attitudes surveys from 1989 to 1993 show that an average of 34 per cent of Catholics favoured remaining within the UK, with an average of only 53 per cent favouring Irish unity. In 1994 these figures were 24 per cent and 60 per cent, respectively. In 1993, the overall figures for Northern Ireland showed that 70 per cent favoured staying within the UK and 20 per cent favoured Irish unity. In 1994, the figures were 63 per cent and 27 per cent, respectively (Breen, 1996). There is an optimism that things are or *ought to be* going the nationalists' way and this has heightened nationalist expectations of significant progress in their favour. However, such projections of a Catholic majority in Northern Ireland presuppose that that community's traditionally high birth rate will be sustained. Since the Catholic birth rate in Northern Ireland has tended to follow the rate in the Irish Republic (which has fallen rapidly since the 1970s) this is now in doubt. As one expert has argued, if the Catholic birth rate begins to match that in the Republic there is a strong chance that Catholics will never form a majority in Northern Ireland (Compton, 1994).

The loyalist paramilitaries had announced their ceasefire by declaring that the 'Union is safe'. The Popular Unionist Party (close to the Ulster Volunteer Force) and the Ulster Democratic Party (close to the Ulster Defence Association) chose to follow publicly a more optimistic line about the peace process than the mainstream Ulster, Democratic or UK Unionist (formed around

Robert McCartney) parties. The leaders of the PUP and UDP have a large personal investment in the peace process and on some issues, in particular, the issue of illegal weapons, republicans and loyalists share common ground. These loyalist parties have been consistently critical of the attitudes of traditional unionist politicians and this criticism has now been compounded by competition for the protestant vote. The main concern of unionists was that their interests would be marginalized by the desire of the British government to consolidate the IRA ceasefire. That ceasefire had devalued somewhat the cards the unionists could play, especially the hand of the UUP. From July 1993 the leader of the UUP, James Molyneaux, had been cautiously trading the voting strength of his party at Westminster in exchange for being taken fully into the confidence of the Prime Minister, John Major. Indeed, it was claimed that Molyneaux was the 'barometer of acceptability' for the British government, explaining his party's measured approach to the Downing Street Declaration. After 31 August 1994, the UUP leadership felt that the priorities of the government had shifted to a position more favourable to nationalist ambition.

The Framework Document and Decommissioning

By way of confirmation of this, on 22 February 1995 the British and Irish governments published proposals entitled Frameworks for the Future which were designed to put institutional flesh on the principled bones of the Declaration. The precise status of the framework document (as these proposals became known) remains unclear. The Irish position appears to be that it represents a blueprint which could be submitted to the people ultimately over the heads of the political parties. The British position appears to be that it would give focus and direction to discussion between the parties but would be capable of substantial amendment.

The framework comprised two distinct but related sets of proposals. The first, 'A Framework for Accountable Government in Northern Ireland', concerned arrangements for devolution. The second, 'A New Framework for Agreement', was, according to Major, 'a shared understanding – prepared at the request of Northern Ireland parties – between the British and Irish governments, as to how relations in the island of Ireland, and between these islands, might be based on co-operation and agreement to the mutual advantage of all' (*Irish Times*, 23 February 1995). It is stressed in the proposals that overall agreement on all issues should be reached by negotiation between the parties and that any outcome should be acceptable to the people of Northern Ireland. The most controversial part was the proposal for a North/South body. This North/South body would have executive, harmonizing and consultative functions. These functions could be extended without limit on the basis of an 'agreed dynamic'. Appropriate executive functions for the North/South body are considered to be those involving 'a natural or physical all-Ireland framework' as well as European programmes and initiatives. Those functions considered appropriate for harmonization range from agriculture and economic policy to health and education. Everything in principle would be open for consultation.

Unionist politicians uniformly rejected the thrust of the framework as an unacceptable basis for agreement. They have argued that the framework would involve even greater Dublin influence within Northern Ireland and would create the 'dynamic' conditions for unity irrespective of the principle of consent accepted in the Downing Street Declaration. Constitutional nationalists generally regard the framework as a meaningful basis for negotiation and welcome both the language of and the 'dynamic' within the proposals. The response of republicans was more ambivalent. Some believed that the framework represented a betrayal of traditional aims. Others, such as Adams, welcomed the 'all-Ireland ethos' of the framework even though the provisions for devolved government were unacceptable. The major party outside the main political camps, the Alliance Party, welcomed the broad thrust of the framework though it was wary of a process of harmonization taking place irrespective of the practicality of or support for such harmonization.

The political framework, though, was overshadowed thereafter by argument about decommissioning terrorist weapons. In an attempt to resolve this impasse, the British and Irish governments, after much hesitation, established in December 1995 an international commission to review the problem. Its chairman was former American senator, George Mitchell, President Clinton's special adviser on Northern Ireland. Mitchell's prominent role –

he was later appointed chairman of the talks – confirmed the increasing US involvement in the process. The Mitchell Report of 22 January 1996 argued that it was unrealistic to expect decommissioning *before* all party talks but that some decommissioning should take place *during* the talks. The Report also outlined six principles of non-violence and democratic procedure to which all parties should subscribe.

Before the Mitchell Report was finalized – indeed, during the visit of President Clinton to Northern Ireland in November 1995 – the IRA was preparing to break its ceasefire. On 9 February 1996, it exploded a massive bomb in London's Docklands, killing two people and causing extensive damage. The IRA justified this act on the grounds of British bad faith, also claiming that the British government's response to Mitchell – the announcement of elections in Northern Ireland as 'a gateway' to all-party talks – proved that it was influenced by the new UUP leader, David Trimble. The real consequence of the Dockland's bomb, however, was the concession of a key Sinn Fein demand – a firm date for all party talks. This was fixed for 10 June 1996, less than two weeks after the elections scheduled for 30 May.

Elections and Talks

Interest in the unique election of 30 May focused initially on the competition for the unionist vote. The Northern Ireland (Entry to Negotiations, etc) Bill 1996 made provision for elections to a forum of 110 members. The form of the election was a hybrid involving the election of five members in each of the 18 Westminster constituencies and province-wide regional list allocating two seats to the top 10 parties. Representatives of the 10 successful parties were eligible to take part in the talks about the Northern Ireland's future. These talks were separate from the forum. Sinn Fein never took up its seats at the forum, while the SDLP resigned from it in July 1996. Of the 23 parties standing in the 18 constituencies, 11 represented varieties of unionism. The real contest, though, remained that between the UUP and the DUP. This was a contest to determine which of the two unionist leaders, Trimble or Paisley, could claim to be leader of their community.

Trimble's party topped the poll with 24.17 per cent of the vote. The DUP was disappointed with its 18.8 per cent. Robert McCartney's UKUP took 3.69 per cent. However, the boundaries to the sort of 'constructive unionism' which Trimble had promised in the talks have been limited by the popular proximity of his fundamentalist rivals. The loyalists, the PUP (3.47 per cent) and the UDP (2.22 per cent) did well enough to secure representation at the talks. The story of the election, however, was the increase in Sinn Fein's vote by 24 per cent over its 1993 council election performance: 12.4 per cent to 15.47 per cent. By contrast, the SDLP's vote was marginally down, from 22 per cent to 21.37 per cent. It was possible to interpret that vote to mean that events since 1993 had republicanized a section of the nationalist vote rather than constitutionalizing the politics of Sinn Fein. The main effect of the election was to confirm the polarization of opinion in Northern Ireland and to emphasize the unlikelihood of any practical compromise emerging from inter-party talks. This polarization was dramatically demonstrated by the confrontations attending Orange marches in the summer of 1996.

Those unversed in the details of Irish policy might ask the obvious question. How is it that commentators have spoken of an overwhelming desire for peace and yet it proves impossible to sustain that peace? The answer goes to the heart of the problem. People in Northern Ireland may express *liberal sympathies* about the need for equality, fairness and compromise. They generally have *illiberal instincts* when it comes to matters concerning identity and belonging. In particular, there is a powerful instinct which tells people that communal solidarity is the basis of political power. It is an instinct which local politicians can rarely ignore. The events of the summer of 1996 only illustrated its malignant consequences in dramatic form. It was not only the Orangemen and Unionists who felt obliged to follow that logic. Their nationalist opponents embraced it as well. The Orange parade at Drumcree revealed much about the disposition of the parties to a political settlement in Northern Ireland.

Unionist determination to force through their march in the face of official opposition (however unwise and possibly self-defeating their action may have been) seemed to confirm that the threat of greater force determines public decisions. Unionists believed that the direction of the 'peace process', especially after the Canary

Wharf bombing, has been determined by the threat of IRA violence. What the Orangemen did at Drumcree was in line with what experience obliges them to believe about British policy. Unionists were determined to make the point that, if the British government was weak, they were not. While few Protestants actually engaged in the disruption and many would have been appalled at the images of confrontation, the concern which that disruption represented does permeate widely. And this puts pressure on unionist politicians not to be seen to be complacent. On the other hand, there can be no doubting the genuine sense of Catholic outrage at what happened. For hardliners within Sinn Fein it became that little bit easier to perpetrate the myth that nothing had changed in Northern Ireland since 1969.

If one had tried to imagine a set of circumstances more conducive to polarization it would be difficult to improve on what had happened in 1996. Post-Drumcree, the atmosphere became sulphurous and the hard-won civilities of political discourse, Anglo-Irish as well as unionist-nationalist, degenerated. Many of the key elements of Anglo-Irish policy in recent years – encouraging Catholic support for the police, constitutionalizing republicanism, calming unionist paranoia – were severely damaged. The British government had no option but to try to make the inter-party talks work. The Drumcree events revealed how unlikely that prospect was.

The Talks

That such talks are intrinsically valuable has been an article of faith in government circles since the beginning of the Troubles. However, such is the practical incapacity amongst the parties locally to engage in *definitive* compromise that the political investment in talks by the two governments has so far brought little reward. The real and very deep suspicions which are focused on negotiations about Northern Ireland's future illustrate the difficulty of establishing a local consensus about a constitutional settlement. One can identify at least three understandings of what is meant by political talks, two optimistic and one pessimistic.

First, there exists an expectation that talks should be about persuading one's opponent by debate and discussion of the justice of one's case. It is thought that, in a free and open debate across the table, parties will be persuaded by the logic or coherence of arguments and agree to move to a plane of understanding where old antagonisms and bitterness will be resolved (or transcended). Despite all the evidence that such an expectation is unrealistic and fabulous, it is a faith which has been held to tenaciously by people who are far from naive. Interestingly, this view has informed the approach of the loyalist parties even though it is by no means the view held by all loyalist paramilitaries.

Second, there is the view that talks are about the parties reckoning the impossibility of either side 'winning' and should be about building alliances to attain one's interests, conceding on some points to gain advantage on others. It is hoped that through such hard bargaining, mutual respect – if not affection – will be built up between the participants and that a balance of compromises can be arrived at to the mutual satisfaction of all sides. This is taken to be hard-headed realism and is the official view held by the British and Irish governments. It is believed that there is a compromise deal to be had if all sides are allowed to participate without violence or the threat of violence.

However, even *harder-headed* realists work on a third (and pessimistic) understanding and this understanding corresponds closely to what has actually been taking place in the inter-party talks. Talks, in this view, are *indeed* about winning and losing, about victory and surrender, about mastery and humiliation. That, it is believed, is the true nature of the political in Northern Ireland. Real enemies have nothing to discuss. They can only manoeuvre. Thus, although there are those within the UUP who would like to operate on the basis of the second view, the party is constrained by the attacks of the DUP and UKUP which believe that the talks are fundamentally skewed against unionist interests. Equally, whatever room for manoeuvre the SDLP might have or want to have is constrained by the fact that Sinn Fein, excluded from the talks because of IRA violence, can be critical without responsibility. And the SDLP does not want to commit itself to any arrangement which would confirm unionist advantage within Northern Ireland. The atmosphere is a suspicious one and politicians in their querulous attitudes represent rather than misrepresent their respective constituents.

Thus the problem for the two governments in their promotion of political talks in Northern Ireland is rather like the conundrum faced by social contract theory. If there were sufficient agreement (or 'consensus') between unionist and nationalist to formulate an elaborate political contract then such a contract – especially of the byzantine sort outlined in the Framework Documents and hoped for from the talks – would be unnecessary. If there were not such sufficient agreement (or 'consensus') then a contract of that sort would be impossible anyway.

It might be suggested, therefore, that talks are only of serious value if the parties already desire to reach an accommodation, the shape of which they are already broadly agreed upon. There is little sign of that. The Northern Ireland problem for the British government and the Irish government continues to be one of struggling to discover whether common ground exists, whether the parties are agreed on the meaning of fair play or, indeed, whether the parties want to reach agreement under any conditions at all. But the two governments themselves are not outside the problem.

For instance, the Irish government is required to act as the partisan advocate of nationalist interests in Northern Ireland. Since the beginning of the peace process this has implied fostering and promoting a nationalist consensus the outer limits of which must embrace Sinn Fein. On the other hand, the Irish government is also interested in seeing the establishment of a stable settlement in Northern Ireland. This would actually require it to operate in an even-handed way and take into account unionist objections. These contradictory demands are read by unionists to illustrate bad faith. This has meant that unionists have difficulty in responding to positive messages from the Irish government concerning their interests because of a deep suspicion that the nationalist objective is to have a settlement imposed on them.

By contrast, nationalists have argued that despite having professed no selfish strategic or economic interest in Northern Ireland, the Conservative government had not been 'courageous' or taken enough 'risks' in the peace process because of its uncertain majority and its dependence on unionists votes at Westminster. As a consequence, they argue, unionists had no need to examine their position and engage in real compromise.

There was an expectation that a Labour government with a large majority would be able to deliver more, an expectation held in common by Sinn Fein and the SDLP. In part this reflected one Sinn Fein view that the British government was only hampered by considerations of prudence. In 1996, the focus of republican violence shifted to England in the hope that opinion in Great Britain wanted peace at any price and that a future Labour government would be able to deliver on that desire.

Unlike the situation in 1992, however, when Kevin Macnamara held the shadow Northern Ireland post, the prospects of a Labour victory in 1997 were not encouraging for those who wanted to see a significant nationalist shift in British government policy. Macnamara was known to sympathize with nationalist interpretations of the Northern Ireland problem and to subscribe to the notion of 'Irish unity by consent', which was generally understood to mean that unity was the objective and talks were designed to engender consent for it. Under Macnamara's stewardship a paper entitled *The Options for a Labour Government* was circulated confidentially. That paper envisaged the breakdown of inter-party talks in circumstances unfavourable to the Unionist position and considered the desirability of an imposed Anglo–Irish framework tantamount to joint authority between London and Dublin. Under Tony Blair's leadership, Macnamara was replaced by Marjorie (Mo) Mowlam who was not associated with the traditional concerns of Irish nationalism and whose appointment signalled New Labour's determination to promote a fresh approach to Northern Ireland policy. She was appointed Secretary of State for Northern Ireland following Labour's 1997 general election victory.

That election also saw some small movement between constitutional nationalists and Sinn Fein in Northern Ireland. Gerry Adams and Martin McGuinness won two seats for Sinn Fein and, although they would not take them up because of their refusal to take the oath of allegiance, gained a good deal of publicity from the consequent denial of access to parliamentary facilities.

The advent of a new government inevitably aroused much expectation of a new peace initiative in Northern Ireland. Tony Blair and Mo Mowlam did everything they could in their early period in office to indicate their commitment to making progress.

Mowlam made an immediate visit to Northern Ireland, and Blair held early talks with the leaders of its political parties, with Irish premier John Bruton and with people on the ground on a flying visit to the province. In words which were calculated to reassure unionists (and which also dismayed Sinn Fein) he stated that a political settlement was not a slippery slope to a United Ireland and that he believed in the UK and valued the Union.

At the same time as Blair moved to calm unionist fears he also extended an offer to Sinn Fein to join the peace talks, and authorized British officials to meet Sinn Fein representatives in an attempt to get the peace process started again, provided that 'events on the ground' did not make such negotiations impossible. Although Sinn Fein claimed that it could not itself guarantee a ceasefire, it accepted Blair's offer which was paralleled by an offer of talks with Irish government officials.

Conclusion

Finding a sustainable policy on Northern Ireland has been a problem for British governments for a generation. Although it is improbable that the traditional format of inter-party talks will deliver a settlement that is acceptable to the mass of the electorate, it is incumbent on the British government to keep trying to square the circle of Northern Ireland's antagonistic politics. The Labour government inherited a strategy which had largely unravelled by 1997. The option of simply consolidating what had gone before was therefore bound to appear less acceptable than embarking on a new imaginative enterprise, regardless of the chance of identifying a consensus on which a settlement could be based, or indeed of being able to protect such a settlement from a militant assault on it. Newly arrived in office, Blair had to be optimistic about the prospects of progress. It remains to be seen for how long that optimism can be maintained, and how much effort the new government will devote to keeping the 'settlement train' on track.

13

Local Governance

PETER JOHN

By the late 1990s, much of the national conflict over local politics had receded. With less disagreement between the main parties over local government issues, the high drama of the 1980s, which reached its apotheosis in the poll tax episode, was succeeded by a more humdrum political environment. Local politics seemed to be returning to a quieter era before Margaret Thatcher made the subject interesting for activist and academic alike. Perhaps the new prosaic politics shows how unusual the period of the 1980s was, and that the attempted restructuring of local government by radical Conservative administrations had not in fact dug deep into local political structures. Once the reforming zeal launched by Thatcher had dissipated, so traditional forms of local party politics and professional service administration, with a few nods in the direction of the language of customer care and partnership, continued as before. But the high politics of the 1980s disguised a more profound transformation in British politics, and in local politics in particular. Many of the grand initiatives launched by the Thatcher administration have been gradually extended, and local government has been transformed from being the dominant legitimate local public institution to just being one body which participates in a more complex framework of governing. In short, local government has been succeeded by local governance.

The Restructuring of Local Politics

It appeared at the end of the 1980s that the stable professional policy communities that had governed local politics in the post-war years had dissolved. It is ironic that, just as academics like Rhodes (1986, 1988) identified the informal relationships between a range of central and local and public and private bodies which ran such policy sectors as education, housing, the inner cities and health, these networks seemed to have been fractured by the reform-minded Thatcher administrations. In housing, for example, with relatively little consultation central policy undermined local government's providing role. Governments directed public investment to housing associations, controlled local authority rents, reformed powers over homelessness and gradually shifted local authority stock into private sector ownership or to housing associations.

The radicalism of the Thatcher decade suggests that local government had a golden age which had been destroyed by a centre which removed functions, restricted finance, and limited the discretion of local democratic bodies. Yet this simple 'before and after' story does not do justice to the complexities of subnational politics. First, there was no period when local government was stable and autonomous. Even in the 1930s and 1940s, commentators speculated that centralization was being brought about by the removal of key local government functions and legal controls (Robson, 1933), particularly in the 1945–51 period. Though these fears were assuaged by the expansion of local government functions and finance during the 1950s and 1960s, the national political consensus was that local government was more an agency administering welfare functions than an entrenched institution of the democratic polity. The expansion of local government in the post-war years extended older practices of administration by convenience, devolving administrative functions from the national executive and reducing the costs of welfare. As such, the weakness of local government is part of Britain's unique 'ungrounded statism' whereby public intervention never became as institutionalized as in some other advanced democracies (Dunleavy, 1989). In addition, as most notably Bulpitt (1983) suggests, no matter how important local government seems as an deliverer of services, its leaders lack status as national politicians to embed local political power into the British constitution.

Second, local democratic institutions were not just the passive recipients of central orders in the 1980s. While the national organizations of local government resisted each legislative change introduced by the Conservatives, many of those changes emanated from the communities of which local government is part.

The contracting out of services to private organized bodies, one of the few policy areas for local government consistently pushed by Conservative governments in the 1980s, was pursued by innovative councils in the 1970s, and built on older practices (Brooke, 1989). Traditions of professionalized administration were questioned by local councils at both ends of the political spectrum. Many features of modern public administration and policy, such as citizen charters, decentralization and cost centres, originated as local government experiments. As local government's role has been transferred to other bodies, such as housing associations and training and enterprise councils (TECs), created to administer centrally funded training programmes in 1989, the resulting fragmentation of decisions over service delivery has also seen a revival of the outward-orientated local authority which has become willing to engage in reciprocal horizontal arrangements with other bodies.

A summary of the evolution of sub-national politics in Britain since the late 1970s would describe it as a gradual process of restructuring and response to new institutions and incentives which has been led and followed by all the actors at the various territorial levels. Rather than a strict periodization of phases of central government inspired policies as 'Labourist' (pre-1979), 'reforming-Conservative' (1979–85), 'radical–conservative' (1986–90), and 'consolidationist' from 1990, the shift in the legal and financial framework, the systems for delivering policy and the management and policy-making styles of local politicians and bureaucrats are part of a wider transformation of the process of governing in western societies toward more fragmented and less co-ordinated institutional structures, but with also a flexible, cooperative and adaptive form of politics to provide co-ordination (Stoker, 1989).

The relative simplicity of government by large locally-elected authorities has given way to governance by networks of public, semi-public and private organizations. The bodies which now exist include the following:

- companies/management buyouts supplying contracted out services, as in waste collection, grass cutting and catering
- private or semi-public bodies providing services purchased by local authorities, such as nursing homes

- hospital trusts and a large complex network of health providers, such as GP fundholders
- new central government agencies administering new or formerly local government functions, particularly in urban economic development, such as TECs, urban development corporations and Housing Action Trusts
- partnership organizations, such as Business Links, Single Regeneration Budget steering groups, and business marketing bodies
- micro agencies formerly under the umbrella of the local authority, such as schools running their own budgets under the local management of schools, schools which have 'opted out' of local authority control, further and higher education institutions, such as colleges and the 'new' universities
- existing public agencies which have been given an enhanced new role, such as housing associations
- the regional officers of central government reorganized into government offices for the regions (GORs) in 1995
- decentralized offices of 'Next Steps' agencies, such as of the Highways Agency
- dynamic voluntary associations, such as community organizations
- revitalized business organizations, such as larger, merged Chambers of Commerce
- large private-sector companies with a renewed interest in local public decisions
- the privatized public utilities, such as water companies
- new or rejuvenated regional organizations, such as regional associations of local authorities, regional organizations of TECs and the regional CBIs and TUCs.

Critics of central government reform regard the emergence of new agencies and organizations as evidence of the weakening of local democracy because local government loses influence to other bodies. There are examples of such a weakening, such as in higher education, where the former polytechnics used to be under local democratic control. There are new evolving aspects of local governance, such as in health, where local authorities are unimportant actors. In some areas, such as in coalitions promoting local economic development, local authorities are just one agency among many and need not dominate the partnership, such in seeking EU funding or in projects funded by English Partnerships. But, as the following sections show, the transition from local government to local governance is highly complex and has diverse implications for local accountability and democratic control.

Central–Local Relations in the 1990s

It is possible to see the end of the 1990s as the continuation of a slow grind of centralization. It is true that a degree of normalization of political relations has been under way since 1989, but the softening of national party politics over local government disguises the continuing radical changes which are likely to take place whatever party in is power at the national level. The best example of apparent normalization is in the formerly turbulent history of local government finance. Since the early 1970s the form of local tax has been hotly debated, particularly as the rates, the property tax based on rental values, was thought to disadvantage key Conservative Party supporters. As early as 1974 the Conservative Party committed itself to abolition of the tax. When the attempt to cut local spending in the early 1980s failed because some local councils responded to central government grant cuts by increasing local rate levels, a policy problem was elevated to a political crisis (Travers, 1985). An alliance of junior ministers, civil servants and consultants produced the half-baked single-person tax which collapsed under its own unpopularity and unworkability (Butler *et al.*, 1994). Yet the surprise is not so much that the poll tax was abolished – one can imagine that at some stage even Thatcher would have weakened it or allowed it to die a slow death – but that its replacement, council tax (a property tax based on eight capital bands and not too dissimilar to the old rates), announced quickly in 1992 should have bedded down so rapidly that local taxation again became a 'non-issue'. Research on the implementation of the tax shows a quick healing of administrative systems for collecting local taxes after the ruptures of the poll tax years (Kneen and Travers, 1994), though councils continue to have some problems collecting local revenues.

Central and local agencies seem to have solved the political problem of local taxation, largely because policy-makers and publics compare the new levy to the manifest injustice of the poll tax, and Conservative governments for a while increased the proportion of local authority finance funded by central government to nearly 85 per cent in 1991. Although consumers continued to pay for local government out of a VAT rate increased from 15 to 17.5 per cent, the political sting was taken out of both the community charge and council tax by the reduced burden of expenditure they bore. Once the political crisis was out of the way, central government transferred the burden of local expenditure to local taxes (see Table 13.1). Local authorities have little latitude because of stringent rules about capping local expenditure and taxes. In the long run, central government is able to use its legal power to control local authority expenditure, and to vary the burdens central and local taxpayers bear.

Abolition of the poll tax did not reverse the more fundamental changes in local government finance. Nationalization of the business rate ensures that local tax and expenditure decisions are more dependent on central government grant allocations than ever before. Eyes increasingly focus on the centrally-determined standard spending assessments, measures of spending need used to distribute central government general grants. There is a powerful centralization at work as local government expenditure increasingly converges on these totals. Although some commentators believe the current system to be unstable because the gearing effect makes steep council tax rises likely (Travers, 1995), there is little chance of a reform of local taxation because governments realize too well the costs of radical changes in local government

TABLE 13.1   Projections for local authority spending and taxes, 1996–9

	1996–7	1997–8	1998–9	1999–2000
Total spending (£bn)	44.407	45.162	45.742	46.592
Central grant (%)	79.3	78.4	77.1	75.5
Council tax revenue (%)	20.7	21.6	22.9	24.5
Tax increase on 96–7 (%)		5.9	13.9	23.8

Source: Association of Metropolitan Authorities.

finance and can rely on the compromise solution of the council tax which even retains some aspect of the community charge through the 25 per cent single person's discount. Thus, belatedly, through policy learning, the centre has increased its control over local financial decisions, realizing an aim of controlling local government expenditure which had been beyond its grasp for so long.

Another sector over which central policy on local government has apparently mellowed, and where there is a growing central manipulation of local decision-makers and policy outputs, is local economic development policy. Whereas up to the late 1980s central government deliberately excluded local government from centrally initiated local development policies and sought to limit local experiments (Harding, 1989), by 1989 it had softened its approach. Central government learnt from the policy failures of property-led regeneration strategies carried out by the urban development corporations (UDCs), and sought to involve a larger number of actors in economic policy formulation and implementation. UDCs were allowed to enter partnerships with local authorities. The Local Government and Housing Act 1989 gave local authorities responsibility in local development (though with new central controls as well). The City Challenge scheme introduced in 1990, a competitive scheme for distributing 'top-sliced' funding for the inner cities, was based on local authority led bids. Its successor is the wide-ranging Single Regeneration Budget (SRB) which has unified many centrally-funded urban schemes into one budget since 1995. Partnerships, led by local authorities, TECs, voluntary or private bodies, make an annual bid for funds. However, while local authorities are often the lead partners, the centrally-run TECs are often the leaders as well (Mawson *et al.*, 1995). In fact, regulations for the SRB state that TECs and local authorities must be partners. In addition, the SRB is administered by the government offices for the regions, a structure introduced in 1995 (Chapter 11). The offices aim to improve central co-ordination and are led by a new civil servant, the regional director. While the SRB scheme welcomed elected local authorities into the fold of centrally-funded urban policy, it also was the spearhead of a more co-ordinated central government approach. The SRB entrenched the new leaders in local economic development, the TECs, and legitimized the many other bodies, such as voluntary organizations, community groups, private companies, which all wish to have a say in urban regeneration. The result is a breaking of the monopoly of local authority decisions and the creation of a complex pattern of governance based on the many organizations involved with funding bids and managing the resulting projects. The principle of competitive bidding has now been extended to capital funding on a pilot basis, with the Capital Challenge distributing £600 million supplementary capital approvals between 1997 and 2000, rural funds in Rural Challenge and European funds in Regional Challenge. The distribution of the national lottery funds, many of which have been won by local authority led bids, often as city regeneration schemes, follows the same procedure.

Even if local authority leadership is accepted more in central government decision-making, it is largely because of the rules on funding and a more general change in the outlook of local authorities toward pragmatism and co-operation (Harding and Garside, 1995). Central government is able to achieve its policy aims by ensuring the implementing actors come to believe in its overall philosophy of market-driven economic development, and the government can exercise a greater choice in allocating where funds go. Again, a process of learning has taken place in local economic development policy where manipulation, precise legal changes, new incentives and ideological change take the place of central diktats. As with finance, it is unlikely that the central framework of local economic policy can be disrupted by the Labour government, and new initiatives, such as regional economic development agencies, are likely to be grafted onto an institutional framework which maximizes the ability of central government to manipulate policy outputs.

The course of the reform of local government since 1990 shows the same mixture of pragmatic compromise and ideological policy making as in other policy sectors. One of the outcomes of the review of local government finance started by Michael Heseltine, when Secretary of State for the Environment from 1990 to 1992, was a parallel review of structure and internal management as a way of examining each aspect of local government 'in the round'. The canvassing of options for a new executive framework for local government was really a vehicle for Heseltine's idea of elected mayors for local government. Once Heseltine moved to the Department of Trade and Industry, the idea receded, though it was never off the agenda as the Department of the Environment (DoE) tentatively suggested trial areas. Given its mercurial status in the policy universe of ideas, it is also no surprise Tony Blair favours elected mayors. Labour will create an elected mayor for London. Conveniently, the idea is a costless measure. Given the lack of enthusiasm in local government and the rapidity of the new Labour Party adoption and rejection of policy proposals it could easily slip back once again into the soup of potential ideas.

While the financial reforms were swiftly proposed and implemented, and the review of internal management disappeared from the agenda, the government pushed ahead rapidly with the reform of local government structure, a surprising course of action given the high political costs that arise from the disputes over boundaries and the uncertain benefits of any change. The original idea was that the two-tier system of non-metropolitan counties and districts was wasteful and confusing, and more efficient and accountable local government would follow from a newly created one-tier system. The proposal was the natural successor to the first rupture of the two-tier system in 1986 when the Conservative government abolished the Greater London Council and the six metropolitan county councils. It also was the final part of the ideological assault against large strategic authorities responsible for planning and co-ordination. Small unitary authorities would be better suited to the residual status for local government when stripped of responsibility for welfare services, a vision first set out in the Adam Smith Institute (1989) publication, *Wiser Counsels*.

In keeping with the incentives produced by an electorally vulnerable English centre and the centrally driven Celtic periphery, the Scottish and Welsh Offices swiftly proposed, consulted on and implemented a one-tier system based on 20 large areas in Wales and 28 in Scotland, replacing the 45 and 65 previous local authorities in these two sub-nations. The most notable casualty was Strathclyde region, which had covered about 48 per cent of the population of Scotland. As against many other London initiatives, the Scottish elite and media reactions were combative but ineffective. While there were cries of gerrymandering in Scotland, the new system bedded down with a Labour victory in most of the new authorities in Scotland in 1996. A similar, less politicized, set of events occurred in Wales.

The solution the government followed in England was more interesting. Because of the political sensitivities of reorganizing English local authorities – national government had little to lose in Scotland and Wales – the vehicle for reform was the Local Government Commission, set up in 1992 as an advisory body which roamed the country reviewing 'tranches' of local authorities under the controversial chairmanship of Sir John Banham, a former director-general of the CBI. Subject to guidance from the DoE, the Commission took views from organizations and groups affected and, at first, recommended a one-tier solution in many areas, but with enough exceptions to show policy confusion. The mix between central direction and local flexibility is a further example of the post-Thatcherite policy-making and implementation style, since decision makers allowed for policy learning and adaptability, but sought to retain their leadership and to translate into reality proposals to improve service delivery and to limit the power of large strategic authorities. The flexible approach of the Commission permitted local variation and allowed the central policy gradually to move from an attempt to impose a single-tier system as was proposed for some counties, such as Avon and Humberside, to the idea that the principal towns in counties could have unitary status while the other districts remained part of a two-tier system. There followed a series of policy shifts influenced by the lobbying positions of the existing bodies, in particular the vacillations in the districts' representation and the power of the counties in the House of Lords. Gradually, a 'new' system of local government emerged amidst the rather chaotic courses of Commission and central government policies. The final pattern, steered by former Secretary of State John Gummer, restored traditional powers to the main cities but left much of the two-tier structure in the rest of non-metropolitan England. The compromise dealt with the main cause of the instability of the 1972 system, the loss of autonomy of England's principal towns, but retained most of the historical counties with their generally good record as strategic authorities able to give leadership to many small rural districts beneath them. Yet the irony is that the new system has much in common with the pre-1972 system of local government. While the outcome has some post-hoc rationality to it, the bizarre turns in central decision-making and the power of one judicial review appeared to suggest a policy mess

(Leach, 1996), a characteristic which observers claim defines the process (Leach, 1995). The move to selective unitary status in tranche two meant that the recommendations adopted in tranche one were based on redundant guidance from the secretary of state. To an extent the inconsistency was overcome by allowing cities to apply later for free-standing status. But the system still has a lop-sided aspect which could be the justification of a further disrupting reform. On the other hand, the final compromise – which had its symbol in the new single local authority association which contains counties, districts, metropolitan authorities and new unitary councils and came into existence in April 1997 – is probably the least bad solution for local government. The reform disposes of the worst features of the 1972 system, such as the unloved counties of Humberside and Avon, gives cities the full range of local government powers and minimizes disruption by maintaining or rationalizing the boundaries of many effective district and county authorities. What disappears from view is much of the original ideological driving force behind the reforms, so in this case policy learning attenuated central government's policy aims. What remains is an increasingly fragmented and differentiated pattern of local administration which reinforces trends toward local governance. The increasing tendency of cooperation between local authorities (Travers *et al.*, 1995) is also driven and required by central government that wishes, through regional planning guidance, to try, if weakly, to remedy the gaps in strategic planning and transport caused by local government reorganization. As such the local government review would seem to have precipitated a centrally driven governance and parallels trends in many other policy sectors.

If gradualism weakened the radicalism of the government's reorganization proposals in England, radical incrementalism is the best oxymoron to capture central government's long-term policy requiring local authorities to contract out services to privately organized bodies. The central policy began modestly in 1980 when legislation required direct labour organizations to operate trading accounts and subject a certain percentage of their work to tender. Over time central government increased the proportion of direct work that had to be contracted out. The Transport Act 1985, and then the Local Government Act 1988, extended legislative requirements to a range of activities, includ-

ing grass cutting, catering, street cleaning and grounds maintenance. Legislation applied contracting to education by the provision that schools could opt out of local authority provided services
and the government aimed for the same result in community care.
In circular 5/96 the government is able to define the quality of
service as way of finding out if the local authority is acting
uncompetitively. In spite of draconian central powers and the
legal requirement that local authorities act competitively, studies
show that progress toward private sector provision of services
funded by local authorities has been slow, with management
buyout organizations winning the bulk of the contracts (Walsh,
1991). Over time private sector involvement has increased because the government has tightened rules on tendering. Here
again is an example of the new policy style: rather than introduce
the policy in one go, the government learnt as it introduced new
measures (Walsh, 1995). As local authorities overcame their
initial hostility to the policy, they were able to use competitive
tendering to reorganize internal management systems. The result
of this gradualism was that local authorities became more market-
oriented and the momentum was based on continual change. The
malleability of the institutional environment allowed the government in 1996 to extend compulsory competitive tendering (CCT)
to the core activities of the local authority: white-collar work, such
as legal services, information technology, finance and personnel.
The radicalism of this policy, pushed by the former local government minister, Paul Beresford (former leader of the Conservative
flagship authority, Wandsworth) could only be implemented
because of the skill central departments had gained in manipulat-
ing legal rules over an 18-year period of one-party government.
The careful evolution of legal control is an example of what
Martin Loughlin has called the juridification of central-local
government relations whereby the informal norms which used
to inform central government policy-making for local government
have been replaced by a centrally-driven regulatory order
(Loughlin, 1996). It suits ministers and civil servants to specify
what is expected from local authorities and to keep on changing
the legal framework until the centre achieves compliance and a
successful outcome.

The central regulation of the education system continues to
display further marketization and the loss of a traditional role for

local authorities. The landmark was the Education Reform Act 1988 which required local authorities to delegate budgets to schools, permitted the opting out of schools from local authority control, and set up the National Curriculum and testing. The logic of the reform was to change the local education authority from a body which both provides core services and drives policy to one which provides residual or market-based services and seeks to influence policy or retreats altogether as a player. The way that logic has been played out in education reflects a complex conjunction of political and bureaucratic interests. On the one hand, as in other policy areas, central government has sought to intensify the move to quasi-markets by further regulation and seeks to strip local democratic bodies of their monopoly. Thus the Major government sought to promote, with limited success, a voucher scheme for nursery education; and the Education Act 1993 extended the type of school eligible for grant maintained status to special and religious schools, set up the Funding Council for Schools and provided greater financial incentives to opt out. On the other hand, the policy vacuum left by the attenuation of local education authorities and the severe implementation difficulties of introducing the reforms reinvents a role, if somewhat different from before, for overarching local democratic bodies. While the government, media and local politicians believed the number of schools opting out would increase dramatically from 1993, in fact the number doing so has levelled off, ensuring the bulk of secondary and primary schools remain within the local education authorities' purview.

The other surprise is that the death of the local education authority is much exaggerated. The legislative framework still leaves much legal discretion in the hand of local authorities, such as setting the formula to distribute school budgets and the final decision about school closures. The education authority is able to carry out a provider function for services, particularly to the smaller institutions, such as primary schools, to promote itself as the leader in the network of policy-makers, and to exercise a democratic and strategic role. Thus all of the agencies involved with education are changing rapidly: central government has to cope with new responsibilities and has suffered reverses in some policy initiatives; there are fierce debates within the national education community about standards and central government policy; local schools are coping at varying states of adaption to the new quasi-market; and local education authorities themselves are seeking a new role.

What is striking about recent developments in central-local relations is the variety of roles of local elected and unelected bodies that has emerged. At various stages since the late 1970s it has been possible to see some coherence to central government reforms, particularly in the mid-point of the 1980s. There appeared to be the common themes of reducing local authority discretion, creating new local unelected quangos, introducing institutional and financial incentives for consumer-driven quasi-markets, increasing national legal regulation and enshrining the role of the private sector in public provision. Yet, at the end of the 1990s, the style of government policy varies greatly from the centralized solution of policy for local taxation and finance, the compromise between central and local government in local economic policy and the confusion in education. Thus the prospect for local authorities is highly variable with some policy areas becoming less important and new ones opening up.

Towards Community Governance?

The waning of both the push to market-based policies and the demise of the traditional welfare-based local authority suggests that a new community-based local government system is in the process of being created. What central government reforms have achieved is the liberation of local authorities from their traditional providing function and have stimulated a more responsive and strategic enabling role. As central government reforms cannot be implemented exactly as ministers and civil servants intended, local elected bodies remain as the one strategic body in a locality which is able to give coherence to the institutional mess created by 18 years of central reforms. Some of the examples referred to above in education and local economic development would support this analysis. That central government gave local authorities the leading role in co-ordinating community care in the 1989 legislation would suggest the central government institutions realized there was a need for co-ordination of otherwise incoherent and fragmented patterns of service delivery. On the other hand, a pessimistic view of the loss of local government's role would suggest the retreat of democratic control as functions were reallocated to non-democratic local bodies, quangos. Indeed, there are now some 5750 agencies (90 per cent operate at the local level) which take about a third of public expenditure and have some 50 000 appointed people sitting on them (Stewart *et al.*, 1994; Hall and Weir, 1996). Yet studies examining partnerships and networks in local areas show local authorities are usually the lead partner in the complex networks of governance (John and Cole, 1997). Other organizations are either too small or under-resourced to function on their own. Often unelected bodies seek to involve local authorities because they have the legitimacy and political resources to function effectively as local actors.

A similar leading role in the pattern of governance is being forged by local authorities in newer policy sectors, such as in EU activity and environmental regulation. In EU matters local authorities have a role as one of the main beneficiaries of regional and social structural funds, and also from community initiatives such as RECHAR (a fund for areas affected by the decline of coal industry) and URBAN (a new fund for urban areas). Local bodies are implementors of swathes of European legislation from rules on tendering, the environment, transport, planning, waste management to weights and measures, and many others (John, 1996a). They have become lobbyists in Brussels in their own right by setting up offices and joining cross-national networks (John, 1994b). UK local authorities are among the most prominent subnational activists on the Brussels scene (Goldsmith, 1993; John, 1996b). Over the environment local authorities have moved from being regulators of economic activities to being activists, with many authorities embracing Agenda 21 documents and developing green strategies for recycling and forming links with activist organizations (Ward, 1996). At the same time central government has enhanced local authority powers in pollution control in the Environment Act 1995.

In the three sectors of local economic development, Europe and the environment, local authorities have become drivers for change, led by new cadres of activist professionals (Mills, 1994). These new policy sectors are testament to the resilience of democratic multi-functional institutions which have the incentive, drive and resources to experiment with new local problems which deconcentrated offices of central departments or quangos cannot engage in so readily. The new functions are also an example of long life cycles of the emergence of public goods whereby pioneering municipalities experiment, others copy, and then central government regulates (and often then removes, as in public heath, the utilities and the relief of poverty in the 1930s and 1940s). Given that many of the younger, more dynamic councillors no longer wish to serve so much on traditional service committees, such as education and housing, but seek a more exciting life on recreation or environment committees (Leach and Stewart, 1992), there is a sense in which central regulation of service functions precipitates a search for new areas of innovation.

There are also signs of a democratic revival in local democracy through experiments designed to remedy the defects of the representative system (Stewart, 1995). Pioneered in the 1980s were the decentralization schemes which transferred as many activities and budgets as possible to local area offices and created community forums in partnership with local councillors (Lowndes and Stoker, 1992). There has been much variation in these experiments. They range from exercises in consumer responsiveness to full-blown decentralization of budgeting and decision making as in Tower Hamlets and Walsall. For reasons that are not clear, the areas where radical decentralization experiments were pushed the furthest were those which had political controversies (Walsall) or political corruption (Tower Hamlets). Thus the politics of democratic renewal has been obscured by the nefariousness of local activism and the excesses of the Liberal Democrat spearheads into safe Labour territories. While the natural recommendation is to restate the safety of traditional representative mechanisms, the media reaction also obscures a large number and range of experiments in consultative and direct democracy which are springing up around the UK: citizens juries or focus groups designed to test out a particular issue with a small numbers of individuals; community forums; experiments with the use of high technology, such as the internet and tele-democracy; user involvement; referenda; the involvement of users in policy implementation; experiments to improve electoral turnout; and greater use of more traditional instruments, such as opinion polls (Stewart, 1995, 1996; Geddes, 1996). The experience of coalitions of parties governing in as many one in three councils makes for experiments in new forms of governing which, if often indecisive and uncertain, involves a more co-operative form of politics than at national level. These positive moves reflect greater citizen activism and discontent, and dissatisfaction among officers and councillors with the ineffectiveness of the representative process (Gyford, 1991). While the search for alternative mechanisms for local democracy confronts the classic problems of democracy – the legitimacy and fairness of the decision-making process – the process undoubtedly reflects a wider dissatisfaction with British governing institutions (Chapter 7). In the context of constitutional reform, local level experimentation can be guide for the national process of democratic renewal.

The other factor favourable to local democratic institutions is the changed political context. The national associations of local government have been let back into decision-making networks, as shown by the effective lobby, in alliance with chief constables, against the proposal to remove locally elected members on police authorities before the passing of the Police and Magistrates Courts Act 1994. A further sign that the era of national elite hostility to local government may be at an end is the plethora of commissions and committees setting out proposals for local government reforms and renewal. First was the Joseph Rowntree Foundation's *A New Accord* (1992), second was the Commission for Local Democracy's report (1995), and third was the report of the House of Lords select committee on relations between central and local government (1996). These bodies produced a series of recommendations which are intended to increase the autonomy of local government, such as a power of general competence, the removal of capping of local authority expenditure and the release of central controls of CCT. Yet, by evidence of the scant media coverage, there is little likelihood that these wish lists will turn into reality except for symbolic actions such as Britain signing the European Convention on Local Self Government. The reason for the weakness of such championing of local democracy is the continuing widespread ignorance and disdain for local government within national elite circles, in particular the London-orientated media and civil service. An interview-based account of views of local government held by civil servants and national politicians is highly revealing on this point (Jones and Travers, 1994).

The trends toward more active local authorities as co-ordinators of the local governance can lead to a more prescriptive approach as put forward by Michael Clarke and John Stewart (1996). The advocacy of community government involves a critique of the incoherence of central government policy, realization of the failures of market-based public administration, advocacy of the learning organization, understanding the limits of service-oriented bureaucratic management, experiments with new forms of democratic accountability and management, the development of a broad notion of local democratic role and a search for all of the community as the constituency of local government. The logic of Clarke and Stewart's argument is that the foundations are being created for a new politics and that the damaging policies of the 1980s can be reversed.

Centralized Local Administration and Local Government Decline?

It is, however, possible to qualify the achievements of local authorities in rebuilding themselves in recent years. The new enabling role in education cannot disguise the reduction of control over what is about half of local government expenditure and control entirely of higher and further education. There is the loss of a role in public transport and housing; central government increasingly regulates environment policy; there is decreasing financial autonomy and declining central resources. New local government activities, such as community care, social services functions and the environment, cannot compensate for these dramatic revisions of local government's role. Moreover, the new areas of policy-making are often short-lived initiatives rather than signs that a new local government function is about to be created. Local authorities have retreated from an ambition to intervene directly in their local economies by funding local enterprises, while local economic development policy becomes a series of bids for central government or EU programmes. Given the findings of a recent survey that local authority responses to Europe are overwhelmingly financially orientated (Martin, 1996), the probable decline in the UK's take of regional and other funds after 2000 is likely to mean that local government's interest in the EU will wane when the financial incentive is removed. Also, as with central government policy, European funding is becoming more directed to other bodies, such as the voluntary sector, universities and central government bodies, creating another sector of complex governance. With the exception of the environment, where a local response is being driven by central government departments, the new activities of local government are vulnerable either to the vicissitudes of fashion or increasing financial constraints. There is also a political dimension to the cultivation of new roles: they need a political justification, particularly to the traditional constituents of local government. A sign of the 1990s is that the leader of England's largest unitary council, Birmingham, should be elected in reaction against the large physical projects and European policies of the 1980s with a mandate to allocate resources to traditional services, such as education.

The move to democratic renewal needs to be seen in the context of a continuing crisis of representative democracy in local government caused by the weaknesses of party politics and an inadequate representative system based on over large constituencies and ill-defined councillor roles. It is remarkable that at the end of the 1990s, after an intense period of local experimentation and central regulation, the core of the decision-making process in most local authorities, the concentration of power in the hands of the leadership of the party group, remains almost untouched. Moreover, the system of party control of local government, dating back to the spread of party government in the early years of the twentieth century, has been strengthened by several parallel trends in the 1980s. The first was the erosion of traditional two-party politics in much of the country which was a consequence of the long period in office of the Conservatives, the anti-local government stance of the 1979–90 governments and the operation of the electoral system, all of which ensured the loss of seats and councils from the Conservatives and the greater security in office in urban areas of the Labour party. In 1973 the Conservatives had 7500 councillors and controlled 93 councils, in 1993 they had 4950 members and were in power in 13. By 1996, 199 local authorities had a majority of Labour councillors. The emergence of one-party government in many cities, though balanced by the growing strength of the Liberal Democrats in the south and the nationalists in Wales and Scotland, and also experiments in coalition politics in 'hung' councils, weakens Conservatism and removes the pressure of loss of office for many local administrations. Even though the Conservatives could bounce back (Rallings and Thrasher, 1996), their electoral demise has contributed to a weakening of a powerful force in local politics, Conservative localism (Holliday, 1996), and the rise of the Liberal Democrats as the main alternative to Labour. The diversity and strength of political traditions at the local level is important for sustaining local political institutions in the state. Paralleling these electoral forces, has been an increase in the turnover in office of councillors (Bloch, 1992) which gives greater security to the party leadership. The trends toward greater party control of local government continue as party politicians have taken greater control of council business (Gyford, 1989), a long-term trend the reforms proposed by Widdicombe Committee left untouched.

Some of the excesses of party politics in local government have been expressed in the exposure of corruption in local government in some high profile cases, most notably with the Conservatives in Westminster, under the leadership of Lady Shirley Porter, who were found in a district auditor's report to have attempted to secure re-election by allocating council houses to households of Conservative political preference. It seems likely that corruption in local government grew in the 1980s, as shown by the public examples of Hackney, Liverpool, Tower Hamlets and West Wiltshire. With the abuses of the current system coming to light, the structure of representation within councils and the scrutiny of the executive are key issues in local government reform. Corruption also draws attention to some of the weaknesses of the new urban governance and the need to strengthen public accountability in the informal relationships between the public and private sectors.

The autonomy of local elites, the murky world of local corruption and the relative ease with which central administrations have restructured local government, such as abolishing the upper tier of metropolitan and London government in 1986, reflect not only the separation of central and local elites and a nationalized and unitary political culture, but popular indifference to local institutions. At first sight this statement is puzzling as most surveys of popular opinion show overwhelming satisfaction with local councils and confidence with local democracy, and people favour elected over unelected agencies (Miller and Dickson, 1996). But the public show satisfaction with a wide range of established institutions when asked to express their view in closed questions. If the evidence is inspected more closely, particularly when attitudes to local government as a organization and the way in which services are administered are examined, the optimistic picture vanishes (Bloch and John, 1991; Rallings *et al.*, 1994). There is growing party politicization and polarization of attitudes to such values as local autonomy. When compared to the satisfaction the public express for railways and electricity, local government scores less with under 20 per cent expressing satisfaction. The weak salience of local government is shown by a recent study which examined explored loyalty to territory and found there does not appear very much community identity for any level of local elected government above the parishes (Young *et al.*, 1996). When these findings are set against the influence of the media on the reputation of local government and the persistent low turnout in local elections, it seems the public have ambiguous attitudes to local democratic institutions and their performance.

What emerges at the end of the 1990s is the conflation of a number of contradictory trends in local and central politics, making for decentralization/centralization, experimentation/statis and content/discontent, occurring at the same time but varying according to policy sector and place. Indeed, the very complexity of local governance and the legacy of the Conservative years is a challenge for all the local bodies now involved in decision-making. With little guidance, they must make sense of the institutional profusion. In part the resilience of organization and the high degree of policy learning that has taken place give much to build upon. Locally-elected authorities are still the main public authorities with a high degree of popular recognition. The slow, bureaucratic and professional culture in many local authorities has broken down and has been replaced by a more consumer-driven, efficient, goal-oriented, open and networking orientation. The new expanded governance sector has the strengths and enthusiasm of new bodies searching for their identities and bases of legitimacy. Often because of their democratic deficits, bodies like TECs are willing to address issues of community representation and citizen views. But also their fragility and instability in the face of the vicissitudes in central government policy mean they are unable to develop stable long-term strategic alliances with traditional policy-makers (John and Cole, 1997).

The Future

Both the achievements and the failures of 18 years of reform and experimentation need to be addressed by succeeding national governments from 1997. In opposition, Labour tried to keep a balance between rewarding its members in local government who wished for new freedoms and financial security after the years of Conservative rule and maintaining policy responsibility and fiscal restraint in the face of a national media obsessed with the machinations of some Labour London and metropolitan local authorities. After all, the turning point of the fortunes of the Labour party in the 1980s was leader Neil Kinnock's public refutation of the policies of the Labour-controlled Liverpool City Council at the Labour Party conference of 1985.

As well as an electoral calculation, the moderation of Labour's main policy document, *Renewing Democracy, Rebuilding Communities,* and the subsequent watering down of many of its commitments, reflect the selective acceptance of slices of what was once regarded as the Conservatives' policy agenda but which have been subsumed into normal politics for much of innovatory local government. Whether the process of adapting to central reforms reflects the underlying strength of local government is a matter of interpretation, yet it is also testament to the power of the ideological revolution which is likely to live far beyond the Conservative governments. Thus Labour's plans for 'best value' and local performance plans in local government have little to distinguish them from the value for money proposals pushed by the Audit Commission since 1982. Even though the government intends to abolish the requirement to contract out by 1 April 1999, the best value criterion will encourage councils to retain competitive tendering, although in the context of a partnership between local and central government. Indeed, the proposal to give powers to the Audit Commission to overhaul inefficient services goes beyond the policies of the Conservatives.

On the other hand, there are many positive proposals. Labour is committed to regional government, starting with regional chambers operating within the government offices for the regions, charged with promoting accountability of EU funding and local economic development policy, and introduced after support in a local referendum (Chapter 11). Councils now have the freedom to spend capital raised by council house sales, spread over a number of years. Labour has a commitment to restoring the autonomy of local government, expressed through the commitment to end the central 'capping' of local expenditure, the return of the national non-domestic rate, the proposal for a general competence and the creation of a directly-elected mayor and strategic authority for London, though these proposals are carefully qualified so they do not give any hint of irresponsibility. Thus the end of capping will still see central government retain reserve powers; the authority for London will only be introduced with the consent of the people of London. Deputy Prime Minister John Prescott is a champion of regional government, and his team at the Departments of Environment and Transport is likely to be sympathetic to elected local government. So too are the many new Labour MPs with local government backgrounds. Though the new century is unlikely to see a rebirth of traditional local authorities as the centre for local democracy, government policy is likely to be more sympathetic than before.

Rather than representing a fundamental break from the policies followed for local government, the Blair government is likely to deliver much of same type of central policies with some of the ideological sting removed and to develop a commitment to community governance. Even though the Blair government will generate more consensual policies for local governance than its predecessors, it will tend to work within the framework of governance that has emerged rather than try to restructure it. The changes enacted between 1979 and 1997 were too radical to give it any other option, and what has emerged is a more flexible form of governing than before, attuned to the complex and shifting policy making environment. Moreover, the central government obsession with quality of local services and control in areas such as education and law and order, plus the ministerial need for successful local policy initiatives, are likely to continue, and thus it is probable that central government will continue to use and create special agencies to implement policy. On the other hand, while central actors have greater power to implement initiatives in the 1990s than before, the sheer complexity of the issues, and the unintended negative consequences of often conflicting central initiatives, means that a cooperative form of governance, operating across central and local institutions and coordinated by dynamic political leaders, is the only practical means of solving modern policy problems. Many of the trends of the last 20 years have yet to be fully worked out as central government continues to restructure the periphery and local authorities have not fully adapted to their new roles, but there are the beginnings of more effective policy making at the local level geared to increase governing capacity. The key factor limiting such a development is the detail of much central control, the weak lines of accountability and democratic deficits of both new and old local public authorities.

Acknowledgment

I am grateful to Dilys Hill, George Jones, John Stewart and Gerry Stoker for comments on an earlier draft of this chapter.

Part III

14

Economic Policy

GAVIN KELLY

The last time Labour won a landslide victory (in 1945), one of its first acts was to nationalize the Bank of England. In 1997 Gordon Brown marked his arrival as Chancellor by announcing, to widespread applause from the City, the CBI and two recent Conservative Chancellors, that the Bank would become operationally independent. The decision neatly symbolized both the fundamental reorientation of economic policy that has taken place in the past 20 years and the growing convergence in the economic thinking of the two main parties, particularly on the institutionalization of a permanently low-inflation economy. This is in sharp contrast to the late 1970s and 1980s, when the demise of the postwar Keynesian consensus and the rise of the New Right led to fierce disagreements on central aspects of economic management. Drawing on monetarism and the new classical economics the New Right advocated a much reduced role for the state, privatization as the flagship industrial policy, cutbacks in public spending on welfare and the control of inflation as the key objective of macroeconomic policy. The left mostly clung to old certainties from the Keynesian era: full employment was to be maintained through active fiscal and monetary policy, privatization was to be fought at all costs, and the structure of the welfare state was to be preserved.

These sharp distinctions between right and left have been diminishing for some time. One explanation is the changes occurring at a regional and global level. Higher levels of international product market competition, the ever increasing importance of multinational companies, and perhaps most significantly of all, the growth of global financial markets have greatly restricted the freedom of national governments to pursue economic policies that are not palatable to international business and finance. These constraints have recently been reinforced at a European level by the convergence criteria set down in the Maastricht Treaty for entry into a new single currency. These spell out in some detail a number of macroeconomic criteria which all governments – whether right or left – are supposed to meet if they wish to qualify for European Monetary Union (EMU) and set the terms of reference by which all macro policy measures will be judged. Taken together these changes have greatly narrowed the parameters within which governments must operate and have contributed to the common view that there is no longer any clear distinction between a 'left' and a 'right' approach to many of the big issues of economic policy.

In Britain the most vivid manifestation of these changes was the rapid shift by the Labour Party after 1987 to a pro-market, pro-business, anti-inflationary economic position. It has sought to leapfrog the Conservatives in its attempt to portray itself as the party of low inflation and sound public finances. Doubtless much of this was a response to Labour's habit of losing elections, but it also reflects the belief that Labour can achieve many of its goals within a capitalist economy. While most of the recent convergence can be explained by New Labour's shift to the centre, the Conservatives have also contributed. The severity of the 1990–2 recession ensured a less self-confident approach to economic policy than during the Thatcher years. Taxes had to be increased, mistakes made during the Lawson years were admitted, the possibility of a beneficial devaluation was accepted, the post office privatization plans were halted and any lingering belief in the ability of money supply figures to predict inflation accurately was abandoned.

The combination of these global and European constraints and the ideological convergence between parties might suggest that economic policy in the 1990s is no longer interesting or contentious. This is not so. The relationship between public policy and economic performance remains vital. Economic performance determines the ability of governments to pursue many other policy agendas in areas such as social policy, health and education. So if government policy improves the performance of the economy it increases its capacity to do other things. Although it may be easier for governments to damage the economy than actually to improve it, different economic policy agendas do lead to different outcomes in terms of growth, unemployment and the distribution of income.

It is also possible to take the convergence view on economic policy too far. Some important differences between the parties do still exist. As the big macroeconomic disputes about how fiscal and monetary policy should be used have faded, so other issues concentrating on supply-side reforms to the economy have taken their place as the focus for policy debate. This shift has given rise to a new set of buzzwords in which the policy debate is conducted. Terms such as competitiveness, worker insecurity, shareholder value, workfare, inward investment and lifelong training have replaced the old vocabularies of monetarism, Keynesianism and corporatism. Future policy divides will therefore tend to be on microeconomic policy. In terms of political rhetoric this was reflected in the 1997 election in which the Conservatives spoke of Britain as the enterprise centre of Europe; a free market economy with low taxes, little labour market regulation and an entrepreneurial culture, while New Labour talked of an economy in which all individuals are encouraged to participate in the world of work, and social justice and economic efficiency go hand-in-hand. Underlying these slogans there are still *some* latent policy differences, but they are more nuanced than those in the old left–right debates. Both parties are now thoroughly committed to capitalism; it is the *type* of capitalism that is in dispute.

After the ERM: Rebuilding the Institutions of Macroeconomic Policy

Kenneth Clarke's 1993–7 Chancellorship is best understood as a reaction to the political and economic upheavals which preceded it. In September 1992 the UK's two year membership of the Exchange Rate Mechanism (ERM) came to a dramatic end. Despite unprecedented rises in interest rates and the use of foreign exchange reserves, selling within the foreign exchange markets ensured that sterling could not be maintained at its central rate of 2.95 Deutsche Marks. The ERM débâcle was a unique moment of political and economic crisis, the first time since 1945 that a Conservative government was forced to devalue. Its impact on the overall macroeconomic framework was equally profound. ERM membership had been hailed by many as a means of overcoming the UK's failure to impose an effective internal monetary discipline by introducing a credible external discipline: a pegged exchange rate. A high value of the pound would maintain downward pressure on prices and ensure that wages remained in line with those in other European countries, particularly Germany. Following the pound's exit this framework lay in tatters and had to be replaced by something new.

The Rise and Fall of the Ken and Eddie Show

At the heart of the new monetary framework were a number of institutional changes. A specific and publicly stated inflation target was initially set at 1–4 per cent, and was revised in June 1995 to a more restrictive 0–2.5 per cent band. Supplementing this was a more open approach towards monitoring compliance with the target. The Bank of England, whose reputation escaped the ERM crisis comparatively unscathed, started publishing quarterly reports on inflation prospects; monthly meetings began to be held between the Governor of the Bank, Eddie George and the Chancellor Kenneth Clarke, the minutes of which were publicly disclosed six weeks after the event; and a panel of independent academic and professional economists was set up to advise government (initially referred to as the 'seven wise men' before it incorporated several women members). More generally the Bank of England was granted *some* operational independence, which proved to be a precursor to the *full* operational independence introduced in 1997.

The new monetary framework formalized the decision making process used to determine the policy stance best suited to meet the inflation target. Chancellor Clarke determined the monetary stance after having been told the Bank's opinion. Initially most commentators argued that this set up would greatly increase the influence of the Bank over interest rate policy, though hindsight suggests that this may not have been the case.

Of course if economists could guarantee accurate predictions about future economic trends there would have been little for the two main figures involved to disagree about. But this was not the case. Uncertainties over future economic trends meant that policy making required difficult judgements which had to be made in the face of contradictory evidence. These differences in the perceived 'balance of risk' involved in meeting the inflation target were given greater coverage due to the improved transparency of decision making.

So did they normally agree or disagree? During 1994 and 1995 there was agreement in 18 of the 24 meetings, with the Bank calling for a harder anti-inflationary approach in the remaining six (that is, they either called for increases in interest rates or argued against cuts made by the Chancellor). More revealing, however, is that at almost one in three of the meetings held up to June 1996 there was either an interest rate change or a change advised, and on almost half of these occasions there was disagreement between the two parties. During much of the period events tended to support the Chancellor's judgements rather than the Bank's, which boosted the Chancellor's credibility in the City.

The monetary framework introduced by Gordon Brown in 1997 represents the most radical change in the UK's economic constitution since the Second World War, a first instalment of the wider constitutional modernization to which Labour is committed. The Bank of England now has 'operational independence' which means that a revised 'monetary policy committee' has complete autonomy to set the interest rates necessary to meet the Chancellor's inflation target of 1.5 to 3 per cent. This committee will consist of the Bank Governor, two Deputy Governors and six other members (two from the Bank with the remainder being external experts appointed by the Chancellor), and is internally accountable to a revised Bank Court consisting of representatives of industry and finance from throughout the UK, and externally accountable to a bolstered Treasury select committee in Parliament.

The stated rationale for this delegation of authority to the Bank is to ensure that monetary policy is set on economic grounds free from political manipulation. The hope is that this will reassure financial markets and thereby reduce interest rates in the long term and increase investment and employment. In this regard it can be interpreted as a political response to the economic imperatives of a global economy. Conversely, critics argue that diminished democratic control of the Bank will lead to a deflationary monetary policy which will be harmful to the economy.

Though the long-run economic effects are as yet unclear, the move provided the new Labour government with the short-term political benefits of reassuring the City and partially fulfilling one of the entry conditions to a future single European currency.

Evidence: Macroeconomic Policy and Trends

In the post-ERM period the broad macroeconomic stance which Clarke pursued involved a relatively loose monetary policy and quite restrictive fiscal policy, a mix that helped ensure a period of low inflation and stable growth. Reliance on any one theoretical or ideological approach (such as monetarism) or policy tool (such as a pegged exchange rate) was firmly rejected. For a period in 1994 it seemed that this new pragmatism had fostered an almost unique set of circumstances as the UK economy seemed poised to enjoy a period of 'export-led growth', something which all post-war governments have sought and few attained. Improved export performance would, it was thought, spur an increase in private sector investment leading to long term improvements in growth and productivity. By 1995, however, it was clear that the rapid growth in exports was short-lived and business investment had failed to respond to a period of record corporate profitability and low inflation. During 1996–7, renewed economic growth was underpinned by the more familiar trends of growing consumer spending, high personal borrowing and rising house prices leading many commentators to recommend the rise in interest rates made by Chancellor Brown on assuming office.

Possibly the most striking aspect of the post–1992 recovery was the remarkably stable and low inflation rate. Since the new monetary framework was introduced inflation has averaged 2.8 per cent, which compares favourably with an average rate of 7 per cent in the 1980s, 12.6 per cent in the 1970s and 3.5 per cent in the 1960s (OECD, 1996). This is all the more notable because in the past devaluations have often fed through into higher inflation. Whether or not this improved performance can be fully explained by the new monetary framework is however open to question. Inflation rates have been almost uniformly low throughout the OECD countries, with the UK's rate being slightly above the average of its main trading partners.

Indeed these international trends have led some economists to talk optimistically of the 'death of inflation' due to increased international competition in product markets and less regulated labour markets which keep downward pressure on prices. The low rate of growth in earnings was also a notable component of the recovery and contributed to the gradual decline in unemployment, which fell below 1.9 million in February 1997 (Figure 14.1).

One of the most persistent problems during this relatively benign macroeconomic period was the poor state of public sector finances. Since the early 1980s the governments' Medium Term Financial Strategy (MTFS) has set targets for forthcoming years which seek to bring the Public Sector Borrowing Requirement (PSBR) back into balance over the medium term (for instance, the 1996 projections anticipated that the public finances would move into a surplus by the financial year 2000–1). During the 1990s there have been habitual adjustments of the predicted

FIGURE 14.1   UK unemployment and inflation (%)

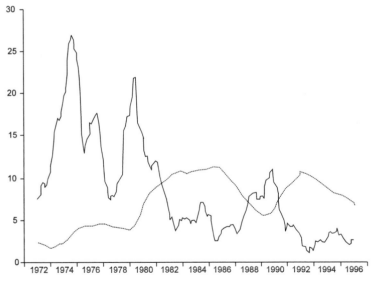

—— UK inflation rate

·········· UK unemployment rate

Source: DATASTREAM.

PSBR due to forecasting errors: occasionally this has led to downward revisions, more typical however are upward adjustments, as occurred in 1995–6. Though estimates vary on the size of the 1997–8 PSBR there is a wide consensus that, given the stage of the economic cycle, the UK has a structural deficit. This suggests that Chancellor Brown will have to find a way of raising the tax take without breaking Labour's election pledge of not increasing personal tax rates.

The budget in July 1997 set out the government's priorities for welfare reform and higher long-term investment. It also implemented a £4.8 billion windfall tax on the privatized utilities to fund Labour's welfare-to-work programme, reduced VAT on domestic fuel to 5 per cent, and cautiously began to deliver Labour's agenda for fair taxation by cutting several tax reliefs. These measures, combined with the use of the budget reserve (£2.2 billion), allowed the Chancellor to proclaim moderate fiscal tightening, adherence to public expenditure limits, and higher spending on education and health. Overall, he sought to convince the Bank and the City that the inflation target could be achieved without excessive increases in interest rates.

Policy Debates

EMU and Economic Policy

In the period after the ERM débâcle there was widespread satisfaction that the UK was following an economic policy which, for the first time in three years, was tailored towards its own domestic requirements. Euroscepticism flourished within the Tory government while enthusiasm for any attempt to advance monetary union seemed to sag across much of the European Union. For a time the whole EMU project was thought to be dead in the water. In the 1997 general election campaign, however, and against a backdrop of continuing tabloid and public scepticism, none of the main parties was willing to make a manifesto pledge ruling out membership of a single European currency during the lifetime of the new Parliament, though all parties committed themselves to a referendum before any decision to join is made. This indicates that for a variety of reasons policy makers are reluctant to exclude the possibility of a renewed attempt at building a truly European economic policy. At one level this simply reflected the precarious position of a bitterly-divided Conservative government seeking to avoid further splits, but it also suggested a tacit acceptance that despite all the rhetoric to the contrary, the UK's economic interests remain linked to the possibility of further EU integration.

The Maastricht Treaty provided a wide ranging extension of the areas of European Community competences and made important changes to the EU's institutional machinery. But Maastricht has now become synonymous with the economic proposals set down as stepping-stones towards EMU (see Wilks, 1993). Specifically the Treaty set out 'convergence criteria' for a number of fiscal and monetary variables which countries have to satisfy as preconditions for membership of the common currency (Box 14.1). With the exception of the UK and Denmark (who negotiated opt-outs) all countries who meet the convergence criteria are bound according to the terms of the Treaty to join a single currency by 1999. The actual decision as to when Stage 3 will in fact start and which countries are able to join it will be taken by the Council of Ministers (voting by qualified majority voting) in early 1998.

As important as the formal criteria for entry is the subjective language in which they are couched. Crucially, this gives scope to the Council of Ministers to use their discretion in interpreting whether a member's economy conforms to the Maastricht conditions, and will doubtless give rise to a strong political pressure from borderline states for a flexible interpretation of the criteria. Indeed, in 1996 and 1997, several member states made plain their strong political desire to meet these criteria by indicating their willingness to employ suspect accounting techniques or plead special circumstances in order to improve their chances of entry. These manoeuvres, combined with budgetary tightening and a liberal interpretation of the convergence criteria, suggest that many countries will soon be in a position to meet the entry conditions in 1999, though others such as Greece will clearly be ruled out, while the decision on countries such as Belgium and Italy is likely to be controversial.

Concerns over the rules governing the operation of EMU extend to the nature of the so called 'stability and growth' pact agreed in December 1996, which sets limits to the fiscal behaviour

Box 14.1   *Maastricht convergence criteria*

The key features of the convergence criteria can be summarized as:

(i)   *price stability*: consumer price inflation no more than 1.5 per cent above that in 'the three best performing' states

(ii)   *interest rates*: long-term interest rates not to exceed the average of 'the three best performing' states by more than 2 per cent

(iii) *exchange rate*: maintaining member currency within the fluctuation margins of the ERM for at least two years, without devaluing against other member currencies

(iv)   *institutional criteria*: statutory independence for the Bank of England

(v)   *fiscal stance*: a budget deficit/GDP ratio below 3 per cent; and a total government debt/GDP ratio below 60 per cent.

Scope for flexible interpretation applies particularly to the fiscal criteria. If the above criteria are breached, the Council is to decide whether or not an 'excessive deficit exists'. The Commission is bound to advise the Council on this according to whether:

(i)   the (budget deficit) has 'declined substantially and continuously . . . and comes close to the reference level'; or

(ii)   the excess is 'exceptional and temporary . . . and remains close to the reference level'; or

(iii) (for government debt) the excess ratio is 'sufficiently diminishing and approaching the reference value at a satisfactory pace'.

of the participating countries once EMU has commenced. This pact gives the Council of Ministers the power to impose stringent fines on states which breach the fiscal criteria unless their GDP has fallen by more than 2 per cent in the preceding year; though the offending states can appeal against this penalty if GDP has fallen by between 0.75 and 2 per cent in this time. But once again political pressures may prevent the Council from invoking this threat against troubled economies.

The Economic Costs and Benefits of EMU

All sides of the debate agree that there would be *some* costs and some benefits to either joining or opting out of EMU, the real debate is about the relative size of these effects. Some of the benefits are very clear. A single currency would eliminate the transaction costs associated with the current conversion between member countries; it would eliminate exchange rate instability (between member countries) which would remove an important source of business uncertainty and benefit export industries; and it would help foster greater intra-EU competition by removing a major obstacle which prevents the current EU from having a truly single market. The size of other alleged benefits is more controversial as they depend upon each country's economic history, but they could be highly significant. For instance, the benefits of the European Central Bank (ECB) maintaining low inflation and low borrowing costs could be highly significant to countries with poor track records on inflation, while countries such as Germany which already have a firmly embedded anti-inflationary culture may have less to gain.

The disagreement over the possible costs of EMU are far more wide ranging (Corrie and Michie, 1997). Most economists accept that the principal cost associated with EMU is that if differences in the structure of national economies lead to different economic cycles, growth rates, or unemployment levels, then national monetary policies could, at least in theory, help to counter these different national trends. Under EMU however there can only be a single monetary policy to cover all member states. How serious this problem really is depends upon several technical considerations upon which there is little consensus. These include, primarily, whether the freedom to devalue is a tool of economic policy that member states should be worried about losing; the extent to which European economies are actually aligned; and the implications of a single monetary policy for the conduct of a fiscal policy. Behind much of the economic debate on EMU are different interpretations of the importance of the ability to devalue and to run an independent monetary policy. Economists divide sharply on this issue, with views ranging from those who see devaluation as a key tool of economic management to those who see devaluation as being unable to have any real effect on economic performance at all in the long and even medium term. Both sides within this debate often point to the ERM experience as supporting their case. Those against EMU repeat the conventional wisdom that the post-ERM devaluation of the pound underlay the following recovery. Most economists would agree that changes in the value of a national currency can and have had strong short-term effects on economic outcomes. The more difficult question is how long these effects are likely to last and whether they will tend to cause an increase in inflation, the typical view being that a devaluation will give the exporting country a temporary boost which will be eroded in the short to medium term by price rises. Those sympathetic to EMU emphasize that while the immediate 14 per cent devaluation led to a rise in exports which helped jolt the economy out of recession, exporters soon raised their prices sharply which in effect eroded the price competitiveness that the devaluation provided. As a result they argue that devaluation is not an effective means of improving long-term economic performance and should not be allowed to obstruct the real long term benefits that EMU would offer the UK.

One way around the problem of the loss of national monetary autonomy inherent in EMU would be for states to use national fiscal policies more proactively as a means of addressing difficulties specific to a country. An impending recession could for example be fended off by a slackening of the fiscal stance. This highlights the importance of the 'stability and growth' pact because a counter cyclical fiscal policy could breach these provisions leaving a member at risk of incurring fines imposed by the Council of Ministers. As a result a lively debate has opened up on whether EMU will require a substantial increase in the size of funds available to the EC to assist poorly performing regions. At present, however, there is little indication that there is political support for a significant shift towards a form of the fiscal federalism implicit in high inter-regional fiscal transfers.

Another fundamental concern voiced by many is the lack of democratic accountability of the proposed ECB. As planned the ECB is to be made up by a nominee from each member state. Once appointed however these individuals operate as members of the ECB not as representatives of member states, and are charged with the single objective of pursuing price stability. The argument in favour reflects that made at a domestic level: it is thought to be a requirement of a truly credible low inflation policy. If monetary policy is placed under direct democratic control the authorities, it is argued, may well buckle under popular pressure for expansionary and inflationary policies.

Those in favour of EMU question how much sovereignty a state like the UK actually has. If much of the UK's monetary policy will inevitably be shaped by the decisions of the Bundesbank, membership of EMU could confer at least as much new sovereignty (through the UK's ability to influence the ECB policy) as is likely to be lost. It can also be argued that it is not in the interests of the economy for the UK to retain whatever residue of sovereignty it still has. While in theory prudent monetary policy can help iron out cycles in the economy, in practice inappropriate UK monetary stances have often accentuated damaging trends. It might be better therefore for the UK to delegate responsibility to an ECB composed of member states with more successful track records in monetary policy.

The British Debate on EMU

Despite all the talk of ideological convergence the great economic issue of the day has still polarized all sections of political opinion within the UK; from the political parties to employers organizations, trade unions, the City and academia it is hard to find a unified voice on the issue (Box 14.2). As a result the debate is replete with ambiguity and paradox. Unlikely cross party alliances have occurred between those with strong views on the issue, while the two front benches went into the 1997 election with positions on EMU which were formally identical though very different in tone: both parties were committed to a 'wait and see' policy of deferring judgement on EMU until a later date. But the

Box 14.2 *Divisions over monetary union*

	Against EMU in principle	Wait and see/ referendum	Willing to support EMU in principle
Left	Avoid a deflationary 'Banker's Europe' Lack of accountability Devaluation a key tool of economic policy	Need for 'real' criteria (e.g. unemployment and growth) Develop a 'people's Europe' Some democratic control of the ECB	Possibility of Euro-Keynesian: reduce exposure to financial markets EMU as a job creator Integral to a 'people's Europe'
	(Campaign Group; much of old Labour)	(most Labour ministers TGWU UNISON)	(TUC; Liberal Democrats; Gordon Brown)
Right	Protect national sovereignty Backlash to the ERM saga/ support for floating exchange rates Global outlook, not 'fortress Europe'	Greater convergence required Wait to see if it succeeds Follow business opinion as it evolves	Lower inflation Assist the City Pro-business and free market Anti-nationalism
	(William Hague and the shadow Cabinet; Institute of Directors; James Goldsmith; Lady Thatcher, *Daily Telegraph*, *Times* and most of the tabloid press)	(John Major and the former Conservative government; much of the small business community)	(CBI; *Financial Times*; Kenneth Clarke; Leon Brittan)

leadership of each party was divided. Kenneth Clarke's dogged defence of the potential merits of EMU was at odds with the view of most of the cabinet. Among Labour-watchers much was made of the supposed rift between the Euro-enthusiast Gordon Brown and the more sceptical Robin Cook, although Cook admits that it will be difficult for a Labour government to stay outside a successful EMU area after 2002 while Brown concedes that it is highly unlikely that entry could occur in 1999.

Overall the whole question of EMU proved deeply divisive for the Conservatives in government and will prove difficult for Labour. It is probably not untrue to say that much of the leadership of both parties would be relieved if the whole EMU project was blown off course. However, given the long standing determination of other EU countries to press ahead this looks increasingly unlikely.

Could the UK Join?

Despite the successful period of growth in the 1992–7 period, there are still several potential obstacles to the UK's membership of EMU (should it wish to join) if the convergence criteria are strictly applied, though if the approach is more flexible the UK should be in a strong position to join. One of the most significant problems is the state of the public finances, specifically the budget deficit/GDP ratio. During 1995–6 the UK overshot the 3 per cent target figure and current projections are divided as to whether this criteria could be met by 1998–9. Another hurdle is sterling's failure to be a member of the ERM for two years prior to the commencement of EMU, meaning that (in theory) sterling would have had to re-enter the wider ERM during 1996 in order to qualify for entry in 1999. But neither of these problems is likely to prove insurmountable. At the entry date the UK is likely to be in a relatively strong and stable fiscal position compared to many EU states and the wording of the exchange rate criterion is sufficiently ambiguous that it is unlikely to constitute a binding constraint. Finally, further legislation would be required to convert the Bank of England's current 'operational independence' into the full statutory independence required under the Maastricht provisions.

Moving from the theme of 'could Britain join' to 'should Britain join' requires a number of further assumptions to be made about institutional decisions that have not yet been made. For a meaningful assessment of the benefits or otherwise of membership requires a judgement not only on which other countries will participate but also the nature of the relationship between the outsider and the insider states of EMU.

Rather than attempt to predict a single outcome it is more useful to map three plausible EMU scenarios. The first concerns the dangers that a split between EMU insiders and outsiders may pose to the continued stability of the single European market. While in theory the single market should carry on functioning regardless of developments in the EMU debate, the post-ERM crisis made clear that a competitive devaluation by those who remain outside of EMU is likely to be met with considerable political pressure from insider states. This exposes the nightmare scenario for many pro-integrationists: that the convergence criteria prevents some countries joining EMU – an initiative which was aimed at strengthening the single market – and as a result leads to tension between insider and outsider states, which threatens the operation of the single market itself. A second gloomy possibility for the EMU project, and one touted by many EMU cynics, is that a liberal interpretation of the convergence criteria will allow many structurally weak and poorly aligned economies into the EMU area which will weaken the new currency and lead to increasing tension between participating states over the stance of monetary policy. Eventually this political turbulence could lead to the unravelling of EMU as countries choose to go it alone in order to reduce the high levels of unemployment brought about by a restrictive ECB monetary policy. A final scenario is that a small number of stronger economies will initially sign up for EMU to be joined by other countries as their economies converge. Over time the financial markets will impose an increasingly high interest rate premium on outsider states, such as the UK, whose currencies will be volatile and sensitive to movements in the euro. Gradually pressure from the business community and the City will feed through into the media which will start to question the wisdom of the UK's outsider status. Eventually an application to join EMU will be made and accepted on terms less attractive than were available at EMU's inception.

Perhaps out of all of this uncertainty, only two clear points can be made. First, there is enough contradictory economic evidence to allow those with strong political views on EMU to be able to invoke some economic reasoning on their behalf. Second, economic calculations about the pros or cons of EMU are highly dependent on continuously evolving political developments which will shape the transitional path to EMU and the insider-outsider relationship once Stage 3 of the process has commenced.

Supply Side: The Competitiveness Debate

The pursuit of the elusive objective of economic competitiveness is a theme which unites all parties and is the yardstick on which nearly all economic and increasingly social policy measures are judged. The former Conservative government published three white papers on the subject, all parties have 'competitiveness' spokespeople, and reports claiming to measure and compare the UK's international competitive position get widespread coverage in the press: the competitiveness bandwagon is almost an industry in itself. If a policy proposal is thought to damage competitiveness there is little chance of it being accepted: no mainstream politician could stand on a platform and be 'against competitiveness'. So what is meant by the term and what policies might promote it? In order to clarify these issues two key aspects of the debate, investment behaviour and the labour market, will be considered in more detail.

Competitiveness is perhaps best thought of at the level of the firm. Porter (1990) argues that firms acquire competitive advantage by 'adding value', either by providing goods of comparable value to those of other firms but at a lower price, or by somehow differentiating their goods from others in the market in a way which allows them to charge a higher price. Either of these approaches allows firms to maintain or expand market share in internationally contested markets. More controversial however is the popular idea that whole countries are, or can be, competitive (Krugman, 1994). Likening countries to firms, this wider approach contends that whole countries compete, slugging it out in international markets with one another, the implication being that if one country increases its 'national' competitiveness and 'wins' then other countries must 'lose'. In fact rising productivity levels in competitor countries (which would presumably increase competitiveness) could benefit domestic industries as it will increase their export markets. This suggests that international trade is often not a 'zero-sum game', it can be mutually beneficial, though exposure to international competition can lead to unequal distributional outcomes: it may hurt particular groups within a given country, even though the country as a whole may benefit. Despite this ambiguity concerning some uses of the term, there is a political consensus that policies which foster corporate competitiveness are the elixir of national economic success.

How Important is Investment?

Low rates of productive investment are routinely accused of being a root cause of the UK's relative economic decline during the twentieth century and a continued challenge to the UK's competitiveness. Higher investment, it has long been argued, is required to remedy these problems. The evidence on investment performance is hotly disputed and, predictably, there is some evidence supporting both sides of the argument. Low historical investment levels have been attributed to a number of different causes. Orthodox views on the factors which boost investment focus on the determinants of business confidence such as stable macroeconomic conditions and corporate profitability. If true the UK should have undergone a significant improvement in its investment performance between 1992 and 1997. Instead this period was characterized by relatively weak private investment which led many, including Howard Davies, the deputy governor of the Bank of England, to question whether 'the markets can respond' to improved conditions. It seems that these factors are necessary not sufficient conditions for higher investment.

This investment puzzle has renewed interest in a long-standing and well rehearsed critique of British capitalism: financial short-termism. Throughout the century many academics, politicians and businessmen have argued that the City has undermined the UK economy due to its alleged unwillingness to provide long-term investment funds to industry. Again the contemporary evidence on this is contradictory. City economists point to the fact that big investors such as pension funds typically hold shares

in the companies they invest in for between three and 10 years
(Self, 1996), hardly evidence of rampant financial short-termism.
Against this is evidence which suggests that UK companies have
to meet exceptionally high hurdle rates before investment projects
are agreed to, and have to pay dividend payments to shareholders
(rather than retaining funds for investment) which greatly out-
strip those in all other OECD countries.

During the 1995–6 period the government adopted a more
robust defence of the UK's investment record, with William
Waldegrave claiming that 'There are a lot of myths about
investment. In fact, it is a British success story' (23 February
1996). This stood in marked contrast to the more defensive tone
struck in 1994 when the Treasury was ordered to conduct an
inquiry into whether the financial system imposed constraints on
investment. The change in government presentation appeared to
be more a result of changing ministerial portfolios than any great
shift in investment behaviour. Comparative data on investment
performance is ambiguous (Table 14.1): it certainly is not a great
success story (and investment shares have hardly improved since
1979) but neither is it greatly worse than that of several other EU
countries, all of which are massively outperformed by Japan
(Bond and Jenkinson, 1996). Others argue that though the share
of GDP going to investment may be comparable with other
countries, this should hardly be reassuring given the UK's
comparatively poor growth record over much of this period.
Moreover it is argued that these figures disguise both the
poor investment performance of the UK during the post-1992
recovery and the particularly weak record in certain sectors
which are thought to be important to growth, such as manufacturing.

TABLE 14.1   Investment as a percentage of GDP

	Japan	*Italy*	*Germany*	*France*	*US*	*UK*
1980–93						
Gross fixed capital formation	30	21	21	21	18	17
1960 – 93						
Gross fixed capital formation	31	23	22	22	18	18

Source: OECD historical statistics (1995).

Post-Neo-Classical Endogenous Growth Theory . . . and All that Jazz

In recent years the debate on investment has taken a new twist. When Gordon Brown invoked 'post-neo-classical endogenous growth theory' in support of New Labour's economic programme he was referring to an important strand of research which claims to offer a new interpretation of the link between investment and growth. Put simply this theory suggests two things: firstly that the level of investment may be a determinant of the long-run growth rate of the economy (contrary to neo-classical assumptions), and secondly that investment in 'non-tangible assets' (education, training and R&D) can be as important for growth as that in tangible assets (machinery and buildings). This approach seemed dovetailed for a party which has long referred to Britain's 'investment problem' as the cause of its relative decline while also seeking to emphasize the importance of education as a key economic policy.

Unfortunately for protagonists of this approach the evidence is not as clear cut as the theory. Some recent work by growth economists suggests that over long periods of time growth rates still may be independent of investment. Others suggest that the theory might well be right but it is not capable of providing any clear case for greater government intervention. Despite these reservations it is none the less clear that the UK's unimpressive record on investment in education and training has led to a clear shortage of skills, particularly during upswings in the economic cycle, which may have had a negative impact on growth. For instance, over the 1979–91 period, 14 per cent of all UK firms reported skills shortages as opposed to a 5 per cent average for the EU as a whole, worse still, the UK figure rose to almost 33 per cent during the Lawson boom (Haskel and Martin, 1994). These shortages tend to choke off recoveries prematurely as skills bottlenecks lead to inflationary wage pressures which prompt the Bank of England to respond by pressing for a tightening of monetary policy. These concerns over investment in human and physical capital suggest that new initiatives on vocational training and an investment promoting overhaul of the corporate tax system will be priorities for the new Labour government.

The Labour Market

Within the wide debate on competitiveness perhaps the most contentious issue and one that has become central to the political

debate is that of the labour market and the issue of 'flexibility'.
The UK has one of the least regulated labour markets of all the
OECD countries following the implementation of measures which
reduced the influence of trade unions and decentralized pay
bargaining, removed procedures to regulate low pay, and cut
restrictions on the conditions of employment, working times and
dismissal rules. This approach was widely supported by the
influential OECD Jobs Study (OECD, 1994) which called for
other countries to follow this shift towards labour market flexibility.

So has greater deregulation improved the performance of the
labour market? Clearly in the 1990–2 recession and associated
recovery employment figures responded more rapidly to changes
in output than in earlier periods. It is also possible that the level of
unemployment at which stable prices can be sustained (referred to
clumsily as the 'natural rate') – which rose dramatically in the
1970 and early 1980s to 9.75 per cent in 1985 – has fallen slightly
to an estimated 7.5 per cent in 1995 (OECD figures). However
whether or not this fall is a direct result of deregulation is not
clear. Similarly the UK's relatively low unemployment rate in the
1990s compared to other EU countries has been attributed to
labour market reform. Against this many economists doubt that
the reforms of the 1980s significantly improved the trade off
between real-wages and unemployment, and there has been
widespread concern about the nature of the jobs created and
how these jobs have been distributed throughout the labour
market. Moreover much of the fall in unemployment can be
attributed to individuals leaving the labour market rather than
the creation of more jobs. These concerns alongside the increased
willingness of employers to lay off large sections of their established workforce has made the issue of job 'security' one of the
most potent political themes of the 1990s.

Labour Market Adjustment: Evolution or Revolution?

The nature of the political debate has to some extent reinforced
the view espoused by many commentators that the 1980s brought
about policy-induced structural change in the labour market.
While the right boast that their reforms have created a mobile
and efficient labour market in which employers are more willing
to take new staff on, leading left-wing critics such as Will Hutton

(1995) have argued that deregulation has created a 'thirty/thirty/ forty' society in which 30 per cent of the population is unemployed or inactive, 30 per cent is in insecure short-term or unprotected part-time positions, and 40 per cent of the population is in relatively secure tenured positions and is paid above median earnings. If true, this would mean an incredibly divided labour market in which the contented minority is outnumbered by an insecure or economically excluded majority. While this interpretation seems in tune with the widespread perception (and oft-cited anecdotal evidence) of job insecurity it is however open to question on several counts (Robinson, 1995). Firstly, the categorizations may be misleading; within each job category (for example, self-employed) there may be a spectrum of job types, some more secure and better paid than others. It is doubtful that all employees within this category are in insecure positions. Another question mark concerns the extent to which the changes which have occurred since 1979 have been a result of government policy. For instance, average job tenure (of those in employment) only fell from nine to eight years between 1979 and 1991, while the increase in part-time work reflects a long-term and stable trend originating in the 1950s and the share of temporary work remained at a constant level of 5 per cent during 1984–91, though it did increase to 7.5 per cent by 1995. However the figures do present some significant changes, particularly as regards the persistently high levels of unemployment and the growth of self-employment: both of which underlie a growing sense of insecurity.

Another much commented on and less disputed trend concerns the concentration of new jobs going to adults who live in households where other adults already have jobs. This has led to a polarization of work between 'job rich and job poor households'. The upward shift in the share of non-pensioner jobless households has been staggering, rising from 6.5 per cent in 1975 to 19 per cent in 1994. These movements combined with the continued escalation of top pay (which was not interrupted by the recession) led to such rapidly increasing levels of income inequality that even pro-free-market institutions such as the OECD were prompted to voice their concern over the damage this could cause to social cohesion.

What type of policies have been advocated to address these labour market problems? There is a consensus that active supply-side policies are required to reduce unemployment and to move people off welfare benefits into work. But there is a left–right split on the form these measures should take and the extent to which interventionist supply-side measures are required both to increase the rewards of work and to increase the financial incentives to employers of taking on the long-term unemployed. Most on the right are content to emphasize training packages for the unemployed but see the minimum wage for instance as an unjustified restriction on business which will only destroy jobs. On the centre-left there is little desire to return to pre-Thatcher forms of industrial relations but there is support for limited forms of regulation (such as the imposition of a minimum wage, a right of recognition for trade unions when the majority of employees support it, and membership of the Social Chapter) in order to counter some aspects of employee insecurity. Some also challenge the general trend towards equating flexibility with a highly deregulated labour market. It is argued that employees will be more willing to accept changing work practices or to undertake demanding training within the context of a more secure employment contract (EC, 1993). From this perspective some employment regulation can help foster a more committed and productive workforce.

Conclusion: New Debates

The post-ERM years have in many ways been the most successful years of economic management since the end of the Bretton Woods era. The policy mix has led to a relatively prolonged stretch of sustained economic growth, low inflation and falling unemployment and high levels of inward investment, which taken together may mean that the UK is in a position to meet the EMU criteria. This is due to a combination of the post-ERM devaluation, prudent economic management and luck. It suggests some of the costs that have been imposed due to the macroeconomic adventurism which deepened the two preceding recessions. These are hard-won and considerable achievements. But they have been accompanied by sharply increased inequality and levels of unemployment which would have been unthinkable 25 years ago. Some of these difficulties can be attributed to changes in technological and demand conditions which are not particular to Britain, but other problems are depressingly familiar: Britain's historically weak record on standards of education and training, and the reluctance of domestic investment to respond adequately to improved macroeconomic conditions. It seems unlikely that macroeconomic stability combined with microeconomic deregulation will be enough to resolve these deep rooted supply-side problems.

The convergence in many aspects of economic policy over these years has been remarkable. Labour's economic programme in the 1997 election would have been unthinkable five, never mind 10 years beforehand. Not only had it completely rejected corporatism, wider public ownership, old-style Keynesian macroeconomics and increased welfare spending, but it also pledged not to raise the standard *or* top rate of income tax within the next parliament *and* to accept the Conservative public spending limits for 1997–8 and 1998–9. No opposition in recent history has been willing to impose such stringent fiscal constraints upon itself. However, in its commitment on a minimum wage, the use of the windfall tax on the privatized utilities to fund more active labour market policies and its pledge to concentrate future tax cuts (should they arise) on the low paid, it did offer a significantly different choice on the role that government can play within a market economy.

Clearly then it would be would be wrong to conclude that the convergence is complete and new divides will not arise. Currently there are many lively debates within the economics profession which have not yet fully filtered through into policy agendas, some of them raising issues which do not fit neatly into what remains of the political divide on economic policy. For instance on the supply side new debates are emerging which could have profound implications for the future of companies and work: for instance whose interests should companies represent? Should company managers be made more accountable to their shareholders or should the interests of other groups (or 'stakeholders') be considered? Will the nature of work in the post-corporatist era spell an ever diminishing role for trade unions in the economy or will current labour market insecurities lead to an upswing in new forms of collective employee organization? Another debate which poses fundamental questions for all future governments concerns the sources of tax revenues. Should there be a further shift away from taxation on employment (both in terms of income tax and employer's contributions) towards other sources of revenue, particularly environmental taxes? It seems likely that this supply-side terrain will see a continued growth of lively policy debates. But debates in macroeconomic policy have also evolved. Many economists are starting to question the central bank wisdom of myopic macro policies which seek to push already low levels of inflation towards zero, while the implications of endogenous growth theory for public incentives to invest are still being worked out. It remains to be seen whether these developments will seriously impact on the policy agenda and are capable of increasing the political emphasis placed on objectives which have long been out of fashion, such as full-employment. But it does seem that intellectual currents have shifted from the crude monetarism which dominated the late 1970s and 1980s and will continue to do so.

The arena in which future policy development is most important but least certain is that of international or at least supranational co-ordination and co-operation. Typically co-ordination of this kind occurs in relation to exchange rate and monetary policy, trade agreements and more recently environmental protection but it could increasingly apply to issues traditionally thought of as being wholly domestic such as fiscal policy, employment, company and competition law, and welfare provision. Increased economic interdependence arising from greater mobility of capital, labour and technology will ensure that Britain's willingness to pool sovereignty by participating in new forms of international economic governance will continue to plague the political debate as it did during John Major's administration. International pressures for more powerful forms of supranational governance, particularly at the European level, are likely to grow, whether or not the UK signs up to EMU. The decision on monetary union will therefore not only determine the future path of Britain's macroeconomic policy, but is also likely to determine the future tone of the UK's approach to pooling sovereignty across a whole range of other economic and social policy issues. Rarely has so much depended upon a single issue of economic policy.

15
Social Policy

CATHERINE JONES FINER

There is a new consensus in British social policy which, ironically, the very scale of Labour's victory has served to confirm. Despite the campaign rhetoric of New Labour for a new Britain, the incoming Blair government's stance on social policy owed more to the example set by John Major and Margaret Thatcher than to original thinking on the part of the Labour Party. The polarizing period of Thatcherism had already been replaced by a coming together period of post-Thatcherism, as both main parties competed for a new centre ground more in managerial than ideological terms. Naturally the dynamics of adversarial politics caused politicians to play down this consensus and to emphasize differences. Yet the values dominating social policy debate in all the main parties are now essentially convergent. Nonetheless, just as the scale of Labour's victory bore witness to the accuracy of Blair's recipe for electoral success, so might the return of so very many Labour back-benchers eager for action serve to undermine his strategy to establish Labour as a middle-class, self-denying party of the 'radical centre'. In social policy the Blairite tendency is certainly likely to prevail for the foreseeable future. But it is unclear how long this future might last.

It is easier to explain the origins of the new consensus than to define its character. New Labour's review of social policy occurred as part of its more general modernization of the party's aims and values. The notion of a 'stakeholder' economy has replaced more traditional approaches based on ideas of redistribution and the pursuit of equality (Hutton, 1996). Tony Blair has extended the terminology of 'stakeholding' to a range of public policy issues and the idea has attracted interest well beyond left of centre circles (Blair, 1996; Field, 1996). Although this chapter will explore the implications of 'stakeholder' social policy, the utilization of the term should not be taken as endorsement of its intellectual incisiveness or coherence. Indeed, as will be seen, the 'stakeholder' idea has gained attention precisely because it is sufficiently vague to facilitate consensus and can be used without giving too many specific policy commitments.

The Stakeholder Idea

The notion of a stakeholder implies a view of society as a form of joint stock undertaking operated on behalf of all its individual 'paid up' members. Irrespective of how unequal the 'stakes' or 'shares' may be, no bona fide member or family or group should fail to *gain something* as a result of membership but reward will reflect the extent to which such members are deemed to have played by the rules of the organization. Interestingly, the values inherent in this conception of society are as reminiscent of *Rawlsian* notions as of the 'Asian values' permeating the 'national corporations' of Singapore, South Korea, Taiwan, Hong Kong, and Japan, or for that matter, of German notions of subsidiarity (Jones, 1993). They do not, however, have much in common with the styles of social corporatism evident in the European Union.

Britain's post-war welfare state was given to proclaiming the virtues of social solidarity and the pooling of risks *precisely* because these values were seen as being under threat, once the unifying force of war had been removed. Britain on the eve of a new century has been urged by both main parties to return to even more basic values which predate the coming of the welfare state. As part of a 'new' consensual approach to social policy, everyone deserves a fair chance; but by the same token everyone is expected to exploit the opportunities which lawfully come their way. Rules are important. Crimes must be properly punished and victims compensated. Families must be properly responsible for their dependents, whether young or old. Communities must contrive as far as possible to be self-supporting. Collective provision – in the form of government support – should be designed to meet only those needs genuinely beyond the capacity of individuals, families and communities to manage for themselves.

The difficulty with this revisionism, much as it might appeal to generations tired of the culture of dependency allegedly induced by the welfare state, is that contemporary Britain is not the Britain of long before the welfare state, waiting to be rediscovered. Society has changed in a number of complex ways. Women, for example, count as full citizens to an extent unheard of a hundred years ago. Concepts of 'the family' have had to take account of varieties of structure and relationship unmentionable for policy purposes 100 years ago. Today's urban 'communities' are a far cry from the needs-be life-long street solidarities of a hundred years ago. Multi-ethnicity and multi-culturalism are no longer confined to the backstreets of a few city ports of entry. There is longer life expectancy and perhaps an unreasonable anticipation of ever rising living standards. Life has become altogether more expensive and expansive and hence less susceptible to being run in accordance with a single uncomplicated set of rules. So, for all the efforts of today's leading politicians to compete with one another in the morality stakes, John Major's 'back to basics' formulation can only give a moralistic gloss to Tony Blair's idea of the stakeholder society. It cannot make it 'decent'.

The real revolution has been much more practical. Whether one dubs this 'post modern', 'post-Fordist' or simply 'post-big government', the *new public management* of social policy stands as one of Thatcherism's outstanding achievements. In place of the monopolistic, professions-led, open-ended, 'jobs-for-life' welfare state industry of the past has come the pluralistic, somewhat *anti*-professional, competitive, short-term contract and target-led managerialism of the present. Understandably, this proved a harder pill for the Labour Party to swallow than for post-Thatcherite Conservatives; but the signs are that the world of quasi-markets in a swirl of welfare pluralism has come to stay. After all, Blair's Labour government is also in a stronger position to face down public sector unionism than Labour ever was before.

The object has been to make 'stakeholders' of everyone involved in the delivery of social policy. In the language of the quasi-marketplace, they must be functioning either as competitive providers of services or else as discriminating purchasers, despite the fact that certain key staff inevitably still have to function as both. At the level of central government, this movement has involved farming out hitherto direct service responsibilities to 'free-standing' agencies contracted to deliver services within a specified framework. Likewise local government is increasingly expected to commission agents to deliver what had previously been provided by local authorities themselves. An internal market has been introduced into the already highly ad hoc arrangements of the National Health Service. In place of old-style statutory services have come new-style *statutorily commissioned* services, which require to be regulated, measured, inspected and league-tabled as never before.

The import of such changes for those most closely involved has been threefold. First, they raise questions as to the point of the exercise itself. To what end are the new nostrums of economy, efficiency and effectiveness supposed to be working? Is the goal of social policy national profitability or collective utility? Is it instead regime legitimation? Or user satisfaction? Secondly, these changes raise questions concerning the role of professionals in the new order. How far are hospital consultants and head teachers also supposed to be able to *manage their enterprises?* Can they be at once expert providers *and* evaluators of their own and each other's performances? How far can general practitioners and social workers operate both as providers *and* purchasers? And to whom, to how many and *how* are they to be held accountable?

Thirdly, and perhaps most fundamentally, these changes raise questions about the identity of welfare's consumers. Manifestly the 'purchasers' of the new public management-speak are not always primarily the users of a particular service. 'Carers', like professionals, tend to intervene. The implications of such potential triangular relationships between service providers, service users and those who 'care for' service users have been best illustrated to date in respect of elderly and disabled people (G. Wilson, 1994; Ungerson, 1997; Morris, 1997). Yet the message holds good for *any* service user not deemed to be sufficiently informed, equipped or willing to decide for themselves in a given situation. Thus it is not just schoolchildren being decided for by their parents in consultation with teachers, but 'ordinary' patients being decided for by their own GP's choice of hospital consultant, let alone 'common criminals' being decided for by their probation officer's capabilities in court. At the other end of the social policy delivery spectrum, by contrast, new market opportunities and deregulation have meant that some of the most vulnerable people in society are being expected to fix such crucial arrangements as pensions for themselves at virtually their own risk and without any professional intervention (Klein and Millar, 1995; Waine, 1995). In such circumstances, the language of empowerment raises important questions about who is being empowered and at whose expense. Without adequate resources and regulation or indeed a coherent philosophy to guide its operation the freedom and flexibility offered by the new public management can look like abandonment for some groups most dependent on welfare provision.

'Stakeholder' Social Policies

Since these consist as much of exhortations, regulations and prohibitions as of benefits in cash or kind, they are not best discussed under the traditional categories of 'social services'. Not that the traditional big five sectors of social security, housing, health care, education and social care have gone away. Rather they have been re-ordered according to a different set of priorities.

Employment and Training

The post-war welfare state was based on a presumption of full employment which seemed valid for the first near twenty years of its existence. So, unlike the high profile reforms of health, education and social security, there was no serious attempt to refurbish employment and training services after the war. Indeed before the late 1960s textbooks on social policy scarcely made reference to employment or labour market issues or even to the economy as a whole. Today the emphasis is quite reversed, with considerations as to the state of the economy prefacing virtually every social policy debate. Nevertheless, the provision of employment and training services has remained one of the least developed and least coherent policy sectors in Britain. Margaret Thatcher's great achievement in this sphere, it should be remembered, was not what she *did* for the unemployed, but rather that she convinced them the guarantee of full employment was no longer to be regarded as the responsibility of government.

True, there have been a series of strategies since the 1970s which have been designed to suggest that something is being done especially for the young and the long-term unemployed. But these efforts were aimed more at the people concerned than at the state of the labour market. For instance, unemployed school leavers have been encouraged and are now effectively *obliged* to undertake some form of training (currently via a Youth Training place). Participation in such training schemes is a requirement for financial assistance from the state. Meanwhile (with effect from October 1996) the adult unemployed have seen their 12 month unemployment benefit or eligibility for Income Support replaced by eligibility for a six month Job Seeker's allowance. Tests govern eligibility for the new allowance. It must be demonstrated at interview that the applicant is actively seeking and is available for work. A 'Job Seeker's Agreement' has to be signed by the applicant and specifies the type of work sought and the steps to be taken by both the individual and the Employment Service to find it. The 'stratagems' are becoming ever more demanding.

New Labour's *welfare to work* programme promises 'proactive' employment/training advice (including advice on after-school care) for every lone mother whose youngest child has reached its second term at school.

Manifestly these are policies more social than economic. It is the behaviour of categories of the non-employed, rather than the structural causes of unemployment, which has been identified as the problem. Thus unemployed young people deprived of a chance to acquire habits of industry constitute not merely an expense but a moral hazard to society, as do the long-term unemployed. The present consensual penchant for varieties of 'workfare' rests not so much on its opportunities to save money on the social security bill as on a shared belief that work, per se, is good for people and that 'getting something for nothing' is bad.

Crime Prevention

What is a stakeholder society to do about its *non*-stakeholders? Several strategies are available.It can keep them out as in the case of economic migrants and suspect asylum seekers. It can police-cordon them, in as in the case of inner-city sink housing estates. Or it can lock them up as in the case of persistent malingerers, burglars and muggers. Although such strategies may seem a parody of the most extreme expressions of right-wing authoritarian wisdom in contemporary Britain, there are signs that public policy is moving in this direction. Michael Howard's tenure at the Home Office was a manifestation of a new approach to law and order issues endorsed by both parties (Chapter 16) No ambitious politician – let alone government – can nowadays afford to look soft on crime, no matter how many reservations they may entertain about the causes of it – or indeed about the efficacy of prison as a remedy.

Probation is out of fashion, save maybe to the extent that it can be rendered more simplistic and punitive in style. Community service orders are likewise out of fashion if only because they *sound* soft, regardless of their results. By contrast, the institution of 'fast-track' punishment (as against 'short sharp shocks') for intransigent young offenders and of longer mandatory prison sentences for specified adult offenders look distinctly *in* fashion, irrespective of *their* respective chances of delivering results. Bona fide stakeholders are not expected to have to concern themselves overmuch with the treatment of apprehended stake-robbers and snatchers, beyond seeing to it that such people are put out of harm's way for as long as possible, both as punishment to them and as a deterrence to others.

Nevertheless, a major practical problem for the new public administration has arisen from the shortage of sufficient suitable prison space. It has proved impossible to construct new prisons, even in the private sector, fast enough to keep up with the escalating demand – hence Howard's enterprising Dickensian plan (since taken up by Jack Straw) to commandeer an offshore ship for temporary prison purposes. Other ideas such as the use of a Pontin's holiday camp risked ridicule and local opposition but they underlined the dilemma inherent in pursuing a tough penal policy in the absence of sufficient prison capacity.

Education

Here we are ostensibly back into the traditional mainstream territory of social policy. Yet much has changed in this sector in recent years and its role in social policy debates has been transformed. Education in the post-war welfare state had been about social reconstruction in the cause of a more egalitarian society, about national manpower investment, and about equality of opportunity for all to make the most of their various talents. If the message had been a 'best of all worlds' *pot pourri*, no less confusing and patchwork had been the manner of its delivery, as 'autonomous' LEAs of all shades of political opinion strove to place their own stamp on local school arrangements, despite such central initiatives as the attempt to impose comprehensive secondary education.

The 1988 Education Act reordered the education universe. It undermined the ability of LEAs to control the activities of what had hitherto been their own schools. It attempted to convince school managements and local parents that the future of what were in truth '*their*' schools lay with them. And, most significantly, it reasserted the right of central government in principle to determine not merely curriculum content of schools in the state sector but to impose forms of assessment and even styles of teaching. In the drive to force an open, competitive and accountable system according to the values of the time, what were seen to be recalcitrant professional and other vested interests were to be subjected to new mechanisms of inspection and control.

Initially the Thatcherite educational agenda was seen as radical and highly confrontational. Now, virtually the same agenda (plus a few additions and refinements) is being pursued along increasingly and unmistakably 'consensual' lines. Witness the 1997 election contest, as party leaderships vied with one another to demonstrate who could advance the same transformative process most efficiently, effectively and economically. Apart from in the most diehard of teaching and LEA circles, increasingly few objections are heard to such ideas as budget management by schools, the retention of grant maintained status, streaming by ability, the retention of some selective schooling involving grammar schools, standardized pupil testing leading to published tables of exam results, or even standardized teacher assessment procedures which might result in removing unsatisfactory teachers from post. The Labour government's promises to cut class sizes and abolish the Assisted Places Scheme are trivial by comparison with what has gone before.

Today's concerns centre more on the adequacy of the measures adopted than on the principles behind them. Witness Labour-inspired moves to refine the tables of examination results by incorporating social and economic information about the catchment areas of schools in order to assess the value being added by the school and to inform parental choice. If the promise of parental choice of school remains more honoured in the breach than the observance, this is frequently because some schools are so popular that not all applicants can be accepted. Labour no less than the Conservatives can see the merit of imposing national standards and market values on the schools system as a whole to ensure that all children benefit from the competition in the long run even if there are bound to be some disappointments about allocation to individual schools. The only problem of course is that virtually all children have to attend school somewhere rather than nowhere. Given the limited capacity of schools to adapt quickly to swings in demand, the so-called 'sink' schools of the system (so long as not actually closed down by central government) are always going to be able to recruit. Education is at best a quasi-market.

Meanwhile a further fundamental ground of debate continues around the vexed question of the curriculum. Too many school leavers are still exiting the system with no formal qualifications whatsoever, yet seemingly unstoppable rates of improvement in GCSE, A-level, university entrance, and for that matter university degree results, continue to provoke suspicion that standards might be slipping. Anecdotal evidence from teachers as well as employers that school leavers cannot actually read, write and 'reckon' properly, whatever their paper qualifications, has combined with concern that 'progressive' teaching methods have deprived them even of a proper grounding in morals to produce a sense of popular outrage at the product of modern education.

Finding answers in place of scapegoats is of course more difficult. Whatever the international evidence linking levels of labour force education to 'ensuing' levels of economic performance, the British – certainly the English – have never seemed much good at transforming education and training into marketplace skills. Even recent moves to devise ever more serious and relevant National Vocational Qualifications (NVQs) as a credible alternative to A-levels for the 'vocationally minded' seem so far to have been more productive of jobs in the education industry than of 'real' jobs outside it. Nor is there much evidence that reform of

A-level syllabuses and reduction in the number of 'competing' examining boards will effect the transformation in their 'usefulness', flexibility and reliability for further education and employment purposes that their advocates suggest.

So what else is to be expected? If the schools system is not to be looked on as a guaranteed route to employability, the least it should be doing, according to one prominent (cross-party) band of critics, is turning out decent law-abiding citizens. Understandably, however, teachers tend to dispute the leading role assigned to them (as against 'family' or 'community') in this scenario, just as members of minority ethnic groups and religions object to the prospect of majority values being imposed on their own ways of life. The vacuousness of the National Forum for Values' draft attempt in the autumn of 1996 to distil 'the prevailing consensus' into a single *moral code for schools* for use by the Schools Curriculum and Assessment Authority is proof, if proof were needed, of the impracticability of this particular project.

Health Care

The National Health Service of Aneurin Bevan's dream promised everyone high quality health care free at the point of delivery. Practical limitations apart, the NHS was *the* flagship programme, symbolic of the spirit of the post-war welfare state. While it might be dismissed as 'socialized medicine' in the United States, opinion polls regularly confirmed its popularity in the United Kingdom.

Yet organizationally the NHS was makeshift from the start. Its so called tripartite structure (hospitals administration, independent practitioners administration, municipal health services administration, in descending order of cost) was indicative of nothing so much as differences of status within the medical profession from senior salaried hospital consultants via 'freely contracting' general practitioners right down to local authority medical officers of health. Hitherto separate, but overlapping, systems of health care delivery had had to be cobbled together at short notice on terms doctors could accept – which had meant largely at the expense of the municipal authorities.

The ambitious goals of the NHS were of course incapable of realization. Optimum health care according to need, without payment at point of contact, constituted a receding target in an age when advancing medical science was joined with an ageing and increasingly health conscious population. Yet attempts to 'reform' the NHS invariably focused on the organizational short-comings of the service, as if, being so obvious, these were somehow the root and cause of all its trouble.

Paradoxically, however, it was precisely this thrown-together structure of the NHS which had ensured its continued subjection to central budgetary control and, by the same token, its unbeatable public image as the brave underdog of the public sector. It also became the envy of cost-conscious governments panicked by 'runaway' health care expenditures elsewhere. In short, the one attribute of the NHS of which its champions in Britain had been most resentful – the ability of a government of the day simply to resist demands for 'sufficient' additional funding – had emerged in the eyes of others by the 1980s (not least in the British Treasury) as being its single greatest strength. Hence, even had British public opinion ever allowed for it, the NHS, as the biggest single public sector employer in Europe, could not be scheduled for privatization under Thatcher, or even for 'demotion' to the form and status of a subsidized system of health insurance. Instead the object, as from 1990, was to transform this vast agglomeration of public sector activity into something as close as possible to a market.

This project was one to which the organizational eccentricities of the NHS might have been thought well-suited from the start. Hospitals have been encouraged to form themselves into self-governing trusts for the purpose of competing for business (as 'providers') from 'purchasers' such as fundholder GPs or district health authorities. The money is in principle supposed to follow the patient, whose GP is notionally supposed to act in the patient's best interest, exploring all the possibilities for treatment prior to recommending a particular 'purchase' or choice of purchases. In turn GP practices themselves are supposed to be free to compete for patients; not least by advertising for them (albeit discreetly) and by offering additional services (such as minor routine surgery) over and above those required by the 1994 *Patient's Charter*.

In retrospect, all this amounted not to one great 'reform' but rather to a cascade of interlocking reform processes, each with its own momentum and capable of impinging on other aspects of the NHS in unpredictable ways. Attempts to cost hospital practices and evaluate performances have alone spawned fresh specialisms and research industries in their own right; all the more complicatedly so, given that the target recipients for the information produced can range from fellow professionals, rival clinical teams, entire rival hospital establishments, central or regional officials, GP fundholders, district health authorities and community health councils (the latter *par excellence* being in search of a fresh rationale in the new climate) even down to real live patients in pursuit of 'their rights'.

Costing general practitioner services, by contrast, seems to have given rise to early complications of a more primitive kind; owing to the fact that pioneer fundholding practices tended to have their budgets calculated on a different 'bottom-up' basis from the 'top-down' way in which budgets were conventionally being calculated for health districts as a whole, with the result that the sums per district tended less and less to add up. An additional complication arose because the entire NHS budget was still in process of being redistributed between the regions to accord more fairly with population needs despite pre-existing problems arising from such factors as the original uneven distribution of fixed stock – as witnessed by an alleged 'excess' of hospital beds in London. The potential for book keeping confusion and popular resentment as the new system generated its own irrationalities was self-evident.

More fundamentally, much has been remarked about the inequities presumed to result from the introduction of even a *quasi* market into what had hitherto been the cost-disregarding culture of the NHS. If the introduction of GP fundholding means that some practices are liable to be more successful than others in purchasing prompt effective treatment for their patients, then other GPs' patients must, by implication, lose out. There was fear that the introduction of budget-holding responsibility could 'force' competitive practices into turning away potentially expensive patients such as the elderly; similarly there was fear that the vagaries of GP preference, once untrammelled by district health authority block bookings, could place entire hospital specialisms at risk. Yet the results to date have been distinctly less dramatic.

To be sure there have been outrages over hospital and ward closures, underfunding in general and the denial of expensive treatments to hard cases in particular. But, short of dreams of unlimited funding all round, it is hard to estimate just how much of this might have been avoided (as against conceivably rendered less visible) had the NHS not had an internal market thrust upon it. Then again, inequalities of treatment with regard to the patients of more – as against less – 'successful' GP practices may be little more than an 'open' version of inequalities taken for granted hitherto, courtesy of the old boy network and the fact that some GPs were keener operators with better contact networks than others. Indeed, apart from hospital managers, the chief gainers in all of this have been precisely the GPs – no longer mere gatekeepers but the veritable playmakers of the revamped system – at the notable expense of hospital consultants. Indeed it has been the 'grudging' satisfaction expressed by GPs (by far the largest single category of doctors working for the NHS) which seemingly obliged not merely the BMA but the leadership of the Labour Party to tone down its opposition to the changes. Significantly, the new government is committed to 'removing the bureaucratic processes of the internal market' but not, by implication, to the dismantling of the internal market per se (Labour Party, 1997, p. 20).

Hardest of all to estimate, meanwhile, has been the balance of benefit or otherwise to the so-called 'patient consumer'. The literature on British doctor–patient relationships is replete with information to the effect that a patient's ability to communicate with a doctor (let alone that of a doctor to communicate with a patient) on anything approaching a 'quasi-market' business basis, will be conditioned by such factors as age, sex, level of education, social class and family status, quite apart from any particularities or peculiarities arising from the patient's actual medical condition. The latest evidence would seem to suggest, unsurprisingly, that most patients still do not see themselves as anywhere near on a par with their GP and are just as reluctant, therefore, to take responsibility for mapping the course of their own specialist treatment as is their GP to encourage them to do so. But, then again, most patients are unlikely to register a complaint against the NHS, however much they might have suffered at its hands, because they are assured that it is doing its best despite a lack of resources.

In short, the NHS may still be a winner in public relations terms, even as its quality of care may be deteriorating. Where, however, patient requirements straddle that most common, but organizationally inconvenient, boundary between 'health' and 'social' care, there would seem to be no public relations victory in the offing at all.

Social Care

Three interlocking themes need to be addressed in relation to the emergence of consensus in respect of community care: the promotion of family/neighbourly responsibilities, the role of voluntary action, and the conduct of an internal market.

Families constitute the first resort as they always have, with or without the insistence of the state. The tradition of regarding social work as essentially a supplement to or substitute for family care in times of stress, dates back to the Charity Organisation Society's first essays in social work of 100 years ago. Social work has come some way since then, whereas the family has arguably been everywhere on the retreat. Every venture in modern social provision can be portrayed as having subtracted somewhat from family responsibilities. Yet few would presumably wish to see services such as education, health care, housing and social security reduced entirely to whatever today's families could fix for themselves. Ironically, however, the current emphasis on 'back to the family' in respect of social care, would seem to be focused on the very sorts of families whose predicaments and prospects render them least liable to be able to cope.

This is not simply a case of assuming that households resident in deprived areas – and especially in 'sink' council housing estates – will consist disproportionately of lone-parent families or families on 'benefit'. Modern varieties of 'family' tend to look less than functional, from a social caring point of view, right across the socioeconomic spectrum. The vulnerabilities of the elongated family (fewer children, longer-lived elderly) have been compounded as much by geographic mobility and the movement of women into the labour market as by the consequences of higher rates of divorced, remarried and unmarried parenthood. The sorry saga of the Child Support Agency constitutes a lesson not merely in how *not* to implement a contentious piece of legislation but how difficult it can be to impose family values on those who do not fit the bill (see Clarke *et al.*, 1995).

Nor can the 'next-up' line of resort, voluntary action, necessarily offer much of an answer. 'Traditional' voluntary action (such as of the Victorian great name variety) took time, money, commitment, social confidence (on the one side) and social acceptance (on the other) based notionally on a shared set of norms and values. Today's society is ostensibly much less hierarchical, less deferential, certainly less 'monocultural' and above all less possessed of a reserve army of well brought up potential volunteers (women especially) with time on their hands and the acquired social conscience once so characteristic of their social position. Today's voluntary action, furthermore, has to operate not merely in the wake of such social upheaval, but in the wake also of a welfare state which had been committed, precisely, to promoting the role and responsibilities of the state on the grounds of its superiority, both moral and practical, to whatever voluntary action could effect.

Thus, for all Beveridge's own championship of voluntary action (Beveridge, 1948), his 'other report' achieved nothing like the status and acclaim of its predecessor *Social Insurance and Allied Services* (1942). Not that the advent of the welfare state meant that voluntary action was prohibited. Just as it had in the past pioneered so many branches of what were later to become statutory social service responsibilities, so it was assumed the pioneering role should continue within the confines of the welfare state. Inevitably the role of voluntary action would be scaled down and mixed with 'partnership arrangements' geared for instance to funding certain voluntary services as a temporary extra resource (as in the case of children's homes) or as a sole commissioned resource in respect of particular groups such as the blind or for particular functions such as the work of Citizens Advice Bureaux. Not until the welfare state unease of the 1970s did the voluntary sector per se again command serious attention (Wolfenden, 1977); and it was only from the 1980s that the language of voluntary-statutory 'partnership' became fashionable again. Since then, however, and especially since the Health Service and Community Care Act of 1990, the object has been to tap much more systematically into non-governmental sectors in general, in an effort to obtain both better value for money on the state's behalf and a greater range of services for consumers and their advisers. If the imposition of an internal market on the NHS had been headline news, the repercussions of this further venture into marketization have been no less far reaching for the management of social care.

First has been the transformation with regard to the status and responsibilities of local authority departments of social service, the hitherto frontline providers of statutory social care. The only terms on which an originally Thatcherite administration could be persuaded to channel additional money for community (as against residential) care via local authorities had been to make it clear that in future the role of local authorities was to be primarily one of *enabling*: i.e. of purchasing care from all sorts of *other* providers of services in the community (and for that matter outside of it, still, in residential care). It was a new world order, not least for the social workers hitherto responsible for 'care-providing' themselves.

Of all the welfare state's social professions, social work has been the one most firmly associated in the public mind, and especially in the media, with the worst excesses and shortcomings of traditional approaches to welfare. This is ironic, since at the institution of the postwar welfare state there was doubt over how far such a fine and universalistic order really needed something so demeaning as personalized social work, save in respect of particularly vulnerable groups such as children at risk. Thereafter, however, it was the very shortcomings of mainstream statutory welfare which ensured an increasing demand for social work, if only to help pick up the casualties and keep the welfare state show on the road. Unsurprisingly it was a thankless task. The efforts of the 1960s–1970s to build 'generic' social work into a single profession served to concentrate its unpopularity. The scandal-ridden years of the 1970s–1980s had social workers being blamed *both* for failures to intervene *and* for officious excesses of intervention. Systems of social worker training have been subjected to repeated review in the cause of 'common sense' and in repudiation of 'excessive theorizing'.

So now, at last, social workers employed by local authorities have been instructed no longer to venture into social care themselves, to the extent they can commission others to provide it on a cost/care effective basis, according to need. It is not a task for which these social workers have been trained nor one for which they necessarily feel themselves equipped. But they have scarcely been alone in being confused. The idea of public authorities subsidizing the activities of voluntary groups is hardly new. Very few voluntary organizations had proved capable of functioning for any length of time quite independently of the public sector in the welfare state, however uneasy they might have been about accepting its 'money with strings'. But today's 'contract culture' is of a different order. In place of the annual local authority grant in support of its activities (however implicitly conditional on 'good performance'), service organizations – whether of the non-profit or for profit variety – are now expected to compete for contracts specifying precisely what is to be provided, to what standard, for how many, at what cost, over what period; and if selected, to deliver accordingly.

To many, the very prospect seemed to spell the end of the voluntary sector as we had known it. Informal local groups wondered how they were continue to attract volunteers once job descriptions were so firmly laid down and the scope for experiment marginalized. Larger, more professionalized organizations expected increasingly to have to ape the private (for profit) sector in the competition for business and thus to become less distinguishable from it. Taken in conjunction with the equally novel prospect of having to compete before a committee of the great and good for a share of the take from the National Lottery at the literal expense (it would seem) of raising their own gifted money direct from the public, this was a new world order indeed.

Yet earliest evidence suggests that the sky has not yet fallen in on the voluntary sector (Deakin, 1996). Local markets in care do not materialize from nowhere, so it is scarcely surprising to find that hard-pressed care purchasers such as local authority departments of social service have tended to turn to those with whom they have had dealings before. Equally it is not surprising to find that most voluntary organizations hitherto in receipt of some form of public funding have tended, if only from want of competition, to be in receipt of it still, albeit on ostensibly different terms.

Meanwhile, what of the ostensible prime movers in this market of community care: the users and their carers? The evidence so far seems depressingly as might have been predicted. Despite the rhetoric, 'markets in community care' cannot at present, save by patronizing presumption, be deemed first and foremost to be serving the interests of those who are now euphemistically termed their consumers. The attitudes and expectations of, for instance, elderly people are unlikely to change overnight, any more than are the attitudes of their carers and those social workers (now in a 'playmaker' position) with whom they come into contact.

If the playmakers tend in practice to prescribe 'care packages' more attuned to the availability of resources in the locality than to the supposed needs let alone stated preferences of the 'consumer' in question (*Have* I been assessed? *When* was I assessed? *When* was I consulted?), this constitutes nothing more than added proof that social service realities do not change on the ground nearly as quickly as they might seem to have been changed at Westminster. Current controversies over the advisability of 'direct payments' to disabled people, to help them fix up their own care arrangements, constitute further 'caring' proof of the same. Who count as stakeholders, indeed?.

Housing

Possession of a stake in society used to depend on possession of a form of property, most obviously (in the case of the urban classes) a house. Subsequent extensions to the franchise eroded this property qualification at the same time as public health legislation sought, in the interests of all, to limit the worst of the country's housing conditions. Housing initiatives, dramatic by European standards, have occurred at least since the imposition of rent controls in 1915 on what was then a 95 per cent private rental market in housing. The year 1919 saw the famous 'homes fit for heroes' promise, heralding the introduction of council housing as a central government-subsidized, local authority-run form of tenure for (broadly speaking) working-class people capable of paying a reasonable non-profit rent. Yet, for all the advances made in the quality and quantity of council housing erected from the 1920s right through to the 1960s (with the exception of notorious tower blocks), the provision of housing per se was never recognized as unquestionably a core function of the British welfare state.

Ironically, however, it was this very institution of council housing which, with all its accumulated unpopularity by the latter 1970s, enabled Margaret Thatcher to kick-start her campaign for a 'property-owning democracy' by the simple but winning expedient of selling off the best of existing council housing stock to sitting tenants at knock-down prices. It was a masterly achievement. At one stroke Labour was wrong-footed, entire ward voting patterns were set at risk and the race to convert as high a proportion of the population as possible to the virtues of 'a property-owning democracy' was on. Not until the end of the 1980s and the collapse of the house price boom did the limitations of this pursuit begin to make themselves felt, not least in the figures for mortgage default and property repossession. Today's apparent recovery in the housing market is not, we are assured by experts of every shade of political and propertied opinion, to be regarded as *in any way* a return to the Nirvana of the 1980s.

Meanwhile, council housing has not gone away. Too much of it had proved unsaleable, on the one hand; and too many people were continuing to report as being in need of accommodation, on the other. So the situation within England and Wales is coming to seem ever closer to that of the US in this respect: council housing, far from being the mainstream equivalent of European-style social housing it once was, now represents a last resort provision for poor people with problems. Attempts in the meantime to reinvigorate independent non-profit forms of housing provision, not least via the housing corporation, seem destined to fall by the wayside for the reasons that *all* attempts to invigorate the private (rental) sector have tended to fall by the wayside: viz. that the provision of accommodation of an acceptable modern standard costs more for builders to build (or renovate) and owners to operate than many if not most households can afford to pay for without help.

Not that this constitutes the whole of the 'housing problem'. Just as housing conditions can feed into all manner of other societal concerns, so can all manner of societal concerns end up looking like a housing – or in this case a *lack* of housing – problem. Today's homeless, however defined, are not primarily to be supposed a 'housing' category. Rather they are an assemblage, more visible if not more numerous than ever before, of today's losers. Their problem is not typically lack of accommodation per se, since there is usually *some form* of accommodation notionally on offer. Rather, their predicaments range right across the spectrum of needs, as already discussed and as compounded by the simple but evident fact that without a *bona fide* address it can be hard to lay claim to anything else, social security benefits included.

Social Security

So we come last to what would typically have ranked first in any social policy sector-by-sector account of only 10 years ago. To be sure the size of the social security *bill* continues to rank first in social spending terms; yet its significance for policy purposes seems now as much to do with how to cope with the legacy of the past as how come to terms with the needs of the present. Which is in itself a portent for the future.

Short-term benefits, whether means-tested or contribution-based, do not represent the same order of hazard for governments as do benefits of a longer-term pensions variety. This elemental truth has been demonstrated at intervals by governments of all shades of political persuasion since the first introduction of short-term (sickness/employment) National Insurance (NI) benefits from 1911 and of NI pension benefits from 1946. The universal undertakings of the Beveridge Plan were seemingly fixed and static in their commitments. But in conditions of rising living standards coupled with 'diminishing demographic returns', con-tractual statutory pensions commitments even minimally liable to revaluation could not but spell long-term trouble for the Treasury and hence for the public expenditure account.

The intermediate problem is essentially simple, but nonetheless intractable. People who are or have been employed in main-stream, 'quality', opt-out occupations may rest assured of their income-related disability/pensions cover over and above their entitlement to contribution-backed base-level benefits from the state. People not so employed in quality opt-out occupations and hitherto reliant, therefore, on the State Earnings Related Pensions Scheme (SERPS) as of 1976, have been encouraged, in the wake of efforts (in 1986) to downgrade SERPS itself, to take out private pension plans of their own. Many have done so to ill-effect, given that these have tended to be precisely the sorts of people with earnings patterns private pensions providers could least satisfac-torily provide for. Add to this the dilemmas currently being faced by some of the same elderly people and their families in the context of paying for intensive social care, and we have a recipe for intergenerational conflict indeed.

One classic stakeholder response has been to urge the case for a re-vamped social security system which would require *everyone* to be making provision for their own future at the same time as requiring *everyone*, in the meantime, to be working for their own living – instead of (too often) being enabled and encouraged to get by without. As Frank Field, Minister of State for Social Security and Welfare Reform has put it:

> Welfare does not operate in a social vacuum. It influences character for good or ill. Because of the growing dominance of means tests, welfare increasingly acts destructively, penalising effort, attacking savings and taxing honesty. The traditional cry that means tests stigmatise is now a minor issue . . . Means tests are steadily recruiting a nation of cheats and liars. (Field, 1996, p. 11)

So much for the efficacy of targeting.

Conclusion

The recurrent themes in analyzing contemporary social policy are money and motivation. If Thatcherism was about dismantling the culture of the welfare state, stakeholdership is about putting something in its place, a structure of incentives and disincentives capable of shaping behaviour in ways which are socially beneficial. Welfare for profit and profitability. It is almost utilitarianism rediscovered.

Unfortunately just as utilitarianism turned out to be less practical than expected so stakeholdership is similarly likely to disappoint to the extent that the problems of this ageing society with its ageing infrastructure lie more than 'social policy deep.' For all the post-1970s nostrums about the burdens of welfare on the economy, it has been hard to establish, cross-nationally, the existence of *any* incontrovertible relationships between patterns of welfare spending and economic performance. (Pfaller *et al.*, 1991). Nor, for all the literature, has there been any surefire formulation for making social policy programmes self-financing let alone profit making for all. The language of stakeholdership is the language of winners and losers, not just winners. So how many losers will there be and who will be blamed for their losses? For that matter how many winners are there likely to be? Stakeholder social policy is as much about covering for retreat as (supposedly) facilitating an advance. To the extent that we are all responsible for the state of society, we cannot blame politicians too much for its shortcomings. Only politicians who make positive promises (as against threats of maybe worse to come) are liable to be held to account, a fact that has been clearly taken on board by New Labour.

Those inclined to look to corporatist Europe for comfort should also think again. Enthusiasm for the very idea of European social policy can cloud the judgement, as was evident in the Delors era (Streeck, 1995). Darker predictions now prevail, notwithstanding Britain's signing of the Social Chapter. If there is to be social policy convergence, this is more likely to be downwards rather than upwards to the extent that it will be market led rather than achieved positively by legislation (Leibfried and Pierson, 1995).

The gift relationship is gone. Stakeholders want bargains, not presents. Or at least this is the best they should expect.

16

Crime and Public Order

JOHN BENYON AND ADAM EDWARDS

In February 1993, the then Shadow Home Secretary Tony Blair stated that the Labour Party's law-and-order policy was to be 'tough on crime and tough on the causes of crime'. This oft-repeated statement indicated how Labour would seek to assert its competence on law and order, overcome its image of being 'soft' on crime, and attack the Conservatives' record. Blair's statement was made shortly after the murder in Liverpool of two-year-old James Bulger by a pair of 10-year-old boys. The shock waves from this case generated a heightened debate about law-and-order policies among politicians and public at a time when recorded levels of crime were at an all-time peak. The time was clearly ripe for the Labour Party to challenge the Conservatives for the mantle of 'party of law and order'. This was a dramatic change from 1979, when the Conservative Party had campaigned for 'less tax and more law and order', and castigated the Labour government for presiding over rising levels of lawlessness.

Law and order maintained a high political salience throughout the Conservative administrations of 1979–97. The Thatcher and Major governments struggled to contain rising crime and disorder, but to little effect. In the 1990s, the Labour Party's claim to be tough on crime and tough on its causes was promoted as an alternative to the Conservatives' limited focus on discipline, punishment and deterrence, but without a return to the traditional 'welfarist' approach. Some argue that New Labour's law-and-order policies reflect a new consensus, but, in practice, the contemporary politics of crime and public order are a more complex mixture of continuity and change. The renewed emphasis on conventional morality, individual responsibility and punishment is accompanied by longer-standing disputes over the social causes of crime and civil unrest and by more recent ideas on managing opportunities for 'anti-social' behaviour. If anything, law-and-order politics when the Blair government entered office were characterized more by a volatile 'short-termism' than by a stable moral consensus.

The Politicization of Crime and Public Order

The Bipartisan Consensus

Until the 1970s there was a broad bipartisan consensus on policing and criminal justice, with general agreement on a causal relationship between 'anti-social conditions' and 'anti-social behaviour' (Downes and Morgan, 1994). However, this 'welfarist' (Hudson, 1993) or social democratic approach was challenged when levels of crime consistently increased in the period 1951–71. This increase coincided with rising incomes, improved welfare provision and full employment, which undermined social democratic arguments that reductions in poverty and disadvantage would lead to decreases in crime (Young, 1988).

One response was to question the reality of the reported rise in crime. Official statistics arise from a process whereby certain behaviour is defined as criminal, reported to the police, or detected by them, and finally recorded. The crime figures are thus a social construction, shaped by a number of variables, including changes in the scale and focus of policing, legislation, levels of household insurance and shifts in public opinion. From a left-intellectual perspective, rising crime and disorder could be explained in terms of 'moral panics' about 'delinquent' youth subcultures, violence on picket lines and at sporting events, and the emergence of 'American' street crimes such as 'mugging' (Cohen, 1973; Hall *et al.*, 1978).

According to this argument, moral panics displace tensions generated by periods of rapid economic and social change on to perceived problems of moral decline and weak government. Political actors, such as parties, pressure groups, and the mass media, play a central role in this process of displacement, whereby crime and disorder is 'amplified' well beyond its real extent (Cohen and Young, 1973). This 'new left criminology' led to a more sceptical view of crime statistics and promoted a more subtle academic debate on law-and-order problems.

The Rule of Law Becomes an Issue

By the late 1970s, law and order had become a major issue of government competence and party conflict. Labour continued to support 'welfarist' principles, emphasizing rehabilitation of offenders and diversion from custodial sentences. The 1979 Labour manifesto called for an attack on 'social deprivation which allows crime to flourish'. In the 1979 election, crime and disorder featured as one of the main issues and opinion polls gave the Conservatives a 30 per cent lead, their largest on any policy issue (Butler and Kavanagh, 1980, pp. 37–8). The Conservative manifesto argued that the 'rule of law' had been undermined by the Labour government, and merged rising levels of crime and public disorder during industrial disputes, particularly the 'winter of discontent' of 1978–9, political demonstrations and violence at leisure and sporting events, into a singular problem of weak government.

The fusion of law breaking, order defiance and strikes formed a central part of the ideological challenge to social democracy mounted under the 'New Right' leadership of Margaret Thatcher. 'Thatcherites' promised to deregulate the economy while reinforcing the rule of law, to provide a 'free economy and a strong state' (Gamble, 1988). The effects of this new ideological framework were dramatic for law-and-order politics. 'Authoritarian populism' meant abandoning the welfarist consensus and embracing 'classical' conceptions of discipline, deterrence and punishment.

Law and Order Under the Conservatives

The high priority of law and order from 1979 onwards resulted in an array of legislation and reform in the organization and practice of the police, criminal justice and penal systems. The Police and Crime (Sentences) Acts passed by Parliament in March 1997 meant that 34 separate pieces of law-and-order legislation had been introduced in 18 years. During that period, it is possible to discern three phases of law-and-order politics, which were the result of the diverse pressures that shaped the Conservatives' policy responses to problems of crime and civil unrest. An examination of these three phases reveals elements of continuity and change in law-and-order policies under the Conservatives and provides the basis for a greater understanding of the 'new consensus' that some people believe has emerged. It also makes clear how the Conservatives' approach constrained their repertoire for policy reform, undermined their capacity to adapt to the changing context of crime and public disorder, and eventually enabled New Labour to emerge as the alternative party of law and order.

1979–87: Restoring the Rule of Law

Expenditure on law enforcement increased considerably after the Conservatives came to power in 1979. Police officers were awarded a 16 per cent pay rise and police numbers were increased. The cost of the police service grew from £1.6 million in 1979 to £3.4 million in 1984 and expenditure on prisons rose by 85 per cent. Important legislation included the Criminal Justice Act 1982, which introduced 'short sharp shock' sentences for juveniles and granted greater discretion to magistrates.

The controversial Police and Criminal Evidence (PACE) Act 1984 gave the police increased powers to stop and search people and to detain suspects, while the Public Order Act 1986 defined new public order offences and set constraints on marches and demonstrations. Public order policing strategies changed rapidly with the advent of new technology and equipment. This 'paramilitarization' of British policing occurred after major disturbances in British cities in the early 1980s, and violent confrontations between police and miners during the coal dispute of 1984–5 (Benyon and Solomos, 1987).

The 'authoritarian state thesis' argued that investment in the police, criminal justice and penal systems had been made to deal with anticipated conflict with the labour movement and disadvantaged communities as a result of economic and social restructuring (Jessop *et al.*, 1988). However, others emphasized the Janus-faced character of the legislative and organizational reforms. The 1982 Act, for example, directed courts to use custodial sentences only as a last resort and to divert offenders into community-based punishments. Given the expense of incarceration, there was pressure from the Treasury to reduce the use of custodial sentences. Lord Scarman's 1981 inquiry into the inner-city riots was critical of many trends in policing and led to a significant re-evaluation of police–community relations and some important reforms.

1987–93: Enlisting the Community

By 1987, government policies appeared to be an expensive failure. Despite large increases in expenditure crime and disorder had continued to rise, and the Conservatives needed a new approach to distance themselves from this lack of success. Ministers began to stress the need for communities to become more involved, prompting a growth in Neighbourhood Watch schemes, the 1988 Safer Cities Programme and creation of Crime Concern. However, an unintended effect was a greater role for Labour-controlled local authorities and a consequent reintroduction of some 'welfarist' ideas. This was exemplified by the Morgan Report (Home Office, 1991), which favoured programmes for employment and training, and rehabilitation of offenders and their families.

The community also featured strongly in the new approach to punishment. The government's revised views were outlined in a white paper, which stated: 'for most offenders imprisonment has to be justified in terms of public protection, denunciation and retribution. Otherwise it can be an expensive way of making bad people worse' (Home Office, 1990, para. 2.7). The Criminal Justice Act 1991 stated that custody should only be imposed for the most serious offences, but greater use of community service orders meant an increasing role for the 'welfarist' probation service, and so national standards were specified to ensure that non-custodial sentences were suitably punitive.

The government also began to introduce 'new public management' techniques into criminal justice agencies. This was intended to make them more 'business-like', drawing a distinction between strategic management and service delivery, or 'steering and rowing' (Osborne and Gaebler, 1992, p. 34). The application of new public management to policing, probation and the prison service enabled the government to devolve responsibility while steering policy by setting budgetary limits, defining goals and measuring performance. This helps to explain the apparent contradiction between community-based crime prevention and punishment and increased central direction of law-and-order policy making and also explains, in part, the privatization of various aspects of the criminal justice system (Johnston, 1996).

The second period of the Conservatives' law-and-order strategy entailed two important changes: first, a displacement of responsibility to 'the community' and law-and-order agencies and, secondly, the introduction of new techniques for managing policy. The former was intended to distance the Conservatives from the increasing crime and civil unrest, while the latter enabled central control to be retained. Both helped to contain public expenditure on law and order.

However, this 'power without responsibility' did not come without political costs. The Conservatives had built their party of law and order claim on appeals to an anxious electorate and to powerful interest groups, including the police and magistracy, but an important consequence of the second-period reforms was to undermine this political support. The electorate became increasingly disconcerted at rising crime rates, the police were antagonized by spending cuts and government criticisms, and judges and JPs were opposed to executive interference in sentencing. There was a growing opportunity for the Labour Party to challenge the Conservatives on crime and public order.

1993–7: Back to Basic Law Enforcement

Increased expenditure, new legislation and organizational reforms conspicuously failed to stop recorded levels of crime from rising. In 1979 the annual recorded level of crime was 2.4 million, but by June 1993 this had more than doubled to 5.7 million offences, while the proportion of offences which were solved (the 'clear-up rate') fell from 41 to 26 per cent. The government's British Crime Survey reported much greater levels of victimization with an estimated 18 million crimes in 1993 (Home Office, 1995, p. 6). There was also concern about outbreaks of serious public disorder, much of which involved youths on deprived estates. The Bulger murder provoked national discussion about serious and repeat offences by juveniles and declining morality. The Criminal Justice Act 1991 was criticized for being 'soft' on young offenders and for engendering contempt for police and court authority. Pressure grew for tougher powers to control and punish juveniles and prompted a further major reappraisal of criminal justice policy (Benyon, 1994).

At the 1993 Conservative Party Conference, new Home Secretary, Michael Howard, outlined a '27–point plan for law and order' which signalled a complete reversal of policy. Howard stated: 'Let us be clear: prison works'. He announced the introduction of secure centres for 12–14-year-old offenders and increased sentences for 15–16-year-olds. These and other measures, including abolition of the right to silence without adverse court comment and limitations on the right to bail, were included in the Criminal Justice and Public Order Act of 1994, which also introduced new laws against squatting, hunt saboteurs, 'rave' parties and trespassers. Many argued that the shift in policies represented the adoption of a naked 'authoritarian populist' approach to cultivate favour with an alienated police and magistracy and a disillusioned electorate.

The Criminal Justice and Public Order Act also included some measures, such as a national DNA database, recommended by the Royal Commission on Criminal Procedure, which reported in June 1993. The Runciman Commission had been established amidst concern about recurring miscarriages of justice, following successful appeals by the 'Birmingham Six' in 1991, who had served 16 years in prison. The Commission made 352 recommendations on virtually every aspect of the criminal justice system, but concern about wrongful convictions remained and was one of the reasons why repeated attempts by backbench Conservatives to reintroduce capital punishment were unsuccessful.

Publication of the *Report of the Inquiry into Police Responsibilities and Rewards* (Sheehy Inquiry) in June 1993 increased police dissatisfaction yet further. Among the Report's contentious proposals were fixed-term appointments and performance-related pay for police officers. Opposition was vociferous and hostile. A 20 000 strong demonstration at Wembley stadium, an extensive media campaign and resignation threats by several chief constables persuaded Howard to reject many of the proposals. However, further criticisms of the police were forthcoming from the Audit Commission and anxieties within the service were heightened by the setting up of a Home Office Review of Police Core and Ancillary Tasks (Posen Inquiry), although its Report in June 1995 did not recommend the far-reaching privatization that many had expected.

In June 1993, the government announced a major reform of police governance, altering the tripartite structure of chief constables, Home Office and local police authorities established by the 1964 Police Act. Police authorities were to be independent corporate bodies, financially accountable for police performance, with elected councillors reduced to one half of the members and a significant proportion and the chair of each police authority appointed by the Home Secretary. Chief constables would have to formulate local police plans, taking account of national policing objectives set by the Home Secretary. National league performance tables of police forces would be produced by Her Majesty's Inspectorate of Constabulary.

The white paper embodied the new public management approach and many of its proposals were incorporated in the 1994 Police and Magistrates' Courts Act. However, this had a stormy passage through the House of Lords and the government was forced to make concessions, especially on the composition of the new police authorities. The Home Secretary was empowered to set national police objectives and performance targets, and those for 1996–7 included increasing detections for violent crimes and burglaries, providing high-visibility policing and responding promptly to emergency calls.

Critics of the Act said it promoted a centrally-controlled police service which undermined local accountability and encouraged political interference, but others saw the possibility of greater local influence through the establishment of police plans and basic command units at neighbourhood level. An important dimension of the evolution of law-and-order policy making under the Conservatives was the *unintended* consequences of reforms, which inadvertently granted various actors increased opportunities to influence the policy process.

Howard's policies produced a rapid expansion in the prison population, from its licensed capacity of 46 994 in late 1993 to

60 000 on the eve of the 1997 general election. The Woolf Inquiry found that the major riot at Strangeways Prison in Manchester, in April 1990, was the result of overcrowding, lack of sanitation and other conditions which had generated a sense of injustice. Published after the reforms introduced by the Criminal Justice Act 1991, the Woolf Report marked the zenith of liberal optimism for penal reform. However, this evaporated with the reversal of policy in 1993 and Lord Woolf himself called Howard's 27–point plan 'short-sighted and irresponsible'.

The Crime (Sentences) Bill, introduced to Parliament in autumn 1996, promised to raise the prison population yet higher. Proposals for 'mandatory' minimum sentences echoed the Clinton administration's 'three strikes and you're out' policy. The Bill proposed tough sentences for burglars and drug dealers on a third conviction, automatic life sentences for those convicted of a second serious violent or sexual offence, abolition of the existing parole and early release system, and powers to impose curfews on more minor offenders. The judiciary was the most vociferous opponent of these measures, which encountered considerable opposition in the House of Lords in 1996–7. To meet the anticipated demand, 12 new 'super-prisons' were announced, and 'high-impact incarceration programmes', more popularly called 'boot camps', were planned for young offenders.

The salience of law and order was increased further by the murder in December 1995 of a London headmaster, Philip Lawrence, by a 15-year-old youth. Three months later the murder of 16 children and their teacher at Dunblane Primary School led to the Cullen Inquiry, and the Firearms (Amendment) Act 1997 prohibited nearly all handguns. The Police Bill, published on 1 November 1996, included the establishment of a National Crime Squad and a Criminal Records Agency and, much more controversially, promised the police powers to enter property to plant electronic surveillance devices to gather intelligence. In the House of Lords, in early 1997, the government was accused of being 'soft on freedom' and suffered a number of defeats on the Bill, which eventually received the Royal Assent on 21 March 1997.

Howard's 27-point plan in 1993 marked a renewed attempt to recapture an electoral issue from which the Conservatives had benefited in previous campaigns, but which they were in danger of losing to a resurgent New Labour. By 1997, the parties were vying with each other to appear the toughest and most effective on crime and public order.

Labour's Law-and-Order Strategy

New Labour's Communitarianism

The Labour Party's new approach to law and order began to take shape following Blair's 1993 pledge. A 1995 policy document listed 'Labour's proposals for tough action on crime', including increased penalties for violence, cutting offending on bail, legislating against criminal neighbours, and undertaking a thorough review of the prosecution process. Proposals on crime reduction included enhancement of community policing, physical security improvements, and greater police accountability. A partnership approach to crime prevention was advocated, with greater powers for local authorities. Other measures included supporting families, improving education, reducing truancy, enhancing training for unemployed youths, and increasing recreational and youth provision. The document also stressed the need for social policy initiatives on unemployment, inner-city decay, child poverty and growing inequality (Labour Party, 1995, pp. 6–13).

Labour's revised approach retained the conventional social democratic emphasis on tackling social causes of crime and deviance, but stressed the importance of discipline and the responsibilities of individuals and families. The approach fitted squarely with the party's stress on 'community' and 'responsibility' in its developing ideological framework. In 1994, for example, Shadow Chancellor Gordon Brown stated that 'people must accept their responsibilities as individuals and as citizens, and community action should never be a substitute for the assumption of personal responsibility' (Brown, 1994, p. 119). In 1997, Tony Blair said: 'I am utterly convinced that the only way to rebuild a strong civic society for the modern world is on the basis of rights and responsibility going together.'

One appeal of 'communitarianism' for New Labour was that it could be presented as a radical alternative to both laissez-faire conservatism and 'statist' social democracy, attracting disen-

chanted Conservatives without alienating traditional supporters in the labour movement and welfare professions. The labour movement has a long history of extraparliamentary campaigning, including marches, demonstrations and industrial action, which enabled the Conservatives to portray Labour as supporting behaviour which undermined the rule of law. Images of the 1978–9 'winter of discontent' and of poll tax protests in the late 1980s bedevilled the Labour Party. However, communitarianism could evoke an alternative, harmonious, vision of law and order – of different groups and individuals helping each other to create safe and secure neighbourhoods. In Blair's view, the solution to crime 'lies in strong communities prepared to act to protect their citizens'.

This approach, however, has attracted criticism, for example over its undifferentiated conception of community which, some claim, fails to recognize internal conflicts of interest, and the special needs of particular groups, such as ethnic minorities, women, and elderly people. Some critics regard it as 'authoritarian corporatism', while others question the acceptance of conventional nuclear family values, and the traditional role for women, viewing such a conception of communitarianism as 'fundamentally regressive' (Hall, 1995, p. 31).

Zero-Tolerance Policing

In 1996, Shadow Home Secretary Jack Straw provoked controversy by calling for action against 'winos and addicts whose aggressive begging affronts and sometimes threatens decent compassionate citizens'. His speech followed a visit to New York to examine the city's 'zero-tolerance' policing strategy, based on the 'broken-windows thesis' (Wilson and Kelling, 1983). This argues that one broken window leads to further vandalism and then more serious criminal acts follow. Intervention against apparently mundane acts of anti-social behaviour, such as begging, street prostitution and graffiti, can arrest a neighbourhood's downward spiral of increasing criminality and disorder.

Rudolph Giuliani, Republican Mayor of New York, claimed that zero-tolerance policing was the primary cause of the city's 15 per cent decline in crime in 1995, and even larger falls in robberies and homicides. In 1996 the murder rate in New York was 983, down from 2245 in 1990 and below 1000 for the first time since 1968. Others, though, maintain that the fall in crime was the result of many factors, including a demographic fall in the number of young men, a decline in the use of crack-cocaine, a large decrease in unemployment, improved community policing and more effective deployment of police into high-crime areas.

In autumn 1996, a number of British police forces, including the Metropolitan, Cleveland and Strathclyde, introduced experimental schemes for zero-tolerance policing. Critics were concerned, however, that this might worsen police–community relations in ethnically diverse neighbourhoods. In 1981, the Scarman Report into the Brixton disorders identified racial harassment as an important factor in the decline of police–community relations. Research into police–black community relations has highlighted the tendency of officers to associate particular crimes with black people, criminalizing whole ethnic minority communities. Intensive stop-and-search tactics, which are central to zero-tolerance policing, might have the consequence of generating public disorder.

Nonetheless, the approach found favour with both Conservative and Labour politicians. In 1997 Blair reiterated his call for zero-tolerance policing, stating: 'To say we should tolerate a certain level of crime is absurd.' Under his leadership, Labour's law-and-order strategy developed a harder line. This was evident in a 1996 policy document which recommended action on the 'underlying causes of disorder', such as homelessness, youth unemployment and care in the community, but concentrated on punitive measures to suppress public disorder, and advocated CCTV surveillance of town centres and tough action against drug dealers. In summer 1996, Straw called for night-time curfews for children.

Before the 1997 election Straw and Howard each advocated high-profile policing of street crime and anti-social behaviour. The degree of convergence was epitomized when Straw accused Howard of 'stealing' Labour's ideas on crime reduction and zero-tolerance policing. Labour was noticeably reticent in parliamentary debates on the Crime (Sentences) Bill, although it eventually moved successful amendments to the Police Bill in the House of Lords in January 1997.

Problems and Prospects

Towards 2000: Policy Challenges

Under the Blair government a high level of continuity on crime
and public-order policies seems likely, partly because of public
demands for tough action, but also because of legislative reforms
and new public management initiatives. One effect of the politicization of law and order is that public demand for action has
risen considerably. With insufficient Treasury money to meet this
demand, concern over 'value for money', particularly in the
rapidly expanding prison system, is likely to intensify and further
experiments with privatization and community-based crime prevention and punishment seem inevitable.

Continued efforts to increase efficiency and effectiveness in the
police service also seem certain, with tighter performance indicators, increased reliance on computers and other technology,
further 'civilianization' of posts, and close scrutiny from the Audit
Commission and Her Majesty's Inspectorate. The Blair government's priorities include greater development of police–community partnerships, more accountability and consultation, and
improved relations with ethnic minorities. It is likely to experiment with different forms of policing, such as neighbourhood
wardens employed by local authorities or private companies.
There is also pressure for further development of a national police
institution, of which the National Criminal Intelligence Service
(NCIS) and the National Crime Squad are harbingers. Another
priority is to reduce police misconduct, which has resulted in large
compensation payments, estimated to amount to £20 million in
the Metropolitan Police alone in the decade up to 1996. Another
challenge facing the new government is how to reverse declining
public confidence in the criminal justice system, in the wake of the
succession of miscarriages of justice and continuing criticism of the
police.

Concerning the most serious types of crime, there is renewed
pressure on the police and MI5 to combat terrorism, which in
Britain involves groups from as far apart as South America, the
Middle East and Asia, as well as the IRA. Other organized crime,
some of which allegedly involves Triads, 'yardies' and eastern
European criminals, includes drug trafficking, extortion, fraud,

theft of high-value vehicles and works of art, and illegal immigration. To combat what is perceived as an increasing threat, there are likely to be further moves to develop European law-enforcement institutions and co-operative arrangements, such as Europol and the Schengen accord, with accompanying demands for satisfactory forms of political and public accountability (Benyon, 1996).

The fall in recorded levels of crime between 1993 and 1996 appeared to be a result of less offences being recorded, rather than of a real fall in crime. Blair's pledge to be tough on crime seems likely to result in local, relatively cheap, initiatives involving private-sector companies and voluntary bodies as well as 'communities'. In view of British Crime Survey findings that much crime is concentrated in relatively few areas, affecting a small number of repeat victims, selective, local schemes are likely to be encouraged. Increased in-built security measures may diminish car thefts, and proactive, intelligence-led, policing, such as Operation Bumblebee, may reduce burglary and other crimes. Post-Dunblane legislation on firearms, and limitations on dangerous knives, which are likely to be increased yet further by the Blair government, may help to stop the rise in violent crimes.

The new Home Secretary, Jack Straw, made it clear that particular attention would be devoted to juvenile crime and low-level disorder, given their extent and increasing public exasperation with nuisance, noise and vandalism. One of the first pieces of legislation announced by the Blair government was the Crime and Disorder Bill, which was expected to include an array of measures, such as curfews on children under 10, parental responsibility orders, the replacement of cautions with 'final warnings', tougher action against persistent teenage offenders, the creation of youth offender teams to oversee intensive community-based punishment, and an emphasis on 'restorative justice', with meetings between young offenders, their parents and victims, and reparations by the offenders. Other planned initiatives included the establishment of a National Youth Justice Board and the introduction of a fast-track system of punishment for young offenders, action to reduce truancy, and measures to tackle anti-social neighbours, racial harassment and problems of public disorder in housing estates and town centres.

At a deeper level, there is concern about the development of an 'underclass' of unskilled and marginalized people, and of social polarization between them and those who are in employment. There are fears of social and cultural fragmentation which, for some, have conjured up a nightmare *Blade Runner* future of insecurity and violence, where prisons, electronic tagging and surveillance are used to control these 'redundant' populations, with 'respectable' people living in residential fortresses, patrolled by private security personnel (Davis, 1990). These rather melodramatic visions do highlight the dangers posed by unemployment, deprivation, selfishness, anomie and falling levels of social cohesion. In such circumstances, crime and disorder tend to flourish.

This, perhaps, presents the Blair government with its greatest challenge, as being 'tough on the causes of crime' will inevitably cost money and take time. Labour has pledged that it will prioritize action on youth unemployment, which seems essential if crime and disorder are to be reduced. However, action is also required to overcome poverty and deprivation, combat homelessness, assist single-parent families, expand the youth service, and improve education and training. It is not clear how an effective attack on these social problems will be mounted during a period of public expenditure retrenchment.

A New Consensus?

Crime and disorder were prominent political issues throughout the Conservatives' years in office but, despite a plethora of penal, policing and criminal justice reforms, and substantial public and private investment, the problems continued largely unabated. To challenge the Conservatives successfully on these issues, Labour needed to dispel an image of being 'apologists' for civil unrest and 'soft' on crime. It adopted principles of individual, as well as collective, responsibilities and advanced communitarianism both as an alternative to welfarism and to the Conservatives' belief in deterrence and punishment. While highlighting the need to tackle the causes of crime, New Labour's policy prescriptions lay stress on personal and family morality and responsibilities as the foundations of 'strong communities', prompting some to talk of a new bipartisan consensus.

However, the extent to which a bipartisan consensus on crime and public order has emerged remains difficult to gauge. For electoral purposes, at least, Labour emphasized tough crime control rather than tough action to tackle its causes. Yet, like its predecessors, the Blair government faces many policy challenges, not least the considerable pressures on public expenditure generated by increased custodial punishment. The conflict between enhanced public safety and tight public expenditure controls was a recurring feature of law-and-order policy throughout the Conservative administrations and will remain so under the Labour government.

Public expenditure constraints may well lead to further innovations in the delivery of law enforcement and criminal justice, including greater devolution of responsibility for public safety away from the central state and toward public–private 'partnerships'. The 'return to community', and stress on individual and collective responsibilities, may offer the basis for bipartisan consensus on law-and-order policies, but it seems unlikely that traditional conceptions of personal and family morality will do so. Traditionalist approaches fail to recognize the cultural and economic transformations which 'postmodern' societies are experiencing and which are generating cultural plurality and economic and social polarization.

In such circumstances, the task facing the Blair government appears daunting. Polls taken during the 1997 election campaign showed that people rated law and order as one of their top five issues of concern, and Home Secretary Jack Straw moved quickly to begin implementing reforms, with the Crime and Disorder Bill promised as one of the central pieces of legislation in the new session of Parliament. The huge parliamentary majority will enable Straw and his team to introduce radical changes, including incorporation of the European Convention on Human Rights into British law, but the sweeping victory on 1 May also seemed to have raised people's expectations of effective action in a public policy field which had proved so difficult for the Conservatives during the previous 18 years. With an electorate impatient for results, it seems clear that one of the main ways that the Labour government will be judged is by success in the fields of crime and public order.

17

BSE and the Politics of Food

WYN GRANT

Britain's experience with bovine spongiform encephalopathy (BSE) offers a clear example of a policy disaster. The losers included those who died from the new variant of Creutzfeld-Jakob disease (NVCJD) (the human equivalent of BSE); other consumers worried about possible health effects; farmers whose livelihoods were disrupted; and the Major government whose reputation for competence and honesty was further damaged. Britain's relationship with Europe also suffered additional strain.

This sequence of events cannot just be seen as an unfortunate set of unrelated mistakes. Dunleavy (1995, p. 52) has argued that 'Britain now stands out amongst comparable European countries . . . as a state unusually prone to make large-scale, avoidable policy mistakes.' One of the characteristics of these policy disasters is the determination of decision makers to pursue a chosen policy in spite of evidence that it is seriously flawed. Dunleavy offers a number of systemic explanations for the regular occurrence of these policy disasters in Britain, but one that is particularly relevant to the present discussion is the insulation of a self-confident administrative elite lacking knowledge of the field in which they are operating but reluctant to make use of the full range of outside expertise.

In order to understand the BSE episode, it is necessary to present a few stylized facts about the politics of food in Britain. The Ministry of Agriculture, Fisheries and Food (MAFF), which the Labour government has said it will re-name, is the only department of government responsible for one particular industry. Historically its orientation was one of securing a secure supply of reasonably cheap food for UK consumers by providing financial support to British farmers. Although the Department of

Health also has responsibilities in the area of food safety, MAFF has generally been the 'lead' department with an orientation towards producers rather than consumers. Members of the various advisory committees dealing with food safety questions have been criticized for acting 'as paid consultants to the commercial organisations whose actions and products they are evaluating' (Lang *et al.*, 1996, p. 18).

Food production in Britain has been increasingly dominated by a profit-oriented agribusiness style in which more and more emphasis is placed on farmers having financial and marketing expertise rather than husbandry skills. Agriculture has become progressively more intensive as farmers have made use of expensive machinery, agrochemicals, computers and antibiotics. The adoption of biotechnology is likely to lead to further moves in the direction of seeing farming as a science rather than a craft. Once food products leave the farm most of them undergo further processing by large agribusinesses and are then sold in highly 'packaged' forms by retail chains with sizeable market shares. Consumers taking the food product off the supermarket shelf usually know very little about the processes that have gone into producing it.

This agribusiness complex has close links to the Conservative Party. Large-scale farmers are particularly well connected with the Tories. At least one or two of them are usually to be found within the cabinet, they are active in local constituency associations, and they overwhelmingly vote Conservative. Many large food-processing companies have historically been generous donors to the Conservative Party. And quite a few Conservative MPs have been drawn from the senior management of the major retail firms. The whole 'food chain' thus has a close network of links with a Conservative government.

BSE: The Disease and a Chronology

Scientific knowledge about BSE is still very incomplete. This mysterious disease is not transmitted by a virus or bacteria but is associated with proteins known as prions. Just because someone has eaten the offal of an animal suffering from BSE does not mean that they will then be stricken with NVCJD. It is possible that there may need to be a genetic predisposition to the disease; that there may be a cumulative effect, so that one would have to eat a considerable amount of contaminated meat to be affected; and that the incubation period is such a long one that many people may die of some other condition before NVCJD becomes evident. Those most at risk are 'people who ate poor quality beefburgers containing tissue from BSE-infected brain and spinal cord before the ban on the use of specified bovine offals was introduced in 1989' (*Agra Europe*, 13 December 1996, p. N/2). Indeed, by the end of 1996, only 14 victims of NVCJD had been identified, far fewer than the 60 or so individuals under the age of 45 who die each year from dementia.

Individuals are a far greater risk driving a car than eating beef, but, as a result of the BSE episode, people are far more likely to have stopped eating beef than driving their car. It has to be recognized that there is considerable disagreement among individuals when it comes to risk perceptions in relation to nature and the body. One of the problems with the BSE episode is that decision makers have adhered to traditional scientific conceptions of rationality in which cause and effect relationships have to be experimentally demonstrated before policy makers take any preventive action.

BSE is a disease which produces microscopic holes in the brains of cattle, leading to their eventual death. It was first identified in 1986. The mechanisms associated with the appearance of BSE are still far from clear, and there are alternative hypotheses to the one presented here, notably the idea that BSE is associated with the use of organophosphate pesticides in agriculture. This controversy about the origins of BSE is interesting because of the light it sheds on the politics of expertise, but the most likely explanation is the one that follows. Britain has a large sheep population and this population has been affected with a disease known as scrapie for at least 200 years. The disease was clinically recognized in 1732, but probably dates from the importation of Merino sheep in the fifteenth century (Ford, 1996, p. 33).

It seems likely that BSE jumped species from scrapie-infected sheep through poorly rendered offal including dead sheep remains fed to cattle in the early 1980s. A less intensive agriculture, of course, might not make carnivores out of ruminants and would have stuck to traditional methods of raising cattle primarily on grass. In 1981 and 1982, the meat rendering industry stopped the use of chemical solvents to extract fat from carcases and started to sterilize them at a lower temperature. These changes were introduced for a combination of financial and environmental reasons, but had adverse implications in health terms. 'Infective agents like scrapie – which may have been inactivated by the process – would be more likely to survive a gentler form of processing' (Ford, 1996, p. 22). It has also been suggested 'that the increasing intensity of milk production and the widespread introduction in the 1980s of the Holstein specialist dairy breed [could] have played a part in the BSE outbreak' (*Agra Europe*, 2 August 1996, p. P/4).

The initial discovery of BSE and its classification as a notifiable disease in 1988 led to a number of government-sponsored reports and policy initiatives, but the public was assured by the Chief Medical Officer of Health in 1990 that beef was absolutely safe to eat. In what came to be recalled as a notorious gimmick, the then Minister of Agriculture (John Gummer) publicly fed a beefburger to his young daughter in an attempt to reassure the public. The discovery of an evident link between BSE and a new human disease in 1996 (only eight years after its identification in cows) produced a 'food scare' that eclipsed previous scares on issues such as listeria in cheese and salmonella in eggs. The most dramatic consequence of the avalanche of adverse publicity was that European Union agriculture ministers inaugurated a complete prohibition of any exporting of British beef or products derived from beef to any other country in the world – a decision taken to try and head off a chain reaction of bans on any EU beef exports which was beginning to look possible. Saturation media coverage of the issue in Britain undoubtedly both reflected and reinforced public concern, with even the broadsheet press producing some scare stories that had little scientific basis. As the *UK Press Gazette* conceded in a leader on BSE on 29 March: 'Lack of sound scientific knowledge has handicapped many of us . . . More journalists should be recruited from among science graduates, more contacts should be established with the scientific community and more national reporters should be drawn from specialist magazines.'

There is no doubt that a series of policy mistakes was made by the British government. The most serious error was undoubtedly committed in 1988 when ministers and senior civil servants at MAFF decided that there should be compulsory slaughter of all cows afflicted by BSE, but set compensation levels to farmers at only 50 per cent of the value of each infected animal, had it been healthy. This decision gave farmers an incentive to conceal BSE cases. Full compensation was not introduced until January 1990, and the number of BSE cases finally reached its peak at 34 370 in 1993.

The initial handling of the 1996 human health crisis was marred by underlying tensions between the Department of Health and MAFF, the former giving priority to public health issues, the latter seeking to protect its traditional clients in the agriculture and food industries. Political commentators agreed that the performance of the Conservatives' Agriculture Minister, Douglas Hogg, was less than distinguished, and responsibility for organizing the cull of cattle was eventually handed over to the Public Services Minister, Roger Freeman. A more decisive intervention by John Major at an earlier stage might have defused the crisis or at least steered it into calmer waters. As the crisis unfolded, the Treasury was a significant player in the policy process, seeking to limit an ever increasing bill for the destruction of cattle thought to be at risk of infection. Although 70 per cent of the cost of compensation was funded by the EU, the public expenditure impact was greater as the flow of compensation funds had the effect of reducing Britain's budget rebate from Brussels. The eventual EU contribution to the total costs of culling cattle in the UK is likely to be nearer 25 per cent (*Agra Europe*, 4 April 1996, p. P/4).

From the beginning of the crisis, the key to rebuilding public confidence in beef was the implementation of an effective eradication scheme through the slaughter of cattle. The EU asked MAFF to propose such a scheme at the end of March 1996. A policy called the 'over thirty month cull scheme' (OTMS) was introduced in May to boost consumer confidence. It was aimed at slaughtering the older cattle most at risk of having contracted BSE, thereby stopping them entering the human food chain. It was beset with problems of implementation. Considerable problems were encountered initially in achieving a sufficiently rapid slaughter rate although, by November 1996, 800 000 cattle had been processed and queues were substantially reduced. The problem was 'not just abattoir capacity but also the limited pool of trained labour and problems in manning inspection posts and securing sufficient transport' (*Agra Europe*, 4 October 1996, p. N/1).

Although it was evident that most of the policy mistakes occurred in Britain, the government decided to attempt to shift blame for what had happened onto the European Union. Ministers hoped that this would increase the government's domestic popularity and also extract more concessions from the European Union. A three week period of disruption of EU business was initiated by the British government, the most serious non-cooperation incident since the French 'empty chair' episode in 1965. It led to some 80 pieces of European legislation being blocked at various Council meetings. However, it did nothing to revive the government's domestic standing, while the prime minister's claim that almost all elements of the EU's ban on beef exports would be lifted by November 1996 was not enshrined in any agreed timetable. It is difficult to see that the final agreement brokered at the Florence summit in June 1996 offered Britain much that it could not have obtained by normal processes of negotiation without embarking on a 'beef war'.

The Florence framework agreement listed five steps towards the lifting of the EU's complete ban on all British beef exports. One of the most important was a selective slaughter scheme (in addition to the OTMS policy) including the additional slaughter of other cattle viewed as most at risk of having been exposed to BSE. On this question, the British government went through a series of policy reversals which suggest that policy was not being driven by any long-term pursuit of coherent and well defined policy goals, but purely by short-term domestic political considerations.

In September 1996, John Major announced that the selective cull of 147 000 cows deemed to be most at risk from BSE was to be put on hold. In part this was justified by reference to a new scientific study from Oxford University which suggested that BSE would die out anyway by the year 2000, conclusions which were at least debatable. Major argued that delaying implementation of the selective cull was compatible with the Florence agreement, citing a clause stating that the UK's BSE eradication plan could be adapted in the light of scientific and epidemiological developments. In Brussels this development was not seen as a technical adjustment to the programme, but as a serious failure to implement an agreed commitment.

In another policy reversal, it was announced in December 1996 that the selective cull would go ahead after all. The principal reason for this *volte-face* was stated by Douglas Hogg to be that opinion within the UK industry had changed. The powerful National Farmers Union, previously hostile to the selective cull, now came out strongly in favour of it, having realized belatedly that there was no other way of restarting beef exports to Europe or anywhere else. It was also evident that hostility to the cull among Conservative MPs had diminished, so that the government would now be able to win a vote on the issue in the House of Commons. In other words, policy was being driven by what was politically expedient rather than by what was necessary for policy efficacy. By the beginning of 1997, it became clear that it would be some time before the worldwide beef exports ban would begin to be lifted and that the whole issue would be a difficult one for an incoming government.

The Politics of Expertise

It is evident that political decision makers were very selective in their treatment of which pieces of expert evidence to treat seriously. The Oxford study was used to justify the suspension of the selective cull, but its findings were questioned by the chair of the EU's expert committee. The arguments advanced by David Purdey, an organic dairy farmer, that the use of organophosphates to control warble fly led to the BSE epidemic have been largely disregarded in official circles in Britain, but are to be reviewed by the EU's multidisciplinary committee on BSE.

Resolving these issues about what constitutes appropriate expertise in relation to food safety questions is not straightforward, however. On the one hand, there are the large number of experts who seek to base their judgements on what they see as relevant and properly collected scientific evidence. On the other hand, there has emerged what could be termed an alternative food establishment, originally associated with campaigning organizations such as the London Food Commission and linked in the public mind with some prominent individuals. From this perspective, 'The dominant constellation of commercial interests is widely perceived to have been in the driving seat of food and agricultural policy for too long' (Lang *et al.*, 1996, p. 6).

Relatively obscure groups of experts who had been used to operating in a sedate technical context suddenly found themselves propelled by the BSE crisis into the political limelight. Being a state vet is one of the more obscure callings in a national civil service and the EU's veterinary committees (the Scientific Veterinary Committee and the higher ranking Standing Veterinary Committee) had operated for many years without attracting any significant attention from either the media or policy analysts. Suddenly, however, the operations of these committees were moved into the centre of political attention. In May 1996, the Scientific Veterinary Committee recommended that the ban on exports of three non-food products (gelatine, tallow and semen) derived from UK cattle should be lifted. After 12 hours of discussion, enough states in the Standing Veterinary Committee voted against the proposal to block a qualified majority for even this modest lifting of the ban. It is difficult to believe that some of the European countries which voted against were not influenced by political rather than scientific considerations. In any event, John Major regarded the decision of the Standing Veterinary Committee as a breach of faith, triggering Britain's policy of non-co-operation with the EU.

A more fundamental issue is what constitutes legitimate expertise. Physical scientists have agreed procedures for testing and evaluating evidence, but their critics have argued that, rather than waiting for something to be established as fact through such procedures they should give greater weight to the risks associated with uncertainty. One research project into policy-making (Grove-Whyte and Wynne, 1995, p. 8) has argued that there is 'a strong tendency in the dominant UK policy and media knowledge cultures towards relatively uncritical reliance on reductionist scientific framings and representations of problems, as providing the "real" accounts of what is at stake'. When problems arise about the public authority of expert knowledge in 'environmental' fields, the political assumption made is that 'such problems are due to incompleteness of public understanding, and hence that steps to generate and promulgate fuller or more precise

knowledge on the same lines are the most appropriate response'
(Grove-Whyte and Wynne, 1995, p. 9).

Inclusion and exclusion are recurrent themes in British policy
formation. Some experts may have been excluded (or exclude
themselves) from the policy process by failing to observe the
prevalent 'rules of the game', for example, by making statements
to the media which appeared to be exaggerated in their content or
which criticized the decision-making process in government. Even
those individuals with milder views have sometimes found it
difficult to challenge established scientific orthodoxy, as David
Purdey's experience shows.

BSE and Devolution

In his analysis of why Britain has been prone to policy disasters,
Dunleavy draws attention to the fact that the UK 'is unusual in
being a unitary country without the regional-level tier of government found in all federal countries' (Dunleavy, 1995, p. 59). The
BSE crisis raised a number of regional issues which it was difficult
to deal with in a unitary system of government. Indeed, the
interests of Northern Ireland had to some extent to be represented
in EU circles by the Irish Republic.

The Scottish Nationalists argued that Scottish beef farmers
belonging to schemes which certified their Aberdeen Angus cattle
as free from BSE might have escaped the European export ban if
only Scotland had been an independent country. The incidence of
the disease was much lower in Scotland and the head of the
biggest meat business in Scotland argued that 'we should do our
own thing. I think it is time that we considered a Scottish solution
to the problem' (*Farmers Weekly*, 5 April 1996). Northern Ireland
also had a significantly lower incidence of the disease and
operated a computer system which allowed all livestock to be
traced from birth to their final buyer. The EU agriculture
commissioner, Franz Fischler, met the three MEPs from Northern
Ireland and farm lobby representatives and indicated that he
would be prepared to treat Northern Ireland as a special case if a
request was made by the British government (*Agra Europe*, 19
April 1996, p. E/3). Anything which looked like treating the

whole of Ireland as one agricultural region (which it is in many respects) raised all sorts of suspicions in London. It appeared in the winter of 1996–7 as if a special deal might be struck for Northern Ireland because it is a containable region with a well developed cattle database. The Irish Republic's Agriculture Minister, Ivan Yates, travelled to the north to meet Northern Irish MEPs and leaders of the farming and meat industry and agreed to press his EU counterparts for an end to the ban on beef exports from there. Ian Paisley claimed to have won support from the German government for excluding Northern Ireland from the export ban (*Agra Europe*, 6 December 1996, p. P/6). 'Suggestions that Northern Ireland might be first out of the ban . . . infuriated Scottish farmers' leaders, who feel their cause will be set back for years by being lumped with England and Wales' (*Financial Times*, 5 November 1996). In the absence of any kind of Scottish assembly, however, Scots farms were lumped in with England and Wales, and could not call on another member state to act on their behalf as in the case of Northern Ireland.

Britain's Relations with the European Union

The BSE episode provoked a serious crisis in Britain's relations with the European Union, leading to a further deterioration in relationships with other member states, particularly Germany (where consumers' reactions against buying beef were most intense). A key underlying problem here was the deep divisions in an electorally unpopular Conservative Party over Britain's relationship with Europe. The need to maintain a facade of unity in Tory ranks between Euroenthusiasts and Eurosceptics, and the presentation of the issue in a way that would boost government popularity, often seemed to be driving the way in which the BSE issue was managed in Britain. Yet, of course, Britain's BSE problem dwarfs that of any other member state. One paradoxical effect of the BSE episode has been the renationalization of beef sales, leading to an undermining of the common market in Europe because consumers are more likely to trust local produce.

The episode started in March 1996 with mutual mistrust on both sides. Accusations were made in Britain that the initial single country bans of British beef exports by individual EU member states were driven by their own commercial objectives. Certainly, member states were worried about the impact of the British BSE crisis on their domestic beef industries. The Commission also felt that the British government had not informed it quickly enough about the impending crisis. Franz Fischler, the EU Agriculture Commissioner, complained to the British Agriculture Minister, Hogg, that he had not warned the Commission about the impending announcement on BSE at the Farm Council in March. Fischler wrote: 'If the new findings of your scientists are as troubling as they sound, then the measures you announced seemed insufficient. If, on the other hand, your findings do not add to the existing body of knowledge about a link with BSE, a more careful reaction might have been preferable' (*Agra Europe*, 29 March 1996, p. P/3).

The British government caused further annoyance in Brussels when it failed to send its key experts on the human form of BSE (NVCJD) to a meeting of the Scientific Veterinary Committee at the end of March. When this committee recommended a world-wide ban on British beef exports which was accepted by the European Commission, John Major rang the Commission president, Jacques Santer: 'In 10 incandescent minutes, the British prime minister distilled the frustration and bitterness his government feels towards Europe in its struggle to contain the crisis over mad cow disease' (*Financial Times*, 27 March 1996). The Commission agreed to a second meeting of the veterinary committee, which the key British scientists attended. According to a British official in the Commission, the British government was paying the price for years of anti-European rhetoric: 'Britain has no political leverage. It also has no goodwill to draw on' (*Financial Times*, 27 March 1996).

When Conservative ministers subsequently waged a 'beef war' against Brussels, a major imperative was to find a means of coping with divisions within the Tory party. This objective was achieved in the limited sense that it bought acquiescence from the Euro-sceptics and hence political survival time for the government, but at the price of widening the gulf between Britain and other member states: 'The residue of ill feeling left by the British tactics was everywhere apparent . . . as they look to Europe's future, others have decided they can no longer accommodate their awkward island neighbours' (*Financial Times*, 24 June 1996).

There was a particularly serious deterioration of relations between Britain and Germany, symbolized by the actions of German farmers burning the union flag. It was not just a question of German farmers being worried about losing their markets. German consumers and voters are among the most environmental and public health conscious in Europe. When it was revealed at the beginning of August that maternal transmission of BSE was possible (so that infected cows could pass on the disease to their calves), German officials demanded that the EU should restore a strict ban on British beef.

The BSE episode has thrown the Common Agricultural Policy (CAP) into further disarray. The normally measured Agriculture Commissioner, Franz Fischler, has described the problems in the beef sector as of a magnitude unparalleled in the history of the CAP. The EU had to take a number of additional measures to buy beef into intervention stores and to pay for the slaughter of calves (the 'Herod premium') to counteract the substantial slump in the market for beef. The total extra cost of BSE-related measures was estimated to be 1.827 billion ECU in 1997. These additional budgetary obligations came at a time when the approaching deadline for economic and monetary union had imposed further budgetary constraints on all EU member states, and when new international trade agreements made it harder to dump surplus produce onto world markets.

Conclusions

As with other policy disasters, the BSE affair highlighted some key underlying deficiencies of the British system of government. These included the lack of a food safety body which enjoyed broad public confidence; the curious role of MAFF in the structure of government as the only ministry primarily serving one client group; the difficulties in getting lay ministers and generalist civil servants to handle technical information and decisions appropriately; and the Treasury's preoccupation with restraining public expenditure in the short run.

Above all, the episode highlighted the British dilemma about whether it should have a constructive and close, or an adversarial and distant, relationship with the EU. The BSE episode produced an outpouring of xenophobic correspondence in the farming press with accusations of plots to undermine British agriculture directed from Brussels. These problems were exacerbated by the divisions on Europe within the Conservative Party, but relations with the EU constitute a potential line of division across the traditional left–right spectrum. Public opinion is fragile and uncertain on the EU, the Labour Party's divisions on the issue are as deep as those of the Conservative Party (if not as evident), and the direction to be taken is far from clear. Episodes like the BSE affair leave Britain with little goodwill to drawn on in Europe and a set of only partially resolved public health problems for the Labour government.

One of the first actions taken by the new Labour government followed the receipt by Tony Blair of the James Report he had commissioned from a food safety expert. This recommended the establishment of an independent Food Standards Agency modelled on the Health and Safety Commission and Executive. The government proceeded to create just such an agency. Despite this, BSE remains a complex and intractable issue for Agriculture Secretary Jack Cunningham. EU resistance to removing the ban on UK beef exports remains substantial, despite the general improvement in UK–EU relations following Labour victory.

With regard to the Food Standards Agency, much has been said about the need for such a body to be independent, and the FSA will be completely independent of ministers, as recommended by Professor Philip James of Aberdeen University. However, there has been much less discussion of how the scientific and technical independence of a publicly-funded body can be ensured while retaining accountability. The problem is, of course, one of policies rather than structure, but the practical constraints the Labour government faces in policy innovation are illustrated by the issue of organophosphate sheep dips. Michael Meacher, as environment spokesperson, stated that Labour would recommend farmers not to use such dips, but admitted that it would not have evidence to justify a full ban. The Labour government is likely to have to face its own food scares and, until it can introduce reforms such as devolution, it will be dealing with the same governance structure as the Conservatives and run a similar risk of encountering policy disasters.

18
Conclusion: Politics 2000

ANDREW GAMBLE

At the end of the twentieth century there are many uncertainties about future developments in British politics. Old narratives and assumptions which used to give coherence and meaning to the British political experience are being challenged by new circumstances and restless intellectual fashions which promote new grand theories and meta-narratives like globalization and postmodernism. Much of what was once taken for granted about politics in the twentieth century is being swept away.

Nowhere is the challenge to old assumptions about British politics greater than in the current reassessment of the future of the British state. With its ancient constitutional order under strain and its long history of overseas expansion and imperial rule finally at an end, Britain faces the next century as a medium-sized multinational state, but with part of its political class still affirming the unique and exceptional character of British history and British institutions and refusing to adjust to the consequences of the long national decline.

All nations claim to be exceptional in some way. British exceptionalism has its counterparts in American exceptionalism and German exceptionalism, but it is a particularly virulent strain of the disease. It has three main aspects: innovation, leadership and continuity. The first celebrates Britain as a pioneer – in exploring and colonizing the globe from the sixteenth to the nineteenth century; in experiencing in the seventeenth century the first of the political revolutions of the modern era; in undergoing the first industrial revolution with its drastic changes to the structure of occupations and the balance between city and country; in providing one of the first and most durable models of parliamentary democracy; and in technological innovation and scientific discoveries. Britain is depicted as a nation which for several centuries has been at the forefront of many of the key developments in politics, economics and culture which have made up modernity.

The second aspect has been Britain's prolonged exercise of leadership in the world economy and world politics despite its relatively modest base of population and resources. This period of leadership reached its zenith in the nineteenth century but cast its shadow long into the twentieth, and shaped many British institutions and attitudes, from the civil service and the armed forces to universities and companies. British dominance was not only economic, political and military but also cultural. The expectation of British superiority and the idea that Britain had something to teach the rest of the world, based upon its exceptional national experience, became deeply ingrained.

The third aspect is the continuity of British institutions. The survival of the British state for so long without internal overthrow or external invasion, although not entirely without parallel, is in marked contrast to the fate of most other states in Europe and is responsible for many particular and idiosyncratic features of British institutions such as the uncodified constitution, the survival of an unelected second chamber based in part on heredity, and the doctrine of parliamentary sovereignty. The degree of continuity has been questioned. The preservation of outward institutional forms can mask deeper changes of substance. What there has not been is the kind of comprehensive modernization of institutions and elites which many other countries have undergone.

At the heart of the thesis of British exceptionalism is the identification of the history of Britain with the history of its state. In contrast with states elsewhere the British state has generally been perceived, not as a body standing above society, but as one closely integrated with it. The cohesion of British elites was captured by the term 'the Establishment', first used in the 1950s. The borders between the British state and the public institutions of British civil society have not been sharply defined. One of the consequences, as reformers have never ceased to complain, is that it has been difficult to modernize British institutions piecemeal because they have always been so interlocked and resistant to comprehensive reform. This unique complex of institutions and traditions gave rise to a distinctive political identity and conception of statehood.

It is, however, precisely this unique and venerable configuration, sometimes referred to disrespectfully as the last ancien régime in Europe, which is now under such challenge (Chapter 7). The challenge is both internal and external. In the course of the twentieth century Britain has been transformed from being one of the undisputed great powers in the international state system and the leading imperial power to a medium-sized nation-state. The adjustment has not been easy and is still incomplete, but the need to determine Britain's relationship with the EU gives it a new urgency (Chapter 2). At the same time successive governments since the 1960s have attempted to grapple with Britain's relative economic decline, raising profound questions about the competence, organization, representativeness and effectiveness of the British state.

Is radical change in prospect? Many doubt it, believing that substantial continuity will be preserved and the British state and its civil society will survive relatively intact with few changes into the next century (Chapter 7). Cultural, political and institutional conservatism and the force of inertia will frustrate any attempts at more radical change. If change is imposed it will be short-lived. Popular support for constitutional change is said to be weak and the need for it unproven. Britain needs to stay constitutionally conservative if it is to remain economically enterprising and innovative (Willetts, 1992).

The counter to this argument is that many of the formulas which sustained British politics and the British state are exhausted, and that following the radical domestic policy changes of the 1980s which changed the balance between the public and private sectors other radical changes are now in prospect (regional assemblies, electoral reform and a single European currency) which may shift Britain onto a quite different trajectory of development (Hutton, 1995). Britain cannot delay much longer in deciding how to participate in the process of deepening European integration. Membership of the European Union has already had major consequences for many British institutions and for the way Britain is governed and further change is unavoidable which will make the British state come to resemble other European states more closely.

A third view, however, is that whether the British state survives or is reformed is a rather trivial matter because like other nation-states, it is rapidly being rendered obsolete and marginal by huge economic and cultural changes which are sweeping the globe. Since the end not only of the century but of the millennium is approaching, there is an increasingly apocalyptic tone to much writing on politics and an outbreak everywhere of 'endism'. The end of history, the end of the nation-state, the end of politics, not to mention the more conventional end of the world, are all being predicted. Taken together these claims suggest that we have crossed or are crossing a major watershed in human affairs which will leave few things unchanged.

Endism is an example of the modern habit of thinking in terms of trends rather than cycles for understanding change. Many key trends such as population, economic output, technological innovation and communications have shown continual upward movement and appear to be cumulative in their effects, creating new stages of social development which do not repeat the past. This modern view of change supplanted the older view that the basic elements of human experience are constant, and that change is cyclical – everything eventually comes round again.

Cycles remain important, however, in thinking about change. Many trends, even when cumulative, develop through a cyclical pattern, while others particularly in culture and ideology are not cumulative at all. Here the same elements often are recycled endlessly, however much their outward forms may change. The distinction between a trend and a cycle depends also in part upon time horizons. No trend persists forever. New counteracting forces come into play, new forms of resistance emerge, new vulnerabilities appear. If the time horizon is long enough even the most irreversible and linear trend may turn out to be part of a cycle.

Much of the literature on endism is flawed because it lacks clear criteria for distinguishing changes that are qualitatively new and establish a new stage of development from those which are part of either short-term or long-term cycles within the existing stage. When thinking about change, whether in terms of trends or cycles, we need a reference point. Much of the current writing on endism assumes as its reference point a 'golden age', (generally located sometime in the 1950s) when nation-states had sovereignty, governments enjoyed legitimacy, citizens participated in public life, houses were left unlocked, men were employed in secure long-term jobs and people were anchored in traditional communities. Golden age conceptions are extremely prevalent, deeply conservative and mostly imaginary. They prevent clear thinking about change by exaggerating trends. But the writing on endism does have its value. Because much of it puts forward extreme positions it is a useful starting point for sorting out ideas and evidence about what is real and what is not in current accounts of change.

The End of the Nation-State

The claim that the era of the nation-state is over is not new. It has been a key theme of the debate on globalization which has been gathering strength since the early 1970s. But the advocates of the thesis have become steadily bolder in their claims, and a kind of popular wisdom has begun to emerge, particularly since the collapse of communism in Europe and the reunification of the world economy, that the nation-state has become an anachronism and is facing forces which it can no longer control. Power is being drained from it and acquired by other actors, particularly trans-national companies and banks.

The basic claim of the globalization thesis is that what is coming into being is a global economy which is replacing the former international economy. The international economy as its name implies was made up of separate national economies, which were controlled to greater or lesser degrees by the states which claimed authority over the national territory and its population and resources. All flows of goods, people and capital were conceived as being flows that had to be sanctioned by political authority and international agreements. Nation-states owed their power to their capacity to control their territory and the legitimacy which flowed from that.

A global economy, by contrast, is one in which the fundamental units are not nation-states and national economies but patterns of production and consumption organized by transnational companies, operating across national borders, and not reliant on any particular national territory or government. Important economic decisions are determined not at the level of national governments but through the workings of the global financial markets and the patterns of international trade. National governments which seek to 'buck the markets', as Britain is said to have done in the 1970s by subsidizing employment, protecting uncompetitive industries or raising spending too high, suffer penalties of deteriorating economic performance, currency depreciation and low investment. National governments can choose to work with the grain of global markets or resist them. But if they choose the latter the globalization thesis predicts they will impoverish their people and precipitate either the fall of the government or political repression. The rise of the global economy means that governments lose their autonomy and become ciphers for global economic forces, which act as a battering ram to break down all obstacles to the free play of competition and exchange. Not only is this process inevitable, it is also benign. By undermining nation-states, hitherto the main actors in the international states system and the world economy, it brings nearer the nineteenth century dream of a global cosmopolitan society which is co-ordinated and managed without the need for politics and governments (Ohmae, 1996).

The globalization thesis does point to some important and real changes which have been taking place in the world economy, and have led to a weakening of nation-states and an erosion of their sovereignty, but in its extreme form the argument is overblown. The evidence for the emergence of a genuine global economy which overrides the modes of governance including markets organized through nation-states is remarkably thin (Hirst and Thompson, 1996). Global economic forces and global markets have existed since the emergence of capitalism, but they have always depended on non-market institutions and in particular systems of governance, both state and non-state. The forms of governance have been changing in response to changes in the world economy, but the idea that global markets themselves could supply their own internal mechanisms of governance is naive.

In considering globalization it is important to distinguish between two meanings: it is used to refer to certain economic trends but also to a normative ideological project which supports particular policies and rules out alternatives. In Britain, for example, in this second sense it has been used to justify substantial changes in domestic policies, particularly on public spending, welfare, industrial intervention, and prices and incomes policy.

Acceptance of the new constraints and the changed balance between national governments and global markets has become part of the new consensus in British politics (see Chapter 14). The implications of globalization as a set of economic trends for policy are uncertain. Does membership of the European Union, for example, help or hinder globalization? Some of those opposing further European integration are protectionists, but others oppose it because they see it as a move towards the creation of a European superstate. Such a state, they argue, would run counter to globalization because it would be centralized, protectionist and bureaucratic, rather than dynamic, enterprising and responsive to rapidly changing costs and markets in the fastest growing economies in the world in East Asia and North America. Maintaining British sovereignty is presented as the means by which Britain can maximize the opportunities which globalization provides.

Supporters of the European Union believe that the creation of supranational as well as subnational levels of governance is essential to create the kind of non-market institutions which can continue to sustain a European economy which enjoys high income and high welfare, and argue that, because the anti-Europeans misunderstand the crucial links between regionalization and globalization, their policies in practice would be protectionist and isolationist. The pooling of national sovereignty is inescapable in a global economy because interdependence creates problems which can no longer be solved at the national level (Cerny, 1990).

The End of Ideology

The collapse of communism in Europe has revived the 'end of ideology' thesis with claims that economic and political liberalism have triumphed, viable alternatives to capitalism no longer exist, the final point in humanity's ideological evolution has been achieved and democratic government and free market capitalism are now universal. The old differences between left and right are redundant because there is no longer any prospect of improving on the basic principles of the liberal democratic state or of escaping from the capitalist world economy. All forms of autarky are dissolving, and although different models of capitalism are possible, no economy can any longer survive outside the institutional forms and pressures of the global market (Fukuyama, 1992).

The implication of this thesis is not only that politics will be conducted within narrow parameters in the future (it often has been in the past) but also that there is no prospect of the parameters changing drastically and no point in challenging them. The sharper ideological conflict which occurred in Britain in the 1970s and early 1980s is from this point of view an aberration, a last spasm of the old politics. The convergence of the parties towards very similar positions on almost all major policy issues since the end of the 1980s, associated with the premiership of John Major and the rise of New Labour, is seen as the shape of things to come. The parties agree on the boundaries between the state and the private sector and on the relationship of the British economy to the world economy. This severely restrains their options in government.

Hegel was the first to argue that history had ended – in 1806 at the battle of Jena. The triumph of Napoleon's armies signified the triumph of the ideals of the French Revolution. While their implementation might require prolonged struggles, the principles themselves could not be improved on. The ideological struggles of the last 200 years, including the struggle between socialism and capitalism, are therefore struggles about the implementation of the principles of the modern world rather than struggles over the replacement of these principles by new ones. Socialism from this point of view is one attempt to fulfil the principles of liberalism rather than an attempt to go beyond them. The long argument between markets and planning concerned means rather than ends. The basic values of equality and freedom are common to both liberals and socialists, and as some libertarians have argued, only socialism can credibly promise to fulfil liberalism. Old forms of socialism may be discredited, but new forms will appear in the future.

If history in Hegel's sense has ended, therefore, it ended long ago, at the start of the modern era rather than in 1989. Cycles of ideological conflict over the best way to realize the fundamental principles and values of western civilization will continue (Hirschman, 1982). The current transformation in socialist ideology and socialist parties throughout Europe, of which New Labour in Britain is one example (Sassoon, 1996), is part of a new phase of the cycle. The lines of argument have shifted but they have shifted for all parties and all ideologies, and the crisis of belief is general, not confined to socialists. Conservatives have been plunged into their own ideological limbo, torn between their enthusiasm for global markets and liberalization on the one hand and their attachment to the nation-state and cultural traditions on the other. What has occurred is a double inversion. On the left–right or socialist–liberal ideological axis which measures attitudes to the role of the state in the economy, liberal ideas are in the ascendancy, but the importance of this axis is waning compared with the axis organized around nationalism, ethnicity and identity.

The picture is further confused because all forms of ideology are also under attack from another direction. The fixity of identity assumed in many ideologies has been criticized by postmodernists who have emphasized difference, fluidity, subjectivity and relativism. The philosophical thrust of postmodernism has been important in challenging the assumptions of the main ideologies about what identity consists in, and emphasizing instead that identity is contingent, multiple, and constantly being negotiated. The meta narratives of liberalism and socialism, nationalism and ethnicity, and gender are criticized for claiming an objective and immutable basis for their accounts of the social world. This approach rejects the idea that a single identity, for instance class, is capable of defining an individual or of determining the issues with which politics should be concerned. Instead it argues that politics has to be pluralistic to take account of the many and overlapping identities and commitments which individuals have: the list includes race, gender, class, ethnicity, neighbourhood, locality, nation, work, household, age and sexual orientation (Laclau, 1990).

One of the implications for British politics is that political parties can no longer base themselves on one particular social identity like the labour movement in the belief that this has some kind of solidity and priority which is guaranteed because it is based on an identity which is considered primary. Instead political parties have to assemble a coalition of interests which is sensitive to the multiple and changing identities which voters have. Crude appeals to class or nation are only likely to mobilize minorities. Identity politics is associated with social movements rather than with mass political parties and electoral politics of the traditional kind, and therefore with increasing distance from traditional forms of politics (Chapter 6).

One of the most durable sources of identity and political legitimacy remains national identity, because nationalism offers the simplest set of loyalties and signs by which individuals can locate themselves in a complex modern society (Hedetoft, 1995). The increasing emphasis upon national identity rather than class, however, in British politics has further exposed the pragmatic and idiosyncratic basis of the British state and the difficulty of defining the British nation (Chapters 11 and 12). The rationale for a multinational state such as Britain with multiple identities might seem quite strong in a postmodern world, but the legitimacy of the Union state is increasingly challenged by nationalist movements, particularly in Scotland, and by a new awareness and assertiveness of national identity in England (Marr, 1992; Hassan, 1995).

The End of Tradition

The modern era has always been understood as a process of transition from status to contract, from particularism to universalism, from feudalism to capitalism. In the course of this process many traditional ways of behaviour have been challenged and supplanted. But the continuing existence of tradition has always been a counterpoint to modernization, and crucial for its success. But, as modernization and secularization have proceeded, so a point has been reached at which the familiar landmarks of traditional society and traditional behaviour have been seriously weakened or, in many instances, have ceased to exist. These developments have given rise to the notion of a non-traditional society (Giddens, 1994) a society which can no longer rely on tradition for guidance as to what it should believe or how it should behave. The death of tradition has not happened suddenly. In countries like Britain which always prided themselves on the strength of their traditions, it has been a long-drawn-out process.

What are the consequences of the weakening of tradition? Politicians and commentators frequently claim that many institutions, particularly communities, families, schools and churches, no longer have the same moral authority which they enjoyed in the 1950s. There is less agreement on the right way to behave. British society is characterized more by moral confusion and moral relativism than by moral consensus and moral certainty. This places greater weight on individuals to make moral choices and to decide for themselves how they should live and what are appropriate standards of behaviour.

Politics may increasingly focus on issues around which there is no moral consensus, but on which some groups seek to use the authority and the power of the state to impose one. One of the consequences of the weakening of tradition is that there is an increase in support for fundamentalist doctrines, mainly but not exclusively religious, claiming that one particular way of life is authentic. Attraction to fundamentalist doctrines is one response to the insecurity which moral relativism and the weakening of tradition create. Fundamentalist movements aim to suppress moral relativism and impose a new authoritarian moral order, insisting on a consensus where none exists on issues from abortion, gay rights and drug use to euthanasia.

Britain has so far not seen the intense polarization around issues like abortion which has taken place in the United States, but there is increasing mobilization of groups around communitarian issues. None of these are straightforward, even when there is clear majority support, as in the campaign for much stricter gun control following the Dunblane massacre. Majority opinion is not the same as moral consensus, and legislation can result in the sacrifice of the rights of minorities. There has been a pronounced swing in Britain towards a social conservative agenda by both major parties, particularly on crime, education, and the treatment of the young (Chapter 16). Attempts to restore traditions, however, are unlikely to succeed, because communities of the old kind which nourished them cannot be re-established. The decline of traditional community is one trend which does seem irreversible, and this explains the attempts by communitarians and others to reinvent tradition by designing new rules to restrict individual liberty in certain areas of activity (Etzioni, 1995).

The End of the Public Realm

One reason cited for the weakening of tradition is the rise of a more individualist culture in which private pleasures and interests are exalted, and individuals withdraw from participation in the public realm. A common view in the 1980s was that changes in the structure of occupations and the organization of work combined with the neo-liberal cult of the individual were responsible for this trend. Politics was increasingly viewed as concerned only with the exercise of power, often in corrupt ways, dominated by self-interest rather than public interest, and more and more remote from the lives of the majority.

Recent research has supplied new evidence on the decline of the mass party in the UK, particularly the fall in party membership and party activism (Seyd and Whiteley, 1992, 1996), but some analysts have ranged wider, citing declining participation in many kinds of voluntary and social activity (Putnam, 1993). As a result of this trend, key institutions of the democratic era such as the mass party are no longer used as a channel for the expression of the views and interests of the members. The requirements of modern electioneering, particularly as expressed through modern media, focus attention on the leader and require the participation of individuals in the party to be drastically curtailed in the interests of unity and electability (Chapters 3, 4 and 5). New Labour under Tony Blair has been criticized for accelerating this trend, although it is easy to exaggerate the extent of active participation in the old mass parties. Many fear, however, that politics is becoming a media spectacle increasingly unrelated to the way in which power is exercised and see the loss of interest and growing cynicism about politics in the electorate as corrosive of a conception of public citizenship and the rights and obligations which that entails.

A further problem is the increasingly technical nature of many policy problems and reliance on the views of experts, which makes it hard for informed public debate to take place. An issue like the BSE crisis in 1996 (Chapter 17) demonstrated the difficulties of evaluating the evidence and allowing wider public participation. The remoteness of government in part stems from the issues with which it has to deal, and which politicians struggle to make intelligible to the public. As a result, either issues become trivialized and caricatured or the public is shut out completely.

The difficulty with many accounts of the end of the public realm is the golden age assumption that there once existed a time when the public realm flourished more than it does now. One of the defining characteristics of politics in the modern era, however, has been the separation of the public and the private and the giving of primacy to the private. The public realm has always been characterized by a tension between hierarchy and secrecy on one side and openness and accountability on the other. The forms of participation in the public realm continually evolve. The decline of a particular form, the mass membership political party, may be accompanied by the rise of new forms, such as new social movements and campaign groups. Recent examples include the campaigns to ban handguns and live animal exports. Many of the trends of the 1980s which so worried communitarians have not in fact persisted in the 1990s. Union membership has stabilized, while communal leisure pursuits such as attendance at football matches and cinemas have risen. There has been a reaction to the excesses of selfish individualism.

The ideal of a public realm in which the pursuit of the public interest is the main concern, and participation is the highest good and the means by which individuals achieve fulfilment has always been a potent idea. The model is ancient Greece. But this is a romantic view unrelated to the realities of modern societies and also misleading about the character of politics of Greek city states and the foundations on which it rested (slavery and the exclusion of women). Many New Right thinkers have dismissed as rubbish the idea of the public realm and the public interest and rejected the possibility of enlightened or benevolent government. In response communitarian thought has sought to keep alive the notion that a conception of the public is important and cannot simply be reduced to the private realm, and that certain relationships and activities such as education and health or the protection of the environment are so important that different principles ought to apply to them (Walzer, 1983). The application of one set of values derived from the interaction of individual agents in competitive markets is a false guide for determining key public issues, including the way in which markets themselves should be organized, regulated and strengthened.

The questions as to what the public realm consists in, how the borders between the public and the private should be defined, how the public interest should be determined and what standards should be expected of those who participate in public life are critical questions for any society. Britain is currently in transition from one model, which was formed in the early decades of this century, to a new model. Many old assumptions are being challenged or discarded. But that does not mean that the public realm is in for irreversible decline. In many areas such as health and the environment the public realm continues to expand. New issues and problems create an agenda for public debate and public action. In some respects government is more active than it has ever been and the public realm extends further than ever before (Sunstein, 1990).

The End of Government

Closely related to the future of the public realm is the future of government itself. Some of the more enthusiastic advocates of globalization expect government, along with politics, to wither away. If nation-states are in decline, many of the functions associated with them in the past, both of policy making and of legitimacy, will no longer be required. The new forms of governance may have little to do with the traditional sites of either government or politics. Instead governance will be performed by self-regulating markets. It will be a politics-free world, with government stripped down to a bare minimum and society depoliticized. There will be no need to take decisions any longer through public processes. Instead all important governance outcomes will flow spontaneously from the decisions which individuals make in market transactions, and will not require the intervention of public authority and public officials.

What has given some credence to this view is the new trends which are emerging in the way in which government is organized. Much writing has been devoted to the different aspects of this process, particularly the hollowing out of the state and the new public management (Chapters 9 and 10). There has been a celebration of the cult of small government and a growing belief that the trend, so dominant throughout the twentieth century, of an ever enlarging public sector is going into reverse.

The withering away of the existing institutions of national government, however, would not mean the disappearance of basic functions of government such as ensuring public order, providing a legal framework and enforcing property rights. They would still need to be discharged, but not necessarily at the level of the nation-state. Realization of this has led to an elaboration of the concept of governance – the mechanisms and procedures which steer and control social activities of all kinds (Rhodes, 1996). National governments and their agencies are one set of mechanisms and procedures, but they are not the only one.

There is certainly evidence for considerable change in the way in which governance is organized, but relatively little for the radical proposition that human society is about to dispense with the need for government as one of the most important modes of governance. Of more interest are the moves towards new roles for the state. There are a number of different aspects. One of the most analysed in Britain has been the rise of the new public management, the separation of policy formulation and implementation, the creation of new executive agencies and reconsideration of the areas in which the state should be involved in a more active way than hitherto (for example, education and training) and those where it should be less involved (for example, industrial policy).

A second development has been the emergence of different levels of governance. The idea of subsidiarity in the European Union has focused attention on the appropriate level at which governance should be exercised, which functions should be transferred to a supranational level, which retained at national level, and which devolved to regional and local level. The bias of subsidiarity is that functions should be handled at the most decentralized level possible. Retaining a monopoly of functions at one level of governance is rejected, but that does not necessarily signify an end of government or even of national government but a changed and more diversified role. In some areas it may mean an expanded role for government, as new forms of governance are established which expand the competences of political organization. One example would be global environmental policies. Another would be regional assemblies and regional development authorities.

The changing role of government with the emergence of new forms of governance has led some political scientists to argue that the real meaning of contemporary developments is not a major reduction in the size of government but the replacement of the interventionist state by the regulatory state. Governments seek to determine the framework of rules within which activities go on and to influence the character of the agencies which deliver services and goods rather than to run the activities directly. This suggests that future areas of political conflict will be over the scope of regulation, as well as over reconciling the prescriptions of different regulators (Grant, 1993). The shape of this kind of politics is already evident within the European Union, with disputes between EU regulators and national governments over issues such as fish stocks.

One of the consequences of the rise of the regulatory state may therefore be an increase rather than a decrease in government. Regulation can be as burdensome as ownership, and the manner in which it is set up can raise serious problems about accountability (Jenkins, 1995). Do these new modes of implementing policy strengthen or weaken national government? Characterization of states as strong or weak have focused on the capacities which states have to further their goals. A state which presides over a very large public sector may appear strong but may actually be so overextended in attempting to manage that state that it falls prey to special interests and fails to establish a clear strategic control of policy. A withdrawal of a state from some functions may strengthen its ability to secure its key objectives.

This idea of the lean state is drawn from analogy with the lean company, the suggestion that if companies slim down and concentrate on their core business they become more effective and more profitable. There is some truth in this, although it is easy to exaggerate it. The British state is most unlikely ever to become just a regulatory state. Eighteen years of Conservative rule failed to reduce the level of state spending very much although the number of civil servants was reduced, and a large number of state enterprises were privatized (Chapters 9 and 10). But the state continues to perform a variety of other roles including direct administration, persuasion and information, and strategic intervention. The balance between the different roles of government will continue to evolve away from top-down, central planning models, but the dreams of libertarian conservatives are unlikely to be fulfilled.

The End of Security

One of the achievements claimed for the twentieth-century welfare state was that it greatly reduced insecurity – from unemployment, sickness, old age, disability – as well as mitigating the effects of poverty by providing a floor income below which no-one need fall (Chapter 15). But in the 1990s there has been a preoccupation with the return of old forms of insecurity and the rise of new ones. Much of this has been analysed under the category of risk: the increasing risks which individuals and their families face (Giddens, 1994).

Risk is a very broad category and, like several of the other concepts discussed in this chapter, care has to be taken not to contrast a present time of heightened insecurity and risk with an imaginary past when there were no risks or much reduced ones. Much of the popular discussion of crime or drugs or new diseases for example, tends to imply that there was once a golden age when these things were not serious problems. Similarly, the period of the 1950s and 1960s is often treated as a golden age in terms of economic performance, particularly as regards unemployment and inflation (in Britain during that time unemployment never rose above one million while inflation stayed below 4 per cent). But in a longer perspective this golden age looks decidedly aberrant, the product of special circumstances rather than especially wise and effective policy. What is true is that the nature of risk and insecurity does change, in particular the perception of them. The consequences of the weakening of tradition and the availability of new sources of information, and the immediacy of events from around the world due to new forms of communication, all combine to make contemporary societies much more aware of certain kinds of risk.

This effect has been enhanced by changing attitudes towards science. The absolute dependence of modern societies upon scientific knowledge and the technologies which spring from it is coupled with awareness of the limited character of scientific knowledge, particularly about the long-term effects of many of these technologies. But what has also become apparent is that the social enterprise of modern science is now so institutionalized and so diverse that it is impossible to prevent either scientific discoveries or their dissemination and application (Williams, 1993). This faces modern societies with increasingly difficult dilemmas. Some of these are already apparent and concern the effects of industrial processes on the ecology of the planet. Earlier fears that unchecked industrial growth would lead to an exhaustion of many basic resources have proved exaggerated, but they have been replaced by fears that the present pattern of industrial development is leading to irreversible changes particularly in the climate through global warming, an effect expected to become more difficult to manage as more countries industrialize. The key problem for sustainability has become the disposal of waste products of industrial activity (Kennedy, 1994). The problem is intensified by the pace at which world population is increasing and the predictions that it is not likely to stabilize until it has reached 10 billion.

Many of the problems associated with the harmful effects of technology on the environment are in principle soluble if there is political will to agree global programmes, and if science can provide the technological solutions which are required. But there is another set of problems which are less easy to resolve because they strike at the heart of the value systems of existing societies. They involve questions to do with new techniques of genetic engineering, such as cloning, and the possibilities of effecting radical alterations in human beings: lifespan, genetic characteristics, abilities and behaviour. At present these have only surfaced into politics in mild ways, but the impact of the debates on abortion and the contraceptive pill shows what potential new medical technologies can have for politics. There is no more radical attack upon tradition than the attack upon the notion that the genetic inheritance of each individual is somehow given and pre-ordained and outside human control. It raises the possibility in the future of many new expectations, demands and conflicts which the political process will find extremely difficult to handle.

Science and technology have changed the nature of the risks individuals face both through providing new knowledge and new opportunities. This has not happened all at once, and in some respects was inscribed in the scientific project from the start. But there is some validity in the notion that a new watershed may be approaching. One of the consequences of a knowledge-based society is that paternalistic models of state support to remove insecurity have less relevance than they did because there are so many forms of insecurity which individuals now face and from which it is impossible for individuals to be protected. The increase in crime, the changing nature of work and employment – particularly the decline of long-term permanent jobs – and the increasing incidence of marital and family breakdown are all symptoms of this new situation. Again, it is important not to exaggerate. To some extent these are all features of modernity which have been present to varying degrees from the outset and some forms of risk, for example many types of health risk, have been reduced rather than increased. Nevertheless, the phenomenon of insecurity is an important feature of contemporary societies and one that is increasingly shaping its politics and the responses of its politicians.

New Beginnings

Endism raises some important questions about the way our world may be changing but because it focuses on trends and because of its golden age assumptions it is inclined to be pessimistic about the future, nostalgic about the past and sceptical about the ability of human beings to change anything. It needs to be balanced by an optimism which is aware of the scope for innovation, novelty and creativity in human societies (Mulgan, 1997). Developments never proceed along a single track. The unexpected and the new are always waiting.

At the end of the twentieth century, Britain can be seen to be at the end of a particular path of development. The transition from being a great power and world empire is almost complete. Some problems remain, not least the constitutional arrangements of the United Kingdom itself. How these are resolved, particularly in relation to the British Union and the European Union, will be critical for the way British politics develops and how other issues such as the definition of the public realm, the role of tradition and the handling of risk are treated. At stake is the character of the

British polity, its accountability, openness and effectiveness in the face of the trends which the various endisms describe.

If new constitutional arrangements for the governance of the British Isles can be worked out and if the relationship with Europe can be clarified, one result may be that the British will cease to think of their institutions as exceptional and their destiny as special. Exceptionalism requires a particular set of circumstances to sustain it. The fight over Britain's place in Europe may be the last great fight to preserve a notion of British exceptionalism in a world in which there is increasingly little room for it. Such a future does not imply convergence on a single model of capitalism or a single political system. There will always be significant divergences and contrasts. But what may disappear as far as Britain is concerned is the belief that these divergences and contrasts confer on Britain a unique status.

Other new beginnings are also discernible. The Labour Party has undergone a fundamental transformation since 1987 in both its ideology and its organization (Perryman, 1996). It has now emerged as the party most in command of the centre of British politics (Chapters 3 and 5) and most in tune with Britain's changing position in the world (Chapter 2). The Conservatives have not experienced such a transformation, but now in opposition they are obliged to rethink the meaning of Conservatism and renew their organization and their leadership or face being marginalized (Chapter 5). For the Conservative Party this is one of the biggest challenges it has ever faced, because all the four institutional pillars on which its political hegemony in British politics was based in the twentieth century – the constitution, the union, property and the empire – have either disappeared or been gravely weakened (Gamble, 1995).

In the new political landscape that is emerging, the old dividing lines between left and right no longer have much meaning, and many of the symbols which helped define political positions have gone. All parties are now pro-business and pro-market. These changes have pushed debate into new areas. On the right the dominant reaction is to advocate a return to core Thatcherite principles – free market economics and national independence, but with increasing emphasis upon the latter. Further liberalization of markets, deregulation and privatization is supported, along with low tax and less government. This position is coupled with an intransigent defence of the British constitution, which involves asserting the sanctity of the principle of the union within the United Kingdom and resistance to involvement in any European structures which involve a dilution of British sovereignty. There are obvious strains between the two positions, because the latter tends increasingly towards nationalism and isolationism, as is evident in the debate on the European single currency (Chapter 14). The anti-European wing of the Conservative Party argues that membership of the European Union should only be retained if the EU becomes no more than a free trade area. Disengagement from Europe is said to be in Britain's interest in order to allow British companies to remain free to develop links with the more important markets of North America and East Asia. Europe is depicted as centralized, inflexible and bureaucratic and likely to interfere with the free market policies which have successfully restructured the British economy, and to undermine British sovereignty and with it the sense of national identity.

Britain's future in Europe has become the major dividing line in British politics, and may lead to further realignment. Majority opinion in the Labour Party, the Liberal Democrats and important sections of the Conservative Party rejects the notion that the European Union is inherently protectionist, centralized and inward-looking, or that there is any alternative to a progressive pooling of sovereignty. The advantages of Britain's links with North America and East Asia are not denied, but the idea of Britain as the Hong Kong of Europe, reverting to its old independent open seas commercial and financial policy outside the European Union, is regarded as a fantasy which would impose significant additional costs on the British economy. Labour and the Liberal Democrats are also persuaded that only decentralization within the UK can keep Scotland within the Union and create the kind of regional structures of government most appropriate for coping with the pressures of the new global economy. The Conservative attempt before 1997 to block any internal constitutional reform, except partially in Northern Ireland, was seen as more likely to break up the union than to preserve it.

In domestic policy the new battleground is over different interpretations of stakeholding: what kind of rights and obligations for individuals should be recognized in different spheres and organizations? What can governments do to promote the inclusion of individuals and combat exclusion through their policies on welfare, work and education (Kelly, 1997)? All parties now speak the language of stakeholding even when they do not use the term itself, because the political discourse has become centred on endowing individuals with rights, assets and opportunities to enable them to exercise autonomy, while demanding from them in return the fulfilment of certain responsibilities and obligations. Liberal communitarianism and civic conservatism, despite their different emphases, have ventured onto this same terrain.

Britain could experience a significant reshaping of its character as a state over the next decade. The degree of centralization and 'ungrounded statism' (Dunleavy, 1989) which made it stand out in relation to similar states will disappear as a result of the impact of privatization, the new public management, decentralization, and European integration. The relative prosperity of the British economy will depend on whether the sharp shift in the balance of the British economy away from manufacturing towards services in the 1980s will provide British companies with significant comparative advantages in the new global markets which are developing (McRae, 1995). Britain's success both as a society and as an economy in the future will depend on the ability of its political class to identify and articulate ways to maintain an open society which can learn and adapt and deal with the new kinds of risks and insecurities which a global economy and a traditionless society create. No political party really disagrees with that. But there is deep disagreement over whether a condition for ensuring that Britain becomes such a society depends on acceptance of the need for radical constitutional change and new ways of organizing politics.

Guide to Further Reading

Chapter 2   Britain, Europe and the World

For a general and readable overview of British foreign policy, see Clarke (1992). Sanders (1990) and Denman (1996) both offer provocative historical treatments. Sharp (1996) offers an update on British defence policy, while Coates (1996) contains a number of useful essays on the international effects of British economic policy. Britain's 'special relationship' with the USA receives treatment in Renwick (1996) and Peterson (1996). The history of Britain's post-war relationship with the European Union is treated by George (1994). Useful general texts on the EU include Dinan (1994), George (1996), Nugent (1994) and Peterson and Bomberg (1998).

Chapter 3   Voting and the Electorate

The best introductions to UK electoral behaviour are Denver (1994) and Norris (1997). The seminal analysis that began the series of British Election Studies (BES) is Butler and Stokes (1974). It should be consulted by anyone seeking to understand the broad methodological approach taken by 'mainstream' UK electoral analysis. Subsequent BES volumes are Sarlvik and Crewe (1983) and Heath et al. (1985, 1991, 1994). For studies of specific general elections, the Nuffield series (for example, Butler and Kavanagh, 1992) and the Britain at the Polls series (for example, King et al., 1992) are particularly useful. For comparative analysis of electoral systems, see Farrell (1997).

An excellent review of the uses and abuses of opinion poll data in UK electoral research can be found in Broughton (1995). For a recent, if technical, analysis that makes extensive use of time-series opinion poll data, see Clarke et al. (1997). Anyone interested in the latest substantive and methodological developments in UK voting research should consult the *British Parties and Elections Yearbook* series, the most recent of which is Rallings et al. (1996). Journals most likely to cover electoral research generally are the *British Journal of Political Science*, *Electoral Studies*, *Parliamentary Affairs* and *Party Politics*. The October 1997 number of the journal *Parliamentary Affairs* is a special edition on the 1997 general election edited by Pippa Norris which provides invaluable early analysis of the campaign, the results and how the electoral system performed.

Chapter 4 Political Communications

For recent developments in campaigning see Kavanagh (1995) and Scammell (1995). Good overviews of the historical developments of the press and broadcasting in Britain can be found in Seymour Ure (1995) and Curran and Seaton (1993). The most systematic survey evidence of the role of the media in a British campaign can be found in Miller (1991). Communications in the 1992 election are discussed in Butler and Kavanagh (1992) and Crewe and Gosschalk (1995), while voting behaviour is covered in Heath *et al.* (1994) and Norris (1997).

Chapter 5 Political Parties

Seyd and Whiteley (1996) offer an overview of the British party system. Shaw (1994, 1996) reviews Labour's recent history. Seyd *et al.* (1996) conveniently covers the role of Labour and Conservative party members. Norris and Lovenduski (1995) provides an overview of the literature on political recruitment. Finally the new journal, *Party Politics*, is a useful source of new writing on Britain's parties.

Chapter 6 Political Participation

The five classic texts on political participation are Almond and Verba (1963), Verba and Nie (1972), Parry (1972), and Barnes *et al.* (1979). The most recent study of political participation in the United Kingdom is Parry *et al.* (1992). On political participation in comparative perspective see the provocative Inglehart (1990) and Jenkins and Klandermans (1995). On feminist politics in Britain, see Lovenduski and Randall (1993). Garnier (1996) provides a useful discussion of environmental politics in Britain. On the politics of new social movements, see Tarrow (1994) and Kriesi *et al.* (1995).

Chapter 7 The Constitution

There is no single book which deals very well with constitutional issues and reform. The political history of how we got to where we are is covered in Brian Harrison's curious work *The Transformation of British Politics 1860–1995* (1996). He manages to leave out discussion of the critical 1917 and 1931 debates on electoral reform; fails to explain why MPs gave away their individual power to their party leaders and the executive between 1880 and 1900; and lapses at the end into complacent editorializing on the wonders of the two-party system. But Harrison does sum up orthodoxy more neatly and completely than anyone else. A useful approach to electoral reform is given in Farrell (1997). The most authoritative analysis of how alternative electoral systems would operate in Britain is given in P. Dunleavy *et al.* (1992). A new 1997 analysis by the same authors will be available from September 1997 from LSE Public Policy Group, Department of Government, LSE, Houghton Street, London WC2A 2AE. The issues surrounding a bill of rights are well explored in F. Klug, K. Starmer and S. Weir (1996) and in the special issue of *Political Quarterly* (April–June 1997) covering 'Human Rights in the UK'. On quangos the best treatment yet remains S. Weir and W. Hall (1996b) and their earlier report (1996a). Most practical aspects of constitutional reform are covered in the reports of the Constitution Unit, 4 Tavistock Place, London WC1U 9RA. The Unit's short summary 'Briefing' reports are available free, while its long reports provide a great deal of detail about practical difficulties, but are dismissed by New Labour loyalists as much too pessimistic.

Chapter 8 Parliamentary Oversight

Norton (1993), Adonis (1993) and Silk and Walters (1995) provide useful introductory texts on the British Parliament; Norton considers relations between Parliament and the citizen as well as between Parliament and government; Silk and Walters are strong on processes and organization in Parliament. Shell (1992) is the principal introductory text on the House of Lords.

Griffith and Ryle (1989) provide substantial data on parliamentary actitivities. Drewry (1989) is a good study of select committees, though now in need of updating. Franklin and Norton (1993) offer the first substantial analysis of parliamentary questions for 30 years. Rush (1990) constitutes a substantial study of the relationship between Parliament and pressure groups. Parliamentary reform is discussed in Garrett (1992), the Hansard Society Commission Report on the Legislative Process (1992) and the Constitution Unit Report 'Delivering Constitutional Reform' (1996b).

Westlake (1994b) and Jacobs *et al.* (1995) provide authoritative introductions to the European Parliament. Jacobs *et al.*, are strong on the procedures of the EP. Westlake puts the EP in a broader political environment, exploring links with other institutions and the electoral connection.

Chapter 9   The Central Executive

For an analysis of the institutions and workings of the British cabinet system with case studies from different policy areas see Burch and Holliday (1996); on the 'core executive' see an edited collection by Rhodes and Dunleavy (1995). Other useful books on cabinet government are by Peter Hennessy (1986) and Simon James (1994). For a history of the civil service since 1945 see Theakston (1995). Current public management reforms and their problems are discussed by Foster and Plowden (1996). The history of a specific policy disaster, the poll tax, is traced by Butler *et al.* (1994). For an analysis of the quango state see the edited collection by Ridley and Wilson (1995). The current 'Whitehall' ESRC research initiative will produce further publications on central government.

Chapter 10   The Regulatory State

Good general introductions to regulatory practice within the UK can be found in Ogus (1994). Bishop, Kay and Mayer (1995) contains a helpful collection of essays, mainly written by economists, about a range of issues concerning regulation in the UK. More theoretical accounts are supplied by Ayres and Braithwaite (1992). A good account of the perceived crisis in UK utilities regulation is offered by Graham (1995). Useful analyses of regulatory challenges within the public sector are provided by Hood and Scott (1996) and Foster and Plowden (1996). The issues raised by regulation within the European Union are addressed in Majone (1996).

Chapter 11   Territorial Politics

No single textbook covers all the issues analysed in this chapter. Aspects of territorial management are classically surveyed from the left by Nairn (1977) and from the right by Bulpitt (1983). Hutton (1995) is a more recent analysis from the left which incorporates territorial issues. From the right, Mount (1992) is prepared briefly to consider territorial political change; Willetts (1992) is not. The Scottish dimension is covered by Midwinter *et al.* (1991) and Marr (1992). England and the English are analyzed by Haseler (1996). Most examinations of Wales are rather old now. Excellent reports have been produced by the Constitution Unit (1996a, 1996c, 1996d). European regionalism is analyzed by Sharpe (1993) and Rhodes (1996).

Chapter 12   Northern Ireland

The best general introductory survey is Aughey and Morrow (1996). An excellent study of the historical complexity of the Ulster question is Bew *et al.* (1996). A sophisticated political science approach is to be found in McGarry and O'Leary (1995), which supplements the useful statistics in O'Leary and McGarry (1993). A sympathetic account of the Unionist position is Wilson (1989). A sympathetic account of the nationalist position is Farrell (1980). A useful collection of essays is Barton and Roche (1994). On the evolution of the peace process, see Mallie and McKittrick (1996).

Chapter 13   Local Governance

The best two textbooks on British local politics are Stoker (1991) and Wilson and Game (1994). For debates about current issues there are a number of collections: Stewart and Stoker (1989), Leach *et al.* (1996) and Stewart and Stoker (1995). Useful too is the report of the Commission for Local Democracy (1995). For consideration of the normative debate see King and Stoker (1996). For management issues there is Kerley (1994). Hill (1994) covers both urban policy and citizenship matters. Stoker and Young (1993) explore the city focus, both in urban policy and the European dimension (1993). A useful review of the theoretical literature on the transformation of local politics is Cochrane (1993).

Gray (1994) is a useful starting point for the research and debate on local governance. Also the publications which have arisen from the quango debate deal with the non-elected sector (Skelcher and Davis, 1995; Stewart, 1992; Whitehead, 1996; Weir and Hall, 1994; Stewart and Stoker, 1995). The ESRC initiative on local governance will produce a wide ranging review of governance structures, and some early publications are Dowding *et al.* (1995) and John and Cole (1995).

Chapter 14   Economic Policy

For a detailed account of economic trends, see the OECD's *Economic Surveys*. The more theoretically ambitious should consult the authoritative *National Institute Economic Review*. The journal *New Economy* offers a very readable and slightly left-of-centre perspective on contemporary policy debates while the *Oxford Review of Economic Policy* is a highly regarded source of detailed policy analysis (see especially the 1996 editions on investment and competitiveness). Buxton (1994) and Buxton (forthcoming) offers a good guide to a wide range of policy issues. An interesting account of the economic arguments surrounding EMU can be found in Taylor (1995). *Political Quarterly* often carries interesting political discussions of general policy developments while the *Financial Times* remains the best guide for day-to-day events. An increasing amount of useful material can also be obtained via the internet. See particularly the Treasury (www.hm.treasury.gov.uk) and the Office for National Statistics (www.ons.gov.uk) sites.

Chapter 15   Social Policy

There is now a reasonably extensive literature taking in the years post-Thatcher, but not much as yet which pays this particular attention as a potential 'period' in its own right. Laybourn (1995) offers a conventional account of the evolution of social policy up to the 1990s and Glennerster (1995) offers his own more personal interpretation of developments (nearly) to date. Stimulating introductory texts which range widely across the contemporary field and make some reference also to the recent history of social policy include Alcock (1996), Gladstone (1995) and Hill (1997). Davies (1997) offers the best and most comprehensive review of the state of social work. Barnat *et al.* (1993) and Payne (1995) between them cover most aspects and issues in community care. Klein (1995) still offers the best insights into NHS reform and Lund (1996) offers the most nearly up-to-date introduction to housing policies and practice. Burrows and Loader (1994), Pascall (1997), Levin (1996) and Samson and South (1996) each offer interesting particular approaches to the analysis of aspects of social policy per se.

Chapter 16   Crime and Public Order

Despite the public and political attention devoted to crime and criminal justice, there is no single text which effectively examines 'the politics of law and order'. The most comprehensive book is the collection of essays edited by Maguire *et al.* (1994), but readers should be warned that the 25 chapters amount to 1259 pages! An interesting set of readings on crime and its causes is Muncie *et al.* (1996), while Brake and Hale (1992) offer a more controversial analysis of how the economic and social policies of the

Thatcher governments led to increases in crime and disorder. Benyon and Solomos (1987) remains a good source of information on the inner-city riots of the 1980s, while Campbell (1993) offers insights into the disorders in 1991, and Waddington (1992) examines hooliganism, industrial disputes and other forms of disorder.

The basic textbook on policing remains Reiner (1992). An interesting collection of essays is Leishman *et al.* (1996). Privatization is examined by Johnston (1992), while Critcher and Waddington (1996) are useful on public order policing. Crime and policing in the EU is explored in Benyon *et al.* (1993). McDonald (1997) includes essays on the 'globalization' of crime and law enforcement. A short, but nonetheless useful, general introduction to criminal justice and penal policy is provided by Newburn (1995). Hudson (1993) is more detailed.

Much interesting material is to be found in sources such as the *British Journal of Criminology* and *Policing and Society*. A number of publications by the Home Office (especially the *Annual Report* and *Statistical Bulletin*) and the Audit Commission (especially 1993 and 1996) are rich and accessible sources of information.

Chapter 17   BSE and the Politics of Food

Ford (1996) provides a readable perspective on the underlying science. Two early reviews of the policy process associated with the BSE crisis are to be found in Baggott, (1996) and Winter (1997). The implications for the CAP are discussed in Grant (1997). The limitations of expert advice and reform options for food safety are succinctly reviewed in Lang *et al.* (1996).

Chapter 18   Conclusion: Politics 2000

For future-gazing from a generally pessimistic standpoint try Kennedy (1994); for optimism about Britain's prospects try McRae (1995). On the shape of the new politics, see Mulgan (1994, 1997), Giddens (1994) and Gray (1995, 1996). An important book for thinking about the nature of political change is Hirschman (1982). For critical reflection on globalization, see Hirst and Thompson (1996) and, for the changing nature of politics in the global economy, see Cerny (1990). For reflections on the British constitution, see Mount (1992) and Jenkins (1995). Different perspectives on New Labour can be found in Perryman (1996) and on stakeholding in Kelly *et al.* (1997).

Bibliography

Adam Smith Institute (1989) *Wiser Counsels*, London, Adam Smith Institute.

Adonis, A. (1993) *Parliament Today*, 2nd edn, Manchester, Manchester University Press.

Alcock, P. (1996) *Social Policy in Britain: Themes and Issues*, London, Macmillan.

Almond, G. A. and Verba, S. (1963) *The Civic Culture: Political Attitudes and Democracy in Five Nations*, Princeton University Press.

AMA (1992) *Bus Deregulation Five Years On*, London, Association of Metropolitan Authorities.

Anechiarico, F. and Jacobs, J. B. (1996) *The Pursuit of Absolute Integrity*, Chicago, Chicago University Press.

Arlidge, J. (1997) 'Peace Until When?', *New Statesman*, 14 February.

Audit Commission (1993) *Helping with Enquiries: Tackling Crime Effectively*, London, HMSO.

Audit Commission (1996) *Misspent Youth: Young People and Crime*, London, HMSO.

Aughey, A. and Morrow, D. (eds) (1996) *Northern Ireland Politics*, London, Longman.

Ayres, I. and Braithwaite, J. (1992) *Responsive Regulation*, Oxford, Oxford University Press.

Baggott, R. (1996) 'Where is the Beef? The BSE Crisis and the British Policy Process', *Talking Politics*, vol. 9, no. 1.

Baker, D., Gamble, A. and Ludlam, S. (1993) 'Whips or Scorpions', *Parliamentary Affairs*, vol. 42, no. 2, pp. 151–66.

Baker, D., Gamble, A., Ludlam, S. and Seavwright, D. (1996) 'A "rosy" map of Europe? Labour parliamentarians and European integration: initial survey results', paper presented to annual conference of the Political Studies Association, Glasgow, April.

Baldwin, R. and Cave, M. (1996) *Franchising as a Tool of Government*, London, Centre for the Study of Regulated Industries.

Ball, W. and Solomos, J. (1990) *Race and Local Politics*, London, Macmillan.

Banham, J. (1994) *The Anatomy of Change*, London: Weidenfeld & Nicolson.

Barker, A. and Rush, M. (1970) *The Member of Parliament and his Information*, London: George Allen & Unwin.

Barkman, K. (1995) 'Politics and Gender: The Need for Electoral Reform', *Politics*, vol. 15, pp. 141–6.

Barnat, J., Pereira, C. and Pilgrim, D. (eds) (1993) *Community Care: A Reader*, Milton Keynes, Open University Press.

Barton, B. and Roche, P. (1994) *Northern Ireland: Policies and Perspectives*, Aldershot, Avebury.

Beer, S. H. (1965) *Modern British Politics*, London: Faber.

Bentham, J. (1983) *Constitutional Code*, vol. 1, ed. F. Rosen and J. H. Burns, Oxford, Clarendon.

Benyon, J. (1994) *Law and Order Review, 1993*, Leicester, CSPO.

Benyon, J. (1996) 'The Politics of Police Co-operation in the European Union', *International Journal of the Sociology of Law*, vol. 24, pp. 353–79.

Benyon, J. and Solomos, J. (eds) (1987) *The Roots of Urban Unrest*, Oxford, Pergamon.

Benyon, J. et al. (1993) *Police Co-operation in Europe: An Investigation*, Leicester, CSPO.

Berger, P. (1986) *The Capitalist Revolution*, New York, Basic Books.

Beveridge, Sir W. (1948) *Voluntary Action*, London, Allen & Unwin.

Bew, P., Gibbon, P. and Patterson, H. (1996) *Northern Ireland 1921–1996: Political Forces and Social Classes*, London, Serif.

Bishop, M., Kay, J. and Mayer, I. (1995) *The Regulatory Challenge*, Oxford, Oxford University Press.

Black, J. (1996) 'Constitutionalising Self-Regulation', *Modern Law Review*, vol. 59, pp. 24–55.

Blair, Tony (1996) *New Britain: My Vision of a Young Country*, London, Fourth Estate.

Bloch, A. (1992) *The Turnover of Local Councillors*, York, Joseph Rowntree Foundation.

Bloch, A. and John, P. (1991) *Attitudes to Local Government*, York, Joseph Rowntree Foundation.

Bogdanor, V. (1980) 'Devolution', in Z. Layton-Henry (ed.), *Conservative Party Politics*, London, Macmillan, pp. 75–94.

Bogdanor, V. (1996) *Politics and the Constitution: Essays on British Government*, Aldershot, Dartmouth.

Bond, S. and Jenkinson, T. (1996) 'The Assessment: Investment Performance and Policy', *Oxford Review Economic Policy*, vol. 12, no. 2, pp. 1–29.

Brake, M. and Hale, C. (1992) *Public Order and Private Lives*, London, Routledge.

Breen, R. (1996) 'Who Wants a United Ireland', in R. Breen et al. (eds), *Social Attitudes in Northern Ireland*, 5th report, Belfast, The Blackstaff Press, pp. 33–48.

Breyer, S. G. (1993) *Breaking the Vicious Cycle*, Cambridge, Mass, Harvard University Press.

Bridges, L., Meszaros, G. and Susker, M. (1996) *Judicial Review in Perspective*, London, Cavendish Publishing.

British Social Attitudes Survey (1996) Aldershot, Dartmouth.

British Youth Council (1995) *The Democratic Deficit*, London, BYC.

Brittan, L. (1994) *Europe: The Europe We Need*, London: Hamish Hamilton.

Brooke, R. (1989) *Managing the Enabling Authority*, London, Longman.

Broughton, D. (1995) *Public Opinion Polling and Politics in Britain*, London, Prentice-Hall/Harvester Wheatsheaf.

Brown, G. (1994) 'The Politics of Potential: A New Agenda for Labour', in D. Miliband (ed.), *Reinventing the Left*, Cambridge, Polity.

Bryan, L. and Farrell, D. (1996) *Market Unbound: Unleashing Global Capitalism*, Chichester, John Wiley.

Brynin, M. and Sanders, D. (1997) 'Party Identification, Political Preferences and Material Conditions', Party Politics, vol. 3, no. 1, pp. 53–77.

Bulpitt, J. (1983) *Territory and Power in the United Kingdom: An Interpretation*, Manchester, Manchester University Press.

Burch, M. and Holliday, I. (1992) 'The Conservative Party and Constitutional Reform: The Case of Devolution', *Parliamentary Affairs*, vol. 45, pp. 386–98.

Burch, M. and Holliday, I. (1993) 'Institutional Emergence: The Case of the North West Region of England', *Regional Politics and Policy*, vol. 3, no. 2, pp. 29–50.

Burch, M. and Holliday, I. (1996) *The British Cabinet System*, London, Prentice Hall/Harvester Wheatsheaf.

Burnheim, J. (1985) *Is Democracy Possible?*, Cambridge, Polity.

Burrows, R. and Loader, B. (eds) (1994) *Towards a Post-Fordist Welfare State?*, London, Routledge.

Butler, D. and Kavanagh, D. (1980) *The British General Election of 1979*, London, Macmillan.

Butler, D. and Kavanagh, D. (1992) *The British General Election of 1992*, London, Macmillan.

Butler, D. and Ranney, A. (eds) (1992) *Electioneering*, Oxford, Clarendon Press.

Butler, D. and Stokes, D. (1974) *Political Change in Britain*, London, Macmillan.

Butler, D., Adonis, A. and Travers, T. (1994) *Failure in British Government: The Politics of the Poll Tax*, Oxford, Oxford University Press.

Butt, R. (1967) *The Power of Parliament*, London: Constable.

Buxton, T., Chapman, P. and Temple, P. (eds) (1994, 2nd edn forthcoming) *Britain's Economic Performance*, London, Routledge.

Cabinet Office (1994) *The Civil Service: Continuity and Change*, Cmnd 2627, London, HMSO.

Cabinet Office (1996) *Next Steps Briefing Note*, London, Cabinet Office.

Campbell, B. (1993) *Goliath: Britain's Dangerous Places*, London, Methuen.

Cerny, P. (1990) *The Changing Architecture of Politics: Structure, Agency and the Future of the State*, London, Sage.

Chancellor of the Duchy of Lancaster (1996) *Next Steps Agencies in Government. Review 1995*, Cmnd 3164, London, HMSO.

Chisholm, M. (1995) *Britain on the Edge of Europe*, London, Routledge.

Christy, C. (1994) 'Trends in Sex Differences in Political Participation: A Comparative Perspectives', in M. Githens, P. Norris and J. Lovenduski (eds), *Different Roles, Different Voices*, London, HarperCollins, pp. 27–37.

Civil Service Commissioners (1996) *Civil Service Commissioners' Annual Report 1995–6*, London, Office of the Civil Service Commissioners.

Clarke, H., Stewart, M. and Whiteley, P. (1997) 'Tory Trends: Party Identification and the Dynamic of Conservative Support Since 1992', *British Journal of Political Science*, vol. 27, no. 2, pp. 299–318.

Clarke, K., Craig, G. and Glendinning, C. (1995) 'Money isn't Everything: Fiscal Policy and Family Policy in the Child Support Act', *Social Policy and Administration*, vol. 29, no. 1, pp. 26–39

Clarke, M. (1992) *British External Policy-Making in the 1990s*, London, Macmillan, for the Royal Institute of International Affairs.

Clarke, M. and Stewart, J. (1996) *Finding Meanings for Community Governance*, Birmingham, University of Birmingham Press.

Cloonan, M. (1996) *Banned! Censorship of Popular Music in Britain: 1967–92*, Aldershot, Arena.

Cloonan, M. and Street, J. (1996) 'Rock the Vote: Politics and Popular Music', School of Economic and Social Studies, University of East Anglia.

Coates, D. (ed.) (1996) *Industrial Policy in Britain*, London, Macmillan.

Cochrane, A., (1993) *Whatever Happened to Local Government?*, Buckingham, Open University Press.

Cockfield, L. (1994) *European Union: Creating the Single Market*, London, Wiley Chancery Law.

Cohen, S. (1973) *Folk Devils and Moral Panics*, London, Paladin.

Cohen, S. and Young, J. (eds) (1973) *The Manufacture of News: Social Problems, Deviance and the Mass Media*, London, Constable.

Commission for Local Democracy (1995) *Taking Charge: The Rebirth of Local Democracy*, London, *Municipal Journal*.

Committee on Standards in Public Life (Nolan Committee) (1995) *Volume 1*: Report, Cmnd 2850–I, London, HMSO.

Compton, P. (1994) 'No Certainty of a Catholic North', *Parliamentary Brief*, October, vol. 3, no. 1, p. 23.

Constitution Unit (1996a) *An Assembly for Wales*, London, Constitution Unit.

Constitution Unit (1996b) 'Delivering Constitutional Reform', London, Constitution Unit.

Constitution Unit (1996c) *Regional Government in England*, London, Constitution Unit.

Constitution Unit (1996d) *Scotland's Parliament: Fundamentals for a New Scotland Act*, London, Constitution Unit.

Corry, D. and Michie, J. (1997) *The Left Debate on EMU*, PERC Policy Paper, no. 4, University of Sheffield.

Cowley, P. (1996) 'From Arena to Transformative and Back Again? The British House of Commons in the 1990s', paper presented at the Second Workshop of Parliamentary Scholars and Parliamentarians, Wroxton, UK.

Cowley, P. and Norton, P. (1996a) *Are Conservative MPs Revolting?*, Hull Centre for Legislative Studies.

Cowley, P. and Norton, P. (1996b) *Blair's Bastards*, Hull Centre for Legislative Studies.

Cradock, S. P. (1994) 'China, Britain and Hong Kong: Policy in a Cul-de-sac', *The World Today*, vol. 50, pp. 92–6.

Crewe, I. (1983) 'Saturation Polling, the Media and the 1983 Election', in I. Crewe and M. Harrop (eds), *Political Communications: The General Election Campaign of 1983*, Cambridge, Cambridge University Press.

Crewe, I. (1986) 'On the Death and Resurrection of Class Voting: Some Comments on How Britain Votes', *Political Studies*, vol. 35, pp. 620–38.

Crewe, I. (1989) 'The Decline of Labour and the Decline of Labour', *Essex Papers in Politics and Government*, no. 65.

Crewe, I. (1992a) 'A Nation of Liars? Opinion Polls and the 1992 Election', *Parliamentary Affairs*, vol. 45, no. 4, pp. 475–95.

Crewe, I. (1992b) 'Changing Votes and Unchanging Voters', *Electoral Studies*, vol. 11, pp. 335–45.

Crewe, I. and Gosschalk, B. (eds) (1995) *Political Communications: The General Election Campaign of 1992*, Cambridge, Cambridge University Press.

Crewe, I. and Harrop, M. (1989) *Political Communications: The General Election Campaign of 1987*, Cambridge, Cambridge University Press.

Crewe, I. and King, A. (1994) 'Did Major Win? Did Kinnock Lose? Leadership Effects in the 1992 Election', in A. Heath *et al.* (eds), *Labour's Last Chance? The 1992 Election and Beyond*, Aldershot, Dartmouth.

Criddle, B. (1996) 'Blair's Recruits Look Well Drilled', *New Statesman*, 8 November.

Critcher, C. and Waddington, D. (eds) (1996) *Policing Public Order: Theoretical and Practical Issues*, Aldershot, Avebury.

Curran, J. and Seaton, J. (1993) *Power Without Responsibility*, 4th edn, London, Routledge.

Curtice, J. and Semetko, H. (1994) 'The Impact of the Media', in A. Heath *et al.* (eds), *Labour's Last Chance? The 1992 Election and Beyond*, Aldershot, Dartmouth.

Daintith, T. (1979) 'Regulation by Contract: The New Prerogative', *Current Legal Problems*, vol. 41.

Daintith, T. (1989) 'A Regulatory Space Agency', *Oxford Journal of Legal Studies*, vol. 9, pp. 534–46.

Daintith, T. (ed.) (1995) *The Implementation of EC Law in the United Kingdom: Structures for Indirect Rule*, Chichester, Wiley.

Dalton, R. (1993) 'Preface' to 'Citizens, Protest and Democracy', *The Annals*, July.

Dalton, R. (1994) *The Green Rainbow*, New Haven, Conn., Yale University Press.

David, W. (1995) 'Foundations for an Open Union', *The House Magazine*, 24 April.

Davies, M. (ed.) (1997) *The Blackwell Companion to Social Work*, Oxford, Blackwell.

Davis, M. (1990) *City of Quartz*, London, Vintage.

Deakin, N. (1996) *Meeting the Challenge of the Change: Voluntary Action into the 21st Century* (Report of the Commission on the Future of the Voluntary Sector in England), London, NCVO.

Denman, R. (1996) *Missed Chances: Britain and Europe in the Twentieth Century*, London, Cassell.

Denver, D. (1994) *Elections and Voting in Britain*, 2nd edn, London, Harvester Wheatsheaf.

Denver, D. and Hands, G. (1992) 'Constituency Campaigning', *Parliamentary Affairs*, vol. 45, no. 4, pp. 528–44.

Dicey, A. V. (1915) *Introduction to the Study of Law of the Constitution*, 8th edn, London, Macmillan.

Dinan, D. (1994) *Ever Closer Union? An Introduction to the European Community*, London, Macmillan.

Dowding, K. (1995) *The Civil Service*, London, Routledge.

Dowding, K., Dunleavy, P., King, D. and Margetts, H. (1995), 'Rational Choice and Community Power Structures', *Political Studies*, vol. 43, pp. 265–77.

Downes, D. and Morgan, R. (1994) ' "Hostages to Fortune"? The Politics of Law and Order in Postwar Britain', in M. Maguire *et al.* (eds), *The Oxford Handbook of Criminology*, Oxford, Oxford University Press.

Drewry, G. (ed.) (1989) *The New Select Committees*, rev. edn, Oxford: Oxford University Press.

Dunleavy, P. (1989) 'The United Kingdom: Paradoxes of an Ungrounded Statism', in F. G. Castles (ed.), *The Comparative History of Public Policy*, Cambridge, Polity.

Dunleavy, P. (1995) 'Policy Disasters: Explaining the UK's Record', *Public Policy and Administration*, vol. 10, no. 2, pp. 52–70.

Dunleavy, P. and Rhodes, R. A. W. (1990) 'Core Executive Studies in Britain', *Public Administration*, vol. 68, no. 1, pp. 3–28.

Dunleavy, P., Margetts, H. and Weir, S. (1992) *Replaying the 1992 General Election: How Britain Would Have Voted under Alternative Electoral Systems*, London, LSE Public Policy Group and Rowntree Reform Trust.

Dunleavy, P., Weir, S. with Subrahmanyam, G. (1995) 'Sleaze in Britain: Media Influences, Public Response and Constitutional Significance', *Parliamentary Affairs*, vol. 48, no. 4, pp. 602–16.

EC Commission (1993) *Growth, Competitiveness, Employment*, The Delors White Paper.

Etzioni, A. (1995) *The Spirit of Community: Rights, Responsibilities and the Communitarian Agenda*, London, Fontana.

European Commission (1996) *Eurobarometer: Public Opinion in the European Union*, vol. 44, spring, Brussels.

Evans, B. and Taylor, A. (1996) *From Salisbury to Major*, Manchester, Manchester University Press.

Farrell, D. (1997) *Comparing Electoral Systems*, London, Prentice Hall/ Harvester Wheatsheaf.

Farrell, M. (1980) *The Orange State*, 2nd edn, London, Pluto Press.

Fernandez-Martin, J. M. (1996) *The EC Procurement Rules*, Oxford, Oxford University Press.

Field, F. (1996) *Stakeholder Welfare*, London, IEA.

Finer, H. (1932 'State Activity Before Adam Smith', *Public Administration*, vol. 10, p. 157.

Foley, M. (1993) *The Rise of the British Presidency*, Manchester, Manchester University Press.

Ford, B. J. (1996) *BSE: the Facts*, London, Corgi.

Foster, C. D. and Plowden, F. J. (1996) *The State Under Stress. Can the Hollow State be Good Government?*, Buckingham, Open University Press.

Franklin, B. (1994) *Packaging Politics*, London, Edward Arnold.

Franklin, M. and Norton, P. (eds) (1993) *Parliamentary Questions*, Oxford, Oxford University Press.

Franklin, M., Baxter, A. and Jordan, M. (1986) 'Who Were the Rebels? Dissent in the House of Commons 1970–1974', *Legislative Studies Quarterly*, vol. 11, pp. 143–59.

Froud, J. and Ogus A. (1996) ' "Rational" Social Regulation and Compliance Cost Assessment', *Public Administration*, vol. 74, pp. 221–37.

Fukuyama, F. (1992) *The End of History and the Last Man*, London, Hamish Hamilton.

Gallup (1994) 'Gallup Poll December 1994', published in the *Daily Telegraph*, 12 December.

Gamble, A. (1988) *The Free Economy and the Strong State*, London, Macmillan.

Gamble, A. (1995) 'The Crisis of Conservatism', *New Left Review*, vol. 214, pp. 3–25.

Garnier, R. (1996) *Environmental Politics*, London, Harvester Wheatsheaf.

Garrett, J. (1992) *Westminster: Does Parliament Work?*, London, Victor Gollancz.

Geddes, M. (1996) *Extending Democratic Practice in Local Government*, Commission for Local Democracy Report, no. 17, London, Municipal Journal.

George, S. (1994) *An Awkward Partner: Britain in the European Community*, 2nd edn, Oxford, Oxford University Press.

George, S. (1996) *Politics and Policy in the European Union*, 3rd edn, Oxford, Oxford University Press.

Giddens, A. (1994) *Beyond Left and Right: The Future of Radical Politics*, Cambridge, Polity.

Gladstone, D. (ed.) (1995) *British Social Welfare: Past, Present and Future*, London, UCL Press.

Glennerster, H. (1995) *British Social Policy Since 1945*, Oxford, Blackwell.

Graham, C. (1995) *Is There a Crisis in Regulatory Accountability?*, CRI Discussion Papers, no. 13, London, Centre for the Study of Regulated Industries.

Graham, C. and Prosser, T. (1991) *Privatising Public Enterprises*, Oxford, Oxford University Press.

Grant, W. (1993) *Business and Politics in Britain*, London, Macmillan.

Grant, W. (1997) *The Common Agricultural Policy*, London, Macmillan.

Grantham, C. and Seymour-Ure, C. (1990) 'Political Consultants', in M. Rush (ed.), *Parliament and Pressure Politics*, Oxford, Oxford University Press.

Gray, C. (1994) *Government Beyond the Centre*, London, Macmillan.

Gray, J. (1995) *Enlightenment's Wake: Politics and Culture at the End of the Modern Age*, London, Routledge.

Gray, J. (1996) *After Social Demcoracy: Politics, Capitalism and the Common Life*, London, Demos.

Gray, P. (1996) 'Disastrous Explanations or Explanations of Disaster? A Reply to Patrick Dunleavy', *Public Policy and Administration*, vol. 11, no. 1, pp. 74–82.

Griffith, J. A. G. and Ryle, M. (1989) *Parliament: Functions, Practice and Procedures*, London, Sweet & Maxwell.

Grove-White, R. and Wynne, B. (1995) *Science, Culture and the Environment: Research Report 1995*, Lancaster, Centre for the Study of Environmental Change.

Gunter, B., Sancho-Aldridge, J. and Winstone, P. (1994) *Television – The Public's View 1993*, London, John Libbey.

Gyford, J., Leach, S. and Game, C. (1989) *The Changing Politics of Local Government*, London, Unwin Hyman.

Hall, S. (1995) 'Parties on the Verge of a Nervous Breakdown', *Soundings*, vol. 1, pp. 19–33.

Hall, S. *et al.* (1978) *Policing the Crisis*, London, Macmillan.

Hall, W. and Weir, S. (1996) *The Untouchables: Power and Accountability in the Quango State*, Democratic Audit Paper, no. 8, Colchester, University of Essex.

Hansard Society (1992) *Making the Law: Report of the Hansard Society Commission on the Legislative Process*, London, The Hansard Society.

Harden, I. (1992) *The Contracting State*, Buckingham, Open University Press.

Harding, A. (1989) 'Central Control in British Urban Development Programmes', in C. Crouch and D. Marquand (eds), *The New Centralism: Britain Out of Step in Europe?*, Oxford, Blackwell.

Harding, A. and Garside, P. (1995) 'Urban and Economic Development', in Stewart and Stoker (eds), *Local Government in the 1990s*, London, Macmillan.

Harries, O. (1993) 'The Collapse of "The West" ', *Foreign Affairs*, September/October, pp. 41–53.

Harris, N. T. (1993) *Law and Education: Regulation, Consumerism and the Education System*, London, Sweet & Maxwell.

Harrison, B. (1996) *The Transformation of British Politics 1860–1995*, Oxford, Oxford University.

Harrison, M. (1993) 'Broadcasting', in D. Butler and D. Kavanagh (eds), *The British General Election of 1992*, London, Macmillan.

Haseler, S. (1996) *The English Tribe: Identity, Nation and Europe*, London, Macmillan.

Haskel, J. and Martin, C. (1994) 'Will Low Skills Kill Recovery', *New Economy*, vol. 1, no. 3, pp. 130–5.

Hassan, G. (1996) 'New Labour and the Politics of New Scotland', in M. Perryman (ed.), *The Blair Agenda*, London, Lawrence & Wishart.

Hawes, D. (1993) *Power on the Backbenches?*, Bristol, SAUS Publications.

Hay, C. (1995) 'Structure and Agency', in D. Marsh and G. Stoker (eds), *Theory and Methods in Political Science*, London, Macmillan.

Heath, A., Evans, G. and Payne, C. (1995) 'Modelling the Class–Party Relationship in Britain, 1964–92', *Journal of the Royal Statistical Society*, vol. 158, pp. 563–74.

Heath, A., Jowell, R. and Curtice, J. (1985) *How Britain Votes*, London, Pergamon.

Heath, A., Jowell, R. and Curtice, J. (1991) *Understanding Political Change*, London, Pergamon.

Heath, A., Jowell, R. and Curtice, J. (eds) (1994) *Labour's Last Chance? The 1992 Election and Beyond*, Aldershot, Dartmouth.

Heclo, H. and Wildavsky, A. (1974) *The Private Government of Public Money*, London, Macmillan.

Hedetoft, U. (1995) *Signs of Nations*, Aldershot, Dartmouth.

Heffernan, R. and Marqusee, M. (1992) *Defeat from the Jaws of Victory*, London, Verso.

Hennessy, P. (1986) *Cabinet*, Oxford, Basil Blackwell.

Heseltine, M. (1989) *The Challenge of Europe: Can Britain Win?*, London, Weidenfeld & Nicolson.

Hill, D. (1994) *Citizens and Cities*, Hemel Hempstead,

Hill, M. (1997) *Understanding Social Policy*, 5th edn, Oxford, Blackwell.

Hirschman, A. (1982) *Shifting Involvements*, Oxford, Blackwell.

Hirst, P. and Thompson, G. (1996) *Globalisation in Question*, Cambridge, Polity.

Hoagland, J. (1996) 'Britain Needs to be at Europe's heart', *The Guardian Weekly*, 21 July, p. 14.

Hogwood, B. W. (1995a) 'Regional Administration in Britain since 1979: Trends and Explanations', *Regional and Federal Studies*, vol. 5, pp. 267–91.

Hogwood, B. W. (1995b) *Quangos in the Skeletal State*, in F. F. Ridley and D. Wilson (eds), *The Quango Debate*, Oxford, Oxford University Press.

Holliday, I. (1994) 'Democracy and Democratization in Great Britain', in G. Parry and M. Moran (eds), *Democracy and Democratization*, London, Routledge, pp. 241–59.

Holliday, I. (1995) *The NHS Transformed: A Guide to the Health Reforms*, 2nd edn, Manchester, Baseline.

Holliday, I. (1996) 'Diversity and Conflict in Conservative Local Government, 1979–96', in I. Hampsher-Monk and J. Stanyer (eds), *Contemporary Political Studies 1996*, Belfast, Political Studies Association.

Holliday, I. (1997) 'Conservative Constitutionalism 1979–97', in I. Holliday (ed.), *Conservative Government in Britain 1979–97*, New York, New York University, Center for European Studies.

Hollingsworth, M. (1991) *MPs For Hire*, London, Bloomsbury.

Home Office (1990) *Crime, Justice and Protecting the Public*, Cmnd 965, London, HMSO.

Home Office (1991) *Safer Communities: The Local Delivery of Crime Prevention Through the Partnership Approach, (The Morgan Report)*, London, HMSO.

Hood, C. (1976) *Limits of Administration*, London, Wiley.

Hood, C. (1991) 'A Public Management for all Seasons?', *Public Administration*, vol. 69, pp. 3–19.

Hood, C. (1996) 'Cultural Theory and Institutional Variety', *Journal of Public Policy*, vol. 15, no. 3, pp. 207–30.

Hood, C. and Scott, C. (1996) 'Bureaucratic Regulation and New Public Management in the United Kingdom: Mirror-Image Developments?', *Journal of Law and Society*, vol. 23, pp. 321–45

Horn, M. (1995) *The Political Economy of Public Administration*, Cambridge, Cambridge University Press.

House of Lords Select Committee on Central/Local Government Relations (1996) *Rebuilding Trust*, London, HMSO.

Hudson, B. (1993) *Penal Policy and Social Justice*, London, Macmillan.

Hughes, C. and Wintour, P. (1990) *Labour Rebuilt: The New Model Party*, London, Fourth Estate.

Hutton, W. (1995) *The State We're In*, London, Jonathan Cape.

Ibbs Report (1988) *Improving Management in Government: The Next Steps*, London, Prime Minister's Efficiency Unit.

Inglehart, R. (1977) *The Silent Revolution: Changing Values and Political Styles Among Western Publics*, Princeton, Princeton University Press.

Inglehart, R. (1990) *Culture Shift in Advanced Industrial Society*, Princeton, Princeton University Press.

Jackson, R. J. (1968), *Rebels and Whips*, London, Macmillan.

Jacobs, F. and Corbett, R. (1990) *The European Parliament*, London, Longman.

Jacobs, F., Corbett, R. and Shackleton, M. (1995) *The European Parliament*, 3rd edn, London, Catermill.

James, S. (1994) *British Cabinet Government*, London, Routledge.

Jenkins, J. and Klandermans, B. (eds) (1995) *The Politics of Social Protest*, London, University College London Press.

Jenkins, J. and Wallace, M. (1995) 'The New Class and Structure of Contemporary Dissidence', *Research in Social Movements, Conflict and Change*, no. 18.

Jenkins, S. (1995) *Accountable to None: The Tory Nationalisation of Britain*, London, Hamish Hamilton.

Jessop, B. *et al.* (1988) *Thatcherism: A Tale of Two Nations*, Cambridge, Polity.

John, P. (1994a) 'Central–Local Relations in the 1980s and 1990s: Towards a Policy learning Approach', *Local Government Studies*, vol. 20, pp. 412–36.

John, P. (1994b) 'UK Subnational Offices in Brussels: Regionalisation or Diversification', *Regional Studies*, vol. 28, pp. 739–46.

John, P. (1996a) 'Centralization, Decentralization and the European Union: The Dynamics of Triadic Relationships', *Public Administration*, vol. 74, pp. 292–313.

John, P. (1996b) 'Europeanisation in a Centralising State', *Journal of Regional and Federal Studies*, vol. 6, pp. 131–44.

John, P. and Cole, A. (1995) 'Models of Local Decision-making Networks in Britain and France', *Policy and Politics*, vol. 23, no. 4, pp. 303–12.

John, P. and Cole, A. (1997) *Urban Governance in Britain and France*, forthcoming.

Johnston, L. (1992) *The Rebirth of Private Policing*, London, Routledge.
Johnston, L. (1996) 'Policing Diversity: The Impact of the Public–Private Complex in Policing', in F. Leishman *et al.* (eds), *Core Issues in Policing*, London, Longman.
Jones, C. (1993) 'The Pacific Challenge: Confucian Welfare States', in C. Jones (ed.), *New Perspectives on the Welfare State in Europe*, London, Routledge, pp. 198–217.
Jones, G. and Travers, T. (1994) *Attitudes to Local Government in Westminster and Whitehall*, Commission for Local Democracy Report, no. 5, London, Municipal Journal.
Jones, N. (1995) *Soundbites and Spin Doctors*, London, Cassell.
Jones, T. (1996) *Remaking the Labour Party from Gaitskell to Blair*, London, Routledge.
Jordan, G. and Maloney, W. (1994) 'How Bumble Bees Fly: Accounting for Public Interest Participation', *British Interest Group Project*, no. 6, University of Aberdeen.
Joseph Rowntree Foundation (1991) *A New Accord*, York, Joseph Rowntree Foundation.
Jowell, R., Witherspoon, S. and Brook, L. (1987) *British Social Attitudes: The 1987 Report*, Aldershot, Gower.
Judge, D. (1992) *The Parliamentary State*, London, Sage.
Judge, D. and Earnshaw, D. (1994) 'Weak European Parliament Influence? A Study of the Environment Committee of the European Parliament', *Government and Opposition*, vol. 29, no. 2, pp. 262–76.
Katz, R. and Mair, P. (1994) *How Parties Organize*, London, Sage.
Kavanagh, D. (1995) *Election Campaigning*, Oxford, Blackwell.
Keating, M. and Jones, B. (1995) 'Nations, Regions and Europe: The UK Experience', in B. Jones and M. Keating (eds), *The European Union and the Regions*, Oxford, Clarendon Press, pp. 88–113.
Kelly, G. *et al.* (eds) (1997) *Stakeholder Capitalism*, London, Macmillan.
Kemp, Sir Peter (1996) 'The Next Steps Approach', *Howard Journal*, vol. 35, pp. 336–40.
Kennedy, P. (1994) *Preparing for the Twenty-First Century*, London, Fontana.
Keohane, R. O., Nye, J. S. and Hoffmann, S. (eds) (1993) *After the Cold War*, Cambridge Mass., Harvard University Press.
Kerley, R. (1994) *Managing in Local Government*, Basingstoke, Macmillan.
King, A. *et al.* (1992) *Britain at the Polls, 1992*, Chatham, NJ, Chatham House.
King, D. and Stoker, G. (1996) *Rethinking Local Democracy*, Basingstoke, Macmillan.
Klandermans, B. (1986) 'New Social Movements and Resource Mobilisation', *International Journal of Mass Emergences and Disasters*.
Klein, R. (1995) *The New Politics of the NHS*, London, Longman.

Klein, R. and Millar, J. (1995) 'Do-it-Yourself Social Policy: Searching for a New Paradigm?', *Social Policy and Administration*, vol. 29, no. 4, pp. 303–16.

Klug, F., Starmer. K and Weir, S. (1996) *The Three Pillars of Liberty*, London, Routledge.

Kneen, P. and Travers, T. (1994) *Implementing the Council Tax*, Joseph Rowntree Foundation, Local and Central Government Relations Research Committee Research findings, no. 26, York, Joseph Rowntree Foundation.

Kohler-Koch, B. (1994) 'Changing Patterns of Interest Intermediation in the European Union', *Government and Opposition*, vol. 29, pp. 166–80.

Kriesi, H. P., Koopmans, R., Duyvendak, J. W. and Giugni, M. G. (1995) *New Social Movements in Western Europe: A Comparative Analysis*, London, UCL Press.

Krugman, P. (1994) *Peddling Prosperity*, New York, Norton.

Labour Party (1995) *Safer Communities, Safer Britain*, London, Labour Party.

Labour Party (1997) *New Labour, Because Britain Deserves Better*, London, Labour Party.

Laclau, E. (1990) *New Reflections on the Revolution of Our Time*, London, Verso.

Lang, T., Millstone, E., Raven, H. and Rayner, M. (1996) 'Modernising UK Food Policy: The Case for Reforming the Ministry of Agriculture, Fisheries and Food', *Discussion Paper*, no. 1, Centre for Food Policy, Thames Valley University.

Laybourn, K. (1995) *The Evolution of British Social Policy and the Welfare State*, Keele, Keele University Press.

Leach, S. (1994) *The Changing Organisation and Management of Local Government*, London, Macmillan.

Leach, S. (1995) 'The Strange Case of the Local Government Review', in Stewart and Stoker (eds), *Local Government in the 1990s*, London, Macmillan.

Leach, S. and Stewart, J. (1992) *Local Government: Its Role and Function*, York, Joseph Rowntree Foundation.

Leach, S., Davis, H. and associates (1996) *Enabling or Disabling Local Government*, Buckingham, Open University Press.

Learmont, Sir J. (1995) *Review of Prison Service Security in England and Wales and the Escape from Parkhurst Prison on Tuesday, 3rd January 1995*, London, Home Office.

Lee, S. (1996) 'Manufacturing', in D. Coates (ed.), *Industrial Policy in Britain*, London, Macmillan.

Le Grand, J. and Bartlett, W. (1993) *Quasi Markets and Social Policy*, London, Macmillan.

Leibfried, S. and Pierson, P. (1995) *European Social Policy: Between Fragmentation and Integration*, Washington, DC, Brookings.

Leishman, F., Loveday, B. and Savage, S. (eds) (1996) *Core Issues in Policing*, London, Longman.

Levin, P. (1996) *Making Social Policy: The Mechanisms of Government and Politics and How to Investigate Them*, Buckingham, Open University Press.

Liberty (1995) 'Criminalising Diversity, Criminalising Dissent: A Report on the Use of the Public Order Provisions in the Criminal Justice and Public Order Act 1994', London, Liberty.

Loughlin, J. and Mazey, S. (1995) 'Introduction', in J. Loughlin and S. Mazey (eds), *The End of the French Unitary State? Ten Years of Regionalization in France (1982–1992)*, London, Frank Cass, pp. 1–9.

Loughlin, M. (1992) *Administrative Accountability in Local Government*, York, Joseph Rowntree Foundation.

Loughlin, M. (1996a) *Legality and Locality. The Role of Law in Central–Local Government Relations*, Oxford, Clarendon Press.

Loughlin, M. (1996b) 'Understanding Central–Local Relations', *Public Policy and Administration*, vol. 11, no. 2, pp. 48–65.

Lovenduski, J. and Norris, P. (eds) (1993) *Gender and Party Politics*, London, Sage.

Lovenduski, J. and Randall, V. (1993) *Contemporary Feminist Politics: Women and Power in Britain*, Buckingham, Open University Press.

Lowell, A. L. (1924) *The Government of England*, vol. II, New York, Macmillan.

Lowndes, V. and Stoker, G. (1992) 'An Evaluation of Neighbourhood Decentralisation', *Policy and Politics*, vol. 20, two parts, pp. 47–61, 143–52.

Lund, B. (1996) *Housing Problems and Housing Policy*, London, Longman.

Lynch, P. (1995) 'From Red to Green: The Political Strategy of Plaid Cymru in the 1980s and 1990s', *Regional and Federal Studies*, vol. 5, pp. 197–210.

Lynskey, J. J. (1970) 'The Role of British Backbenchers in the Modification of Government Policy', *Western Political Quarterly*, pp. 333–47.

Lynskey, J. J. (1973) 'Backbench Tactics and Parliamentary Party Structure', *Parliamentary Affairs*, vol. 27, pp. 28–37.

Macdonagh, O. (1961) *A Pattern of Government Growth 1800–1860*, London, MacGibbon & Kee.

MacRae, H. (1995) *The World in 2020*, London, HarperCollins.

Maguire, M., Morgan, R. and Reiner, R. (eds) (1994) *The Oxford Handbook of Criminology*, Oxford, Oxford University Press.

Maher, I. (1995) 'Legislative Review by the EC Commission: Revision without Radicalism', in J. Shaw and G. More (eds), *New Legal Dynamics of European Union*, Oxford, Oxford University Press.

Maher, I. (1996) 'Limitations on Community Regulation in the UK: Legal Culture and Multi-Level Governance', *Journal of European Public Policy*, vol. 3, pp. 577–93.

Majone, G. (1994) 'The Rise of the Regulatory State in Europe', *West European Politics*, vol. 17, pp. 77–101.

Majone, G. (ed.) (1996) *Regulating Europe*, London, Routledge.

Major, J. (1996) 'The Future of Europe', speech, Goldsmiths' Hall, London, 19 June.

Mallie, E. and McKittrick, D. (1996) *The Fight for Peace*, London, Heinemann.

Maloney, W. and Jordan, G. (1995) 'Joining Public Interest Groups: Membership Profiles of Amnesty International and Friends of the Earth', in J. Lovenduski and J. Stanyer (eds), *Contemporary Political Studies 1995*, vol. 3, Exeter, PSA, pp. 1137–53.

Mandelson, P. and Liddle, R. (1996) *The Blair Revolution*, London, Faber.

Market Research Society (1993) 'The Opinion Polls and the 1992 General Election', London, Market Research Society.

Marr, A. (1992) *The Battle of Scotland*, Harmondsworth, Penguin.

Martin, S. (1996) 'Local Authorities and Europe', paper to ESRC seminar series, *Local and Regional Responses to Europe*, University of Warwick, 20 September.

Mawson, J. *et al.* (1994) *The Single Regeneration Budget: The Stocktake*, for Association of County Councils, Association of District Councils, Associations of Metropolitan Councils, School of Public Policy, University of Birmingham.

Mazey, S. and Richardson, J. (eds) (1993) *Lobbying in the European Community*, Oxford, Oxford University Press.

McConnell, A. (1994) 'A Concluding Thought: Should Parties be Funded by the State?', in L. Robins, H. Blackmore and R. Pyper (eds), *Britain's Changing Party System*, London, Leicester University Press.

McCullum, R. B. and Readman, A. (1947) *The British General Election of 1945*, London, Geoffrey Cumberlege/Oxford University Press.

McDonald, W. (ed.) (1997) *Crime and Law Enforcement in the Global Village*, Cincinnati, Ohio, Anderson Publishing.

McEldowney, J. (1995) 'Law and Regulation: Current Issues and Future Directions', in M. Bishop, J. Kay, and C. Mayer (eds), *The Regulatory Challenge*, Oxford, Oxford University Press, pp. 408–22.

McGarry, J. and O'Leary, B. (1995) *Explaining Northern Ireland: Broken Images*, Oxford, Blackwell.

McGowan, F. and Seabright, P. (1995) 'Regulation in the European Community and its Impact on the UK', in M. Bishop, J. Kay, and I. Mayer (eds), *The Regulatory Challenge*, Oxford, Oxford University Press, Ch. 10.

McLaughlin, A. (1993) 'Representing Interests in the European Community', paper prepared for the panel, 'Decision-making in the European Community', at the 1993 European Community Studies Association Annual Conference, Washington DC, 27–29 May.

Mellors, C. (1978) *The British MP*, Aldershot, Saxon House.

Melucci, A. (1989) Nomads of the Present: Social Movements and Individual Needs in Contemporary Society, Philadelphia, Temple University Press.

Messina, A. (1989) *Race and Party Competition in Britain*, Oxford, Oxford University Press.

Mezey, M. (1979) *Comparative Legislatures*, Durham, NC, Duke University Press.

Midwinter, A., Keating, M. and Mitchell, J. (1991) *Politics and Public Policy in Scotland*, London, Macmillan.

Miliband, R. (1984) *Capitalist Democracy in Britain*, Oxford, Oxford University Press.

Miller, W. and Dickson, M. (1996) *Local Governance and Local Citizenship*, Glasgow, ESRC.

Miller, W. L. (1991) *Media and Voters: The Audience, Content and Influence of Press and Television at the 1987 General Election*, Oxford, Clarendon Press.

Mills, L. (1994) 'Economic Development, the Environment and Europe: Areas of Innovation in UK Local Government', *Local Government Policy Making*, vol. 20, pp. 3–10.

Minns, R. and Tomaney, J. (1995) 'Regional Government and Local Economic Development: The Realities of Economic Power in the UK', *Regional Studies*, vol. 29, pp. 202–7.

Mitchell, A. (1995a) 'Backbench Influence: A Personal View', in F. F. Ridley and M. Rush (eds), *British Government and Politics Since 1945*, Oxford, Oxford University Press.

Mitchell, A. (1995b) *Election '45*, London, Fabian Society.

Morris, J. (1997) 'Care or Empowerment: A Disability Rights perspective' *Social Policy and Administration*, vol. 31, no. 1, pp. 54–60.

Mount, F. (1992) *The British Constitution Now: Recovery or Decline?*, London, Heinemann.

Mulgan, G. (1994) *Politics in an Antipolitical Age*, Cambridge, Polity.

Mulgan, G. (ed.) (1997) *Life After Politics: New Thinking for the Twenty-First Century*, London, Fontana.

Muncie, J., McLaughlin, E. and Langan, M. (eds) (1996) *Criminological Perspectives*, London, Sage.

Murroni, C. Collins, R. and Coote, A. (1996) *Converging Communications: Policies for the 21st Century*, London, Institute for Public Policy Research.

Nadeau, R., Niemi, R. G. and Amato, T. (1996) 'Prospective and Comparative or Retrospective and Individual? Party Leaders and

Party Support in Great Britain', *British Journal of Political Science*, vol. 26, no. 2, pp. 245–58.

Nairn, T. (1977) *The Break-up of Britain: Crisis and Neo-Nationalism*, London, New Left Books.

Negrine, R. (1994) *Politics and the Mass Media*, 2nd edn, London, Routledge.

Negrine, R. (1996) 'The "Americanization"', of Political Communication: A Critique', *Harvard International Journal of Press/Politics*, vol. 1, no. 2, pp. 45–62.

Nellis, M. (1995) 'Probation Partnerships, Voluntary Action and Community Justice' *Social Policy and Administration*, vol. 29, no. 2, pp. 91–109.

Newburn, T. (1995) *Crime and Criminal Justice*, London, Longman.

Niemi, R. *et al.* (1996) 'Elite Economic Expectations', paper presented to the PSA specialist conference on Elections, Public Opinion and Parties, London Guildhall University, 17–19 September 1995.

Nikaren, W. A. (1971) *Bureaucracy and Representative Government*, Chicago, Aldine.

Norris, P. (1996) *Electoral Change Since 1945*, Oxford, Blackwell.

Norris, P. (1997) *Electoral Change Since 1945*, Oxford, Blackwell.

Norris, P. and Lovenduski, J. (1995) *Political Recruitment*, Cambridge, Cambridge University Press.

Norton, P. (1978) *Conservative Dissidents*, London, Temple Smith.

Norton, P. (1981) *The Commons in Perspective*, Oxford, Martin Robertson.

Norton, P. (1984) 'Parliament and Policy in Britain: The House of Commons as a Policy Influencer', *Teaching Politics*, vol. 13, no. 2, pp. 198–221.

Norton, P. (1985) 'The House of Commons: Behavioural Changes', in P. Norton (ed.), *Parliament in the 1980s*, Oxford, Basil Blackwell.

Norton, P. (1987) 'Dissent in the House of Commons: Rejoinder to Franklin, Baxter and Jordan', *Legislative Studies Quarterly*, vol. 12, pp. 143–52.

Norton, P. (ed.) (1991a) *Parliaments in Western Europe*, London, Frank Cass.

Norton, P. (1991b) 'The Changing Face of Parliament: Lobbying and its Consequences', in P. Norton (ed.), *New Directions in British Politics?*, Aldershot, Edward Elgar.

Norton, P. (1993) *Does Parliament Matter?* London, Harvester Wheatsheaf.

Norton, P. (1994a) 'Select Committees in the House of Commons: Watchdogs or Poodles?', *Politics Review*, vol. 4, no. 2, pp. 29–33.

Norton, P. (1994b) 'Showing Dissenters the Red Card', *Parliamentary Brief*, December, pp. 39–40.

Norton, P. (1995) 'Parliamentary Behaviour Since 1945', *Talking Politics*, vol. 8, no. 2, pp. 107–14.

Norton, P. (1996a) 'Are MPs Revolting? Dissension in the British House of Commons 1979–92', paper presented at the Second Workshop of Parliamentary Scholars and Parliamentarians, Wroxton, UK.

Norton, P. (1996b) 'The United Kingdom: Political Conflict, Parliamentary Scrutiny', in P. Norton (ed.), *National Parliaments and the European Union*, London, Frank Cass.

Norton, P. (1997) '*Think, Minister . . .*' *Reinvigorating British Government*, London, Centre for Policy Studies.

Nugent, N. (1994) *The Government and Politics of the European Union*, 3rd edn, London, Macmillan.

O'Leary, B. and McGarry, J. (1993) *The Politics of Antagonism: Understanding Northern Ireland*, London, Athlone Press.

OECD (1994) *The OECD Jobs Study*, Paris, OECD.

OECD (1996) *Employment Outlook*, Paris, OECD.

Ogus, A. (1994) *Regulation: Legal Form and Economic Theory*, Oxford, Oxford University Press.

Ohmae, K. (1996) *The End of the Nation-State*, London, HarperCollins.

Osbourne, D. and Gaebler, T. (1992) *Reinventing Government*, Reading, Addison-Wesley.

Packenham, R. (1970) 'Legislatures and Political Development', in A. Kornberg and L. D. Musolf (eds), *Legislatures in Developmental Perspective*, Durham, NC, Duke University Press.

Parry, G., Moyser, G. and Day, N. (1992) *Political Participation and Democracy in Britain*, Cambridge, Cambridge University Press.

Pascall, G. (1997) *Social Policy: A New Feminist Analysis*, London, Routledge.

Patterson, T. (1993) *Out of Order*, New York, Vintage.

Pattie, C., Johnston, R. and Russell, A. (1995) 'The Stalled Greening of British Politics', *Politics Review*, vol. 4, no. 3, pp. 21–5.

Paulson, B. (1994) 'Was 1992 Labour's Golden Chance?', in Heath *et al.* (eds), *Labour's Last Chance? The 1992 Election and Beyond*, pp. 85–106.

Payne, M. (1995) *Social Work and Community Care*, London, Macmillan.

Percy-Smith, J. (1996) 'Downloading Democracy? Information and Communication Technologies in Local Politics', *Policy and Politics*, vol. 24, pp. 43–55.

Perryman, M. (ed.) (1996) *The Blair Agenda*, London, Lawrence & Wishart.

Peterson, J. (1994) 'Policy Networks and Governance in the European Union', in P. Dunleavy and J. Stanyer (eds), *Contemporary Political Studies 1994, vol. 1*, Exeter, PSA, pp. 151–69.

Peterson, J. (1996) *Europe and America: The Prospects for Partnership*, 2nd edn, London, Routledge.

Peterson, J. and Bomberg, E. (1998) *Decision-Making in the European Union*, London, Macmillan.

Pfaller, A., Gough, I. and Therborn, G. (1991) *Can the Welfare State Compete?*, London, Macmillan.

Political Quarterly (1997) Special issue covering 'Human Rights in the UK', vol. 86, no. 2, April–June.

Porter, M. (1990) *The Competitive Advantage of Nations*, London, Macmillan.

Power, M. (1994) *The Audit Explosion*, London, Demos.

Prime Minister, Chancellor of the Exchequer and Chancellor of the Duchy of Lancaster (1995) *The Civil Service: Taking Forward Continuity and Change*, Cm 2748, London, HMSO.

Pulzer, P. G. J. (1967) *Political Representation and Elections in Britain*, London, George Allen & Unwin.

Putnam, R. (1993) *Making Democracy Work: Civic Traditions in Modern Italy*, Princeton, Princeton University Press.

Rallings, C. and Thrasher, M. (1996) 'Where Have all the Local Tories Gone?', paper to 1996 annual conference of the Political Studies Association, University of Glasgow, April.

Rallings, C., Farrell, D. and Denver, D. (eds) (1996) *British Elections and Parties Yearbook 1995*, London, Frank Cass.

Rallings, C., Temple, M. and Thrasher, M. (1994) *Community Identity and Participation in Local Democracy*, Commission for Local Democracy Report, no. 1, London, *Municipal Journal*.

Rawls, J., (1990) *A Theory of Justice*, Cambridge, Mass., Harvard University Press.

Redwood, J. (1994) *Global Marketplace: Capitalism and its Future*, London, HarperCollins.

Redwood, J. (1996) 'EMU Would Mean misery', *Financial Times*, 16 May, p. 23.

Reiner, C. (1992) *The Politics of the Police*, London, Harvester Wheatsheaf.

Rentoul, J. (1996) *Tony Blair*, London, Warner Books.

Renwick, R. (1996) *Fighting with Allies: America and Britain in Peace and War*, London, Macmillan.

Review Body on Senior Salaries (1996) *Report Number 37: Eighteenth Report on Senior Salaries* Cm 3094, London, HMSO.

Reynolds, P. and Coates, D. (1996) 'Conclusion' in D. Coates (ed.), *Industrial Policy in Britain*, Basingstoke, Macmillan.

Rhodes, M. (ed.) (1996) *The Regions and the New Europe*, Manchester, Manchester University Press.

Rhodes, R. A. W. (1995) 'From Prime Ministerial Power to Core Executive', in R. A. W. Rhodes and P. J. Dunleavy (eds), *Prime Minister, Cabinet and Core Executive*, London, Macmillan.

Rhodes, R. A. W. (1996) 'The New Governance: Governing Without Government', *Political Studies*, vol. 44, p. 4.

Rhodes, R. A. W. and Dunleavy, P. J. (eds) (1995), *Prime Minister, Cabinet and Core Executive*, London, Macmillan.

Richardson, J. J. and Jordan, A. G. (1979) *Governing Under Pressure*, Oxford, Martin Robertson.

Ridley, F. F. and Doig, A. (eds) (1995) *Sleaze*, Oxford, Oxford University Press.

Ridley, F. F. and Wilson, D. (1995) Th Quango Debate, Oxford, Oxford University Press.

Robinson, P. (1995) 'Evolution or Revolution', *New Economy*, vol. 2, no. 3, pp. 167–73.

Robson, W. (1933) 'The Central Domination of Local Government', *Political Quarterly*, January–March.

Rose, R. (1983) 'Still the Era of Party Government', *Parliamentary Affairs*, vol. 36, pp. 282–99.

Rose-Ackerman, S. (1978) *Corruption*, New York, Academic Press.

Rowan, B. (1995) *Behind the Lines*, Belfast, Blackstaff Press.

Rowbotham, S. (1996) 'Introduction', in M. Threlfall (ed.), *Mapping the Women's Movement*, London, Verso.

Rush, M. (ed.) (1990) *Parliament and Pressure Politics*, Oxford, Oxford University Press.

Saggar, S. (1992) *Race and Politics in Britain*, London, Harvester Wheatsheaf.

Samson, C. and South, N. (eds) (1996) *The Social Construction of Social Policy: Methodologies, Racism, Citizenship and the Environment*, London, Macmillan.

Sanders, D. (1990) *Losing an Empire, Finding a Role: British Foreign Policy Since 1945*, London, Macmillan.

Sanders, D. (1991) 'Government Popularity and the Next General Election', *Political Quarterly*, vol. 62, pp. 235–61.

Sanders, D. (1992) 'Why the Conservative Party Won – Again', in A. King *et al.*, *Britain at the Polls 1992*, Chatham, NJ, Chatham House.

Sanders, D. (1993) 'Foreign and Defence Policy' in P. Dunleavy, A. Gamble, I. Holliday and G. Peele (eds), *Developments in British Politics 4*, London, Macmillan.

Sanders, D. (1995) 'Forecasting Political Preferences and Election Outcomes in the UK: Experiences, Problems and Prospects for the Next General Election', *Electoral Studies*, vol. 14, pp. 251–72.

Sanders, D. (1996) 'Economic Performance, Management Competence and the Outcome of the Next General Election', *Political Studies*, vol. 44, pp. 203–31.

Sandholtz, W. and Zysman, J. (1989) '1992: Recasting the European Bargain', *World Politics*, vol. 42, pp. 95–128.

Sarlvik, B. and Crewe, I. (1983) 'Decade of Dealignment: The Conservative Victory of 1979 and Electoral Trends in the 1970s', London, Cambridge University Press.

Sassoon, D. (1996) *A Hundred Years of Socialism*, London, I.B.Tauris.

Scammell, M. (1995) *Designer Politics*, London, Macmillan.

Scarman, Lord (1981) *The Brixton Disorders, 10–12 April 1981: Report of an Inquiry by the Rt Hon. the Lord Scarman, OBE*, Cmnd 8427, London, HMSO.

Schwarz, J. (1980) 'Exploring a New Role in Policy Making: The British House of Commons in the 1970s', *American Political Science Review*, vol. 74, pp. 23–37.

Scott, R. (1996) *Report of the Inquiry into the Export of Defence Equipment and Dual-Use Goods to Iraq and Related Prosecutions, vols 1–5*, London, HMSO.

Select Committee on Sittings of the House (1992) *Report from the Select Committee on Sittings of the House*, Session 1991–92, HC 20, London, HMSO.

Self, R. (1996) 'Lifting the Veil', *Professional Investor*, February, pp. 12–14.

Semetko, H. (1996) 'Political Balance on Television: Campaigns in the United States, Britain and Germany', *The Harvard International Journal of Press/Politics*, vol. 1, no. 1, pp. 51–71.

Seyd, P. (1987) *The Rise and Fall of the Labour Left*, London, Macmillan.

Seyd, P. and Whiteley, P. (1992) *Labour's Grass Roots: The Politics of Labour Party Membership*, Oxford, Clarendon Press.

Seyd, P. and Whiteley, P. (1996) 'Conservative Grassroots: An Overview', in S. Ludlam and M.J. Smith (eds), *Contemporary British Conservatism*, London, Macmillan.

Seyd, P., Whiteley, P. and Parry, J. (1996) *Labour and Conservative Party Membership: Social Characteristics, Political Attitudes and Activities*, Aldershot, Dartmouth.

Seyd, P., Whiteley, P. and Richardson, J.J. (1994) *True Blues: The Politics of Conservative Party Membership*, Oxford, Clarendon Press.

Seymour Ure, C. (1996) *The British Press and Broadcasting Since 1945*, 2nd edn, Basil Blackwell, Oxford.

Sharp, J. M. O. (1996) *About Turn, Forward March with Europe*, London, Rivers Oram Press, for Institute for Public Policy Research.

Sharpe, L.J. (ed.) (1993) *The Rise of Meso Government in Europe*, London, Sage.

Shell, D. (1992) *The House of Lords*, 2nd edn, London, Harvester Wheatsheaf.

Sieber, S. (1981) *Fatal Remedies*, New York, Plenum.

Silk, P. and Walters, R. (1995) *How Parliament Works*, 3rd edn, London, Longman.

Skelcher, C. and Davis, H. (1995) *Opening the Boardroom Door: Membership of Local Appointed Bodies*, London, LGC/JRF.

Social Policy and Administration (1994) 'Special Issue on Health Care Reform', vol. 28, no. 4.

Social Trends, 1995 (1995) London, HMSO.

Sowemimo, M. (1996) 'The Conservative Party and European Integration', *Party Politics*, vol. 21, pp. 77–97.

Steele, R. (1995) 'The Domestic Core of Foreign Policy', *The Atlantic Monthly*, vol. 275, no. 6, pp. 84–92

Stewart, J. (1992) *Accountability to the Public*, European Policy Forum.

Stewart, J. (1995) *Innovation in Democratic Practice*, Birmingham, University of Birmingham.

Stewart, J. (1996) *Further Innovation in Democratic Practice*, Birmingham, University of Birmingham.

Stewart, J. and Stoker G. (eds) (1995) *Local Government in the 1990s*, London, Macmillan.

Stewart, J. and Stoker, G. (eds) (1989) *The Future of Local Government*, London, Macmillan.

Stewart, J., Greer, A. and Hoggett, P. (1994) *The Quango State: An Alternative Approach*, Commission for Local Democracy Report, no. 10, London, *Municipal Journal*.

Stoker, G. (1989) 'Creating a Local Government for a Post-Fordist Society: The Thatcherite Project', in J. Stewart and G. Stoker (eds), *The Future of Local Government*, London, Macmillan.

Stoker, G. (1991) *The Politics of Local Government*, London, Macmillan.

Stoker, G. and Young, S. (1993) *Cities in the 1990s: Local Choice for a Balanced Strategy*, London, Longman.

Streeck, W. (1995) 'From Market-Making to State-Building? Reflections on the Political Economy of European Social Policy' in Leibfried, S. and Pierson, P. (eds), *European Social Policy Between Fragmentation and Integration*, Washington, DC, Brookings, pp. 389–431.

Studlar, D. (1986) 'Non-White Policy Preferences, Political Participation and the Political Agenda in Britain', in Z. Layton-Henry and P. Rich (eds), *Race, Government and Politics in Britain*, London, Macmillan.

Sunstein, C. (1990) *After the Rights Revolution: Reconceiving the Regulatory State*, Cambridge, Mass., Harvard University Press.

Swanson, D. and Mancini, P. (eds) (1996) *Politics, Media and Modern Democracy*, New York, Praeger.

Tarrow, S. (1994) *Power in Movement: Social Movements, Collective Action and Politics*, Cambridge, Cambridge University Press.

Taylor, C. (1995) *EMU 2000? Prospects for European Monetary Union*, London, Pinter/Royal Institute for International Affairs.

Theakston, K. (1995) *The Civil Service since 1945*, Oxford, Blackwell.

Thomas, S. (1992) 'Assessing MEP Influence on British EC Policy', *Government and Opposition*, vol. 27, pp. 3–26.

Titmuss, R. (1967) *The Gift Relationship: From Human Blood to Social Policy*, London, Allen & Unwin.

Topf, R. (1989) 'Political Change and Political Culture in Britain, 1959–87', in J. Gibbins (ed.), *Contemporary Political Culture: Politics in a Postmodern Age*, London, Sage, pp. 52–80.

Travers, T. (1985) *The Politics of Local Government Finance*, London, Allen & Unwn.

Travers, T. (1995) 'Finance', in Stewart, J. and Stoker, G. (eds), *Local Government in the 1990s*, London, Macmillan.

Travers, Y., Biggs, S. and Jones, G. (1995) *Joint Working Between Local Authorities*, London, Local Government Communications.

Treasury (1994) *Fundamental Review of HM Treasury's Running Costs*, London, HM Treasury.

Treasury and Civil Service Committee (1990) *Eighth Report: Progress in the Next Steps Initiative*, HC 481, 1989–90, London, HMSO.

Ungerson, C. (1997) 'Give Them Money: Is Cash a Route to Empowerment?' *Social Policy and Administration*, vol. 31, no. 1, pp. 45–53.

Waddington, D. (1992) *Contemporary Issues in Public Disorder*, London, Routledge.

Waine B. (1995) 'A Disaster Foretold? The Case of the Personal Pension', *Social Policy and Administration*, vol. 29, no. 4, pp. 317–34.

Wallace, H. (1995) 'Britain out on a Limb?', *Political Quarterly*, vol. 66, no. 1, pp. 46–58.

Wallace, M. and Jenkins, J. (1995) 'The New Class, Postindustrialism and Neocorporatism: Three Images of Social Protest in the Western Democracies', in J. Jenkins and B. Klandermans (eds), *The Politics of Social Protest*, London, University College London Press.

Walsh, K. (1991) *Competitive Tendering for Local Government Services*, London, HMSO.

Walsh, K. (1995) 'Competition and Public Service Delivery', in J. Stewart and G. Stoker (eds), *Local Government in the 1990s*, London, Macmillan.

Walzer, M. (1983) *Spheres of Justice: A Defence of Pluralism and Equality*, Oxford, Blackwell.

Ward, H. (1996) 'Green Arguments for Local Democracy', in D. King and G. Stoker (eds), *Rethinking Local Democracy*, London, Macmillan.

Weir, S. and Hall, W. (1994) *Ego Trip: Extra Governmental Organisations in the United Kingdom and their Accountability*, London, Democratic Audit and Charter 88.

Weir, S. and Hall, W. (1996a) *EGO Trip: The Quango State in Britain*, London, Democratic Audit of the UK/The Scarman Trust.

Weir, S. and Hall, W. (1996b) *The Untouchables: Power and Accountability in the Quango State*, London, Democratic Audit of the UK/The Scarman Trust.

Westlake, M. (1994a) *Britain's Emerging Euro-Elite*, Aldershot, Dartmouth.

Westlake, M. (1994b) *A Modern Guide to the European Parliament*, London, Pinter.

Wheare, K. (1995) *Government by Committee*, Oxford, Clarendon.

Whitehead, A. (1996) *Holding Quangos to Account*, London, Local Government Information Unit.

Whiteley, P., Seyd, P. and Richardson, J. (1994) *True Blues: The Politics of Conservative Party Membership*, Oxford, Clarendon Press.

Wilks, S. (1993) 'Economic Policy', in P. Dunleavy *et al.* (eds), *Developments in British Politics 4*, London, Macmillan.

Willetts, D. (1992) *Modern Conversatism*, Harmondsworth, Penguin.

Williams, R. (1993) 'Technical Change: Political Options and Imperatives', *Government and Opposition*, vol. 28, no. 2, pp. 152–73

Wilson, D. and Game, C. (1994) *Local Government in the United Kingdom*, London, Macmillan.

Wilson, G. (1994) 'Co-Production and Self-Care: New Approaches to Managing Community Care Services for Older People', *Social Policy and Administration*, vol. 28, no. 3, pp. 236–50.

Wilson, J. Q. and Kelling, G. (1983) 'Broken Windows', *Atlantic Monthly*.

Wilson, T. (1989) *Ulster: Conflict and Consent*, Oxford, Blackwell.

Winter, M. (1997) 'Intersecting Departmental Responsibilities: Administrative Confusion and the Role of Science in Government: The Case of BSE', *Parliamentary Affairs*.

Wolfenden, J. (1978) *The Future of Voluntary Organisations*, London, Croom Helm.

Young, H. (1996) 'Prophet of Armageddon', *The Guardian*, 12 October.

Young, J. (1988) 'Radical Criminology in Britain: The Emergence of a Competing Paradigm', *British Journal of Criminology*, vol. 28, pp. 159–83.

Young, K., Gosschalk, B. and Hatter, W. (1996) *In Search of Community Identity*, London, Local Government Communications.

Young, S. (1993) *The Politics of the Environment*, Manchester, Baseline.

Index

accountability, public sector, 216–17
Action Centre for Europe, 104
Adam Smith Institute, 261
Adams, Gerry, 33, 242, 245, 251
agriculture, 343
Aitken, Jonathan, 142–3
Alarm UK, 117
Al-Fayed, Mohammed, 143
Alliance Party (NI), 245
Anglo-Irish Agreement (1985), 241
animal rights protests, 116, 117, 118
arms sales, 36–7, 197
    Scott inquiry, 37, 142, 181, 183
Ashdown, Paddy, 16, 108
Audit Commission, 190, 197, 217, 274,
    333
audit of public services, 189–90, 196–7
Austria, 26, 27, 78

Banham, Sir John, 262
Bank of England
    control of interest rates, 9, 17, 208
    Governor's meetings with
        Chancellor, 282–3
    operational independence, 279, 283,
        293
Battle, John, 208
BBC (British Broadcasting
    Corporation)
    coverage of election campaigns, 79,
        80, 83–4, 85
    future, 87
    World Service, 36
beef crisis, 24–5, 41, 175, 342–54
Beresford, Paul, 264
BES (British Election Study), 54–5,
    61, 76, 85
Beveridge Report, 318
'Birmingham Six', 332
'Black Wednesday', 24

    see also exchange rate mechanism
Blair, Tony
    attempts to postpone shadow
        cabinet elections (1996), 97
    attitude to EMU, 15
    attitude to electoral reform, 149–50
    centrist policies, 14
    claim of 'one-nation' party, 5, 13
    commitment to progress in
        Northern Ireland, 251–2
    decision to hold referendum on
        devolution, 92–3
    favours elected mayors, 261
    leadership, 11–12, 52, 94–5
    in 1997 election campaign, 12,
        17–18
    philosophical influences, 92
    reform of Labour Party under, 51
    reform of PM's Question Time, 170
    'stakeholder' social policy, 304–5
    on law and order, 326, 335, 337
Blair government, 16–18, 207–8
    creation of Securities and
        Investment Board, 211
    divisions within, 94–5
    economic policies, 93, 302
    establishes Food Standards
        Agency, 354
    European policy, 15–16, 21, 23, 27,
        29–30
    foreign policy, 40
    fragmented opposition, 6
    free vote on handgun legislation, 118
    to incorporate European
        Convention on Human
        Rights, 145
    law and order policy, 338–41
    and Northern Ireland, 251–2
    promises Freedom of Information
        Act, 144–5

proposals for devolution, 137–9,
    229–30
proposals for electoral reform, 123–5
proposals on local
    government, 274–6
proposed changes in parliamentary
    procedures, 145–6
to sign Social Chapter, 29
Blunkett, David, 208
Bosnia, 33, 38
bovine spongiform encephalopathy
    (BSE), 343–5
see also beef crisis
British Commonwealth, 36
British Crime Survey, 331, 339
British Election Study (BES), 54–5,
    61, 76, 85
British exceptionalism, 355–6, 374
British Medical Association
    (BMA), 316
Brittan, Sir Leon, 38
Brown, Gordon
    and Bank of England, 9, 17, 279
    budget (1997), 286
    centrist ideas, 14
    economic policies, 51, 93, 95, 283–4,
        298
    opinion on EMU, 15, 293
    on responsibility of individuals, 335
Bruton, John, 252
BSE crisis, 24–5, 41, 175, 342–54
budget (July 1997), 286
Bulger, James, 326
Bulpitt, J., 254
Burch, M., 180

Cabinet, 178–81
Cabinet Office, 178, 190, 208
Callaghan government (1976–9), 131,
    163, 220–1
Campaign Group (Labour Party), 94
Campbell, Alistair, 97
Campbell, Menzies, 108
Carlisle, Alex, 108
Cash, William, 98
'cash for questions' scandal, 143
central executive, regulation of, 181–3
Central Policy Review Staff, 39
Charter 88, 170
Child Support Agency, 317–18

China, 42
Chirac, Jacques, 28
Christopher, Warren, 33
Citizen's Charter, 198, 217
City Challenge scheme, 259
City Technology Colleges, 185
civil service, 183–4
    critical of government policy, 197
    departmental reorganizations, 17
    'market testing', 195–6
    recruitment and promotion, 189,
        194–5, 200–2
    regulation and control of, 190, 191,
        193, 195, 197–8, 199
Clarke, Kenneth
    economic policies as Chancellor, 70,
        281–3, 284
    in leadership contest, 8, 106
    supports European integration, 25,
        99, 293
Clarke, M., 270
class dealignment and voting
    patterns, 53–8
Clinton, President Bill, 32–4, 246
Common Agricultural Policy, 26, 353
communitarianism, 335–6, 365, 367
community care, 317
community charge, 258
community-based local
    government, 266–70
community service orders, 330
Conservative Party, 98–108
    and beef crisis, 351, 352–3
    and class voting, 53–7
    decline in membership, 78, 89–90,
        107–8, 113–14
    divided over Europe, 70, 98–101,
        175, 286, 351–2, 375
    economic and social policies, 101–2,
        280
    election campaign (1997), 49–50
    electoral disaster (1997), 3–4, 5–7
    factions within, 102–3
    future prospects, 7–11
    in House of Lords, 99
    ideological crisis, 363, 374
    law and order policies, 326, 328–35
    leadership contest (1997), 8, 10, 98,
        106
    and local government, 257–8, 271–2
    loss of morale, 89

Conservative Party (*cont.*)
  misjudged public opinion, 9–10
  opposed to devolution, 226, 232–4
  organization and funding, 106–7,
    140, 143, 343
  pledge to prune quango state
    (1979), 185
  rebels, 162–4
  regional differences in
    support, 223–4
  support in opinion polls, 58–61,
    66–70
  support from press, 82
  see also Heath government; Major
    governments; Thatcher
    governments
constitutional reform
  Constitution Unit reports, 225
  Labour agenda for, 171
  possible effects of, 123
  problems in achieving, 130–3
convergence criteria for EMU, 280,
    287, 293
Cook, Robin
  aims for better relations with
    EU, 17, 23, 27, 29–30
  contacts with Liberal
    Democrats, 108
  Eurosceptical views, 95
  favours constitutional
    reform, 14–15
  opinion on EMU, 15, 293
  seeks to sign Social Chapter, 208
Corbyn, Jeremy, 95
corruption, *see* sleaze
Creutzfeld–Jakob disease, new variant
    of (NVCJD), 342, 344
Crewe, I., 56
crime, levels of, 331–2, 339
Crime and Disorder Bill, 339, 341
Crime (Sentences) Bill (1996), 334,
    337
Criminal Justice Act (1982), 329
Criminal Justice Act (1991), 330, 332
Criminal Justice and Public Order Act
    (1994), 118–19, 332
Criminal Records Agency, 334
Critchley, Julian, 104
Cullen Inquiry, 334
Cunningham, Jack, 354
Currie, Edwina, 99

Daily Express, 82
Daily Herald, 80, 82
Daily Mail, 82
Daily Telegraph, 82
Dalton, R., 123
Davies, Howard, 296
Davies, Ron, 229
Dayton Peace Accord, 34
Democratic Unionist Party
    (DUP), 246–7, 249
Department of the Environment
    (DoE), 261, 262
Department of Health, 342–3, 346
deregulation
  of labour market, 299–300
  of trade, 210–11
devolution of government, 136–9
  economic case against, 226–7
  issue in 1997 election contest, 8
  possible effects of, 16–17, 123–4,
    203
  potential problems in
    effecting, 236–40
  referenda on, 137
Dewar, Donald, 229
Dicey, A.V., 221
Dorrell, Stephen, 106
Downing Street
  Declaration, 241–2
Drucker, Henry, 97
Drumcree marches, 247–8
Dunblane massacre, 118, 334
Duncan Smith, Ian, 103
Dunleavy, P., 204, 342, 350
Dykes, Hugh, 99, 105

economic and monetary union
    (EMU), 286–95
  Brown (Chancellor) supports, 15
  Conservative Party split over, 10–11,
    26, 100
  costs and benefits, 30–1, 289
  effect on economic policy, 280
  obstacles to UK joining, 293–5
  single currency, 93–4, 100, 153, 280,
    287
economic policy
  convergence of main political
    parties, 279–81, 302
  future debates, 302–3

education and training
investment in, 298
reform of local authority
control, 264–6, 270, 311
'stakeholder' policies, 310–13
UK lags advanced states, 23
Education Act (1993), 265
Education Reform Act (1988), 265
Efficiency Unit, 216
election campaigns, 76–87
1997 general election, 49–53, 90–1
influence of mass media, 79–80, 82,
83–6
personalization of, 83, 366
electoral system, British, 5–6, 122,
147–50
electoral reform, 123–4, 150–4
employment and training, 308–9
EMU, *see* economic and monetary
union
endism, 358–60
England
proposed regional government, 137
reform of local authority
structure, 262–3
regional offices, 222
Enterprise and Deregulation
Unit, 210
environmental issues, 372
protest over, 116–19
Environment Act (1995), 267
ERM, *see* exchange rate mechanism
European Central Bank, 289, 291
European Commission
in beef crisis, 352
interacts with UK government, 34,
178, 352
obliged to consult interest
groups, 114–16
referrals for violation of internal
market rules, 26
and regional funding, 134
power over European
Parliament, 159–60
European Convention on Human
Rights, 208
European Court of Audit, 190
European Court of Human Rights, 145
European Court of Justice, 26, 27, 173
European Fighter Aircraft, 39
European Foundation, 104

European Parliament (EP), 172–6
elections (1994), 48
lack of power, 155, 159–60
European Union
and beef crisis, 24–5, 345, 346, 349,
351–4
Common Agricultural Policy, 26,
353
Council of Ministers, 115, 173–4,
287–9
directive on 48-hour week, 26–7
enlargement of, 27
Florence summit (June 1996), 25,
347
interest representation
within, 114–15
Maastricht Treaty, 159, 173–4, 212,
287
Major government's relations
with, 24–32
move towards superstate, 361
need for reform, 31–2
regional funding, 134–5, 225–6, 267
regulatory rules and standards, 207,
211–12, 213
UK's future in, 375
see also economic and monetary
union
Evans, David, 102
exchange rate mechanism (ERM), 24,
65, 180, 281–2
executive agencies, 184, 205–6, 207,
214, 267

Fair Trading Act (1973), 211
Falklands War, 32
families and social care, 317–18
Field, Frank, 17, 324
Financial Services Act (1986), 211
Finland, 26, 111
firearms legislation, 334, 339, 365
Fischler, Franz, 350, 352, 353
Florence European summit (1996), 25,
347
Food Standards Agency, 17, 208
Forsyth, Michael, 99, 233
Foster, C.D., 183
France, 26, 27, 28–9, 111
franchising of public services, 214–16
Freedom of Information Act, 202–3

Freeman, Roger, 346
'Fresh Start' group, 104
Friends of the Earth, 117
Funding Council for Schools, 265
Fukuyama, F., 21

Gaitskell, Hugh, 91
Gardiner, Sir George, 98, 105
general elections
  (1970), 7
  (October 1974), 4
  (1983), 3, 4, 48, 148
  (1992), 4, 58, 111
  (1997), 49–53, 82, 90–1, 111, 169,
    251
  see also voting patterns
George, Eddie, 282–3
Germany
  electoral system, 150
  public opinion on EMU, 27
  regions within, 239
  in EU, 26, 28–9, 39, 351
Giuliani, Rudolph (Mayor of New
    York), 336
globalization, 21–2, 279–80, 295–6,
    359–62, 368
Goldsmith, Sir James, 42, 90
  Referendum Party, 4, 10, 90–1
Gorman, Teresa, 98
government
  centralization of, 133–6
  end of, 368–71
Grant, W., 116
Greater London Council (GLC),
    abolition of, 9, 133–4, 261
Greece, 111
Green, Damian, 103
Greenpeace, 117
Gulf War, 32, 38
Gummer, John, 222, 262, 345
gun control, 334, 339, 365

Hague, William, 8, 18, 106
Hamilton, Neil, 52, 143
health policy, 313–17
  see also NHS
Health Service and Community Care
    Act (1990), 318–19
Heath, Anthony, 56
Heath, Sir Edward, 99, 103, 163

Heath government (1970–4), 105,
    163, 222, 232
Heclo, H., 190
Helms–Burton Act, 34
Henderson, Doug, 27
Heseltine, Michael, 25, 37, 181, 210,
    260
Hicks, Robert, 104
Hogg, Douglas, 346, 348, 352
Holliday, I., 180
Hong Kong, 37
House of Commons, 146, 155, 156,
    161–72
House of Lords
  forced concessions on law and
    order, 333, 334, 337
  proposals for reform, 146–7
housing, 321–3
Howard, Michael
  anti-European, 99, 106
  as Home Secretary, 214, 310, 332
  in leadership contest, 8, 106
Howe, Geoffrey (Lord), 70, 104
Hume, John, 242
Hurd, Sir Douglas, 103
Hutton, Will, 13, 299–300

ideology, end of, 361–4
Independent Television Commission
    (ITC), 84–5
inflation, 284–5
information superhighway, 119–21
Inglehart, R., 121
Inspectorate of Constabulary, 216
interest rates, 9, 17, 208, 282–3
Intergovernmental Conferences, 25,
    27, 212
International Monetary Fund, 38
investment, 23, 226–7, 296–8
IRA (Irish Republican Army), 242,
    246
Iraq
  arms sales to, 37, 142, 181, 183
  Gulf War, 22, 32, 38
Irish republic
  in beef crisis, 350–1
  electoral system, 152
  in Northern Ireland peace
    process, 241–2, 244–5, 249,
    250, 252

Irish Republican Army (IRA), 242, 246
Irvine, Lord, 229
Italy, 27, 111

James Report, 354
Jenkins, J., 111, 112
Job Seeker's allowance, 309
Jordan, G., 123
judicial review, 182–3, 189–90

Kingsdown, Lord, 104
Kinnock, Neil, 91, 149, 231, 274
modernization of Labour Party
under, 12, 71, 91
Kissinger, Henry, 32
Kohler-Koch, B., 115
Kreisi, H.P. *et al.*, 122
Kuwait, 22

labour market, 298–302
Labour Party
attitudes to EU within, 29–30, 354, 375
and class voting, 53–7
divisions within, 90, 91, 94
economic policies, 72, 93, 279–80, 298
education policies, 311–12
funding, 97
health policy, 316
law and order policies, 326, 328, 335–7
leadership of, 12, 96–7
manifesto (1997), 92–4
membership, 78, 113–14
New Labour, 71, 91–4, 98, 362
in 1983 general election, 10
in 1997 general election, 1, 2–3, 46–53, 366
organization, 95–6
Parliamentary Labour Party (PLP), 11, 12
promises referendum on single currency, 26
proposals for constitutional reform, 129, 132, 171–2
proposals for devolution, 92–3, 231–2
proposals for local government, 274
proposals for party reform, 97
rebels, 162–4

regional differences in support, 223–4
support in opinion polls, 58–61
see also Blair government; Callaghan government; Wilson governments
Lamont, Norman, 70
law and order
convergence of two main parties' policies, 337
crime, 309–10, 331–2, 339
prisons, 206, 208, 310, 333–4
welfarist consensus, 327
Lawrence, Philip, 334
Lawson, Nigel, 70
Lewis, Derek, 214
Liberal Democrats, 108–9
and class voting, 53–4
decentralist orientation, 236
on electoral reform, 152
future prospects, 16, 74
Labour's relations with, 14, 15, 108, 129, 132, 146
in 1997 general election, 5, 6, 90
support in South West, 223
views on Europe, 16, 375
Lilley, Peter, 8, 23, 99, 101, 103, 106
Livingstone, Ken, 95
local government
compulsory competitive tendering, 205–6
Conservative governments' reforms, 253–7, 261–3
contracting-out of services, 255, 263–4, 274
corruption, 272
council housing, 321–2
finance, 257–9, 270–1
loss of control to central government, 133, 270, 311
proposals for further reform, 269
social services, 319–20
weakness of party politics in, 271–2
Local Government Commission (1992), 262
Local Government and Housing Act (1989), 259
London, proposed strategic authority for, 9, 220, 275
London Evening Standard, 9
Loughlin, M., 264

Maastricht Treaty, 159, 173–4, 212, 287
McAllion, John, 92
McAlpine, Lord, 90
McCartney, Robert, 243–4, 247
McConnell, A., 78
McGuinness, Martin, 251
Macleod Group, 104
MacMurray, John, 92
Major, John
  appoints Nolan Committee, 52, 144
  in beef crisis, 24–5, 346, 347, 349, 352
  considers resigning (1992), 72
  on Europe, 27, 30
  leadership challenge, 104, 180
  in Northern Ireland peace process, 242, 244
  and opinion polls, 67
  opposed to devolution, 8, 233
  promises review of administration in Scotland and Wales, 228
  prorogues Parliament early (1997), 143
  resigns as party leader, 8
  support within the party, 103
  unable to unite party, 52, 99, 100, 105–6
Major governments (1990–2; 1992–7)
  in beef crisis, 347, 351–3
  creates single regeneration budget, 134–5
  divisions within, 10–11, 91–101, 118
  economic policy, 41–2, 101–2, 280
  ERM crisis, 65, 67–8
  and freedom of information, 144
  law and order policies, 326
  and local government, 133
  misjudges public opinion, 17
  in Northern Ireland peace process, 244–5
  nursery voucher scheme, 265
  parliamentary rebels within, 105
  presentation of government policy, 181
  relations with EU, 24–32, 34
  returns Stone of Scone, 227
  scrapped poll tax (1992), 136
  'sleaze' under, 140
  social policies, 101–2
Malaysia, 37, 197

Maloney, W., 123
Mandelson, Peter, 14, 97, 181
manufacturing, investment in, 23
Market Research Society, 58, 79
Marlow, Anthony, 98
mass media, 41, 79–88, 116, 366
Matrix Churchill, 37
Mawhinney, Brian, 29
Meacher, Michael, 354
members of parliament (MPs), 111, 161–4, 165, 167–9
  see also House of Commons; voting patterns
Mexico, 25
Miliband, Ralph, 156
Ministry of Agriculture, Fisheries and Food (MAFF), 342–3, 346
ministerial power, 218
Mitchell, Austin, 155–6
Mitchell, George, 245–6
Mitchell Report, 246
Molyneaux, James, 244
Morgan Report, 330
Mowlam, Marjorie, 251–2
Moyser, G., 125
MPs, *see* members of parliament
Murdoch, Rupert, 82
Muslim parliament, 116

Nadir, Asil, 143
National Audit Office, 171, 181, 197, 217
National Crime Squad, 338
National Criminal Intelligence Service, 338
National Farmers Union, 348
National Forum for Values, 313
National Health Service, *see* NHS
National Lottery, 18, 320
National Youth Justice Board, 339
nationalism, 364
nationalist political parties, 15, 223–5
nation-states, decline of, 359–61, 368
NATO (North Atlantic Treaty Organization), 34, 38
neo-liberal theories, 21, 22, 30–1, 39, 42
neo-realist theories, 21, 22, 30, 39, 42
Netherlands, 25, 27, 111
New Labour, 91–8
  economic policies, 72, 281, 298

focus on leader, 366
ideological momentum, 13–14
takes over centrist ground, 46–53,
  57, 71, 362
new public management
  (NPM), 140–2
in criminal justice system, 330–1,
  333, 338
effects of, 203, 369
'humanized', 18
New Right, 207, 279, 367
New Zealand, electoral system in, 150
newspapers, 41, 79, 80–2
NHS (National Health Service)
clinical audits, 201
public opinion of, 313, 314
reforms, 206, 226, 314–16
removal of inernal market, 18, 208
Nicholson, Sir Brian, 41
Nicholson, Emma, 102, 104
1932 Committee, 104
'92 Group, 104
Niskanen, W.A., 202
No Turning Back Group, 104
Nolan Committee on Standards in
  Public Life, 52, 107, 143, 144,
  168–9, 183
non-departmental public bodies, 184–7
Northern Ireland
all-party peace talks, 248–52
in beef crisis, 350–1
constitutional position, 221–2
decommissioning terrorist
  weapons, 245–6
Forum elections (1996), 246–8
IRA, 242, 246
loyalist paramilitaries, 243, 249
public opinion on united
  Ireland, 243
Sinn Fein, 33, 242, 246, 247, 250
US influence in, 33
Northern Ireland Office, 222

OECD (Organization for Economic
  Co-operation and Development)
Jobs Study, 299
OFSTED (Office for Standards in
  Education), 198, 216
Opraf (Office of Passenger Rail
  Franchising), 215

Olympic Games (1996), 23
opinion polls, 58–62, 79, 82
Orange order, 247–8
Oxleas Wood, 117

Paisley, Revd Ian, 246, 351
Parliament (UK),
House of Commons, 146, 155, 156,
  161–72
House of Lords, 146–7, 333, 334,
  337
proposals for reform, 146, 170–2
role of, 155–8
select committees, 166, 168, 181
sovereignty of, 221
volume of legislation, 158–9
Parliamentary Commissioner for
  Administration, 181
Patients Charter (1994), 314
Parry, G., 110, 125
pensions, 323–4
Pergau dam affair, 197
Peterson, J., 115
Plaid Cymru, 223, 225, 235–6
Plant Commission, 149, 152
Plowden, F.J., 183
plurality rule system, 147–9
police, 332–3, 337
Police Bill (1997), 334, 337
Police and Crime (Sentences) Act
  (1997), 328
Police and Criminal Evidence Act
  (1984), 329
Police and Magistrates' Courts Act
  (1994), 269, 333
policy convergence, 361–3
policy disasters, 136, 204, 342, 345–6
political parties
membership and activism, 76–9,
  113–14, 366
must assemble coalition of
  interests, 363–5
policy convergence, 374
see also under individual party names
political participation, 110–25
political protest, 111, 116–18
poll tax, 136, 257
Popular Unionist Party (PUP), 243–4,
  247
Porter, Lady Shirley, 272
Portillo, Michael, 99

Posen Inquiry, 333
Positive Europeans group, 104
postmodernism, 363
Prescott, John, 229, 275
press, 41, 79, 80–2
Prime Minister's Question Time, 165,
    170
prisons, 206, 208, 310, 333–4
Prisons Agency, 17
Prisons Inspectorate, 216
Prisons Ombudsman, 198
Private Finance Initiative, 196
privatization
    under Blair government, 17–18
    of post office, 164
    of public utilities, 208–9
    regulation of bodies, 208–10
proportional representation, 14–15
    for devolved assemblies, 228, 231
public opinion
    on beef crisis, 41
    on constitutional change, 357
    on Europe, 9–10, 40, 41
    on foreign policy, 40–1
    on freedom of information, 144
    on law and order, 341
    on local government, 134, 135,
        273
    of Parliament, 144
public order, 329
public realm, end of, 366–8
public sector, regulation of, 212–17
Public Sector Borrowing
    Requirement, 285–6
public utilities, 18, 142, 208–9
Pulzer, Peter, 224

quangos, 184–8, 267
quasi-governmental agencies, 17,
    133–4, 139, 141–2

radio and television, political coverage
    by, 79–80, 83–6
railways, 215–16
Railways Act (1993), 216
Rayner, Lord, 201
Raynsford, Nick, 229
Reagan, Ronald, 32
Redwood, John, 98, 99, 103, 106
    in leadership contest, 8
    Euroscepticism of, 41

referenda
    on electoral reform, 151, 153
    on devolution, 220, 229, 239
    on EEC (1975), 10
Referendum Party, 4, 10, 90–1
regional administration
    government offices, 259
    reforms of, 226, 228
regional assemblies, 237–8
regional development agencies, 220,
    229, 238
regulatory state, 18, 205–8
Republic of Ireland, *see* Irish republic
Reynolds, Albert, 242
Rhodes, M., 136, 253
Rhodes, R.A.W., 121
Rifkind, Malcolm, 35
right-wing fringe parties, 4–5
roads, protests over, 117, 118
'Rock the Vote', 115–16
Rogers, Adrian, 102
Royal Society for the Protection of
    Birds, 116, 117
Runciman Commission (1993), 332

Salmond, Alex, 234
Santer, Jacques, 352
Sawyer, Tom (Gen. Sec. of Labour
    Party), 97
Scarman Inquiry (1981), 330, 337
schools, 185, 206, 265–6, 311–13
Scotland
    arts in, 228
    beef crisis, 350–1
    demand for autonomy, 131, 134,
        228, 235
    Edinburgh parliament, 137–8, 150,
        151, 220, 230, 237
    Labour Party in, 93
    over-represented at
        Westminster, 222
    poll tax piloted, 225
    reform of local government
        structure, 227, 261
    Scottish Grand Committee, 166,
        227
    union with England, 221
    weakness of Conservative Party in, 7
    see also Scottish National Party
Scott Inquiry (1996), 37, 142, 181,
    183

Scottish Constitutional
   Convention, 134, 228, 235
Scottish Economic Council, 226
Scottish Grand Committee, 166, 227
Scottish National Party (SNP), 134,
   223, 225, 234–5, 350
Scottish Office, 222, 228
Scottish Parliament, 137–8, 150, 151,
   220, 230, 237
SDLP, *see* Social Democratic Labour
   Party
Securities and Investment Board, 17
security, end of, 371–3
Seitz, Raymond, 35
Sheehy Inquiry, 332
Shore, Peter, 95
Sillars, Jim, 234
Single European Act, 159, 173
single European currency
   Conservative Party divided
      over, 10–11, 100
   convergence criteria, 280, 287, 293
   dangers of UK opt-out, 31
   referendum promised, 93–4, 153,
      286
single European market, 294
single regeneration budget (SRB), 222,
   259
Sinn Fein, 33, 242, 246, 247, 250
Skinner, Dennis, 95, 97
sleaze, 52–3, 140–4, 168–9, 204
Slovenia, 25
Smith, Chris, 92
Smith, John, 12, 51, 71, 91, 149
Smith, Tim, 143
Snowdrop campaign, 118
social care, 317–21
social class and voting patterns, 53–7
Social Democratic Labour Party
   (SDLP), 242, 246, 247, 249
social policy, 304–25
social security, 323–4
socialism, 362–3
Spring, Dick, 242
'stakeholder' society, 14, 304–8, 375–6
   social policies, 308–25
Stewart, J., 270
Straw, Jack, 108
   contact with Liberal
      Democrats, 108
   on curfews for children, 337

   as Home Secretary, 17, 208, 214,
      310, 339
   opposes electoral reform, 151
   on zero-tolerance policing, 336
   subsidiarity, 369
Sun, The, 82
Sunday trading, deregulation of, 164
   supporters' networks, 118–20
Sweden, 26, 27, 78, 111

Tarrow, S., 122
TECs, *see* training and enterprise
   councils
television and radio, political coverage
   by, 79–80, 83–6
Temple-Morris, Peter, 99
terrorism, 23, 338–9
Thatcher, Margaret
   in Anglo-Irish agreement, 241
   could not privatize NHS, 314
   law and order policies, 328
   leadership challenge, 180
   in Pergau dam affair, 197
   on 'property-owning
      democracy', 322
   relations with US under Reagan, 32
   support within party, 103
   and unemployment, 308
   weakening of Cabinet
      government, 179–80, 180–1
Thatcher governments (1979–83;
   1983–7; 1987–90)
   benefited from privatized
      utilities, 209
   centralization of power under, 133,
      136, 226, 253–5
   defence policy, 39
   dissent under, 105
   law and order policies, 326
   poll tax, 69
   social and educational policies, 306,
      311, 319
   Westland crisis (1986), 65
Times, The, 80, 82
Townend, John, 104
trade unions
   decline in activism, 111–12
   loss of influence in Labour Party, 12,
      95
   opposed to new public
      management, 17

tradition, end of, 364–5
training and enterprise councils
    (TECs), 255, 259
transport, protests over, 117–18
Treasury, HM, 178, 193, 200, 346
Treaty on European Union
    (Maastricht), 159, 173–4, 212,
    287
Trident submarine system, 39
Trimble, David, 246–7
two-party system, 122, 130, 147–50
Twyford Down, 117

UK (United Kingdom)
    constitution, 356
    economy in 1990s, 22–3
    international role, 23, 32, 34–40
    investment in, 226–7, 296–8
    relations with EU, 24–32, 351–4,
        375
    relations with US, 32–5
    subnations, 221–2
    trade, 36–7
UK Independence Party, 4, 10
Ulster Democratic Party
    (UDP), 243–4, 247
Ulster Unionist Party (UUP), 244,
    246–7, 249
unemployment, 285, 309
universities, funding of, 202
urban regeneration, 259–60
US (United States)
    foreign policy, 33–4
    relations with EU, 20, 28, 35
    relations with UK, 32–5
    role of Congress, 156
    trade policy, 34

voluntary organizations, 318–19, 320
voting patterns
    aggregate models, 62–70
    and class, 57
    declining support for
        Conservatives, 48–53, 66–70
    regional differences, 48, 223–5
    share of seats (1997), 5–7
    share of votes (1997), 2–5
    survey data, 46–62
    volatility of, 73

Wakeham, John, 164
Waldegrave, William, 297
Wales
    education in, 198
    constitutional position, 221
    previous proposals on
        devolution, 131
    proposed Cardiff assembly, 137–8,
        150, 151, 220, 228, 230
    reform of local government in, 227,
        261
    union, 221
    weakness of Conservative party in, 7
    Welsh Office, 222
Wallace, M., 111, 112
Walters, Alan, 90
welfare
    consumers, 307–8, 315–16, 320–1
    rejection of welfare state, 206, 305–6
West European Union, 34
'West Lothian question', 138–9, 238
Westminster model of
    government, 37–8, 129–30
Whiteley, P. *et al.*, 114
Whitney, Ray, 99
Widdecombe Committee, 272
Wildavsky, A., 190
Willetts, David, 103
Wilson, Harold, 12
Wilson governments (1964–70;
    1974–6)
    proposed reform of House of
        Lords, 131
    parliamentary defeats (1974–6), 163
    unable to introduce
        devolution, 220–1
women
    in Parliament, 95, 96, 111, 169
    participation in politics, 112, 122
Woodward, Sean, 103
Woolf Inquiry, 334
World Bank, 38
World Trade Organization
    (WTO), 38
World Wide Fund for Nature, 117

Yates, Ivan, 351
young people, political participation
    among, 112–13, 115–16